College Readings in

CONTEMPORARY
THOUGHT

Selected and Edited by KENDALL B. TAFT
JOHN FRANCIS McDERMOTT, DANA O. JENSEN
Department of English, Washington University, Saint Louis

---

*I do not agree with a word that you
say, but I will defend to the death
your right to say it.* — VOLTAIRE.

Boston · New York · Chicago · Dallas · San Francisco
HOUGHTON MIFFLIN COMPANY
The Riverside Press Cambridge

The Riverside Press
CAMBRIDGE · MASSACHUSETTS
PRINTED IN THE U.S.A.

PREFACE

A COMPLETE culture," says Lewis Mumford, "leads to the nurture of the good life."

Two phases of a complete culture are acquaintance with a large variety of subjects and tolerance toward the many divergent points of view on those subjects. In this book the editors have tried to bring together definitely conflicting expressions of opinion on a number of important topics. It is hoped that many of the included essays will provoke thoughtful discussion — perhaps even bitter and fiery debate. After all, the main purpose of the writers here represented has been to make their readers think. If the reader does not agree with the opinions expressed, so much the better — if he knows why he does not agree, and can support his beliefs by valid evidence. Recognition of both the weakness and the strength of the other point of view is characteristic of the cultured, the open mind.

Since the purpose has been to select essays which are clearly stated and understandable, very little attention has been paid to the relative importance of their authors. However, it will be observed that a number of the "great" names of contemporary thought and contemporary letters have found their way into the volume. In all cases, brief biographical notes have been given, so that the reader may know by what authority of experience each writer is privileged to speak.

When the book is used in connection with college courses in composition, the suggested theme-plan in the Appendix may prove helpful. The student who enters into the spirit of the essays, and who writes freely and individually upon the various topics suggested, at the end of the course will find that he has produced a series of papers which is, in essence, a sort of mental autobiography. Such writing may be, as regards both thought and expression, interesting and valuable.

The editors wish to express their gratitude to the publishers and authors who have permitted the reprinting of copyrighted material, and to the several people who, by suggestions or in other ways, have helped in the making of the book.

K. B. T.
J. F. McD.
D. O. J.

ACKNOWLEDGMENTS

ACKNOWLEDGMENT must be made to the various publishers and individuals who have generously permitted the reprinting of essays of which they hold the copyright. The editors wish to express their indebtedness to the following authors and publishers:

James Truslow Adams, for "The Mucker Pose." Reprinted from *Harper's Magazine.*

Frank R. Arnold, for "The Mating Season of Co-Education." From *Scribner's Magazine.* Copyright, 1926, by Charles Scribner's Sons.

George S. Brooks, for "Gas and the Games." From *Scribner's Magazine.* Copyright, 1928, by Charles Scribner's Sons.

Lewis F. Carr, for "Unknown America." Reprinted from *The Century Magazine.*

Stuart Chase, for "The Dogma of 'Business First.'" Reprinted from *Harper's Magazine.*

Edwin Grant Conklin, for "Science and the Faith of the Modern." From *Scribner's Magazine.* Copyright, 1925, by Charles Scribner's Sons.

Harvey Wiley Corbett, for "New Heights in American Architecture." Reprinted from *The Yale Review* by special permission of the author and the editors.

Thomas Craven, for "The Great American Art." Reprinted from *The Dial.*

The John Day Company, Inc., for "The Great Sports Myth," from *Sports, Heroics, and Hysterics,* by John R. Tunis.

Bernard De Voto, for "The Co-Eds: God Bless Them!" Reprinted from *Harper's Magazine.*

Dodd, Mead and Company, Inc., for "Oxford as I See It," from *My Discovery of England,* by Stephen Leacock; "Americanism," from *Imaginary Obligations,* by Frank Moore Colby; and "On Vulgar Optimists," from *I For One,* by J. B. Priestly. Copyright by Dodd, Mead and Company, Inc.

Doubleday, Doran and Company, Inc., for "Drink" and "Hustle," from *The Savour of Life,* by Arnold Bennett, copyright, 1928, by Doubleday, Doran and Company, Inc.; and "Voices Crying in the Wilderness," from *The Doctor Looks at Love and Life,* by Joseph Collins, copyright, 1926, by George H. Doran Company.

Robert L. Duffus, for "Where Do We Get Our Prejudices?" Reprinted from *Harper's Magazine.*

Katharine Fullerton Gerould, for "Our Passion for Lawmaking." Reprinted from *Harper's Magazine.*

Harcourt, Brace and Company, Inc., for "Puritan Resistance to Freedom of Thought," from *America Comes of Age*, by André Siegfried; "Pigskin Preferred," from *Read America First*, by Robert Littell; "Thanks to the Artists" and "Sentimental America," from *Definitions*, by Henry Seidel Canby; and "Well Read," from *American Estimates*, by Henry Seidel Canby.

Harper and Brothers, for "Will Science Displace God?" from *Adventurous Religion*, by Harry Emerson Fosdick.

Houghton Mifflin Company, for "New Varieties of Sin," from *Sin and Society*, by Edward A. Ross.

Robert Edmond Jones, for "Art in the Theatre." Reprinted from *The Yale Review* by special permission of the author and the editors.

Alfred A. Knopf, Inc., for "Conclusions of a Man Gone to the Devil," from *Up from Methodism*, by Herbert Asbury; and "The Novel and the Spirit," from *Portage, Wisconsin*, by Zona Gale.

Don Knowlton, for "The Anatomy of Jazz." Reprinted from *Harper's Magazine*.

Harold J. Laski, for "The American Political System: As Seen by an English Observer." Reprinted from *Harper's Magazine*.

Horace Liveright, for "The Business of Education," from *Upstream*, by Ludwig Lewisohn.

W. O. McGeehan, for "Our Changing Sports Page." From *Scribner's Magazine*. Copyright, 1928, by Charles Scribner's Sons.

Robert A. Millikan, for "Science and Modern Life." Reprinted from the April, 1928, issue of *The Atlantic Monthly*.

The Nation, for "Mr. Babbitt's Spiritual Guide: A Review of Sinclair Lewis's *Elmer Gantry*," by Joseph Wood Krutch.

The New Republic, for "On the Industrial Scrap Heap," by A Worker.

W. W. Norton and Company, Inc., for "The Harm that Good Men Do," from *Sceptical Essays*, by Bertrand Russell.

James B. Pratt, for "Religion and the Younger Generation." Reprinted from *The Yale Review* by special permission of the author and the editors.

Henry F. Pringle, for "Politicians and the Press." Reprinted from *Harper's Magazine*.

Arthur H. Quinn, for "What's Right with the Colleges?" Reprinted from *The Century Magazine*.

Agnes Repplier, for "On a Certain Condescension in Americans." Reprinted from the May, 1926, issue of *The Atlantic Monthly*.

Charles Scribner's Sons, for "Poetic People," from *The Enjoyment of Poetry*, by Max Eastman, copyright, 1913; "The Shifting Centre of Morality," from *The Genius of America*, by Stuart P. Sherman, copyright, 1923; and "The Comedy of Leadership," by Christian Gauss, which is a chapter in a book on college problems to be published by Charles Scribner's Sons in the fall of 1929.

Edwin E. Slosson, for "The Changing Mind of Man."

Jesse R. Sprague, for "Prosperity Without Profit." Reprinted from *Harper's Magazine*.

Frederic F. Van de Water, for "My Son Gets Spanked." Reprinted from *Harper's Magazine*.

Carl Van Doren, for "The Spring Lesson: A Review of Sinclair Lewis's *Elmer Gantry*." Reprinted from *The Century Magazine*.

The Viking Press, for "The Sickbed of Culture," from *Horizons*, by Francis Hackett. Copyright, 1918, by B. W. Huebsch, New York.

Thomas Jefferson Wertenbaker, for "What's Wrong with the United States?" From *Scribner's Magazine*. Copyright, 1928, by Charles Scribner's Sons.

CONTENTS

COLLEGE READINGS IN CONTEMPORARY THOUGHT

∴

I. PREJUDICES

WHERE DO WE GET OUR PREJUDICES?

By ROBERT L. DUFFUS

Robert L. Duffus (1888–   ), who was educated at Stanford University, has been an editorial writer on two New York papers, the "Globe" and the "Herald," and he is now a free-lance journalist. Besides contributing many interesting articles to various magazines, he has published three novels: "Roads Going South" (1921), "The Coast of Eden" (1923), and "Tomorrow Never Comes" (1929), and one study in art education, "The American Renaissance" (1928).

WHAT, if you will pardon my asking, does the word "Bolshevik" mean to you? Or "Nordic"? Or "Jew"? Or "Catholic"? Or "German"? Or "Mexican"? Or "tariff"? Or "pacifist"? Or "militarist"? Or "prohibition"? Or "automobile"? Or "motion picture"? Or "chewing gum"? Or any one of a thousand other words?

One answer you may safely make. They do not mean the same to you that they do to me, or to your uncle, your wife, your next-door neighbor, Mr. Coolidge, Mr. Ford, Mr. Wayne Wheeler, Mr. Wrigley, Douglas Fairbanks, or the milk man. We assume that there is such a thing as the English language — and perhaps there is. But each of us speaks a different dialect. All we say is like an imperfectly heard conversation over the telephone. The connection is always poor. We are always getting the wrong number. This is because every important word has to carry around, in addition to its dictionary definition, the meaning that each one of us has attached to it as the result of his life's experiences. "Automobile" signifies one thing to a man who is in the hospital recovering from an argument with one, and quite another to a man who has just made a successful speculation in General Motors.

In order to get at the basis upon which these generalizations rest, let us assume that a representative group of the readers of this article — say twenty or thirty — are given such a list of words as I have mentioned, though preferably a much longer one. Each will receive a large sheet of paper, which will look something like this:

Directions: A. Read through the words and phrases listed below. Consider each one not more than five seconds. If it calls up a disagreeable association, cross it out. You may cross out many or few words. Work as rapidly as you can, but be sure you cross out every word which is more annoying than pleasing, more antagonizing than appealing, more distasteful than attractive.

1. Nordic
2. Disarmament
3. Jew
4. Prince of Wales
5. Immigrant
6. Protestant
7. Pole
8. World Court
9. Ku Klux Klan
10. My Country Right or wrong
11. Roman Catholic
12. 100 per cent American
13. Mohammedan
14. Socialist
15. Nationalism
16. Propaganda
17. America First
18. American Legion
19. Made in Germany
20. Pacifist
21. Monroe Doctrine
22. Defense Day
23. Foreigner
24. League of Nations
25. Japanese

26. Chinese
27. Reserve Officers' Training Corps
28. Quaker
29. West Point
30. Radical
31. Non-resistance
32. Independence of Philippines
33. Treaty of Versailles
34. War Veterans
35. National Security League
36. Protective Tariff
37. Turk
38. Armenian
39. Slav
40. Mexican
41. Fascisti
42. Russian
43. French
44. Italian
45. Greek Catholic
46. Irish
47. Mussolini
48. Preparedness
49. German
50. Patriot

The result will be that we shall get, not the sober second thought upon which all good citizens are supposed to act, but the emotional impulses upon which, to some degree, we all do act.

Next we will ask how the pleasant or unpleasant pictures arose in each individual's mind. We may begin with the impression that we have already weighed the pros and cons with regard to these more or less controversial subjects — that our processes of decision have been purely mental. But before we are through, if we are entirely honest with ourselves, we shall see that our conclusions are, in fact, the result of a mixture of thinking and feeling. Every word is topheavy with what we have seen and felt.

Any representative committee of the readers of this article would be expected to be open-minded on inter-racial or international questions. Let us suppose that we are trying to measure the exact extent of that open-mindedness. We each take a sheet of paper on which is printed:

According to my first-feeling reactions I should willingly admit members of each group (as a class, and not the best I have known, nor the worst members) to one or more of the relationships under which I have placed a cross (X).

(If you are wholly unfamiliar with any one of the groups, you need make no marks for it. Note that crosses may be put in any number of the six columns.)

	To Citizen-ship in my Country	To my Church as Full Members	To my Street as Neighbors	To my Employ-ment as Fellow Workers	To my Club as Personal Chums	To close Kinship by Marriage
British.....	....	....	....	....	....	....
Chinese....	....	....	....	....	....	....
Czechs.....	....	....	....	....	....	....
French.....	....	....	....	....	....	....
Germans...	....	....	....	....	....	....
Italians....	....	....	....	....	....	....
Japanese...	....	....	....	....	....	....
Jews.......	....	....	....	....	....	....
Mexicans...	....	....	....	....	....	....
Poles.......	....	....	....	....	....	....
Russians ...	....	....	....	....	....	....

Again, if we are honest, we may find that our instinctive attitudes do not conform exactly to what we have been accustomed to regard as our opinions. And again, if we dig deeply into our emotional life, from childhood up, we may find that the key to our state of mind lies in some ludicrously trivial episode.

The first of these tests I have cribbed from Mr. G. B. Watson, of Teachers' College, Columbia University. The second was invented by Professor E. S. Bogardus of the University of Southern California. Both have been widely used in a study into the sources of public opinion which is now being conducted by *The Inquiry*, of New York City, under the direction of Mr. E. C. Carter. Mr. Carter and his associates are trying to throw light on what it is that makes our wheels go round.

Mr. S. M. Keeny, working under Mr. Carter's direction, tried a variation of the Watson test on a thousand persons. These "martyrs to science," as Mr. Keeny calls them, were selected from groups who already happened to be interested in the discussion of public questions. They were above the average in education and intelligence — as much so, probably, as the readers of this article. This is important to remember. We are not dealing with the ignorant or the subnormal, but, if I may indulge in a bit of intellectual arrogance (I shall be less arrogant before I am through) with ourselves.

Of Mr. Keeny's thousand thinking Americans, put to tests such as these, 98 per cent crossed out "Bolshevik," 90 per cent crossed out "Turk," 50 per cent crossed out "Mexican," and 30 per cent crossed out "immigrant." That is, these words had unpleasant associations for those fractions of the group. It was fairly obvious that some of these reactions of distaste — whether justifiable or not is beside the question — could be traced to the newspapers and the motion pictures. We may not think we believe what we read in the newspapers, but if we read it often enough we do believe it. The films are even more persuasive, for they carry the illusion of reality. To see a Mexican, Japanese, or Russian villain on the screen is only a little less convincing than seeing one in real life. For the immature mind (and all minds are immature at some stage), it may be just as convincing.

The results, on the words just mentioned, and on nearly all racial or national names, are almost the same the country over. When the unpleasant reactions to the mention of a foreign nationality decline perceptibly it is a sure sign that some unusual influence — usually an educational one — has been at work. In the City Normal School of Rochester, New York, courses were given in the history and culture of a number of races. They proved interesting and enjoyable. Consequently the hate-and-fear reactions of the students, when given the Watson test, were abnormally low. Their former racial attitudes had been altered by a little judicially furnished information.

But at least half of Mr. Keeny's cases had — fortunately for our present purpose — escaped this civilizing process. Some of their prejudices were still sufficiently intact to be examined. With Mr. Keeny's permission I am able to present a few of their confessions. Some of them may appear fantastical, but the whole point is that the insides of what we call our minds, if we examine them courageously, *are* a little fantastical.

"When I was a little girl," a woman wrote, "just starting to school, some one told me that in all the Catholic churches the Catholics kept weapons and ammunition in the basements, all ready at the slightest provocation to make war on the Protestants and kill them. The same person told me that she knew a Catholic lady who had said that she could wade in Protestants' blood up to her knees with a smile on her face. I have had Catholic girl friends since then, some of the best friends I have known, but I could never get rid of my first impressions."

Another correspondent, a college student, found it hard to eliminate the picture of a Catholic as one who "hoped to wade knee-deep in Protestant blood in a religious war." Multiply by a few millions and we have the Ku Klux Klan.

"I have always had a prejudice against foreigners," another letter ran. "When we lived in the East and went to Massachusetts each summer, we would pass Poles and Italians owning and working farms which our forefathers owned. This sight of the foreigners always aroused in me an intense dislike of them." The dislike stuck. It affected the writer's thinking on all subjects connected with "foreigners" and "foreign" countries.

Then there was the story of Henry B. "My early childhood," this confession began, "was spent in a suburban district of the city of Chicago, and in this place there lived but one family of Jews. This family consisted of Mr. and Mrs. B., and their son Henry. As we were neighbors Henry and I used to play together until one fatal day. While playing house I happened to break one of Mrs. B.'s white milk pitchers, for which Henry admonished me and frightened me terribly. . . . From that day I never played with Henry again, for I both hated him and at the same time was afraid of him. . . . Since my childhood days I have had many pleasant dealings with Jews and Jewesses. Yet when one mentions the name 'Jew' I am liable to grow very angry or condemn the Jewish race in a terrible manner, for then . . . the recollection of my childhood experience comes to mind."

A trivial incident, no doubt, but a million such trivialities make a mountain of prejudice. Put this beside it: "When I was quite young my mother read me the story of Oliver Twist. I remember quite plainly how angry I became when I learned the full extent of Fagin's operations as affecting Oliver. There was also a picture of the old Jew, showing him in all the horror imaginable — stooped, filthy, ragged, sly, sneaking, all the worst possible traits. Then I saw a few years ago Lon Chaney play the part on the screen. This performance capped the climax. Since then I have looked upon most Jews with somewhat of aversion."

One of Mr. Keeny's correspondents disliked Spaniards because he had read of Spanish cruelties in the conquest of America. To another, a Jew, the word "Turk" called up "a vivid picture of a malignantly cruel, black-skinned man in oriental garb who stood triumphant over the prostrate body of a blood-stained victim." A boy of twelve tied a can to a Mexican's dog, was terribly alarmed when its irate master chased him, and now, as a grown man, still feels "a natural repugnance whenever I see or hear the word 'Mexican.'" One woman admits "a rather decided prejudice against the negro." She adds, "I don't know why I have this feeling, unless it is because when I was a small child a story was told me of a white girl who was kidnapped by two negro renegades. The picture, even to-day, is very vivid to me."

A child acquired a lifelong fear and dislike of Mexicans because, when she was six years old, her father went to Mexico City on business and during his absence her mother "frequently voiced apprehensions for his safety."

"When the word 'foreigner' is mentioned," another young lady admitted, "I think of limburger cheese. In grade school an immigrant girl of respectable family sat opposite me. During school hours she was continually eating limburger cheese, keeping a great smelly piece in her desk. I was talking about it to some friends. They laughed and said, 'Oh, well, she's a foreigner.'"

Sometimes the pictures are too personal to generalize about. A certain woman finds the mention of "flag drill" disagreeable. Is it because she is defective in what a member of the American Security League might regard as patriotism? Not at all. "This feeling," she writes, "is probably due to an incident that occurred when I was about seven years old. On one occasion our class gave a flag drill. All the girls wore white fluffy dresses except me. I didn't have any, and so had to wear an old blue striped dress that I had always greatly disliked. I was very much humiliated, and my heart ached for a white, ruffly dress. . . . From that time to this I have invariably associated flag drill with an old blue striped dress, and it is a decidedly unpleasant association."

In *all* these cases the incidents lay sufficiently near the surface of the memory to be readily brought up. In most cases they were *always* brought up by the mention of certain words. Just how far these pictures controlled the individual's actions is not easy to say. Probably it was more than the individual himself, or herself, realized. Nor is it a simple matter to determine why certain incidents should be remembered so vividly, and not others. Nor can one more than guess at the forgotten experiences, each doing its share toward determining our emotional attitudes, that are buried in our subconscious minds. At the best that is a job for the psychoanalyst. It does seem certain, however, that much which our conscious minds seem completely to have forgotten still helps to guide our opinions and our prejudices. The weight of evidence is that the trail leads back to the experiences of childhood.

Mr. Bruno Lasker, also of *The Inquiry*, has analyzed the results of a questionnaire on race attitudes in children. The data seemed to indicate that we are not born prejudiced. Nature does not plant in our hearts such convictions as one youngster expressed: "The Italians are a very unclean and sneaking race. The Chinese and Japs are a stealing and distrustful people. The Mexicans are a stingy and conspiracy people. The Portuguese are a very bloodthirsty and dishonest people. Germans are hateful because of their love for war and bloodshed." Or these: "Chinese, too crafty. Cannibals, eat up people. Serbians, not clean people. Germans, war makers. Turkeys, torturers."

Children acquire beliefs like this exactly as they acquire their language, their games, and their gang traditions. They learn from their parents, their school teachers, their companions, and, as they grow older, from motion pictures, newspapers, magazines, and books. Being human, they learn what isn't so just as thoroughly as what is so and believe it just as firmly.

The most primitive form of race prejudice is fear — the savage's hostility to a member of a tribe not his own, the child's dread of a stranger who differs in some marked way from its own father or mother. But even this doesn't seem to be inborn. It is put into the child's nature by some outside influence, or influences, after the child comes into the world. Let a parent manifest race prejudice by a word or even a gesture, or a facial expression, and the child will imitate. Race prejudice may begin before the boy or girl has learned to talk.

When the child is five or six years old the fear may turn into hostility — a race riot in miniature. There will be a stage when foreigners are merely absurd and amusing. Finally, among children of different races attending the higher grades of the same school there will be jealousy arising out of the competition for marks and honors. By this time the child of the "superior" breed has learned that the child of the "inferior" should be kept in his place. Groups form, sharp social lines are drawn, and the chasm between black and white, white and yellow, or "American" and "Wop" is likely to become permanent. Even though in a fit of deliberate liberalism we try to bridge it in later life, we frequently cannot.

Most of us don't try. We merely rationalize. The middle-aged business man who swallows the Nordic gospel hook, line, and sinker to-day, may believe that he got his reasons from Lothrop Stoddard, or that his shrinking from contact with the lesser breeds is the will of God. But the chances are that he learned it all at school, along with his arithmetic and geography, or at home, along with his table manners.

Girls, being earlier responsive to group traditions and loyalties, are found to become race conscious sooner than their brothers. As they grow older the social pressure arising from a dread of intermarriage becomes stronger. They begin to fear, not without reason, that broad-mindedness in their relations with the "inferior" races may cause them to lose caste. A boy's caste, somehow, seems less fragile. Yet boys of sixteen are commonly found to be more snobbish than boys of twelve. There has been more time and more experiences with which to build prejudice — to educate in jealousy and dislike.

All this affords a hint as to how our opinions get into us. They are not made what they are by heredity. They are not produced by accurately digested facts. They are all that our lives are — colorful, unreasonable, egoistic?

But what, aside from the natural interest in playing a game, is the use of knowing this? Simply that we may come a little closer to real thinking, the greatest game of all. It is not until we get out just such a mental mirror as these tests provide, and look ourselves squarely in the eye, that we realize how far we are from unbiased thought, and how fascinating the thinking process might be made.

As this is being written a general strike is going on in Great Britain. I take two morning newspapers. One of them continually irritates me because of what seems to me the prejudices shown by its correspondents. With the other I feel a warm glow of sympathy. It is on my side. Though I try to weigh the evidence carefully, its reports seem to be nearer the truth than those of the other paper. But have I actually given the subject judicial consideration? I suspect not. If I deliberately pull up my opinions by the roots and examine them I find clinging to them fragments of my own life — early friendships, early antagonisms. I have greatly admired So-and-So, and he has influenced me tremendously. I know what he would think of the strike, I still want his approval (though he may be dead, or thousands of miles away), and so I try to think as he would think. And he is but one of many influences, pulling me in the same direction.

I live, let us suppose, in a factory town. A strike is going on. I pass along a certain street and see the strikers brutally knocked about by the police. My emotions are aroused. I become pro-labor. I may even develop into a Socialist or a Communist. But assume that I take another route and hear a peculiarly unattractive orator — a foreign one, perhaps — making a speech. I go a little farther and come on a crowd of strikers beating a "scab." In this case, too, my emotions are stirred up, and unless other and more powerful influences act upon me, I may ultimately join the Chamber of Commerce, vote for Mr. Coolidge, and throw up my hat for Mr. Churchill. These are, necessarily, crude illustrations. Yet the forces which actually do shape some of our most important beliefs are certainly no less haphazard.

The liveliest issue in America at this moment is prohibition. I have an opinion with respect to it. Of what is this opinion composed? I seem to distinguish a number of components. Item one: a great-uncle, a man of brilliant promise in his youth, who drank himself to death in late middle age. Item two: John Bailey, reeling down past our house on a Sunday afternoon, falling helplessly over a barbed wire fence and being carted off to the lockup. Item three: certain poetic allusions to wine, which I came upon in early youth and which call up visions of the vintage in ancient Greece, of the Mermaid Tavern, of good talks across a spotted tablecloth. Item four: an argument *for* prohibition by a man I didn't like. I add up these and other items, subtract the minus quantities, and have what I call an opinion. It may be reinforced with a selected lot of sociological and economic data, but it is not based upon such data. I really don't feel that I ought to be allowed to vote on any prohibition measure. My only comfort is that neither ought very many others. For I do not believe that what I may call my political turpitude is beyond the average.

We are accustomed to think of the nation *as making up its mind* on great public questions. On the theory that masses of people can and do make up their minds in a rational and purposeful way democracy rests. But if the line of thought we have been following means anything, nothing of the sort occurs. Remove the lid from a great political upheaval — remove the catchwords and slogans, the verbal insignia of class and occupation — and something like chaos appears beneath. How crude are all political tests when we examine even one individual, selected more or less at random! Our elections, courts, and legislatures are the clumsiest of recording instruments. They can measure only undigested lumps of opinion; they cannot dissect and analyze and so come at the truth.

But what is necessary, I take it, is not the abolition of democracy or the installation of new political machinery. We need humility, especially among the so-called leaders of opinion. We need tolerance — and not so much that tolerance which is a Christian virtue as that which arises from a scientific recognition of the high percentage of fallacy and irrationality in our own beliefs. The wisest man at this stage of the world's affairs is he who knows that none of us is wise.

PURITAN RESISTANCE TO FREEDOM OF THOUGHT

By ANDRÉ SIEGFRIED

André Siegfried (1875–   ) became widely known in America upon the publication of his "America Comes of Age" (1927). Before this volume appeared, M. Siegfried had written books on Great Britain, Canada, and New Zealand. He is a professor of economics in the Paris School of Social Sciences and, as an expert on economics, is attached to the French Foreign Office.

THE future of American civilization would work out quite differently if the Lutheran or the Catholic conception of the State were to become more powerful than the Calvinist. The recent revival of Calvinism is a sign of its struggle to retain supremacy in order to safeguard the national customs from foreign influence. Countless crusades of every description are undertaken to convert the unbeliever and impose by force the conditions of life advocated by the majority. The minority, they say, have no right to complain, for it is being done for their good. In anything that touches the life of the community, the American is in reality a sort of "collectivist." He is as intolerant as a convert, especially since in religious matters he is an absolutist.

The opposition to this program comes either from scattered groups or from the business interests that are unable to fall in with the plans of the moralist, for business will not agree unless it either profits by these campaigns or guides them.

The Lutheran is out of sympathy partly owing to his hereditary respect for the State, and partly because he is determined to keep his German customs. The Catholic, and even at times the Anglican ritualist, is indignant that the State should submit to the dictates of individual consciences instead of to the Church, for both prefer ecclesiastical authority and family traditions. The Irish colonies of the great cities have imported an original viewpoint of their own with regard to methods of government, and their half-Catholic, half-cynical outlook has become Americanized. The English idea of government by disinterested gentlemen devoting themselves to the general good, which existed in America before the wave of Irish immigration of 1840, has not been entirely stamped out. The Irish newcomers, however, looked upon the State as the property of the people and especially as a means of obtaining the greatest possible advantages for themselves and their friends. A clash was inevitable between the ideals of the Puritan democracy and that extraordinary *pot-pourri* of farce, intrigue, hurly-burly, and whimsicality that goes to make up Irish politics, and which we must admit has, with all its faults, saved America from becoming as dreary as a prayer-meeting!

The reformers have had to reckon with still another power. In America as elsewhere business competition follows the natural laws of the struggle for existence. It does not conform to the standards of brotherly love, and all the "service" in the world cannot change it. Therefore nothing can be done against the wishes of the manufacturing interests, especially since they have been amalgamated and disciplined by the evolution of modern industry. When the religious élite wish to modify the national customs or preserve those that are dying out, they are accordingly careful not to antagonize the business world. Whenever the self-interest of the capitalist coincides with the idealism of the apostle, the "urge" for moral uplift becomes irresistible; for in America the wealthy are Christians, and nothing forbids Christians to be wealthy. In such an alliance lies the vital force of this community. Though it receives its inspiration from Puritan mysticism, it really expresses itself in material wealth, and it is not at all concerned with the liberty of the individual.

It is essential to realize that the liberalism of the eighteenth-century philosophers counts for little among these social forces. It is sometimes held that American political thought is based on the Constitution, which was largely drawn up by Jefferson and is very French in its disregard of religion. In actual fact, however, as may be seen by the renaissance of Puritanism and the extraordinary irruption of the Ku Klux Klan, the political thought of the Protestant masses is very different from that of Franklin, Paine, Jefferson, or Washington. Instead of going back to these great liberals who were so close to secular thought, we must turn rather to the narrow fervour of the Cromwellian Roundheads, who were totally opposed to such ideas. If we overlook this, we are bound to be shocked when we find in America certain intolerant aspects of Protestantism which in Western Europe are now supposed to belong to the past.

It is generally believed that the First Amendment to the American Constitution in 1791 [1] assured complete religious equality, and the Americans were free to choose God, Jehovah, or Buddha as they pleased, or even to maintain that there was no God at all. This, however, is not the case, though it is true that there is no established church. It is nevertheless understood that America is a Christian nation and that Protestantism is the national religion. This distinction seems perfectly plausible to the Protestants, for though their idea of a church is attenuated, their religious zeal is vigorous in the extreme. A Catholic who is not used to separating religion from the Church is apt to find the distinction too subtle. President Wilson in 1917 had printed on the title page of the New Testament that was distributed to the soldiers, "The Bible is the word of God. I request you to read it," and the public did not feel that he had exceeded in the least his rôle as head of a Christian government.

In many States of the Union, Protestantism was the established religion in the eighteenth century; for in those days a nation without a religion was an anomaly. Jews, atheists, and in certain cases even Catholics did not enjoy the full rights of citizenship. Under these conditions the First Amendment did not really secularize the State, but aimed more at holding the balance between the numerous Protestant sects. What the American liberals desired both at that time and since was to divorce the State from the churches, but not to separate it from the Christian religion, and certainly not from Protestantism. The official indifference to religious matters which characterizes French secular thought seems scandalous even to-day to most Americans.

Even after a century of progress, laws protecting religion still exist in many States. To work on Sunday is everywhere an offence, and the unfortunate Jew, after having observed Saturday as his own Sabbath, is obliged by the Christians to respect the next day as well. In North Carolina the law forbids the sale of gasoline during church hours. In Maryland it is a crime to utter impious words about our Lord. In New Hampshire it is heresy to deny the existence of God. In several States — Maryland, Arkansas, and South Carolina — Jews have not, for a long time, been accorded the same legal status

---

[1] "Congress shall make no law respecting an establishment of religion, or prohibiting the free exercise thereof."

as Christians.   In Massachusetts in 1921 a Finnish lecturer who had
mocked the Bible was condemned as follows under the Blasphemy
Act:

> The religion of Christ is the prevailing religion of this country and this
> State. . . . Congress and the State legislature open their sessions with prayer
> addressed to the God of the Christian religion. . . . Shall we say that any
> word or deed which would expose the God of the Christian religion or the
> holy scriptures to contempt and ridicule would be protected by a constitu-
> tional religious freedom?   We register a most emphatic negative.

It is wrong, therefore, to speak of religious liberty or equality as
traditionally American.

Christianity in its Protestant form is so closely woven into the whole
fabric of society that it is impossible to conceive of a separation, even
suppose it were desired.   The recent passage of a law in the State of
Tennessee, forbidding the teaching of evolution in the public schools,
and the famous trial which resulted in 1925 from the violation of this
law are not isolated and interesting facts, but are quite in line with
the traditions of secular legislation.   The intolerance thus denoted is
not simply a relic of the past, but a reflection of present-day sentiments and of a type of nationalism that cannot distinguish between
patriotism and religion.

In the stubbornly insular State of Tennessee on the western slope
of the Alleghanies are some of the most backward people in the South.
Its population consists of honest, frugal farmers of pure Anglo-Saxon
origin who have preserved their Protestant faith on ice.   Dayton,
where the trial took place, is little more than a village, having at most
a few thousand inhabitants, all eminently respectable.   Their ideas
of the world are narrow, for they are not intellectual; neither have
they travelled.   On the other hand they are anything but fools.
They are the prototype of millions of other Americans in the Mississippi Valley who live in hundreds of other Daytons, and whom we of
the Old World can never hope to meet.   One point, however, must
be noted: in Dayton there are no Catholics, no Jews, and no Angli-
cans.   Every one belongs to the Protestant churches, of which two
are Methodist, two Baptist, one Presbyterian, and one Christian
Brotherhood.   All the social life of the town is centred around these
churches, and nine-tenths of the population turns to them for recrea-
tion and distraction, for the poetic relaxation of which every one

feels the need, and indeed for all that art, music, and conversation can give in such an atmosphere.

What a light the trial sheds on this reservoir of Methodist emotions, preserved intact in this far-off country a hundred and fifty years after the death of Wesley! Under the direction of the Fundamentalist ministers, who preached mediæval dogmas with the fervour of the Inquisition, the little community obstinately shielded itself behind the Bible to avoid the contamination of modern ideas and foreign influences. The Eastern States, with their Catholics, Jews, and foreigners, were almost as abominable in their eyes as decadent Europe; and they felt that they must at all costs avoid contagion. We can easily see how the people of Tennessee have remained impervious to outside influence. They believe themselves to be legally masters in their own house, and they intend to worship God in their own way without advice. Both the Federal and their own local State Constitution forbid favouritism in the schools toward any one church to the detriment of the others; so no genuine religious teaching can be given by the State, although the majority undoubtedly wish to legalize their own faith.

Now at long last they hear tell in Tennessee of the doctrine of evolution, and they consider it dangerous to their faith. Darwin's works are publicly burned in the Mississippi Valley by Baptist ministers assisted by enthusiastic crowds. Evolution is considered scandalous and is cursed by ministers who preach the physical resurrection of the body, the reality of hell fire, and literal belief in the Book of Genesis. The South has been converted to such orthodox views for reasons of its own, which touch it very closely. If the monkey can become a man, may the negro not hope to become white? The Southerners prefer to believe that the various species have been fixed once and for all, by divine wisdom, at the level that Providence has decreed.

As the Fundamentalist sects control the Tennessee legislature, it was only natural that they should profit by the fact to forbid legally any teaching in the public schools of theories contradicting their particular interpretation of the Scriptures. Under their influence the following text was adopted:

Be it enacted by the general Assembly of the State of Tennessee, That it shall be unlawful for any teacher in any of the universities, normal and other public schools of the State, which are supported in whole or in part by the public school funds of the State, to teach any theory that denies the story of the Divine creation of man as taught in the Bible, and to teach instead that man has descended from a lower order of animals.

In the newspapers of the time we find John Washington Butler, the proposer of this law, described as a man of "solid physical stature, slow in movement and in words, burnt as brown as an Indian by working in the fields, and above all full of self-confidence." And the paragraph concludes: "These people, who fear God, do not doubt themselves." When he brought in his bill, Butler simply hoped to defend his faith, nothing more. "I know nothing of evolution," he said, "but I have read in the papers that boys and girls have come home from school and told their parents that all that is contained in the Bible is nonsense. For myself I think that all right-minded people believe in the Bible."

John Thomas Scopes, professor of biology in the Rhea County High School at Dayton, was guilty of teaching his pupils that man was evolved from a lower species of animal. He thus came under the displeasure of the law, and the State of Tennessee initiated the prosecution. It was upheld by the great popular champion of Fundamentalism, William Jennings Bryan, former candidate for the presidency of the Republic, and Secretary of State under President Wilson. The trial was like a regular circus performance and was attended by fervent crowds. To it came celebrated lawyers, countless experts, scientists who had been dragged from their laboratories for the purpose, and witnesses from every corner of the country. To improve matters it was July, and in the South the weather was as hot as an oven. With the exception of two, the jurymen were all farmers of the old type. According to the papers, the majority of them wore belts; for suspenders, that hallmark of the European intellectual, upheld the trousers of only a small minority — no doubt about this, for every one was in shirt-sleeves, including the lawyers, the jury, the judge himself, and even the ministers who inaugurated each session by prayer. He may be narrow as regards dogma, but the God of the Americans is certainly liberal in matters of style! A delighted America saw herself portrayed to the life in the naïve discussion in which the *vox populi* was called upon to pronounce in defence of the faith.

When we study the opposing theses of this extraordinary trial, we are at the very heart of the struggle that is perpetually recurring between the tryannical ambitions of the majority and the liberal attitude of the minority in defence of their rights. The desire of the churches to obtain the sanction of civil authority for their dogmas is as old as the hills, and when the Fundamentalist Bible was installed as the official fountain of truth in the public schools, it was after all exactly what local public opinion and the authors of this law desired. If one reads the declarations of Bryan, that religious demagogue who throughout the trial was the faithful interpreter of these ideals, it is obviously hopeless to look there for any separation of Church and State.

Power in this country [he declared] comes from the people; and if the majority of the people believe that evolution breaks down religious faith and threatens Christianity, they have the right to demand that it be suppressed or at least confined to the little group of research men, who may study it as a theory not yet proven. The only morality comes from the Bible, all our institutions and our social life are founded on an implicit belief in it, and without that belief there is no ground on which moral teaching may be founded.

Far from being a dispute over dead constitutions, texts protecting minorities, or the philosophic liberalism of the eighteenth century, this was a burning question to these simple folk who dreaded lest their faith might be contaminated by agnosticism. The great Fundamentalist leader stirred them to the core when, with arms extended as on the cross, his eyes raised to Heaven, he cried pathetically, "Would they have me believe that I was once a worm and writhed in the dust? Will they take from me my hope of a hereafter? I want to go beyond this world, to where there is eternal happiness for me and others!"

The Attorney General, who had been elected by the people, went him one better, but he fully represented them when he said:

When science treads upon holy ground, then science should invade no further. . . . They say it is a battle between religion and science. If it is, I want to serve notice now, in the name of the great God, that I am on the side of religion.

Advertisements plastered all over the walls of Dayton during the trial tersely summed up the popular point of view: "Shall we tax ourselves to damn our children?" The defence hadn't a hope in the world.

They began by contesting the use of public authority for sectarian ends, maintaining that it was a breach of the principle of the separation of Church and State. They argued that no legal authority, no matter what it might be, had the right to impose religious conditions on the exercise of a public function. To consecrate a dogma or even an interpretation of the Bible by means of legislation was not in accordance with the Constitution of Tennessee, as established in 1790, for which the Jefferson Constitution of Virginia had been used as model. At first the defence maintained this thesis brilliantly. Soon, however, unable to resist the insidious atmosphere of the trial, they allowed themselves to be drawn into religious controversy. Using all their skill to prove that evolution was not contrary to the Bible, they pleaded that their client had not violated the law. Although their best plan would have been to contest the bigotry and intolerance of the law as being unconstitutional and anti-American, in the end they practically accepted it by trying to exonerate him on the ground that he had not violated it.

When the discussion drifted into theology, the real character of the trial was shown to be religious rather than judicial. In order to succeed or obtain a hearing in such an atmosphere of blind faith, every one had to prove himself a true believer. Even the Court, although a State institution, was not neutral in this respect. Every session began with prayer, and its impartiality consisted in asking first a Fundamentalist minister and then a Modernist to invoke the Almighty, each side officiating according to a sort of proportional representation. When one of the lawyers began to be a bit bored by the length of these insidious and demagogic prayers, which in truth were addressed more to the jury than to the Creator, he proposed that they should be suppressed. He was firmly put in his place by the Attorney General: "I find it necessary to advise you, in order to govern your conduct, that this is a God-fearing country."

The crowd that filled the room was sulky and excitable, and it kept close watch on the infidels from New York. A free-thought propagandist who was let in by mistake was conducted to the police station, but was released on condition that he would keep quiet. Judge Raulston, who presided, was a genuine product of the Tennessee mountains.   This lay preacher lost no opportunity of affirming, with the full authority of the bench, his respect for the Bible and the faith. Before such a tribunal the position of an atheist would indeed have been enviable.   Though Europe may have laughed and the Atlantic States made sheepish excuses for this outburst of fanaticism, the impression caused in the South and West was tremendous.   When Bryan died, struck down in the middle of the trial by a cerebral hemorrhage, it was as a saint and martyr that they conducted him to the tomb.

In the end Scopes was found guilty, and so he should have been; for he had undoubtedly broken the law.   The real problem is whether the law in question is constitutional.   That has yet to be decided by the Supreme Court of Tennessee, and finally by the Supreme Court of the United States.   Following in the wake of Tennessee, Mississippi passed a law forbidding the teaching of evolution, and a similar resolution was adopted by the Florida legislature, while other States show tendencies to work in the same direction.   If this current of opinion becomes general, will it not threaten all freedom of thought?   The rampart which protects such freedom is simply a text in the Constitution, drawn up over a century ago, and though it is scarcely probable that it will be abrogated or amended, who knows how judges may not interpret it under the pressure of heated public opinion?

If it can be made a crime to-day to teach evolution in the public schools, why should such an interdiction not be extended to private institutions to-morrow?   Will not the very existence of free schools be threatened by sectarian majorities intent on moral unity and impatient of any deviation from it?   A law in the State of Oregon, passed in 1922 but later declared unconstitutional by the Supreme Court, shows the menace clearly.   It also exposes the existence at the other end of the country of the same intolerance as in Tennessee. Oregon represents the centre of Anglo-Saxon Puritanism in the Northwest.   In contrast to the persistent Liberalism of the exotic and charming San Francisco, the nationalism of Portland and Los Angeles is very extreme.   The revivals of Billy Sunday, the evangelist, not to mention prohibition, find a fertile soil in both cities.   Two Puritan migrations from the Mississippi Valley made for these points, one in the second half of the nineteenth century going to Oregon, and one in the beginning of the twentieth century toward Southern California. Though in appearance more modern than the people of the Alleghanies, we find here the same bias, the same fears, and the same religious intolerance.

By popular initiative Oregon passed a law in 1922 declaring that all children between the ages of eight and thirteen years had to be educated in the public schools, although it meant the suppression of private elementary education. The inspiration of this measure appears to be astonishingly like those of the anti-evolutionists of Tennessee. In Oregon they wish to use the public schools, which are controlled by the Protestant majority, to protect from Catholic, Jewish, and even Lutheran influence that portion of the younger generation which for religious or ethnic reasons has not been assimilated with sufficient rapidity. A pamphlet published at the time of the vote by the initiators of this law gives their reasons without beating about the bush:

Our public schools . . . are the creators of true citizens by common education, which teaches those ideals and standards upon which our government rests. Our nation supports the public school for the sole purpose of self-preservation. The assimilation and education of our foreign-born citizens in the principles of our government, the hopes and inspiration of our people, are best secured by and through attendance of all children in our public schools. We must now halt those coming to our country from forming groups, establishing schools, and thereby bringing up their children in an environment often antagonistic to the principles of our government. Mix the children of the foreign-born with the native-born, and the rich with the poor. Mix those with prejudices in the public school melting pot for a few years while their minds are plastic, and finally bring out the finished product — a true American.

This is the classic argument against allowing two types of youth to develop. It is with growing impatience that the true Americans tolerate the separate point of view that is being systematically encouraged by the Catholic Church, through the family and its own schools. Ranged against this determination to remain distinct though loyal is the full force of the free masons, the Protestant masses, and the Ku Klux Klan. If it were not for out-of-date constitutions upheld by the authority of the courts, the organized majority would have demonstrated ere now as it did in Tennessee that unity comes before liberty.

The anti-liberal legislation of Oregon, Tennessee, and Mississippi is at once less dangerous legally and more dangerous actually than it appears at first sight to be.   These bigoted outbursts are still scattered, and if it is finally decided that they are unconstitutional they will not survive, although of course similar laws may be enacted elsewhere, and judges under the pressure of public opinion may further weaken their timid resistance to such innovations.   The real peril is that instruction of every kind will be constantly under suspicious supervision.   It would not be so bad if education were superintended by professional inspectors whose competence and impartiality were assured.   The supervision is more likely to be exercised by a hysterical public, extraordinarily lacking in critical sense, and always likely to be inflamed by some eloquent evangelist.

In the Fundamentalist States and in all the Protestant States generally, the schoolmaster is given very little rope, and even the universities do not escape pressure.   In the case of State universities supported by public funds, the budget is at the mercy of the legislature; that is to say, of universal suffrage; and any unorthodox course of lectures runs the danger of being suppressed.   In the independent universities there are always the trustees to be considered, and although these controllers of the purse-strings are generally well disposed, they have no marked leanings toward extreme ideas.

Under these conditions a liberally minded professor who is anxious to teach what he believes to be the truth runs the risk of raising a scandal either in the local press or in the university itself, and so losing his appointment.   In 1924, to take one example out of hundreds, the professor of biology at the University of Minnesota discussed the Fundamentalist theory of creation in his class and refuted it.   The effect was immediate.   Mr. Bryan hurried to the scene, and before a vast assembly of over eight thousand people in the largest auditorium in Minneapolis, he fulminated against the iniquitous doctrines of evolution and the godless professor who taught them.   The newspapers, knowing their public, reproduced his speech *in extenso*, and so spread the message from one end of the country to the other.   With the danger of such a campaign of indignation always imminent, the professors' hands are bound.   They soon realize, not only from the atmosphere in which they live, but also from their immediate chiefs, that they are expected to be as conventional as possible.   A good professor in the West or the South does not flaunt his independence of thought, and utters nothing that might offend the susceptibilities of the trustees of the university, the important manufacturers and bankers of the town, the ministers of the leading denominations, or the local Congressman.

Of course this may only be a passing phase in the history of the United States, but there is no doubt that at the present time the great Protestant majority is clinging to the old, old belief that has been disputed by philosophers throughout the ages, namely, that there is only one social truth, and unless every one accepts it the unity of the nation is imperilled. We thus have the extraordinary paradox of the descendants of English and Scotch Nonconformists being changed into the narrowest of conformists, and the United States becoming a country where a man who does not fall in line socially and morally runs the risk of not being allowed to express himself freely. In a word, a transformation of the rights of the individual is taking place under our very eyes. The principles of the freedom of speech, of the press, and of association, the inviolability of the individual and of the home, the right to be judged by a jury according to regular procedure, are all solemnly guaranteed by the Constitution, and were handed down to America as part of the sacred heritage of British freedom. Now, however, a new doctrine, vigorous but undefined, is trying to undermine them by teaching that the rights of the community are almost unlimited, if it is defending itself against alien ideas, or against a germ of dissolution threatening its integrity. For the past thirty years, and especially since the War, it is not only the liberty of speech and the press that has been dangerously censored, but even the liberty to unite and the elementary rights of the citizens against an arbitrary police.

The American Constitution still survives, however, without essential alteration, and its revered text upholds in writing the rights of the individual against the State. We must admit that the present tendency of public opinion is out of harmony with it on many points; for, aroused by the menace of foreign ideas, the people are preoccupied with the problem of assimilation and moral standardization. The letter of the law which restrains them was written at an earlier date, and it is doubtful whether the Constitution would be drawn up in the same spirit if it had to be done over again to-day. Jefferson, that great liberal aristocrat whose vague theism has since been denounced as atheistic by generations of rural ministers, is less popular in the West at present then the Fundamentalist demagogue of Dayton. If any relic of the Jeffersonian tradition still survives, it is to be found, strange to relate, in the democratic centres of the great Eastern cities, for ethnic or religious minorities are always in favour of liberty although they may be without doctrinal convictions. But what are we to think of a country of British origin where liberalism has to seek its champions among foreigners and Catholics? The reason is clear enough. In its pursuit of wealth and power, America has abandoned the ideal of liberty to follow that of prosperity.

ON A CERTAIN CONDESCENSION IN
AMERICANS

By AGNES REPPLIER

Agnes Repplier (1858–   ), one of America's most distinguished essay writers, has published books of essays on almost every conceivable phase of American social life. Her first volume of collected papers, "Books and Men," appeared in 1888, and since then, among other works, "Points of View" (1891), "Americans and Others" (1912), and "Points of Friction" (1921).

I

FIFTY–SEVEN years ago Mr. James Russell Lowell published in the *Atlantic Monthly* an urbanely caustic essay, "On a Certain Condescension in Foreigners."   Despite discursiveness (it was a leisurely age), this *Apologia pro patria sua* is a model of good temper, good taste, and good feeling.   Its author regretted England's dislike for our accent, France's distaste for our food, and Germany's contempt for our music; but he did not suffer himself to be cast down. With a modesty past all praise, he even admitted, what no good American will admit to-day, that popular government "is no better than any other form except as the virtue and wisdom of the people make it so"; and that self-made men "may not be divinely commissioned to fabricate the higher qualities of opinion on all possible topics of human interest."   Nevertheless he found both purpose and principle in the young nation, hammered into shape by four years of civil war.   "One might be worse off than even in America," mused this son of Massachusetts; and we are instantly reminded of William James's softly breathed assurance: "A Yankee is also, in the last analysis, one of God's creatures."

Fifty-seven years are but a small fragment of time.   Not long enough surely for the civilizations of Europe to decay, and the civilization of the United States to reach a pinnacle of splendor. Yet the condescension which Mr. Lowell deprecated, and which was based upon superiority of culture, seems like respectful flattery compared to the condescension which Americans now daily display, and which is based upon superiority of wealth.   There has been no startling decline of European institutions, no magnificent upbuilding of our own; only a flow of gold from the treasuries of London, Paris, and ·Rome into the treasury of Washington.   Germany's atavistic belief in the economic value of war, fruit of the evil seed sown in 1870, has been realized in a fashion which Germans least expected. England is impoverished in money and men.   The casualties in the British army were over three million; the killed numbered six hundred and fifty-eight thousand.   France is impoverished in money, men, and resources.   A conscientious destruction of everything that might prove profitable if spared marked the progress of the invading Teutons.   But the tide of wealth did not flow to Berlin.   It leaped the sea, and filled the coffers of the nation that had provided the sinews of war, and that had turned the tide of victory.

Under these circumstances, the deep exhaustion of countries that have been struggling for life as a drowning man struggles for breath is hardly a matter of surprise.   Cause and effect are too closely linked to need elucidation.   When an American newspaper syndicate tells us that "Dr. Frank Crane Explains Europe," we wonder how he comes to know more than the rest of us about it, until we find he doesn't.   "There is only one thing the matter with Europe," says "the man with a million friends," "one root trouble from which all its difficulties spring.   And the matter with Europe is that it has not yet learned to work and to love work.   Europeans still idealize idleness. . . . What is happening now is that the people who are coming into power under the influence of democracy are getting tired of this sort of thing."

My only excuse for quoting these words is that they were written by an American adult, syndicated by American adults, and read by American adults, and that they may therefore be taken as representing one layer of the American adult mind.   Now it is all very well for an ironical scientist, like Dr. Joseph Collins, to intimate that there is no such thing as an American adult mind, and that the great body of the people think like children until they reach senility and cease thinking at all.   The fact remains that nobody but a moron has any right to think like a child after he has ceased to be one.   He goes on doing it because it is an easy, pleasant, and vastly self-sufficient thing for him to do.   But the value of our thinking is the test of our civilization.   If we apprehend the exact nature of our offering to the great depositories of human thought, we know where we stand in the orderly progress of the ages.

There does not seem to be much doubt on this score in the mind (I must continue to use the word) of the average American. The *Atlantic Monthly* published, in February, 1924, a paper by Mr. Langdon Mitchell on "The American Malady." The writer quoted a few lines from an editorial in the *Ladies' Home Journal*, August, 1923. "There is only one first-class civilization in the world to-day. It is right here in the United States and the Dominion of Canada. Europe's is hardly second-class, and Asia's is about fourth- to sixth-class." I verified this quotation, finding it a little difficult to credit, and borrowed it for a lecture I was giving in New York. My audience took it at its face value, and cheerfully, I might say enthusiastically, applauded the sentiment. It was evident that to them it was a modest statement of an incontrovertible fact, and they registered their cordial agreement. They seemed — so far as I could apprehend them — to believe that we were, like the Jews, a chosen people, that our mission was the "uplift" of the human race, and that it behooved those who were to be uplifted to recognize their inferior altitude.

Is this an unusual frame of mind among educated Americans? Is it confined to Main Street, or to those who cater with shameless solicitude to our national self-esteem? Where can we find a better spokesman for the race than Mr. Walter Hines Page, a man to whom was given a hard and heart-rending job, who did it superlatively well (even the animadversions of his critics are based upon the success of his activities), and who died in the doing of it, worn out, body and soul and mind, as if he had been shot to pieces in the trenches. Yet this able and representative American thought and said that Latin civilization was a negligible asset to the world. He could see little good in people who did not speak English, and no good at all in people who did not speak English or French. "Except the British and the French," he wrote to his son, Arthur Page, in December, 1917, "there's no nation in Europe worth a tinker's damn when you come to a real scratch. The whole Continent is rotten, or tyrannical, or yellow dog. I wouldn't give Long Island or Moore County for the whole of continental Europe."

It was a curious estimate of values. Long Island is a charming place, and very rich. Moore County is, I doubt not, one of the most beautiful tracts in a supremely beautiful state. Nevertheless, there are those who would think them dearly bought at the price of Rome. No one can truly say that Switzerland, Denmark, and Holland are rotten, or tyrannical, or yellow dog. Indeed Mr. Page admitted that the Danes were a free people, and that Switzerland was a true republic, but too small to count — a typically American point of view. To interpret life in terms of size and numbers rather than in terms of intellect, beauty, and goodness is natural for a patriot who has more than three million square miles of country, and over a hundred million countrymen. As Walt Whitman lustily sang:

I dote on myself — there is that lot of me, and all so luscious.

That Mr. Page clearly foresaw the wealth and strength that would accrue to the United States from the World War proves the keenness of his vision. In 1914 he wrote to President Wilson: "From an economic point of view, we *are* the world; and from a political point of view also." That he was sure this wealth and strength were well placed proves the staunchness of his civic pride. "In all the humanities, we are a thousand years ahead of any people here," was his summing-up in a letter to Mr. Frank Doubleday, 1916. Even our reluctance to credit Prussia with militarism showed the immaculate innocence of our hearts. "There could be no better measure of the moral advance that the United States has made over Europe than the incredulity of our people." Finally, in a burst of enthusiasm, or sentiment, or perhaps homesickness, comes a magnificent affirmation and elucidation of our august preëminence: "God has yet made nothing or nobody equal to the American people; and I don't think He ever will or can." Which is a trifle fettering to omnipotence.

Mr. Page's Americanism being what it was, I cannot help thinking that his countrymen might have more readily forgiven his admiration for the admittedly inferior qualities of Great Britain. His regard for England was not wholly unlike the regard of the English for the United States in Mr. Lowell's day: a friendly feeling made friendlier by a definite and delightful consciousness of superiority. Ten months before the war, he wrote to President Wilson: "The future

of the world belongs to us. . . . Now what are we going to do with
this leadership when it falls into our hands?   And how can we use
the English for the highest uses of democracy?"

The last sentence is a faultless expression of national condescension.
It would have given Mr. Lowell as much entertainment as did the
comments of his British acquaintances.   I know nothing to put by
its side, because it is so kindly meant.   Our lordliness is, as a rule, a
trifle more severe, tinged with reproof rather than sweetened with
patronage.   When the Locarno Conference progressed to its satisfactory conclusion without our help or hindrance, a leading American newspaper seized the opportunity (which was not a good opportunity) to assert our domination over Europe, and to remind her of
the finality of our verdicts.   If our President urged "international
agreements," his words must be received outside the United States
as "a warning that this government, as represented by Mr. Coolidge,
will accept no excuse for war anywhere."

But why, in heaven's name, should any European nation offer an
excuse to Mr. Coolidge for anything it feels disposed to do?   If it
belongs to the League of Nations, and undertakes, however lamely,
to go to war on its own account, excuses are in order, but not to
Washington.   Even in the World Court we share our rights and
responsibilities with other governments, and accept or reject excuses
in accordance with the will of the majority.

II

The Locarno Treaty has, in fact, given us food for thought.   It
does not in any way impair our safety or our interests.   We are as
big and as strong and as rich as we were before.   But it does show
us that something can be accomplished without our controlling
influence.   Our help is needed in the reconstruction of battered
Europe; but, while we can withhold it at pleasure, giving it does
not warrant too sharp a tone of authority.   A little boy, who has
since grown into a distinguished man of letters, once stepped with
deliberation into a pond and stood there, to the detriment of his
health and of his shoes.   An indignant aunt summoned him to dry
land.   The little boy, being well out of reach, remained water-
logged and defiant.   The aunt, indisposed to pursuit, said sternly:
"Do you know what I do when youngsters refuse to obey me?   I

whip them." The little boy, aware of moral as well as of physical immunity, replied with decision: "You don't vip other people's children, I pwesume." And neither, when it comes to the point, does the United States.

It is natural, though regrettable, that inferior nations, crowded together in Europe, which they have somehow contrived to make glorious and beautiful ("Thank God," cried Henry James, "for a world which holds so rich an England, so rare an Italy!"), should resent our presenting ourselves to them as an example. They have troubles and traditions of their own, inheritances great and grievous which reach back to

> ... old, unhappy, far-off things,
> And battles long ago.

They cannot wipe the slate clean and begin afresh after a new and improved model. We keep on telling them (I quote now from recent American utterances) that our "accumulated heritage of spiritual blessings" is theirs to command; that our idealism "has made itself felt as a great contributory force to the advancement of mankind," and that "the Stars and Stripes are a harbinger of a new and happier day for the lesser nations of the world." We explain to them that we demand payment of their debts in order to maintain "the principle of the integrity of international obligations"; and that our connection with a World Court is in the nature of a public notice "that the enormous influences of our country are to be cast on the side of the enlightened processes of civilization." "Lord, gie us a guid conceit o' ourselves" is about the only prayer which the American has no need to utter.

If Europeans pay insufficient regard to our carefully catalogued virtues, Americans are far too deeply impressed by them. It is as demoralizing for a nation to feel itself an ethical exhibit as it is demoralizing for a young woman to win a beauty prize — by virtue of her nakedness — in an Atlantic City contest. The insult offered to our country by calling such a prize-winner "Miss America" is not greater than the insult offered to our country by calling every expansive wave of self-esteem "Americanism." If our civilization be "infinitely the best so far developed in the ages," we have all the less need to say so. If we are giving to the world "supreme grandeur in service," we can afford to be modest in calling attention to the fact. If we are, by virtue of precept and example, "working great changes in the spirit of international morality," it would be more self-respecting to give other nations a chance to express their un-prodded appreciation and gratitude.

America has invested her religion as well as her morality in sound income-paying securities. She has adopted the unassailable position of a nation blessed because it deserves to be blessed; and her sons, whatever other theologies they may affect or disregard, sub-scribe unreservedly to this national creed. Scholars, men of letters, and the clergy lend it their seasonable support. Professor Thomas Nixon Carver of Harvard, who has written a clear, forceful, and eminently readable book on *The Present Economic Revolution*, seems to have no shadow of doubt that our good fortune is due to our good behavior. "Prosperity is coming to us," he says, "precisely because our ideals are not materialistic. It is coming to us because we are pursuing the exalted ideal of equality under liberty, as it must of necessity come to any nation that pursues that ideal whole-heartedly and enthusiastically. . . . All these things are being added to us pre-cisely because we are seeking the Kingdom of God and His righteous-ness, as they are always added, and must of logical necessity always be added, unto any nation that seeks those ideals of justice which are the very essence of the Kingdom of God."

I wonder if righteousness can be linked so securely to the elements of success; and if food and raiment — all that is promised in the Gos-pel — can be magnified into the colossal fortunes of America. The American may not be materialistic; but he has certainly hallowed commercialism, and made of it both a romantic and a moral ad-venture. He sings its saga at banquets, and he relates its conquests to his sons in magazines and in much-read books. There is great satisfaction in doing this, and we are told it is well done. If some-thing be lacking in such a philosophy, that something is not missed. It is easy to count up the value of the proprieties in a watchful world; but exceedingly hard to put the spiritual life on a paying basis. The Old Testament consistently taught that goodness and piety were rewarded with material well-being; but Christianity has committed itself to no such untenable proposition. "He that findeth his life shall lose it" sounds inconceivably remote from the contemplation of well-merited affluence.

III

A point of difference between the condescension of foreigners in 1869 and the condescension of Americans in 1926 is that the magniloquence which amused and ruffled Mr. Lowell was mainly spoken (he was in a position to hear it both at home and abroad), and the magniloquence which to-day ruffles without amusing sensitive foreigners and Americans is, as I have shown by liberal quotations, printed for all the reading world to see.   An editorial in *Current Opinion* modestly suggests that "Europeans might learn a good deal if they would come over here, study the history of America since the war, and try to imitate our example. . . . We may be crass and uncultured; but at least we have been good sports, and have been honest enough, farsighted enough, and sagacious enough to render the United States the soundest and healthiest nation in the world to-day."

A "good sport" recognizes handicaps.   He knows and he admits that poverty is not the equivalent of wealth, that dead men are not equal to live men, that ruined towns are less habitable than sound ones.   A "good sport" may honestly believe that the one hope for mankind is "the Americanization of the world"; but he does not coarsely call on Europe to "clean up and pay up"; he does not write with comprehensive ignorance: "Europeans will have to abandon their national vanities, and get together, before they can expect to get together with us"; he does not second the Congressman from Ohio who informed the American Chamber of Commerce in London that "right now the United States wants to see Europe do some housecleaning without delay."   He may even venture a doubt when the Honorable David F. Houston, writing ably and reasonably in *Harper's Magazine*, June, 1924, affirms our superior spotlessness. "The United States," says Mr. Houston, "is in a position of leadership in all the fundamental idealistic, moral, and spiritual forces which make a nation great, and constitute a worthy civilization.   It seeks as its highest aim to have a clean national household from cellar to attic."

Seeks it, yes.   All civilized countries seek political integrity, and justice in the administration of law.   Sufficiency, security, and freedom are not the exclusive ideals of the United States.   We may be as good as we are great, but our distaste for sincere and searching

criticism blurs our national vision.   A blustering, filibustering,
narrow-minded Senate is not a source of legitimate pride.   To lead
the world in crime should be a source of legitimate humiliation.
President Coolidge called the attention of the State Governors last
January to the fact that twenty-four thousand persons had met their
deaths by highway fatalities within twelve months.   He said it was
too many for one country in one year, and he was right.   Yet
twenty-four thousand deaths by accidents — some of which were
unavoidable — are less appalling than eleven thousand deaths by
violence in the same length of time.   The combined numbers are
worth the consideration of peace-loving Americans who write
eloquently about the sacredness of life.

The crime waves in every State of the Union have now reached a
stage of permanent inundation; and the ever-increasing youthfulness
of criminals (the American Bar Association has called our attention
to this point) promises more complete submersion in the future.   It
is gratifying to know that twenty-five million American children go
to school every day; but some of them appear to spare time from
their studies for the more exciting pursuits of robbery, housebreak-
ing, and pathetically premature attempts at banditry, to say nothing
of such higher flights as firing their schools and murdering their
grandmothers.   The *Ladies' Home Journal* has recently told us that
"everywhere in Europe the ambitious youngsters of the new generation are learning English, and studying American geography and
political history.   They want to get the spirit of what American
Democracy really is."   We can but hope that these innocent offspring of effete civilizations will not extend their studies to American
newspapers.   If they do, they may give their backward countries
an unexpected lesson in progress.   In 1923, Scotland, with a population of five millions, had only eleven murders, while Massachusetts, with a population of four millions, could boast of one hundred
and seven.   It almost seems as if we could do a little housecleaning
of our own.

The superiority complex is, however, as impervious to fact as to
feeling.   It denies the practical, it denies the intellectual, and it
denies the spiritual.   The Sorbonne and the Institut Pasteur make
no more appeal to it than does the girl Jeanne d'Arc, or the defenders
of Verdun.   France as the inspiration of the artist, the stimulus of

the thinker, the home of those who seek to breathe the keen air of human intelligence, is lost in the France that cannot stabilize the franc, or keep the peace of Syria. She is, in our eyes, a nation reprehensible because she demands the security which two oceans guarantee to us, and contemptible because she has failed to readjust herself after such calamities as we have never known.

What the American likes and respects is what he is happy enough to possess: efficiency, moral uniformity, and a fairly good brand of standardized thought. Conventions are the life and soul of the country, and there is nothing like a convention (except perhaps a political campaign) for making us think well of ourselves. The importunate virtues of small communities are nourished by oratory, and by uplift-mongers on platforms, and in the editorial columns of widely circulated periodicals. Uplifting has become a vocation, and its practitioners enjoy the esteem and gratitude of the public. There is a poignantly funny description in one of William James's letters of a lady, the wife of a Methodist minister, whom he met at Chautauqua, who told him she had his portrait hanging in her bedroom, and underneath these words: "I want to bring balm to human lives." "Supposed," said the horrified — and modest — philosopher, "to be a quotation from *me*."

Americanism has been defined as "the more or less perfect expression of the common belief that American ideals realize themselves in American society." This belief is wholly disassociated from the austere creed of the patriot. It was not patriotism which made foreigners in Mr. Lowell's day so sure that they were conferring a favor on the United States by visiting our shores. It is not patriotism which makes Americans to-day so sure that they are conferring a benefit on Europe by advice and admonition, by bidding her study our methods and imitate our example. There is an intellectual humility which is another name for understanding. It enables us to measure the depths of tragedies which have brought us no personal pain, and the height of supremacies which have failed to arouse our ambitions. It is the key to history, and the open sesame to the hearts of men. It may even come as close to deciphering the mysterious ways of God as the complete assurance that we are His deservedly favorite children.

It takes a great deal to make an enjoyable world. It takes all we have to give to make a world morally worthy of man. Efficiency is an asset; but, without a well-balanced emotional life, it gets us no further than the door of human happiness. Peace and wealth are serviceable possessions; but only intense personalities can create art and letters. Good-will, which Santayana says is the great American virtue, shines like a lamp; but even good-will must be intelligently directed if it is to light up the dark places of the earth; and the dark places of the earth are not confined to other continents than ours. The desire to taste the pleasure of contrast — which is a cruel delight — has disposed us to ignore those things which may be conceived as lowering us to our neighbor's level. "In judging others," says the wise and singularly ironic à Kempis, "a man usually toileth in vain. For the most part he is mistaken, and he easily sinneth. But in judging and scrutinizing himself he always laboreth with profit."

ON VULGAR OPTIMISTS

By JOHN BOYNTON PRIESTLY

John Boynton Priestly (1894–   ) *was born in England and attended Cambridge University. As a critic, reviewer, and essayist his works are varied. Among other books, his "I For One" appeared in 1923, his "Figures in Modern Literature" in 1924, "George Meredith" in 1926, and "Open House, A Book of Essays" in 1927.*

THERE is a certain kind of optimism that is easily the most depressing thing in the world. To meet one who professes it, one who may fairly be called a vulgar optimist (for this kind of optimism is vulgar), is to long for the sweet consolations of Leopardi and Schopenhauer and the blithe despair of the "Shropshire Lad." Who does not know and shrink from that metallic and inflexible cheerfulness, that brutal determination to make what is very absurdly called "the best" of everything, which mark such optimism and set it apart from all reasonable attitudes toward life? Its unmistakable vulgarity, the sign of it everywhere, is easily discovered in its favorite aphorism on the subject of dark clouds and silver linings. There is nothing more beautiful, in their own season, than dark clouds, and no man with a healthy mind — and a healthy mind is a poetical mind — has failed to be strangely exalted, uplifted in spirit, at some time or other at the sight of these somber masses and fantastic shapes which for a few brief moments can transform the whole world into a battlement of Elsinore; yet this vulgar optimist, like some importunate bagman, must come bustling in with his talk of silver linings. He cannot be content with having his pockets and coffers lined with silver, he must line the night sky as well, and all with the same cold, glittering stuff. He lives in a brummagem universe, silver-lined and silver-plated. What does he know of that wise melancholy which is the familiar companion of all good men and true thinkers? He presses all the world and the sun, moon, and stars into the service of maintaining his fixed grin, and he can wring bright conclusions from twilight and the moaning sea, from old, unhappy songs and the pitiful remembrance of first love. For him the strings are muted in vain; he will have nothing but the loud trombone. Now that he and his fellows have swarmed into pulpits and newspaper offices, the whole population is steadily sinking into a deep fit of depression. He it is who is responsible for all these cheery messages and bright services and talks we hear so much about at the present time. Is there anything more hateful than a bright talk?

This vulgar strain of optimism may affect a man's ordinary manners and talk, or his opinions, his philosophy of life, or it may affect them all. In their manner, a great many parsons are optimists of this kind, though they are not so much vulgar as morbid, the victims of a curious sort of nervous disorder. A good deal of the current prejudice against clergymen has nothing at all to do with their religion, their opinions in general, their peculiar functions; it is simply the result of a distaste for the manner they affect in ordinary society. Many of them have a suspicion that their ministrations are not wanted, and as they are compelled to meet all kinds of people who may possibly be hostile, and are anxious to carry it off bravely and prove that they are good fellows and men of the world, they finally adopt a manner that irritates every sensible person they meet. Their grimly determined cheerfulness and hectic goodfellowship are appalling. They drench the world in rosewater. Never will they permit the faintest shadow to cross their faces; they will not be serious for a single moment, but will break into loud, though distinctly nervous, guffaws at every turn. They appear to exist in a universe designed by the editor of *Punch*, and by their kettle-drum counsels of good cheer drive even children toward a bleak but less depressing agnosticism. In America, where extremes flourish, the popular preachers and orators seem to have reached such a frenzy of vulgar and intolerable optimism that perhaps nothing but the reintroduction of gin into the country will save its millions from idiocy. There, a mechanical cheerfulness, the result of nothing but astigmatism and insensitiveness, passes for the very height of wisdom. To read Dr. Samuel Johnson, who meditated and wrote much on the vanity of human wishes, is to be heartened to face the inevitable ills of life; but to read Dr. Frank Crane, who screams into millions of ears every day that everything is for the best and that nothing can go wrong, is to be depressed beyond belief, to be dazed and deafened by the brass band of cheap optimism.

The men who are forever slapping one on the back and saying that everything will come right are bad enough, but more intolerable are those persons who will persist in slapping humanity itself on the back and regarding all life with an unchanging grin of approval. We have not had so many of these vulgarly optimistic philosophers among us of late, but their influence is still felt in the opinion of our time. There are not more things in heaven and earth than are dreamed of in their philosophy, because, in the first place, their philosophy does not dream. Stupidity, downright insensitiveness, is the secret of such optimism, which fits as much as it can of life into its bright little boxes and blandly ignores the rest. It is at its worst when it is based upon a creed of mechanical progress, believing that humanity can be saved by its comforts and conveniences. Who does not know the man who, in his heart of hearts, is convinced that the fact of twenty-five pins being sold for one halfpenny is a blow at, say, the doctrine of original sin? Or him who can now ignore the "still, sad music of humanity," simply because the voice of Mr. George Robey can be heard at both Dundee and Gloucester in the same evening? Or those who prefer to concentrate upon the future, and believe that once all rooms are built without corners and electric light is found in every village, desire shall not fail and the mourners shall go about the streets no more? It is such thinkers as these who — to borrow once more the words of their greatest enemy, the Preacher — come in with vanity and depart in darkness, and whose names shall be covered with darkness.

The reason why such shallow optimism always succeeds in depressing us is that blindness, stupidity, and insensitiveness are always depressing. It is plain to us that those who profess it are living in a world of their own, a much smaller world than ours, a world without atmosphere, and therefore without either sunlight or shadows, and so their words mean little or nothing to us. They are denied both tears and laughter and much of what we call poetry. Shelley, with his belief in human perfectibility and his beautiful anarchy, was an optimist if ever was one, but he is neither vulgar nor depressing, simply because he sings and does not speak, sings out of a vision; he gives us not thought, but the intoxication that thought always induced in him, and it is for this noble intoxication that we treasure him. He is everybody's adolescence, or at least the nobler part of it, transmuted into song.   Thanks to his untimely death, we see him and his work forever in the golden haze of his youth and panther-like beauty, and we ask for nothing better.   What we should have thought of a fat, spectacled, middle-aged Shelley still uttering the same sentiments is another matter.   In the meantime, we go to him neither for wisdom nor for consolation, but in moments of great stress turn rather to that plain, long-nosed gentleman who lounged about the shores of Grasmere, even though we do not care a snap of our fingers for his moral cottagers and celandines.   Another great poet, Browning, was an optimist, but was saved by his passion and dramatic genius from the vulgar strain, though even he came dangerously near it at times.   Tennyson spent sixty years trying to become a vulgar optimist, but fortunately for us he could never destroy (though he could cheapen) his natural dreamy melancholy, and now when his voice returns to us it is mournfully declaiming such things as —

> The lights begin to twinkle from the rocks:
> The long day wanes: the slow moon climbs; the deep
> Moans round with many voices. . . .

There are a number of great men of letters, and they are, on the whole, those with whom we spend the most of our time, whose attitude, not to be lightly labeled either optimistic or pessimistic, seems to be the right one; they are neither intoxicated youths, clothing the world in their bright dreams, nor bitter hobbledehoys, cursing the world for their own awkwardness and bad manners, but grown men, ripe, experienced, knowing the worst, but still smiling, a little sadly sometimes, but smiling.   There are Shakespeare among the poets, Fielding and Thackeray among the novelists, Lamb among the essayists, and Johnson among — shall I say — the literary figures; and when I remember what they have known, drudgery, poverty, and disease, mad sisters, and young wives dead or insane, and all the smaller ills of life besides; when I remember these things and read their work, noting their humor and pathos, their flashes of indignation, their wise wonder, their lasting kindliness, I understand how life, that is neither rosewater nor bitter aloes, should be approached.   There is about all such men a certain sweet melancholy, as far from the studied gloom of the pessimist as it is from the metallic cheerfulness of the optimist, that pervades their work rather than finds direct expression in it; a sweet melancholy that is an air, an atmosphere, a background to their laughter and junketing, a vague curtain before which the little things of this life appear small and bright, pitiful and lovely, an expression that steals over their faces when the fighting and clowning and feasting are done with, and they think they are unnoticed. So it is, I fancy, with all good and wise men, except those who are prophets and mystics. So it is not with the vulgar optimists, who have never meditated upon vanity and have no values. They stand crowing in the darkness, and they will never raise our spirits until they have depressed their own.

II. THE AMERICAN SCENE

UNKNOWN AMERICA

By LEWIS F. CARR

Lewis F. Carr has studied at Yale and Cornell. After graduation he worked as a farmhand in Ohio and New York, and has managed farms in Connecticut, Arkansas, and Georgia. For a time he was editor of "Country Life," a farmers' paper, and for two years was the agricultural expert at Loomis Institute, Windsor, Connecticut. He is now a free-lance writer.

APPARENTLY, we do not know our America. Perhaps nobody does. Any casual conceits we may have entertained about our own knowledge on the subject have been punctured by Bernard Shaw's statement that Americans simply do not know their own land. Shaw contends that only a foreigner, viewing the country objectively, can really know America; he then clinches his point by demonstrating how well he doesn't know this country! Many critics agree that he would never have written his latest book as he did, if he had known and understood us fully. The question arises: Who, if anybody, really knows these United States?

I do not claim to. But the existence of a certain kind of ignorance about America has been impressing itself upon me for some time. After many years in the hinterlands of this country, in the rural districts along the backroads, I have come to dwell among your skyscrapers. And though I remember that my country friends had rather quaint and queer ideas about you city people, I find that you have just as hazy notions about them. We of the country are almost as numerous as you of the cities. Yet I find that you leave us largely out of the picture. You do not know us; yet you presume to speak for America. You make statements that may be true as regards your half of this nation; but they appear quite questionable with respect to the other half.

Your position is of course understandable. You have lived in an environment of progress and well-being; you assume that environment for the whole of America. You travel from New York to Chicago or St. Louis; you see a countryside sleek with prosperous farms and dotted with prosperous cities. You take it as a matter of course that the rest of America is like that which you see.

But it isn't. It's so different that neither I nor anybody else — I verily believe — can tell you the extent of that difference. Perhaps you cannot be told. Possibly the feat is psychologically impossible. If conceptions do not exist in the mind to match the words the ear hears or the eye reads, very possibly those words must remain meaningless. We of the land use the same words that you use, speak a similar language. True; but our talk is based on the facts of a different environment — an environment which you do not understand and which apparently can be learned only by experience. If we speak, for example, of hiring a good cook for three dollars a week, or of contracting with a good seamstress to make children's dresses for the sum of thirty cents each, you may assume, as my friends do, that there's an error some place, typographical, oral or mental; you will gravitate toward the conclusion that somebody's crazy. Most of you will pass on to the consideration of more intelligible facts in your experience.

Yet withal there still may be some hope of understanding each other. Starting at one definite point which is probably in your experience, you may remember the character of "Mrs. Cagle" in the recent play, *Sun Up*. She, at least, was different from your idea of existing American women. A woman of the mountain people of the Southern Appalachians, she was essentially a seventeenth-century person, though living in the twentieth. She and her people used Elizabethan word forms. Her conceptions were equally archaic. The law to her was something that killed her men-folks or deprived them of their lawful means of livelihood, moonshining. The greatest distance imaginable to her was "forty miles beyond Asheville." All enemies were to her "Yankees," and any one who came from farther than ten miles away from her cabin was a "furriner."

"Mrs. Cagle" was part of our unknown America, a part aptly portrayed. Yet I wonder if she was able actually to tell the rest of America anything of her people, to connote to you the facts and conditions of her environment. I doubt it. I had occasion to study several audiences at various performances of the play. These people liked the play exceedingly, were enthusiastic about it. It had entertained, amused, thrilled them — all it was supposed to do. But the situation reminded me of a lecture on the beauties of the sunset before a group of blind people. They heard the words, but they did not see the whole picture. "Mrs. Cagle" was to them a mere fictional character. She was this of course; but she was also true fiction. She was taken from life. Her part was that of a contemporary American, a fact which the audience did not seem to grasp at all. She was the wife, portrayed in the flesh, of another person you may remember, the Forgotten Man, delineated by Walter Hines Page. And the number of Mrs. Cagles and Forgotten Men in progressive, rich, educated America to-day is appalling. Until we know them and their conditions, we cannot be said to know America.

These Forgotten Women exist not only in the Big Smokies, but almost throughout America. E. C. Branson, of the University of North Carolina, has followed the trail further. He tells us there are nearly half a million replicas of "Mrs. Cagle" in this country to-day — poor, ignorant, native-born, white women, "thin and wrinkled in youth from ill-prepared food, clad without warmth or grace, living in untidy houses, working from daylight to bedtime . . . the mothers of joyless children, worn-out by excessive child-bearing, and encrusted in a shell of dull content with their lot in life."

He tells us there are 1200 in Aroostook County, Maine, 1400 in Clinton and Franklin counties, New York, 2000 in Berks, Lancaster, and York counties, Pennsylvania, 3600 in Wisconsin, many in Michigan, Ohio, Missouri, 44,000 and 43,000 in North Carolina and Kentucky, respectively, and so on. These poor women make up America too. The facts and conditions of their existence are largely unknown to the rest of America. And they make up the smallest class that I would mention as being unknown to the urban population.

More appalling is the larger class of illiterates of which the Forgotten Woman is but a part. Our national percentage of illiteracy is six per cent. This is higher than in nine other nations of the world! Applied to the 1927 estimates of population over ten years of age, we find that we have about six million Americans who cannot read or write. The number runs over eighteen per cent in some of our States, higher than among twenty other nations of the world. The percentage of illiteracy even *among native-born white people* in some of our States runs over eight per cent, higher than the national percentage in seventeen other nations of the world.

The fact of illiteracy must be reckoned with in the hinterlands. There, you may not assume as in the city that every one can read and write. Other assumptions are equally dangerous. That rather bright-looking boy over yonder may be able to read and write. But you will probably find on experiment that he draws his letters and figures in the slow painful way of a first-grader drawing the picture of a dog. If you settle in that section, you may have to send elsewhere — as I did — for competent office personnel.

As an illustrative experience: I once sold six car-loads of cattle to a cow-man at so much a head. He was fairly well dressed — gold watch and chain — well spoken of and well spoken; and he knew his business. Together we made the count of the cattle. Then I asked him to compute the gross amount, check it with my figures and write his check. Imagine my surprise — the man could neither read nor write, though he could count cattle going through a gate. I did the figuring; I wrote the check; I signed his name; he made his cross mark. The amount was about eight thousand dollars.

So, when you look at a map, do not assume that those great areas that you have not traversed are like the America that you know. For probably they aren't. That one county that happens to catch your eye because of its peculiar name probably isn't at all like the county just outside your city. It may have a population that is sixty per cent illiterate! And the remainder — though able to read and write — may be so ignorant and benighted, excepting the few professional men, that they would not seem like modern Americans at all. Such counties do exist in America, like transplanted areas of the dark continents.

Perhaps you have had a glimpse of the conditions I am talking about. You may have seen from your Pullman window some pitiably poor shacks, and in the field, two bull yearlings with their tails tied together yoked to a piece of a plow — or perhaps a single steer hitched to a primitive cart. You may have wondered — and rightly. For though oxen are not to be despised for certain tasks — I have owned as many as six yoke — still the use of them for general farm purposes as pictured above indicates, to me at least, a whole set of circumstances and conditions that I find are inconceivable to most of my urban friends. The family living in that shack is probably totally illiterate, is probably suffering from two, three, four or even five serious diseases, is living in dirt and squalor, has no idea of sanitation and finally presents a challenge to the statements that have been issuing for the past several years from this nation's leaders of thought.

It has been rather the fashion of late among certain economists and business men to prophesy that within five years we shall have an America without poverty, without illiteracy and with a minimum of disease. It has also been the fashion — I regret to say — among certain medical authorities and foundations to represent to the American people that certain diseases have been controlled and eradicated. These general "blurbs" about America, made by urban leaders of thought, may be true as regards the urban population. But as regards the rest of America, I for one hold them to be largely unacceptable, generally misleading and in some cases wholly untrue.

I take it that these prophecies and statements — if they mean anything at all — mean that the makers of them are so imbued with the philosophy and religion of modern Americanism that they believe that this cult of progress, intelligence, and confidence — so well typified by our cities — can be extended throughout the rest of America within five years. I do not believe it can. There is too much territory to cover, too much distance to travel, too large a void to fill, too many obstacles to overcome and too much lack of knowledge on the part of those who would spread this gospel and who now prophesy its early general acceptance.

Let us consider for a moment a few of the attributes that we associate with the word "Americanism." The word progress will probably suggest itself to our minds first. America is progressive, especially in the matter of efficiency. She is apt at engineering things, so that one man can do the work of from two to fifty. Yet on forty per cent of our farms, according to estimates of authorities, one man is doing the work of only one man, or of one man and a fraction. In many sections, in New England, in parts of Wisconsin, Michigan, in sections even of Ohio, Indiana, Illinois, and Missouri, and in the border States and in the South, you will still see one man plowing one horse after the fashion of one hundred and fifty years ago. Sometimes you will see one man plowing and another leading, as Poor Richard described — that is, two men doing the work of one. In the more progressive sections, of course, you see one man plowing with four or more horses or a tractor; but this does not erase the fact of the one-horse farmer.

This one-horse farming has serious consequences. There is a farm population of about thirty million, and a village population of about eight million, dependent directly on the farm. Of this thirty-eight million, about forty per cent, or fifteen million people are depending on this archaic, one-horse farming. The actual wages of such labor cannot be higher than thirty-five or forty cents a day; by actual survey such wages have been found to approximate twenty cents a day. It is in sections where such farming exists that one can hire good cooks for three dollars a week and get very pretty little dresses for the children made for thirty cents each.

It is in such sections too that the maximum salary of school-teachers ranges around sixty-five dollars a month, paid generally in county vouchers or warrants maturing usually in two or three years, but which can be discounted only with difficulty. Often, in such sections, there is only one small bank to a county or trade area, a bank with a capital of about ten thousand dollars. Such banks usually do not have the money to discount these teachers' warrants. And if they do, the rate is high, from eight to twelve per cent. The result is that only those of minimum qualifications are attracted to the teaching profession.

As an illustration of these meager qualifications: I lately asked the principal of such a school what mischief certain rowdy boys had done. "Well," he said, "I don't think they done much. They throwed some bricks at the door. . . ." A principal of an American school, teaching English "as she is spoke" to young Americans!

Associated with the word "Americanism," is the idea of material well-being. But this condition does not hold in general for the rural population, though it does in certain favored sections — in most of the Corn Belt, for example, in the Blue Grass, in the Mississippi delta lands, the black lands of Texas, and to a lesser degree in those of Alabama, in parts of the West and the Coast, and so on. Outside of these sections, the great majority of our farmers are on a standard of living far below that which you would consider as a satisfactory American standard.

It has been stated that forty dollars a week — or $2080 a year is about the minimum income which will support a family on an American standard of living to-day. In contrast to this, the National Industrial Conference Board found that our average farm operator receives his house rent and part of his living from the farm and has only the meager sum of $170 a year left over for other living expenses. Under any construction this must be taken to indicate a great difference in the standards of living of farm and city dwellers.

A few years ago, Branson and Dickey, of the University of North Carolina, made an exhaustive study of conditions in three agricultural counties. A reported decrease in the number of farmer-owners and an increase in the number of renters and croppers occasioned the investigation. They found that the average renter lived on a family income of about $250 a year, the cropper family on about $150. There are probably about ten million of such people throughout this country, people who do not own their homes, who make no property return whatever, who seldom see newspapers or magazines and who almost never read books. The investigation showed that not even a Bible was to be found in many of these homes.

It is of these people in one section that Herman Steen wrote lately:

For sixty years, poverty and distress and misery have stalked across the plantations of Dixie, and a dozen States are blinded by illiteracy. Every year, 1,000,000 children are robbed of their birthright of school and opportunity. . . . The standard of living . . . is the lowest of any class of farmers in the United States.

And in 1918, at the beginning of the last year of the war, George Pattullo wrote:

We are beset continually by wails from our sob-sisters, both male and female, relative to Europe and her starving millions. The truth is that there is no more distress, hardship, and privation among the people of Europe, *in spite of war and every attendant horror* than is suffered annually by the poor cotton-farmers in the United States.

These statements are not exaggerations. I have lived among the people described above — within the past year and a half. I have spent a month among them within the past six months. And I know that their condition as set forth by Steen and Pattullo is not overstated. I have tried at various times to describe to my urban friends something of these people, without much success at making myself understood.   My friends in your half of America do not seem to be aware of these people or to be able to comprehend anything of the facts and conditions of their existence or to understand any of the causes which are responsible.

Another vast difference between the America that you know and that which I know is apparent in the study of land values.   You urban people assume as a matter of course that all land values in America naturally increase.   But that is not true when you venture into the other half of America, as many have found to their sorrow.

A friend of mine tells of a certain corner in the outskirts of my town that sold five years ago for $8000.   The loan company would not advance more than $6000 at that time.   Six months ago, that property sold for $30,000, and the loan company advanced $25,000.   To-day, the corner is held at $38,000.   This is perhaps exceptional, but advances of this kind seem to lie more or less in the natural course of things in America.

But across the street from my window, is the office of a firm of lawyers.   Twenty-five years ago they put some of their investment funds in farm lands.   Have they ever been able to get their money out?   No.   Can they get to-day what they paid for their land?   No. Without doubt they could have done so if they had invested in farm lands in the favored sections mentioned before.   But they put their money in farm lands in average sections.   And they lost.   Land values increase only to a limited extent — and more often not at all — in the half of America that I know best.   If you doubt it, look up the records of almost any abandoned farm in a section untouched by industrial development, find out what it has sold for, then ask what it can be bought for to-day.

And you — my urban friends — assume as a matter of course that the bank you do business with will always be in business and will always be able to lend you money on a record of earnings.   But we of the farm persuasion do not assume anything of the kind.   Such an assumption, in our half of America, wouldn't be justified.   We've had experiences — such as my own.   I had a bank "bust right in my face" one day.   With country bank failure increased some 550 per cent over the normal in the past eight years, and with farm bankruptcies increased one thousand per cent over the normal in the same time (while the rate among industrial concerns remained normal) we cannot share with you your confidence in financial institutions; or in commercial ventures. In our part of the world commercial ventures do not succeed very well. We have seen too many sawmills, heading-mills and country merchants fail. And this is why we seem so slow and stupid when you come to us talking investment. The wisest among us put our dollars in the safest place imaginable and no promises of profit can pull them out.

The real point I am making is that there is a tremendous difference between the economic life of our world and that of yours. In my experience in farming in four States, and in my study of farming conditions in as many more, I have known only one man to get rich out of farming, "eight-cylinder rich" I mean, able to live in a "residence" with servants, to send his boys to college without stinting, and so on. One other runs a poor second. But, in your half of America, it seems that every whipper-snapper one knew yesterday is rich to-day.

Drawing illustrations from my acquaintance: In a little farming village where I lived for several years, the richest man was worth perhaps thirty thousand dollars. He was of Scotch name, and Scotch ancestry, a shrewd, able, hard-working business man. But his ability if it had been applied in your half of America would have netted him much more. Again — a few doors down the street from where I write is a department store doing a business of over twenty-five million dollars a year. It was started by a local man, now a millionaire. In contrast, I would mention a merchant friend of mine in the Northwest. He too was a good merchandizer. He ran a good store and for a while made money. His investment funds he put in land, in bank stocks, and in city property. The land went down in price, the banks failed, the cities didn't progress. To-day, he is bankrupt. Others like him have done slightly better, others worse. But none has been able to approach the success that the owner of the store across the street — the man who lives in your half of America — has attained.

This difference I am speaking of is expressed aptly in the vernacular of the day. In your half of America a ten-dollar bill is hardly more than "chicken-feed"; in our half, it often seems "bigger than all outdoors and then some."

And you assume something else that we do not take as a matter of course, except in the more favored sections. You assume health. We do not. We are troubled with strange maladies which you know not of. You probably think of "chills and fever" as something that affected your great-grandfather, possibly, but not as a disease which menaces you. It menaces us. I have before me a morbidity report for this Corn Belt State, a report that is admittedly incomplete. Yet it shows the existence of malaria here. My urban friends do not realize it, but down in the southwestern part of this State, chills and fever still exist. In that section, so the cattle-buyers tell me, people still live in log houses, drink from open shallow wells and take no precaution about stagnant water. (And if you become sick down there, you can get a complete physical examination by a registered and reputable physician for only fifty cents!)

Morbidity statistics for the nation are likewise incomplete. An adequate idea is obtained only from estimates. I have heard it claimed that there are ten million people suffering from malaria in this country; and I think such a figure is reasonable. Malaria has been characterized as "the most destructive disease known to the human race." Its ravages in the United States are not understood. As a side-light: of the six men with whom I was associated most closely in a certain section, three are now dead. They died in their early thirties, two of acute malaria, one of complications with malaria. As I have had malaria, I have had occasion to observe something of it.

And then hookworm! Its existence is denied in many localities, denied as existing in America. But such denial seems to me absolutely false. In 1910, certain responsible authorities estimated that from twenty to fifty per cent of the populations of various States were suffering from hookworm. How then can its existence be denied, when in many sections of those States, almost no work has been done to eradicate it? During 1924, 1925, and 1926, I was manager of a plantation. I needed tenants and I learned from experience something about selecting them. I learned to recognize — and to shun — the hookworm sufferer. I should say that about thirty per cent of the applicants were sufferers. A local doctor helped me in my diagnosis of the human factor. Here were people more hopelessly degraded than any I had ever met before, poor beyond description, shiftless, hopeless, unkempt, and yet withal rather

well-spoken and coming from good original stock. They were reduced to a condition so low that I could hardly describe it to you.
And if I could, you would probably not understand. They were
miserably sick, and yet they were so ignorant that they did not even
know they were sick. Many of them could read and write after a
fashion. But they were hopelessly ignorant just the same. Their
condition could be explained only on the ground of serious physical
derangement.

Hookworm is not conquered. It is not eradicated. When we
realize that by actual examination, infestation was found to extend
to from fifteen to eighty per cent of the population in certain sections,
we must conclude that the disease could not have been eradicated
without a tremendous campaign. If such had been carried on, we
would have heard more about it.

And then pellagra and malnutrition. The people of the hinterlands suffer from these conditions. Dwelling in the midst of a garden
of plenty, our farmers too often "live out of a tin can and a paper
sack." Especially is this true in sections devoted to one-crop farming. In one farming section where I lived it was almost impossible
to buy fruits and vegetables, or milk and eggs. A dieting millionaire
would have starved to death. Why? Because that section had
grown nothing for the past century but a single crop. That crop
was the only crop they knew and the only one they wanted to know.
And it wasn't edible. Their food was "store-bought" stuff, and
they suffered from that fact. Our prophets of Americanism who
would reduce disease in America to a minimum in five years must
contemplate a vast campaign of education in dietetics.

Other diseases plague us too; but they are familiar to you and
you understand them. However, the existence of the three I have
mentioned seems generally overlooked in most statements about
America.

Finally, I would mention certain surveys and studies that have
been made by responsible people in regard to the agricultural systems of whole sections of America. It has been proved beyond
question that certain types of our agriculture, practised by millions
of people, do not pay at all. The sections following these systems
manage to exist only through the sale of natural resources, timber,
turpentine, oil, clays, the products of quarries, and the like, and by

day-labor in other lines. Our prophets who would give us an America without poverty must devise in the short space of five years profitable systems of agriculture for those sections; and what is more difficult they must get the systems they devise adopted by the people.

So you see that all these things combined give us of the hinterlands a slightly different conception of America from yours, an America that can hardly accept the statements that your leaders of thought are making. What few ten-dollar bills we have still appear large to us, and we intend to hold on to them. At the end of five years, we don't expect to find money growing on trees, or that our doctors will have gone out of business. In case we succeed in a personal way according to our hopes, we shan't look forward to a country-club existence, punctuated by trips on yachts and so on, but to the modest home of the retired farmer. Our whole conception of things is different. In fact, almost all our thoughts about life are different from yours, except perhaps our thoughts on the subject of patriotism. We admit that we don't know very much about you and we find that you don't really know very much about us. For this reason, we have to grant the truth of the term, "Unknown America."

HUSTLE

By ARNOLD BENNETT

One of the most prolific of modern writers, Arnold Bennett (1867–   )
has had a varied career as lawyer, editor, and man of letters.   Since
1900 he has devoted his time to the production of novels, short stories,
plays, essays, and other literary forms.   A complete list of his writings
would seem almost incredible merely because of its length; however,
mention may be made of "The Old Wives' Tale" (1908), "Hilda
Lessways" (1911), "These Twain" (1916), "Riceyman Steps"
(1923), "Lord Raingo" (1926), "Books and Persons" (1917),
"Things that Have Interested Me" (1921, 1923, 1925), and "The
Savour of Life" (1928).

THE verdict of certain specialists in Harley Street is that we are a
nation in a state of nerves, and that this state of nerves is the result of too much hustling.   To hustle, so far as I can ascertain, from
those terse and tantalizing sources of information, the dictionaries,
means to hurry and bustle over one's work, and it appears to include
the ideas of fussing, pushing, thrusting, and being generally noisy,
breathless and unceremonious — to the laudable end of "getting a
move on."   Now I have noticed four very marked qualities in all the
great workers and doers of my acquaintance.   They are never in a
hurry; they are never late; they are calm and quiet persons; and
they always have time to spare for any job that may turn up un-
expectedly.   You never hear them say, in response to an appeal:
"Haven't a moment!"

I think that most people will agree with me that the really great
workers do as a rule possess these qualities.   Hence it would appear
that hustling is not a necessary accompaniment of genuine and
consistent industry.   I would go further and say that, if the example
of the great workers is worth anything at all, regular hustling is a
positive hindrance to accomplishment.   For if hustling helped work
the great workers would hustle, and the fact that they don't hustle is
an indication that hustling hinders work.

At any rate it is obvious that nobody can satisfactorily live in a
permanent condition of hurry and bustle.   Such a form of existence
must end in exhaustion, muddle, inefficiency, "nerves," and even
a breakdown.   One often reads in the papers that some mighty

hustler has had a breakdown. He disappears for a time from the field of fuss, and when he returns he is usually a chastened man — unless he happens to be incurable, which is another way of saying that he is a born fool.

That the habit of hustling is fairly widespread among us I would not deny; nor would I deny that in so far as it exists it is apt to bring about a state of nerves. But when I hear, as I do hear, the deduction that because we hustle we are working too hard I grow hot, or I should grow hot, did I not laugh. For if anything is clear on this misty island, it is clear that as a nation we are not working too hard. And if the Harley Street specialists meant to warn us against overwork, then I would spurn them; I would have none of them. However, I do not accuse the Harley Street specialists of anything so enormously stupid as warning us against overwork. The Japanese may work too hard; also the Germans; but not the British, nor the Americans. There is no sign of overwork in Britain. On the contrary, there are a thousand signs of underwork — and in all ranks of society. And hustle itself is a sign, among other things, of underwork.

Hustle is hurry, and hurry implies either a miscalculation of time or deliberately lost time — generally the latter — which time must be made up. (Not that lost time ever can be made up; time lost is lost forever — you cannot possibly find it again like a dropped sixpence.) A sense of the value of time — that is, of the best way to divide one's time into one's various activities — is an essential preliminary to efficient work; it is also the only method of avoiding hurry. People without a due sense of time spend half their working lives in a hurry. They disorganize all the world by unpunctuality — which is a direct and prolific cause of hurry and hustle. Every efficient person carries a clock inside his head, and this wonderful self-winding clock rings a warning signal at frequent intervals.

I am told that punctual persons are a terrible nuisance to their friends. Quite! But an honest man is a terrible nuisance to a thief. I am told also that punctual persons are the slaves of time. Not so. It is the unpunctual who are the slaves of time, which constantly rushes them to and fro with whips and scourges. Further, unpunctual persons are unmannerly. To be late is to be selfish and silly, because the late person wastes other people's time for his own inconvenience.

Unpunctuality, however, is seldom deliberate; the waste of time due to it is merely the unhappy consequence of muddle-headedness. Far more time is wasted deliberately than is wasted by unpunctuality. It has become almost the rule to work only five days a week, and many men will in addition take a day off in the middle of the week for purposes of amusement and distraction. This is notorious. Consciences are uneasy, and consciences urge the wasters to the ridiculous attempt to cram the work of five and a half days into five days or four days. The attempt fails, and must fail. Hurry, hustle, bustle, and fuss ensue, but not achievement.

Nor is this all. Behold the multiplicity of resorts where apparently sane individuals dance nightly until one, two, three, four, five, or even six o'clock in the morning. What jolly scenes — the women so beautiful and bright, the men so chivalrous and hospitable! The brilliant lights! The tinkling of glass, the enheartening hullabaloo of saxophone and drum! This is what we are supposed to live for. And, considered by itself, it is doubtless worth living for. But what about the next day? Is any first-rate work going to be done the next day? It is not. I have watched these peacockian assemblies, and they have faded away before my eyes, and by the vision of my third eye (in my mind, near the self-winding clock) I have seen neglected homes, late meals, aspirin, scornful servants, yawns in offices, pick-me-up cocktails, lost tempers, bullied clerks, and a grand general mess in inefficiency.

I am all in favor of fun — but to please me it must be fun with a sense of proportion, and it must be earned before it is enjoyed. The mischief with us is that our fun is not being paid for. We are undoubtedly securing our fun on credit, and running up enormous bills of fatigue, hurry, hustle, etc., etc., which we cannot discharge. Our budget is not balanced. And I am convinced that one of the main causes of to-day's "nerves" and dissatisfaction and inefficiency is the nocturnal life we lead. If everybody bolted his front door (on the inside) at midnight we should soon see more work and a change for the better in the national existence.

So much for one end of society, the employing end. The other end, the employed end, is equally suffering from underwork, but the cause of the underwork is quite different. The working man and woman, with all their doubtless frightful defects of character and behaviour, do not make a practice of turning night into day and day into purgatory. Nor do they in any way attempt to do five and a half days' work in five days or four days. No! If they belong to a union they use every effort to do the work of three days or four days in five and a half. Hurry, hustle, and bustle emphatically do not count among their sins.

The employed section of society, at any rate the larger part of that section, is suffering as regards its work from one specific malady: payment by time instead of payment by results. I admit that payment by time is the logical result of events in the industrial life of the country during the last hundred years. I admit that it can be explained, and to a certain extent even justified. But it remains the curse of labor. It robs the energetic man of the incentive to use his energy. It reduces the real worker to the level of the shirker. It ministers to and encourages the worst characteristics in human nature. And it lessens the total volume of work done.

Further, because it is unnatural, it dulls the conscience and affects the nerves. A man who spends his days carefully and deliberately doing much less than he can do must perforce get himself into a strange and dangerous state of mind. His unused energy must find some outlet, and it finds an outlet in searching for trouble. And note that it is the best men who are demoralized, not the worst. Payment by time amounts to a canker, which is another word for cancer. Though the operation may be highly dangerous to the body-politic, the cancer will have to be cut out before there can be any genuine improvement in the general state of society.

With one half of the nation hustling and fussing to make up for lost time, and the other half hustling and fussing in order to avoid the unavoidable consequences of enforced, continuous sloth, the pickle we are in may justly be called very acute. It is. It is much more acute than some folks imagine. And it will be worse before it is better. The first step toward the cure is to realize clearly the nature of the disease. I have tried to show what the disease is, and in particular to show that hustle is not work, but the enemy of work.

SENTIMENTAL AMERICA

By HENRY SEIDEL CANBY

Henry Seidel Canby (1878–   ) received his education at Yale, and was later a professor of English there. For a time he was an editor of the "Yale Review," and then of the "Literary Review." He is now editor of the "Saturday Review of Literature," a magazine which is influential among the intellectual classes. Besides a textbook on rhetoric, his "Definitions" (1922), a collection of critical essays, is well known.

THE Oriental may be inscrutable, but he is no more puzzling than the average American. We admit that we are hard, keen, practical — the adjectives that every casual European applies to us — and yet any book-store window or railway news-stand will show that we prefer sentimental magazines and books. Why should a hard race — if we are hard — read soft books?

By soft books, by sentimental books, I do not mean only the kind of literature best described by the word "squashy." I doubt whether we write or read more novels and short stories of the tear-dripped or hyper-emotional variety than other nations. Germany is — or was — full of such soft stuff. It is highly popular in France, although the excellent taste of French criticism keeps it in check. Italian popular literature exudes sentiment; and the sale of "squashy" fiction in England is said to be threatened only by an occasional importation of an American "best-seller." We have no bad eminence here. Sentimentalists with enlarged hearts are international in habitat, although, it must be admitted, especially popular in America.

When a critic, after a course in American novels and magazines, declares that life, as it appears on the printed page here, is fundamentally sentimentalized, he goes much deeper than "mushiness" with his charge. He means, I think, that there is an alarming tendency in American fiction to dodge the facts of life — or to pervert them. He means that in most popular books only red-blooded, optimistic people are welcome. He means that material success, physical soundness, and the gratification of the emotions have the right of way. He means that men and women (except the comic figures) shall be presented, not as they are, but as we should like to have them, according to a judgment tempered by nothing more searching than our experience with an unusually comfortable, safe, and prosperous mode of living. Every one succeeds in American plays and stories — if not by good thinking, why then by good looks or good luck. A curious society the research student of a later date might make of it — an upper world of the colorless, successful, illustrated by chance-saved collar advertisements and magazine covers; an under world of grotesque scamps, clowns, and hyphenates drawn from the comic supplement; and all — red-blooded hero and modern gargoyle alike — always in good humor.

I am not touching in this picture merely to attack it. It has been abundantly attacked; what it needs is explanation. For there is much in this bourgeois, good-humored American literature of ours which rings true, which is as honest an expression of our individuality as was the more austere product of ante-bellum New England. If American sentimentality does invite criticism, American sentiment deserves defense.

Sentiment — the response of the emotions to the appeal of human nature — is cheap, but so are many other good things. The best of the ancients were rich in it. Homer's chieftains wept easily. So did Shakespeare's heroes. Adam and Eve shed "some natural tears" when they left the Paradise which Milton imagined for them. A heart accessible to pathos, to natural beauty, to religion, was a chief requisite for the protagonist of Victorian literature. Even Becky Sharp was touched — once — by Amelia's moving distress.

Americans, to be sure, do not weep easily; but if they make equivalent responses to sentiment, that should not be held against them. If we like "sweet" stories, or "strong" — which means emotional — stories, our taste is not thereby proved to be hopeless, or our national character bad. It is better to be creatures of even sentimental sentiment, with the author of *The Rosary*, than to see the world *only* as it is portrayed by the pens of Bernard Shaw and Anatole France. The first is deplorable; the second is dangerous. I should deeply regret the day when a simple story of honest American manhood winning a million and a sparkling, piquant sweetheart lost all power to lull my critical faculty and warm my heart. I doubt whether any literature has ever had too much of honest sentiment.

Good Heavens! Because some among us insist that the mystic rose of the emotions shall be painted a brighter pink than nature allows, are the rest to forego glamour? Or because, to view the matter differently, psychology has shown what happens in the brain when a man falls in love, and anthropology has traced marriage to a care for property rights, are we to suspect the idyllic in literature wherever we find it? Life is full of the idyllic; and no anthropologist will ever persuade the reasonably romantic youth that the sweet and chivalrous passion which leads him to mingle reverence with desire for the object of his affections, is nothing but an idealized property sense. Origins explain very little, after all. The bilious critics of sentiment in literature have not even honest science behind them.

I have no quarrel with traffickers in simple emotion — with such writers as James Lane Allen and James Whitcomb Riley, for example. But the average American is not content with such sentiments as theirs. He wants a more intoxicating brew — to be persuaded that, once you step beyond your own experience, feeling rules the world. He wants — I judge by what he reads — to make sentiment at least ninety per cent efficient, even if a dream-America, superficially resemblant to the real, but far different in tone, must be created by the obedient writer in order to satisfy him. His sentiment has frequently to be sentimentalized before he will pay for it. And to this fault, which he shares with other modern races, he adds the other heinous sin of sentimentalism, the refusal to face the facts.

This sentimentalizing of reality — to invent a term — is far more dangerous than the romantic sentimentalizing of the "squashy" variety. It is to be found in sex-stories, which carefully observe decency of word and deed, where the conclusion is always in accord with conventional morality, yet whose characters are clearly immoral, indecent, and would so display themselves if the tale were truly told. It is to be found in stories of "big business," where trickery and rascality are made virtuous at the end by sentimental baptism. If I choose for the hero of my novel a director in an American trust; if I make him an accomplice in certain acts of ruthless economic tyranny; if I make it clear that at first he is merely subservient to a stronger will, and that the acts he approves are in complete disaccord with his private moral code — why then, if the facts should be dragged to the light, if he is made to realize the exact nature of his career, how can I end my story? It is evident that my hero possesses little insight and less firmness of character. He is not a hero; he is merely a tool. In, let us say, eight cases out of ten, his curve is already plotted. It leads downward — not necessarily along the villain's path, but toward moral insignificance.

And yet, I cannot end my story that way for Americans. There *must* be a grand moral revolt. There must be resistance, triumph, and not only spiritual, but also financial recovery. And this, likewise, is sentimentality. Even Booth Tarkington, in his excellent *Turmoil*, had to dodge the logical issue of his story; had to make his hero exchange a practical literary idealism for a very impractical, even though a commercial, utopianism, in order to emerge apparently successful at the end of the book. A story such as the Danish Nexö's *Pelle the Conqueror*, where pathos and the idyllic, each intense, each beautiful, are made convincing by an undeviating truth to experience, would seem to be almost impossible of production just now in America.

It is not enough to rail at this false fiction. The chief duty of criticism is to explain. The best corrective of bad writing is a knowledge of why it is bad. We get the fiction we deserve, precisely as we get the government we deserve — or perhaps, in each case, a little better. Why are we sentimental? When that question is answered, it is easier to understand the defects and the virtues of American fiction. And the answer lies in the traditional American philosophy of life.

To say that the American is an idealist, is to commit a thoroughgoing platitude. Like most platitudes, the statement is annoying because, from one point of view, it is indisputably just, while from another it does not seem to fit the facts. With regard to our tradition, it is indisputable. Of the immigrants who since the seventeenth century have been pouring into this continent, a portion large in number, larger still in influence, has been possessed of motives which, in part at least, were idealistic. If it was not the desire for religious freedom that urged them, it was the desire for personal freedom; if not political liberty, why then economic liberty (for this too is idealism), and the opportunity to raise the standard of life. And of course all these motives were strongest in that earlier immigration which has done most to fix the state of mind and body which we call being

American. I need not labor the argument. Our political and social history supports it; our best literature demonstrates it; for no men have been more idealistic than the American writers whom we have consented to call great. Emerson, Thoreau, Hawthorne, Whitman — was idealism ever more thoroughly incarnate than in them?

And this idealism — to risk again a platitude — has been in the air of America. It has permeated our religious sects, and created several of them. It has given tone to our thinking, and even more to our feeling. I do not say that it has always, or even usually, determined our actions, although the Civil War is proof of its power. Again and again it has gone aground roughly when the ideal met a condition of living — a fact that will provide the explanation for which I seek. But optimism, "boosting," muck-raking (not all of its manifestations are pretty), social service, religious, municipal, democratic reform, indeed the "uplift" generally, is evidence of the vigor, the bumptiousness of the inherited American tendency to pursue the ideal. No one can doubt that in this generation we believe, at least, in idealism.

Nevertheless, so far as the average individual is concerned, with just his share and no more of the race-tendency, this idealism has been suppressed, and in some measure perverted. It is this which explains, I think, American sentimentalism.

Consider, for example, the ethics of conventional American society. The American ethical tradition is perfectly definite and tremendously powerful. It belongs, furthermore, to a population far larger than the "old American" stock, for it has been laboriously inculcated in our schools and churches, and impressively driven home by newspaper, magazine, and book. I shall not presume to analyze it save where it touches literature. There it maintains a definite attitude toward all sex-problems: the Victorian, which is not necessarily, or even probably, a bad one. Man should be chaste, and proud of his chastity. Woman must be so. It is the ethical duty of the American to hate, or at least to despise, all deviations, and to pretend — for the greater prestige of the law — that such sinning is exceptional, at least in America. And this is the public morality he believes in, whatever may be his private experience in actual living. In business, it is the ethical tradition of the American, inherited from a rigorous Protestant morality, to be square, to play the game without trickery, to fight hard but never meanly.   Overreaching is justifiable when the other fellow has equal opportunities to be "smart"; lying, tyranny — never.   And though the opposites of all these laudable practices come to pass, he must frown on them in public, deny their rightness even to the last cock-crow — especially in the public press.

American political history is a long record of idealistic tendencies toward democracy, working painfully through a net of graft, pettiness, sectionalism, and bravado, with constant disappointment for the idealist who believes, traditionally, in the intelligence of the crowd.   American social history is a glaring instance of how the theory of equal dignity for all men can entangle itself with caste distinctions, snobbery, and the power of wealth.   American economic history betrays the pioneer helping to kick down the ladder that he himself had raised toward equal opportunity for all.   American literary history — especially contemporary literary history — reflects the result of all this for the American mind.   The sentimental in our literature is a direct consequence.

The disease is easily acquired.   Mr. Smith, a broker, finds himself in the environment of "schemes" and "deals" in which the quality of mercy is strained, and the wind is decidedly not tempered to the shorn lamb.   After all, business is business.   He shrugs his shoulders and takes his part.   But his unexpected fund of native idealism — if, as is most probable, he has his share — seeks its due satisfaction. He cannot use it in business; so he takes it out in a novel or a play where, quite contrary to his observed experience, ordinary people like himself act nobly, with a success that is all the more agreeable for being unexpected.   His wife, a woman with strange stirrings about her heart, with motions toward beauty, and desires for a significant life and rich, satisfying experience, exists in day-long pettiness, gossips, frivols, scolds, with money enough to do what she pleases, and nothing vital to do.   She also relieves her pent-up idealism in plays or books — in high-wrought, "strong" novels, not in adventures in society such as the kitchen admires, but in stories with violent moral and emotional crises, whose characters, no matter how unlifelike, have "strong" thoughts, and make vital decisions; succeed or fail significantly.   Her brother, the head of a wholesale dry-goods firm, listens to the stories the drummers bring home of night life on the road, laughs, says to himself regretfully that the world has to be like that; and then, in logical reaction, demands purity and nothing but aggressive purity in the books of the public library.

The hard man goes in for philanthropy (never before so frequently as in America); the one-time "boss" takes to picture-collecting; the railroad wrecker gathers rare editions of the Bible; and tens of thousands of humbler Americans carry their inherited idealism into the necessarily sordid experiences of life in an imperfectly organized country, suppress it for fear of being thought "cranky" or "soft," and then, in their imagination and all that feeds their imagination, give it vent. You may watch the process any evening at the movies or the melodrama, on the trolley-car or in the easy chair at home.

This philosophy of living, which I have called American idealism, is in its own nature sound, as is proved in a hundred directions where it has had full play. Suppressed idealism, like any other suppressed desire, becomes unsound. One does not have to follow Freud and his school into their sex-pathology in order to believe that. And here lies the ultimate cause of the taste for sentimentalism in the American *bourgeoisie*. An undue insistence upon happy endings, regardless of the premises of the story, and a craving for optimism everywhere, anyhow, are sure signs of a "morbid complex," and to be compared with some justice to the craving for drugs in a "dry" town. We must look for psychological as well as economic and geographical causes for mental peculiarities exhibiting themselves in literature. No one can doubt the effect of the suppression by the Puritan discipline of that instinctive love of pleasure and liberal experience common to us all. Its unhealthy reaction is visible in every old American community. No one who faces the facts can deny the result of the suppression by commercial, bourgeois, prosperous America of our native idealism. The student of society may find its dire effects in politics, in religion, and in social intercourse. The critic cannot overlook them in literature; for it is in the realm of the imagination that idealism, direct or perverted, does its best or its worst.

Sentiment is not perverted idealism. Sentiment *is* idealism of a mild and not too masculine variety. If it has sins, they are sins of omission, not commission. Our fondness for sentiment proves that our idealism, if a little loose in the waist-band and puffy in the cheeks, is still hearty, still capable of active mobilization, like those comfortable French husbands whose plump and smiling faces, careless of glory, careless of everything but thrift and good living, are nevertheless figured on a page whose superscription reads, "Dead on the field of honor."

The novels, the plays, the short stories, of sentiment may prefer sweetness, perhaps, to truth, the feminine to the masculine virtues, but we waste ammunition in attacking them. There never was, I suppose, a great literature of sentiment, for not even the *Sentimental Journey* is truly great. But no one can make a diet exclusively of "noble" literature; the charming has its own cosy corner across from the tragic (and a much bigger corner at that). Our uncounted amorists of tail-piece song and illustrated story provide the readiest means of escape from the somewhat uninspiring life that most men and women are living just now in America.

The sentimental, however — whether because of an excess of sentiment softening into "slush," or of a morbid optimism, or of a weak-eyed distortion of the facts of life — is perverted. It needs to be cured, and its cure is more truth. But this cure, I very much fear, is not entirely, or even chiefly, in the power of the "regular practitioner," the honest writer. He can be honest; but if he is much more honest than his readers, they will not read him. As Professor Lounsbury once said, a language grows corrupt only when its speakers grow corrupt, and mends, strengthens, and becomes pure with them. So with literature. We shall have less sentimentality in American literature when our accumulated store of idealism disappears in a laxer generation; or when it finds due vent in a more responsible, less narrow, less monotonously prosperous life than is lived by the average reader of fiction in America. I would rather see our literary taste damned forever than have the first alternative become — as it has not yet — a fact. The second, in the years of world-war, we placed, unwillingly, perhaps unconsciously, upon the knees of the gods.

All this must not be taken in too absolute a sense. There are medicines, and good ones, in the hands of writers and of critics, to abate, if not to heal, this plague of sentimentalism. I have stated ultimate causes only. They are enough to keep the mass of Americans reading sentimentalized fiction until some fundamental change has come, not strong enough to hold back the van of American writing, which is steadily moving toward restraint, sanity, and truth. Every honest composition is a step forward in the cause; and every clear-minded criticism.

But one must doubt the efficacy, and one must doubt the healthiness, of reaction into cynicism and sophisticated cleverness. There are curious signs, especially in what we may call the literature of New York, of a growing sophistication that sneers at sentiment and the sentimental alike. "Magazines of cleverness" have this for their keynote, although as yet the satire is not always well aimed. There are abundant signs that the generation just coming forward will rejoice in such a pose. It is observable now in the colleges, where the young literati turn up their noses at everything American — magazines, best-sellers, or one-hundred-night plays — and resort for inspiration to the English school of anti-Victorians: to Schnitzler with his brilliant Viennese cynicism; less commonly, because he is more subtle, to Anatole France. Their pose is not altogether to be blamed, and the men to whom they resort are models of much that is admirable; but there is little promise for American literature in exotic imitation. To see ourselves prevailingly as others see us may be good for modesty, but does not lead to a self-confident native art. And it is a dangerous way for Americans to travel. We cannot afford such sophistication yet. The English wits experimented with cynicism in the court of Charles II, laughed at blundering Puritan morality, laughed at country manners, and were whiffed away because the ideals they laughed at were better than their own. Idealism is not funny, however censurable its excesses. As a race we have too much sentiment to be frightened out of the sentimental by a blasé cynicism.

At first glance the flood of moral literature now upon us — social-conscience stories, scientific plays, platitudinous "moralities" that tell us how to live — may seem to be another protest against sentimentalism. And that the French and English examples have been so warmly welcomed here may seem another indication of a reaction on our part. I refer especially to those "hard" stories, full of vengeful wrath, full of warnings for the race that dodges the facts of life. H. G. Wells is the great exemplar, with his sociological studies wrapped in description and tied with a plot. In a sense, such stories are certainly to be regarded as a protest against truth-dodging, against cheap optimism, against "slacking," whether in literature or in life. But it would be equally just to call them another result of suppressed idealism, and to regard their popularity in America as proof of the argument which I have advanced in this essay. Excessively didactic literature is often a little unhealthy. In fresh periods, when life runs strong and both ideals and passions find ready issue into life, literature has no burdensome moral to carry. It digests its moral. Homer digested his morals. They transfuse his epics. So did Shakespeare. His world is predominantly moral; but his stories are not forged into machines contrived to hammer home neglected truth.

Not so with the writers of the social-conscience school. They are in a rage over wicked, wasteful man. Their novels are bursted notebooks — sometimes neat and orderly notebooks, like Mr. Galsworthy's or our own Ernest Poole's, sometimes haphazard ones, like those of Mr. Wells, but always explosive with reform. These gentlemen know very well what they are about, especially Mr. Wells, the lesser artist, perhaps, as compared with Galsworthy, but the shrewder and possibly the greater man. The very sentimentalists, who go to novels to exercise the idealism that they cannot use in life, will read these unsentimental stories, although their lazy impulses would never spur them on toward any truth not sweetened by a tale.

And yet, one feels that the social attack might have been more convincing if free from its compulsory service to fiction; that these novels and plays might have been better literature if the authors did not study life in order that they might be better able to preach. Wells and Galsworthy also have suffered from suppressed idealism, although it would be unfair to say that perversion was the result. So have our muck-rakers, who, very characteristically, exhibit the disorder in a more complex and a much more serious form, since to a distortion of facts they have often enough added hypocrisy and commercialism. It is part of the price we pay for being sentimental.

The American sentimentalists, two million readers strong, are intrenched behind ramparts of indifference, which no shrapnel fire of criticism or countermine of honest writing can ever destroy. We can take a trench or two, blow up some particularly obnoxious citadel, and trouble their security by exploding bombs of truth; but defeat must come finally from within their own lines.

If I am correct in my analysis, we are suffering here in America, not from a plague of bad taste merely, nor only from a lack of real education among our myriads of readers, nor from decadence — least of all, this last. It is a disease of our own particular virtue which has infected us — idealism, suppressed and perverted. A less commercial, more responsible America, perhaps a less prosperous and more spiritual America, will hold fast to its sentiment, but be weaned from its sentimentality.

VOICES CRYING IN THE WILDERNESS

By JOSEPH COLLINS

Joseph Collins (1866–   ) *is a nationally known neurologist who resides in New York. He has studied at New York University and at Frankfort, Germany. Three of his books, "The Doctor Looks at Literature" (1923), "The Doctor Looks at Biography" (1925), and "The Doctor Looks at Love and Life" (1926), contain psychological criticism of contemporary writers and social problems.*

WE say that we carried and still carry the torch of liberty; yet, year by year, we restrict increasingly man's conduct by legislation. We say that we are idealists, but by word of mouth and by example we strive to convince ourselves that it is more important to succeed than to live. We proclaim altruism and our determination to foster the welfare of our fellow nations, but we content ourselves with the proclamation. We are satisfied with ourselves, and with our neighbors who agree with us and who conform their conduct to ours, but we are dissatisfied with all others, and determined to make them mend their ways.

This, it will be said, is an intemperate statement, a grotesque exaggeration, a purposeful falsehood. But consideration of some of the trends and activities in this country to-day will show that it is naught but the truth.

First, the Klan, champion and defender of what is called Americanism, whose purpose is to rescue America from aliens — Catholics, Jews, and negroes — and to thwart liberalism of any and every kind that seeks to make boil the "melting pot" or to extend the welcoming hand to any save one hundred per cent Americans. Though it is little more than ten years since its charter was granted, it is to-day a political and social organization of enormous power. Five years ago the *New York World* made scathing arraignment of its methods and startling exposure of its accomplishments, the record of which was published in a score of important newspapers. Instead of being discredited to the American people, it was endeared to thousands. Its membership has increased tenfold since Congress investigated it in 1921.

Ku Klux Klanism alleges that it is concerned with the needs, the purposes, and the convictions of the great mass of Americans of the old stock.   It maintains that the pioneers who built America bequeathed a priority right in it to their children; the control of it and its future; that it is the mission of Americans to perpetuate and develop the kind of nation and civilization that the pioneers created; that mixture of races makes for national evil; that the American stock shall not be mongrelized; and that all foreigners adopted by this country are to agree that they will adopt our ideas and ideals and not try to thrust *theirs* upon us.   Their belief is that our aliens are constantly trying to change our civilization into something that will suit them better; that the Catholic Church is an organized, disciplined, powerful rival to our government, determined to win control; that the negro does not belong here; that he cannot be segregated; that he is not an equal and that equality should not be vouchsafed him; and that the Jew cannot last long in the free atmosphere of America; therefore his parting should be speeded.

In one word, the Klan is anti-liberal.   It is the summation of all the religious and race prejudice of the nation.   Those opposed to it say that it has its greatest development in sections of the country where illiteracy and ignorance are densest, but in reality it flourishes like the green bay tree in the middle and south West, on the Pacific coast and in New England.   Recently it has had its greatest growth in a section of the country that prides itself on its culture and illumination, Ohio and Indiana.   It has fostered, and in most instances effected, legislation against teaching science in public schools; it has sponsored and stimulated the movement against religious research which aims to reconcile religion with reason; it has made religion a political issue and it controverts the fundamental principles upon which the nation was founded.   It probably has more sympathizers than it has adherents though Robert L. Duffus in 1923 estimated its membership to be two and a half millions.

"I am really a Klanner at heart," said a man who had achieved a most distinctive place in the commercial and cultural world and who had a commanding position in his community, to me "though I do not approve of their methods or accomplishments; but they are right about the Catholics."   That hatred is the diastole of the Klan's heart, and the determination for thirteenth-century thought and conduct.   When it seems to transcend my understanding that a man of parts can believe that an individual's loyalties to his religion come before that to his country and his people, I go to hear Bicknell Young, C.S.B., lecture; then for a time at least I can believe anything.

One often hears it said by Americans, ashamed that their country should have gestated and nourished such a monster of bigotry, that its members are mostly ignorant and illiterate. Nothing could be further from the truth. Oregon has less illiteracy than any State in the Union, one and a half per cent; the "melting pot" is unknown there; its population is less than ten per cent Catholics and there are practically no Jews or negroes. Yet the Klan is more powerful, more aggressive and more dominant there politically and socially than anywhere else. It is the State with a law that all children between eight and sixteen must go to a *public* school, or their parents must go to jail. All of which seems to show that religious animosity is directly proportionate in this country to what is called education and enlightenment.

What is the explanation of the Ku Klux Klan? The explanation is that a million or more one hundred per cent Americans have feelings of inferiority for which they seek compensation. Their repressions are showing themselves in intolerance of the rights of others, in assumption of moral superiority; in display of intolerance with liberalism of every form, and in a quality of bigotry from which the whole world has been free for five hundred years.

The belief of the Klanner has close kinship to that which maintains that though we lie down a peaceful nation, we wake up a nation of warriors; that we are invincible in any field; that there is nothing we cannot do as well as any one else and a lot better. It is a belief that is dependent upon our youth, and only time, the greatest of all therapeutists, can cure it. Meanwhile, we must exercise a care that those most severally afflicted do not cause us to die of shame, or to become permanently invalided of humiliation.

The history of the Ku Klux Klan will be the enduring monument to our preposterous hypocrisy. We profess kindliness and hospitality; we admit a truism and humility; we shout loyalty to God and country, but the conduct of millions of us testifies our cruelty, selfishness, narrow-mindedness, and more than all, our ignorance of the meaning of liberty.

What does it avail us to be told that the taproot of the Klan is the prosperity of the Scotch-Irish, of the South and Southwest? Why should their transformation from Presbyterian to Baptist have made them more narrow-minded than their forebears? They have been nourished on liberty, for until the present generation a measure of it existed in this country, both ideally and practically. Nor is their bigotry an irradiation of the small town mind operating upon weaklings, dependents, and illiterates. It is the stereotype of national dementia. For a time it is bound to immobilize us. We shall begin to re-acquire flexibility when we begin to realize that all work and no play, all materialism and no idealism, make Jack not only dull but deadly.

Just in proportion as our material prosperity has increased, our spiritual prosperity has diminished. Liberty, as the architects and builders of the nation understood it, does not exist any more. Our government gets more paternalistic and centralized every year and the time is in sight when all of man's conduct will be regulated by law. It will tell him where he can go and when; what he can indulge in and what he must avoid; what he may study and what he shall not read; how he must dress and what he cannot put on or leave off. Probably everything has been said about the Eighteenth Amendment to our Constitution that can or should be said. We know all about its conception, genesis, and display. The only thing about it that we do not know is who, by furnishing the money, made it possible. So far we have not been able to transform our suspicions into certainties. We know that the most serious infringement of man's liberty ever made was effected in the United States in the beginning years of the twentieth century and that it was accomplished by persons who arrogated to themselves knowledge which they could not possibly possess, viz., that the world would be a better world and that its inhabitants would be healthier, happier, and more efficient were they to cease from a certain day a custom which had existed from time immemorial. They believed it would be, and they proceeded to thrust their belief upon millions of their fellowmen who believed the contrary. The world has never seen greater tyranny.

Employers of labor have convinced themselves that their workmen are more efficient and productive when they do not drink alcohol than when they do, but that is no justification for making it illegal for them to make or take alcohol. They might easily convince themselves that all clerks, scriveners, and accountants are more efficient and productive when their diet is deprived of meat. Few would be willing to see added to the Constitution an amendment that would taboo the consumption of animal proteid.

It seems impossible to convince a certain type of man that it is more important to live than to succeed; more vital to be happy than to be rich; more essential to have peace of mind than to have radios; tranquillity will always be preferable to apprehension; courage to fear; resignation to agitation. Alcohol, properly used, is the most important tangible means in the world to secure these *desiderata*. And so long as that remains so, the gates of reform and the power of money shall not prevail against it. Laws forbidding its manufacture, distribution, and sale may be made. The national exchequer may be drained to enforce them. The army, navy, state, county, and municipal officers may be pressed into service, but until every roof in the land is lifted and every residential wall razed, alcohol will be obtained, manufactured, and drunk. The only way to make man stop drinking is to kill him. The way to make man drink is to have another man tell him he must not. Hence thousands, probably millions, who a few years ago had small inclination to take alcohol, now have an urge to do so which they coddle.

I can understand why the head of a great corporation like the U.S. Steel should be pleased with a law whose operation makes the output of its employees greater, providing he is more beholden to its stockholders than he is to the ideal that it is every man's duty — and the greater the man the more incumbent the duty — to make the world more livable for others, that is, to contribute to man's happiness.

I can understand, too, that a man finding himself the possessor of fabulous inherited wealth, and being without distinctive vision of understanding, can, under the dominion of an idea, believe that he must use his money to salvage the morals of his fellows and to swell the slush funds of coercive legislation. The worst of all tyrants is one who has wealth, dwarfed intellect, and warped emotions. If he is convinced that God has selected him for assistant or coadjutor, woe to his country that suffers his activities. What I cannot understand is why immodest John Smith should know what is better for sane Jim Brown's welfare than he does himself, when they have had equal opportunities for enlightenment, save that John has believed from his infancy that he knows more than Jim and that his father knew more than Jim's father.

I cannot understand what there is about administering a five-and-ten-cent store, even though it is done with such success that the proprietor accumulates fifty or more millions of dollars, that entitles him to tell me how to play the game of life. Nor does the determination to give some of it away seem to me a source of information. Even an amateur philanthropist who has made it a rule never to give a dollar to a church whose pastor smokes, has no conception of what life means to me, and would not have if he lived as many years as he has dollars. It would never occur to me to thrust my conception of life down his throat nor to suggest to him directly or indirectly that I know more about it than he does. Unless he should seek my advice as physician, I shall never tell him he should or should not take alcohol, use tobacco, drink tea or chew gum. Even then I should confine myself to counsel that would encourage his bodily health. Should his spiritual health give him concern, he must look to Drs. Straton, Shields, Goodchild, or other sapient specialists. He, however, does not hesitate a moment to thrust his conception of life, its possibilities and obligations, upon others, and to drive it home with the most powerful of all engines, money.

As a result of the paranoiac determination of such seers and decalogists, we have become a nation of law breakers, and are on the way to become a nation of drunkards. Many of those to whom we look for spiritual guidance, ethical orientation, moral and material direction are the worst offenders. Hypocrisy stalks in the land. Some of those who were instrumental in thrusting the most ignominious legislation of modern times upon us and who support the measure in congressional hearings serve alcoholic liquor to their guests and drink it themselves. The liberty of others displeases us; and yet we will not have our own desire denied us.

Finally, though immigration has been profoundly restricted for nearly a generation, a maelstrom of criminality has struck this country, the like of which it nor any other country has ever experienced, and it flows as directly from the legislation of the Anti-Saloon League as the Mississippi River flows from Lake Itasca.

I have no intention of becoming a participant in the discussion as to whether alcohol is beneficial or harmful to man, though as a physician and observer of human conduct I am entitled to an opinion and possibly to an expression of it.   I refer to the subject only to cite another illustration of our emotional enslavement and to the dominion of our emotions over us when they are repressed, and to point out the peril of our neighbor's wishful thinking.

Nothing testifies our emotionalism so directly and truthfully as the conduct of the Fundamentalists, men wise in their own eyes and prudent in their own sight.   They are determined to put God in the Constitution, and more determined that science prejudicial to literal acceptation of the Old Testament shall not be taught in public schools, and institutions of learning supported by State funds.   It was not generally known that several States had such laws until the Scopes trial of a year or so ago.   That told the world.   An Anti-Evolution bill was introduced into North Carolina legislature last year and now a committee of one hundred has been formed "to rout the forces of modernism" in that State, and to select a personnel for the next legislature that will ensure passage of the Bill.   The secretary-treasurer of the committee, "speaking as the representative of a large body of the Christian people in the State," says, "We object to pay taxes to support professors and teachers to teach subjects in the Schools and State Colleges that are subversive to the doctrine the citizenship of the State holds to be true."   He and his Christian people are opposed to sending men to the legislature who hold to these views.

The Fundamentalists, like the Klanners, are increasing in number and power; one is the complement of the other and they are both parents of protective legislation.   Again I have to repeat that I am not attacking Fundamentalism.   It is Fundamentalists that make me seek, like the first Joseph, a place *where* to weep.   They are doing more to convince me that we are involuting mentally than any activity, organization or institution in existence.   When I hear one of their most trusted spokesmen say that the doctrine of evolution is the most serious issue that confronts the world to-day, and see his audience rise up, applaud and embrace one another to manifest their approval of his words and to show their determination to unite that this judgment may be smashed and obliterated, I realize as I never realized before the hatefulness of arrogance, the menace of the "group mind," the peril of wishful thinking, the blight of ignorance.

The most intolerable thing in the world for me is to have some one attempt to save my soul.   I can do it successfully enough to satisfy myself.   The result may not be acceptable to my neighbor, but he should keep in mind that his efforts in his own behalf are entirely acceptable to me.   The interest I have in him is his health, mental and physical.   The former is bound up with education and enlightenment, the latter with right thinking and living.   Therefore they have my advocacy.   If from study, experiment, and experience I have gained skill in directing a seeker after them, it is at his disposal.   But I do not threaten him with the perils of the law or the pain of hell if he does not accept them.   And I resent his threats, or efforts to put them into effect.   I find no difficulty in accepting the revelations both of the Bible and of science.   Why should I be persuaded by men whose ideas or accomplishments I cannot respect that they are irreconcilable?   They believe that in so far as science contradicts the literal acceptation of the Scriptures it is in error, and that it should not be taught in institutions of learning supported by public funds. The logical thing to do is to have two kinds of schools with appropriation of public funds proportionate to the attendance.   It is probable that we are coming to it, and the sooner it comes the better, for my belief is that it is the quickest way to put an end to the discussion as to whether evolution shall be taught in public schools, and to avoid the blights on civilization that are flowing from it.

At the moment, religion and science seem to be irreconcilable. But they must be reconciled, for man cannot live without religion and he should not (and it is safe to say he will not) without science. What then is the solution?   Ecclesiasticism claims that the convention known as religion never changes.   Its claims are neither well founded nor allowed.   Religion has always changed, and now it must change more radically, that we may be saved.   The major ethical conceptions of Christianity are all consistent with science. Then we seem to forget that science is a weather-cock; it changes with the wind, and fortunate for us that it does.   It has never yet told the whole truth, but what it has told us in the past generation or two has been startling and most useful.   Had theology kept pace with it, we should not now be treated to the humiliating spectacle that is going on within the American Protestant Church.

III. GOVERNMENT

WHAT'S WRONG WITH THE UNITED STATES?

By THOMAS JEFFERSON WERTENBAKER

Thomas Jefferson Wertenbaker (1879–   ) *attended the University of Virginia, receiving from that institution the degrees A.B., A.M., and Ph.D. Since 1905 he has been engaged in teaching and newspaper work. At present he is Edwards Professor of American History at Princeton. Among his published books are: "Patrician and Plebeian in Virginia" (1910), "Virginia under the Stuarts" (1914), "Planters of Colonial Virginia" (1922), "The American People — A History" (1926), "The First Americans" (1927).*

RECENTLY I received a bundle of books for review. They all dealt with conditions in the United States, and most of them were extremely pessimistic. One author believes that the horde of immigrants who poured into the country in the years just preceding the World War have brought us to the verge of ruin. Unrestricted immigration, he says, has filled our cities with morons, criminals, and the physically unfit, has lowered wages, imperilled our institutions, and impaired the racial stock. We have now closed the doors, it is true, and we are trying to keep them closed, but it will be centuries before we can assimilate the conglomerate mass of humanity which we have admitted. It is a permanent disaster, perhaps an irretrievable disaster.

With a troubled mind, I turn to the next volume. But it, too, sounds the alarm-bell. This time it is our tendency toward undirected reproduction which appears as the great peril. The best classes, leaders in every walk of life, we are told, are restricting the size of their families, while the unfit — the lowest classes of workers, the ignorant, criminals, defectives — are reproducing with great rapidity. It is the survival of the unfittest. The race ascends the ladder by centuries of laborious striving, only in the end to cut off its own head. Seeing in this volume only the blackest future for the United States, I lay it aside more troubled than ever.

The next is a volume by a foreign observer — a diplomat who had dwelt long in this country. Perhaps he can see something of good in us. Alas! He is of opinion that we have bartered off our souls to Mammon. "Big profits overshadow liberty in all its forms," he says, "and the exercise of intelligence is encouraged only if it fits in with the common aim. Any one who turns aside to dabble in research or dilettanteism is regarded as almost mentally perverted. ... In the universities the majority of the students are satisfied if they memorize an array of ready-made facts, and they seek from their professors not culture but the fundamentals of a successful career. ... The material advance is immeasurable in comparison with the Old World, but from the point of view of individual refinement and art the sacrifice is real indeed. Even the humblest European sees in art an aristocratic symbol of his own personality, and modern America has no national art and does not even feel the need of one."

In disgust I leave my study and wander to the university library. There, by chance, I happen upon a well-known novel, the work of an American. In it the average, middle-class American is pilloried. Self-assertive, crude, ignorant, provincial, blind to the better things of life, satisfied with his overdecorated house or his drug-store, with its soda-fountain and marble-topped counter, he brings a blush to the face.

I lay the volume down, and take up a newspaper. It informs me that the United States is the most unpopular nation in the world. In one column there are strictures upon Uncle Shylock, in another complaints from Japan at the abrogation of the Gentlemen's Agreement, in a third accusations from Latin America of international hypocrisy. A fourth column is devoted to the crime wave in Chicago. It states that in the six years ending last spring there were 1795 murders in Cook County; that in four years 45 policemen have been killed; that crime is open, and criminal gangs in control. Rum-trucks are plying merrily, the city is wide open, bootleggers and bookmakers are prospering, while the mayor is valiantly defending his flock from the British lion, and ordering the Mississippi back to its proper bounds.

What of all this? Is it true? Are we on the road to perdition? Are we incapable of self-government? Are we of low-grade racial stock, criminally inclined, sordid, without national art, vainglorious, aggressive, unjust to our neighbors? I take my hat and leave the library for a walk on the campus. A walk through our beautiful campus is often very helpful. The dignified old trees and the lovely buildings calm the nerves and clarify the thoughts. What is the meaning of America? I ask myself. What part has it played in world history? What lies before it?

I picture the first settlers at Jamestown and at Plymouth. Simple, sturdy folk, face to face with unlimited opportunities, and almost unlimited difficulties. Theirs were the riches of a continent, but only on condition that they wrest it from stubborn Mother Nature. It required courage, physical endurance, and an iron will to desert a safe and comfortable home, to risk starvation, disease, and the tomahawk, to hew out a clearing, build a cabin, and face the task of rearing a family under wilderness conditions. The Virginians and New Englanders of three centuries ago may have contributed little to science, art, and literature, but they did their part in a work no less important. They added a great continent to the civilized world.

In no sense inferior to their fellow Europeans whom they left behind, their talents were of necessity turned into different channels. This man might have been another Milton had he remained in England; in Massachusetts he had to become a soldier in the unending war against the wilderness; this man might have been an artist, this one a statesman, this a scientist. The colonial period of American history produced few great names. Benjamin Franklin alone stands out above the general level of mediocrity. But if Europe, in the years from 1607 to 1775, boasted of its Harvey, Boyle, Milton, Newton, Kepler, Galileo, Molière, and a host of others, the Americans could rightfully claim that they had done their full duty toward civilization by advancing its borders into a New World. To fell trees or to open a corn-field seems an ignoble task when compared with investigation into the mysteries of nature or the writing of epic poems, but the effect upon human welfare may be as great in one case as in the other.

When, with the dawn of the national period, settlers began to push along the narrow valleys of the Appalachian ranges, out into the Mississippi Basin, a new and rich world opened before America. There were great plains waiting for the plough and the sickle, prairies ready for the ranchman's herd, hidden treasures of coal, iron, and oil, a network of rivers spreading out like a system of natural canals. Was it not the duty of the nation to pour out its energy and its talents in the development of this land, endowed so lavishly by Nature's hand? Wonderfully well was the task performed. In a century the frontier advanced three thousand miles to the Pacific. In another half-century the frontier disappeared. Where formerly were only prairies, deserts, mountains, and interminable forests, are now millions of industrious people, great cities, fields of wheat and corn, smoke-covered industrial centres, concrete roads, railway lines, hospitals, colleges, schools.

This great work, accomplished in so remarkably short a period, cannot be explained entirely by the abundance of natural resources. Mexico is a land of untold natural wealth, but it has experienced no such development as that of the United States because the Mexicans lack the resourcefulness, energy, and industry of our people. Says J. Ellis Barker, the noted English economist, in *America's Secret*:

> The country was settled by men possessing the conquering spirit and the spirit of leadership. These men fought among themselves, fought the Indians, and conquered the wilderness around them. . . . They created a new race, possessed of daring enterprise, of boundless energy, and of the passionate desire for achievement and success. . . . American economic success is less due to the vastness of its natural wealth and to the excellence of its machinery than to the ambition, good sense, ingenuity, and industry of the people and the wisdom and energy of the leaders.

But American energy could not have accomplished so much had it not been aided by labor-saving machinery, which in turn was the product of American inventive genius. In this country there has always been an urgent demand for labor. With natural resources so abundant and cheap, all that has been needed to make them yield rich returns was workers and ever more workers. It was this, as Captain John Smith explained to the London Company, which made it difficult for the infant colony of Virginia to compete with the potash, iron, and glass manufactures of Europe. It was this, also, which brought on the country the curse of slavery. But it brought one great benefit — the urge to create machinery which would economize in human labor.

It became the object of every American inventor to devise machines which could do the work of twenty men. Eli Whitney led the way with the cotton-gin. This device made it possible to multiply many times over the output of raw cotton, with the result that cotton cloth came within the means of many millions who formerly had had to do without. It was Thomas Jefferson who worked out the proper curves for the plough, and his fellow Virginian — Cyrus McCormick — who was chiefly responsible for the reaper. To-day our great agricultural areas are cultivated largely by means of machinery — the tractor, the gang-plough, the reaper, the thresher, the wheat-drill, potato-planters, hay-stackers. In 1850 the value of our agricultural machinery was $151,000,000; in 1920 it had mounted to $3,600,000,000. Under present conditions the average farm-worker in the United States produces far more than his fellow laborer in any other country in the world.

At first America was content with exploiting her agricultural resources. But with the opening of the nineteenth century there came an all-important change — the American industrial revolution. To-day not only is the bulk of our wealth created by manufactures but we produce a larger quantity of manufactured goods than all the other nations of the world combined. Six per cent of the world's people produce approximately fifty per cent of the world's manufactured goods.

Here, too, the explanation is found in the use of labor-saving machinery. Eli Whitney is known chiefly as the inventor of the cotton-gin, yet he is responsible for another achievement quite as important. It was Whitney who worked out the principle of standardization, or interchangeability, in manufacture, the very foundation of large-scale production. Turning his attention to firearms, he announced that he intended to make the same parts of different guns " as much like each other as the successive impressions of a copperplate engraving." He was ridiculed by the ordnance officials of France and England. Yet he succeeded so well that standardization began to make its way into the manufacture of other articles, lowering production costs, increasing the output, and emancipating workmen from killing toil.

In the footsteps of Whitney followed other inventors of tool-machines, or machines for making machines. American copying-lathes and American gun machinery became the best in the world. It was a long cry from the day when the youthful Slater stole away from England to set up the first spinning machinery in the United States, to the time when the British Government purchased in America a full set of machines for the Royal Small Arms factory at

Enfield and imported American workmen to run them. In the years which followed, American inventive genius carried the use of machinery in industry to undreamed-of lengths. There came new machinery in printing, in shoemaking, in the manufacture of automobiles, of furniture, of clothing, clocks, firearms.

With what result? That one American worker produces to-day about as much as four British workers. That the wealth per inhabitant in the United States increased from $308 in 1850 to $2731 in 1922. That the annual income of the American people mounted from $62,000,000,000 in 1921 to $90,000,000,000 in 1926. That the annual income of the United States to-day is as great as the entire wealth of Great Britain, and is five times as great as the annual income of England, nine times as great as Germany's, and twenty-two times as great as that of Italy. It is ten times as great as that of China, despite the fact that there are four times as many workers in China as in the United States. In other words, one worker produces forty times as much in the United States as one worker in China. In short, the result has been that in this country to-day human beings have reached a higher state of material welfare than in any other era of world history or in any other nation of the world.

I know that some will say: "It is for these very things that we are criticised. We have been accused of worshipping material gain to the neglect of literature, art, music, and science." But, after all, is not the material more fundamental? What boots it if we produce a Shakespeare or a Michelangelo, if there are millions living in misery and degradation? There once lived in England a devotee of beauty. He had the painter's sensibility to color, the sculptor's grasp of form, the poet's gift of language. Regarding beauty as the visible revelation of God, he devoted himself with the apostle's fervor to the task of arousing the British public to a more genuine love of beautiful things. But in the midst of his career he turned aside to become a social reformer. We find him trying to reclaim the slums, organizing a gang of street-sweepers, investing in coöperative enterprises. To many this seemed an unaccountable shift. What connection was there between painting and architecture, on the one hand, and the earning of bread in the mills of Sheffield, on the other? To Ruskin's mind the two were intimately associated. He had learned that a people cannot lift their souls to the clouds while their feet are stuck in the mire of hunger and overwork. "I am tormented," he wrote, "between the longing for rest and lovely life, and the sense of the terrific call of human crime for resistance, and of human misery for help."

After all, as an English writer tells us, "The most precious possession of a nation consists in the productive power of the people." In a country where the masses labor early and late for a bare living, where they have insufficient food and clothing, where there is little time for things of the mind and spirit, the scale of civilization must of necessity be low. The great contrast between China and the United States is that China depends for production upon manpower, the United States upon machinery. Under any form of distribution there will be in the United States hundreds who can be placed in what has been called the builder class — leaders in science, architecture, business, invention, art — to one in China.

If Ruskin found England sterile soil for his seeds of beauty, how much more hopeless would his task have been in India or China? India and China developed a promising civilization centuries ago, but these civilizations stagnated. They stagnated because, while the methods of economic production remained fixed, the population doubled and quadrupled. The margin over the barest necessities gradually dwindled, until life became one long, bitter struggle to keep hunger from the door.

Why, then, ask our critics, has not the United States outstripped all rivals in the cultural fields? Why has it not produced a Shakespeare, a Beethoven, a Raphael? The answer is found in our history. We have barely emerged from the stage of preparation. The passing of the frontier is still fresh in the memory of us all. We are even now forging our giant industrial system and widening each year the margin between the worker and the bare means of subsistence. The future — we claim the future as our own. I know that Sidney Smith said of us a century ago: "Others claim honor because of things done by a long line of ancestors; an American glories in the achievements of a distant posterity. . . . Others appeal to history; an American appeals to prophecy." But in the years which have passed since Smith made this mocking statement, the prophecies of the Americans of his day have been fully justified. "Who in the four quarters of the globe reads an American book?" he asked, "or looks at an American painting or statue? . . . What new substances have their chemists discovered? Who eats from American plates? . . . or sleeps on American blankets?" To-day this brings a smile. Yet, I venture to say, the gibes of our present critics may seem equally amusing before the passing of many decades.

Already, while yet in the stage of preparation, American civilization has done its full share for human welfare. In invention our record stands without a parallel. Says J. Ellis Barker: "Americans invented the steamboat, the cotton-gin, the sewing-machine, the telephone, the typewriter, the talking-machine, the incandescent lamp, the linotype, and the single-type composing-machine, the motion-picture machine, the airplane, vulcanization of rubber, modern agricultural machinery, modern bootmaking machinery. These American inventions have revolutionized transport and industry, agriculture and commerce, and have vastly increased man's power over nature." In the fields of invention Edison alone is enough to place the United States among the foremost.

In medical research this country has done noble work. An American, William T. G. Morton, gave suffering humanity the boon of anæsthesia. His priority in this great discovery has been disputed, it is true, but all the other claimants were also natives of the United States. Theobald Smith is the founder of one of the most important branches of bacteriology — for it was he who first discovered the part played by insects in conveying infectious diseases. It was Doctor Smith, also, who conquered that scourge of childhood — diphtheria — by his discovery of toxin-antitoxin. Equally important was the work of the American Federal Commission, under Doctor Walter Reed, in demonstrating that a certain species of mosquito is the agent for spreading yellow fever. But it is only within the past few decades that the United States has taken its place as the undisputed leader in medical research. The founding of the Rockefeller Institute has not only brought to this country some of the world's greatest investigators but it has organized and financed preventive work in almost every part of the world. The headquarters of the scientific army which is warring against disease is now in the United States.

It was two Americans, the Wright brothers, who gave the world the airplane. True, during the World War the leadership in aeronautics seemed to have slipped from our grasp, and many an American soldier in the Argonne or on the Meuse, as he gazed above at the German planes hovering over his head, wondered why his own government could not furnish as many planes and as good as the enemy. But to-day the wonderful exploits of Lindbergh, Chamberlain, and Byrd in conquering the Atlantic have aroused universal enthusiasm. On all sides it is acknowledged that American engines are the best in the world, and that American aviators are inferior to none in daring and skill.

In exploration, Americans have done their full share. The names of Meriwether Lewis, William Clark, and Zebulon Pike loom large in history, while Peary has the distinction of being the first to reach the North Pole. In recent days the exploits of Byrd and the dirigible Norge in flying over the Pole have added new lustre to American exploration.

In the strictly cultural aspects of her life, America already is entering the stage of accomplishment. In no field is there greater hope than in painting. Charles L. Buchanan, the distinguished critic, says: "There are persons who believe that American painting — our landscape-painting in particular — is, in a way, the finest development that this phase of the art has so far shown. . . . We find that the average person is talking about the possibility of a problematic future for American painting, without the slightest notion of the fact that a superb American painting is in our very midst." That Mr. Buchanan is not alone in this view is shown by the recent statement of the great French painter Henri Matisse: "You have made enormous progress during this generation. Before, you had almost nothing. Now you are a nation of painters to be considered alongside the European nations, with their long artistic histories and traditions."

If in literature the fulfilment has not been so prompt as in painting, the promise is equally great. Says the English writer John Boynton Priestly: "I believe that [America] has a greater mass of what we might call the raw material of literary genius than any other contemporary national literature." Another critic gives it as his opinion that within a reasonable time the United States "will produce as glistening a galaxy of geniuses as any other country can boast." Certain it is that in fiction this country leads the world, and that New York has become the theatrical producing centre of the world — the place to go, above all others, to study modern drama.

And what of architecture? Has America produced anything worth while in that important field? Perhaps we have our best answer in an incident which occurred a few years ago in London. An American was visiting some of the architectural gems of the old city — Saint Mary-le-Bow, Saint Brides, and others. With him was a distinguished Englishman, a Fellow of the Royal Society of British Architects. As they stood gazing up at the noble dome of Saint Paul's, the American remarked: "I suppose Sir Christopher Wren's work has a profound influence on modern British architecture." The Englishman turned to him: "Listen. Do you really want to know the greatest influence in British architecture to-day? Well, it's the United States of America." The measured judgment of Thomas E. Tallmage, the distinguished American architect, is as follows: "Previous to 1893 there was not a single class of building in which we excelled or equalled contemporary work of the mother countries. . . . To-day there is hardly a single class of structure in which an excellent claim cannot be advanced for either our supremacy or our equality."

In the field of political science America has accomplished much. No assemblage in world history can surpass the Constitutional Convention, at Philadelphia, in its combined knowledge of the history and science of government; and many have thought the Constitution the greatest political document ever struck off by the hand of man. And throughout their history the American people, despite an occasional tendency to be led astray by bosses and demagogues, have displayed a capacity for self-government, a saneness in public affairs, which has aroused the admiration of foreign observers.

Nor need Americans blush at their record in the field of pure science. A conservative summary of the situation seems to be that of J. McKeen Cattell, the psychologist: "It is my general impression . . . that the United States is in advance of Great Britain and Germany in the biological and geological sciences, and in astronomy; behind them in physics, chemistry, and physiology; about on even terms with them in mathematics."

Professor Joseph Mayer, of Tufts College, in the January *Scientific*

Monthly, states that in the last hundred years the United States, France, Great Britain, and Germany each has produced more than thirty outstanding scientists, while no other country has produced more than six.

In the eighteenth century, when the forests and the Indians were still unconquered, America produced two eminent scientists — Benjamin Franklin and Benjamin Thompson. They were the forerunners of a numerous and distinguished band which followed in the nineteenth and twentieth centuries. One of the greatest was Josiah Willard Gibbs, who has been called the "Newton of chemistry." Among the noteworthy accomplishments of recent years must be included the interferometer experiments of two American physicists, Michelson and Morley; Millikan's measurement of the electron; the work of Rutherford, Pickering, Abbe, Newcomb, and Russell in astronomy; of Newbury, Powell, Gilbert, Dalton, Chamberlain, and Daly in geology; of Morgan, Wilson, Jennings, Wheeler, Osborn, and Loeb in biology. America produced "the world's greatest psychologist" in William James, and since the publication of his *Principles of Psychology*, in 1890, has been the centre of activity in this field.

Professor Mayer's estimate of America's future is indeed optimistic. "The star of her scholarly accomplishment rose comparatively late, but it is quite apparently of first magnitude, and every sign points to its becoming the most brilliant spectacle in the firmament before the second quarter of the new century has passed."

As for our educational system, our organized charity, our public health system, there is every reason for pride. Certainly the American surgeons and dentists are the best in the world, American hospitals the most complete and efficient.

It is not the purpose of this article to answer all the criticisms aimed at the United States. Some of these criticisms are inspired by ignorance or jealousy, others are matters of controversy, still others are trivial. Some, beyond question, are sound in character, and point to real defects in our system, real dangers for the future. But let us not lose our proper perspective because of the present volley of abuse. We may agree that unrestricted immigration has produced a very real problem; that undirected reproduction has its dangers; that there is need for curbing crime in our large cities; that there are too many boxlike little cottages spread out over the country; that our fellow citizens are sometimes aggressive and a bit trying when they visit foreign countries.

But let us pity those critics who see nothing beyond these blemishes, when the most amazing spectacle in all history stretches out before their eyes — the chaining of the forces of nature, the freeing of man from the bondage of killing labor, the creation of a huge surplus above the needs of the hour and its diversion to the higher and better things of life, not only to greater comforts and opportunities for the individual, but to education, to research, to literature, to art.   After all, we have a right to view with pride a past of splendid accomplishment; to look forward with confidence to a future of unprecedented promise and hope.

OUR PASSION FOR LAWMAKING

By KATHARINE FULLERTON GEROULD

Katharine Fullerton Gerould (1879–   ), the wife of Professor Gordon Hall Gerould, of Princeton University, has been a welcomed contributor to numerous magazines for over two decades. She has written successful fiction as well as timely and forceful articles on a wide variety of subjects. Among her books are: "Vain Oblations" (1914), "The Great Tradition" (1915), "Modes and Morals" (1919), "Valiant Dust" (1922), and "The Aristocratic West" (1925).

I

IN a recent article the ever-stimulating Mr. Duncan Aikman declares that we Americans are "not quite standardized yet," and that there is a good deal of individual freedom even in Kansas, yes, even in Tennessee. He refers to an argument he heard, in the latter State, about the "monkey laws." "So long as they remained largely ineffective," the arguer maintained, "little harm was done, and that little might in time be repaired."

"So long as they [the laws] remain largely ineffective, little harm is done" is perhaps one of the most common and perilous American formulæ. I have long tried to determine the mental and moral conditions that underlie our willingness to permit the enactment of unenforceable and ridiculous laws, our tendency to tithe ourselves mentally for the benefit of virtue, it being understood that nine-tenths of the mind revolts. Our general social hypocrisy, as expressed by the discrepancy between laws and the observance of them — our dozens of impossible or tongue-in-the-cheek statutes, openly flouted — has been matter for foreign comment these many years, and now, thanks to Prohibition, is being freely mentioned at home. Perhaps most of us are more light-minded than hypocritical. Mr. Hoover's reference to Prohibition as a "noble experiment" is presumably not hypocritical; but surely it is light-minded to confess blandly, without horror, that we have been experimenting within the Constitution of the United States. If you are testing a new serum, you do not inoculate the whole population. The Constitution is no place for experiment, whether noble or ignoble.

As far as Prohibition goes, so much has been ably said by prominent and learned men that it would be tedious to use the Eighteenth Amendment even for illustration.   Though it is an extreme case of legislative turpitude, we are all tired of it.   We have not lacked men in high place to point out that we multiply laws to the point of absurdity; that the American's fondness for legislation is as inordinate as his love of motor cars or ice-cream soda.   "Why don't they make a law about it?" is on the lips of every irritated citizen.   Usually "they" do make a law about it, and irritations, alas! multiply. President Butler referred publicly, only a few days ago, to the fact that in many States the average citizen would be estopped from most of his normal Sunday activities if he paid any attention to laws actually on the statute-books.

It is not these facts, which are undisputed, that need detain us. The state of mind that permits conditions to be such is another matter.

No loyal lover of America is going to admit our hypocrisy, and let it go at that.   He is going to try to find out why we are hypocritical; analyze the vicious or virtuous national traits that result in hypocrisy.   He is not going to believe that the great body of his fellow-citizens has deliberately declared for evil.   There must be some reason, besides moral turpitude, why millions of Americans acquiesce daily in the passing of laws, ordinances, statutes that no intelligent man or woman believes can, or perhaps should be, enforced.   The blame cannot all be laid on legislators, though legislators are more or less without honor in America, for the legislator's chief fear is of his constituents.   If he did not think the people at home would like his vote, he would not vote that way.   No: we are all guilty, voters as well as representatives.   Most of us are not fanatics; I doubt if fanatical legislation could ever be put through on a big scale unless it were supported by non-fanatics for reasons of their own.   We are not concerned at the moment, however, with the people who support such measures cynically, because they see private profit in them.   We are concerned rather with the reasonable men and women who see the absurdity, who have no axe to grind, and who yet support the absurdity, or at least fail to fight it. What are their motives?   Have they anything so definite as a motive?   Why do they permit themselves to back impossible legislation about amusements, bed sheets, cigarettes, radical fraternities, and apple pies?

Most of them, one fears, feel with the Tennessean that "so long as the laws remain largely ineffective, no harm is done." Thus, presumably, they salve their consciences — with poison. But just what is gained by putting them on the statute-books at all? Surely no sane and righteous man really prefers to live under the shadow of laws that he has no intention of obeying. The answer, one supposes, is that American hypocrisy is a tribute — a blind, a stupid, yet, paradoxically, a sincere tribute — to virtue. Also, we lack, on the whole, a sense of humor. Or perhaps it is more accurate to say that we keep our humor apart; that we do not let it penetrate our attitude to life. We park it with Will Rogers, and rent it out when we want it. We leave our humor, as we leave our public utilities, to experts; it plays little part in our private philosophy. We do not, you might say, really own it. This is not unimportant, for Americans have been wont to pride themselves on their humor. It seems fairly clear that if a sense of humor were truly inwrought into the American character, we should lack many of our most notable possessions, from the Eighteenth Amendment to Tall Cedars of Lebanon.

The fact is, I believe, that most Americans want to be good; and being good is a difficult business. We want so much to be good that we simply cannot bear to admit, publicly and formally, that we are not. Also, we are verbalists — also, we are solemn.

In former days, there used to be much sociological discussion of the advantages of licensed and inspected houses of prostitution. Elaborate surveys of foreign cities were made and reported on. Every one knew that our cities were full of prostitutes, and the experts argued as to whether protection protected. I dare say they discovered that it does not; but whichever way the experts had decided, it would have made no difference. No American municipality, I imagine, could have brought itself to admit officially, by regulating it, that prostitution was normal. No more than any European nationals, did our citizens believe that it could be really abolished in their time — but they could not confess it. Laws, to the American mind, are not so much expedients as counsels of perfection. If we cannot all be good, let us at least say that every one must be good. Hypocrisy, yes; but rather pathetic, on the whole, than detestable. It may make us an easy instrument for cynics, yet in itself it is a sort of last-ditch protest against the Devil. We shall be lured by him, we shall fall, we shall compromise with him, we shall even serve him, since we are all miserable sinners; but we will not confess to the acquaintance, and officially we shall cut him. If we once recognized him, the last barrier would be gone, and perhaps there would be no saving us. Our hypocrisy, let our critics inveigh as they will, has been, in its deepest intent, a tribute to virtue.

A more experienced, more humorous, more practical people would have objected to the waste and absurdity of increasing legislation, increasingly defied; but we are verbalists, and still feel that words have a mystical value. Many of us feel, even, that a law once phrased and recorded develops some power of enforcing itself automatically, as if it were not a formula but a dynamo. When we pass a law we have a sense of having done something outside the realm of mere words. We may know that we ourselves cannot enforce it; but surely it will do something, of its own nature. This is mere fetishism, of course; all verbalists are dabblers in the magic art. If you say the right words, something far off will concretely happen, though your hand is not raised and only your lips have moved. I do not doubt that many of the people who supported Prohibition actually believed that the inclusion of it in the Constitution would turn a nation sober — not merely by the aid of guns and poisons, but by some miracle involved in the words of the amendment. Many intelligent Englishmen, I have heard, despise us for derogating from the dignity, altering the nature of the Constitution, more than they dislike us for our position in regard to foreign debts. Prominent Americans have been pointing out at home, for some years, the political disgracefulness of the amendment. But the average American has only a vague conception of politics as a science or an art. Consistency, logic, principle, do not mean much to him. Political virtue, for him, consists in refraining from graft. He ignores the spirit of law, the theory of statecraft. Yet he does desire a diffused and general virtue, and he will take the most unethical means to achieve it. His attitude towards good-looking legislation is like that of the man who wants his wife to go to church. It is a gesture that may appease Something, a feeble signal in the direction of holiness. He is vague about it, stupid, superstitious — but well-intentioned. He truly wants to be on the side of the angels; and, unable or unwilling to analyze and understand the angelic strategy, he pays with words. This, it seems to me — not cynicism, greed, or dishonesty — is the real heart of American hypocrisy.

II

Besides this, being verbalists and being solemn, we rather like laws. We could never do with an unwritten constitution, like our friends, the British. We have a strong sense of "the majesty of the law" — so long as we are permitted to take it rhetorically. Law-abiding we are not, and never have been — men seldom are in new country; but we do like a grave formula, properly engrossed, to express our most violent decisions. We are capable of rolling under our tongues, with delight, even the phrases of a statute we expect to ignore. We divorce precept from performance, yet we do really love the precept. We love making laws; probably because we are able to regard them as existing in and for themselves, to isolate them, imaginatively, from all the chain of events and circumstance that they draw in their wake.

One need not cite instances, since we all live and suffer under some statutes which are a disgrace to us because disregarded, and under others which are an annoyance because enforced. We do not like to repeal anything. As I said, we love laws; we regard them mystically. It can have escaped no observer that the tendency of American reformers is almost never to teach, to educate public opinion, to prove gradually to the citizenry the value of the reform, but always, alas! by intimidation, blackmail, bribery, any quick means whatsoever, to jam legislation through, and then to depend on the strong arm of the government, State or Federal, to carry out the reformers' ideas. We are not logical: loving to make laws, we make them hastily, looking neither before nor after, we go in for "noble experiments" — and we have not the willingness to repeal that should go with the haste to legislate. Even the law that was passed for some dirty political reason, to profit the cynical few, has a tendency to remain on the statute-books forever. We will break it at our convenience, for we are not law-abiding; but we will keep it there, in its completeness, because we are law-adoring. Ju-ju:

plain Ju-ju. Though the idol was made by our own hands, it has now become a god.

The State of New Jersey, in which I live, cannot be reckoned among the fanatical communities of the country. Our minor children may buy and use Colt automatics and cigarettes; bed sheets may be of any length the proprietor of the bed chooses; divorces may be granted on reasonable grounds; parochial schools flourish unmolested; and, for all I know to the contrary, evolution may be taught in State-supported institutions. But we cannot have Sunday movies or Sunday baseball; and some years ago there was a serious if ineffectual attempt to prevent, in New Jersey, the Sunday delivery of ice or milk. Undoubtedly the State Commissioner for Motor Vehicles has had his troubles. He has been stern about revoking licenses, merciless indeed to transgressors. He has made an admirable commissioner, and many of us hope that he will be the next governor of New Jersey. But if it is at his recommendation that recent legislation has been enacted, he has fallen into the easy American habit of "making a law about it" — a law that cannot be enforced.

After January 1, 1929, I understand, no one under the age of twenty-one will be able to acquire a driver's license in this State. Any one who lives on the Lincoln Highway between New York and Philadelphia knows perforce something about the dangers of traffic. Any one who has watched the driving of cars knows who does the best driving. Apart from the occasional tipsy driver, the people who imperil us all most frequently are the citizens of voting age who drive busses and trucks; and it is pretty safe to say that the younger you are, the better you drive. In California, one can get a license at the age of fourteen. There are, I believe, more cars in proportion to the population in California than in any other State — to say nothing of the heavy tourist travel — and there are far fewer serious accidents. "Hitch-hiking," if the hiker stands in the roadway, has become illegal in New Jersey. To refuse a license to any one under twenty-one can actually be done, however unjust and unwise the doing of it; but hitch-hiking cannot be stopped unless every road in the State is patrolled, day and night, by policemen a hundred yards apart. In other words, it cannot be done at all. Just another statute for citizens to ignore and — preserve. Many of us (especially parents!) disapprove of hitch-hiking. Yet the truth is, one supposes, that unless something worse than the begging of a ride is attempted, there is no moral harm in it. The motorist is free to ignore the begging signal; no one need ever give any one else a lift. Perhaps the intent of the law is to warn all motorists that any one begging a ride after September 1st thereby registers himself a lawbreaker and, therefore, one not to be trusted with life or property.

Unfortunately, these classifications do not work. The children who, year after year, transgress local ordinances by buying and using firecrackers throughout the month of July are not necessarily murderers or thieves. Though they disturb the neighborhood peace, they are doing it no more effectually than the citizens who place their loud-speakers in open windows — who are breaking no law. The schoolboys who beg rides have no criminal intent, and indulge in no harmful gestures. Yet they are to be known as lawbreakers. These classifications do not work, for they do not really classify. The object of legislation, presumably, is to separate sheep from goats; by forbidding malefactions, to define malefactors very clearly. No one can pretend that this is the achievement of a lot of statutes which we are familiar with. In Massachusetts one can go to movies on Sunday, though I believe one must forego, on Sunday, the longer clinches. In New Jersey, we cannot even go to "The Ten Commandments" or "The King of Kings" on Sunday. A malefactor in New Jersey is an honest citizen in New York or Massachusetts. Which in itself shows that statutes do not correctly classify.

III

It has been sufficiently shown by others that this spawning of laws is bad for our morals, since the citizenry that flouts one law with a good conscience tends to lose respect for all laws. We cheapen law itself, the whole principle of self-government, by enacting laws that public opinion will not sanction. Crime waves more or less naturally result from the national attitude to legislation. This, thank Heaven, is becoming a platitude; one need not dwell on it. What is interesting, deeply concerning, is the reason for our acceptance of these conditions. How did we get to the point where a good citizen can say that "so long as the law remains largely ineffective, little harm is done"? I doubt if it was cynically meant.

We got a good distance on the way to it, no doubt, when we began to look upon legislation not as a vital necessity, something the community could not safely exist without, but as an opportunity for "noble experiment." The more we were convinced that legal experimenting was noble, the more experiments we tried. Laymen turned loose in a laboratory . . . the difference being that, in a laboratory, the experiment that does not work is frankly called unsuccessful, and discarded. It is not hallowed and perpetuated. If you have once proved that like poles do not attract each other, you do not, in a laboratory, go on pretending that they do. As citizens, we have not learned — or perhaps we have forgotten — that we should accumulate our evidence before we pontificate; that no law should be passed at all until there is overwhelming reason to suppose that it is both necessary and workable. All governance of a changing world must in a sense be plastic, and new conditions imply new needs. Unfortunately, along with our willingness to experiment, goes this reverence for the original hypothesis, this determination to preserve the formula though it be proved out of date or simply vicious. It is notorious that it is far easier to get the most absurd or patently corrupt law passed than to get the same law repealed. Why?

Because, as we have said, our laws are mostly well-meant. Being, on the whole, an unpractical people, outside of whatever happens to be our own individual business, we do not envisage government as a practical problem. We expect our mere intentions to count more heavily than they possibly can. We expect, as has been said, a law to show some mystic power of its own to bring about the things we virtuously desire. If it does not work, we do not sufficiently blame ourselves for not having foreseen its impracticability. Our hearts were pure; we hoped for the best; and at least the world must see how nobly we intended. It would be a pity, merely because original sin is always complicating matters, to expunge that proof of our pure intent from the statute-books.

No, not wholly hypocrisy, I maintain, though even the dullest of us are becoming hypocrites, since even the dullest of us can see that we are legislating beyond the bounds of common sense. We have come to this condition of affairs through a pathetic belief in the formula, through our too great theoretical respect for laws, which we balance (perhaps inevitably) by an increasing practical disrespect. It arose, in the beginning, not from cynicism, but from over-much faith. Our unwillingness to repeal bad laws bears witness to that theoretical respect, still lurking in our hearts. When we non-fanatics support fanatical legislation we do not do it with a wink or a sneer; we do it, rather, in hope, with some measure of that superstitious faith still left in us. Besides, like children, we like to make contraptions that will "go" even if they wobble dangerously. We are a little intoxicated by our power to phrase something which can bring policemen and penalties in its train. We are solemn, but not, perhaps, very serious. Our lack of the humor which is part of the equipment of the serious man — humor being, presumably, a lively sense of the incongruous, in whatever field — is offset by our light-mindedness. It is perfectly possible to be both solemn and light-minded: to pull a long face, yet shirk one's job.

It is notorious — I seem to be mentioning only notorious facts — that, as citizens, we Americans do shirk our job. Look at the statistics of non-voters. If municipal, State, or National Governments are at any time in the hands of corrupt or selfish or stupid men, the voting population has, in the last analysis, only itself to thank. The men who had nothing to gain from office, in money or prestige, long since (with rare exceptions) ceased to give their time and energy to politics. Politics was (or is it only that for this reason it became? — the circle seems to be vicious, wherever you start) a "dirty game." It is not fair, however, to put all the blame on the politicians. They must, after all, obey their mandates or eventually lose their posts. Who can say that our representatives do not represent? If we have foolish laws, it is because we either like them or do not take sufficient interest in the matter to see to it that laws shall be sensible. Most of us, I believe, really do not like foolish laws, but we cannot take the trouble to analyze our discontent. And there is always the possibility that the counsel of perfection will perfect — somebody. If our legislators are representative citizens — and one assumes that they are — they too, no doubt, like counsels of perfection, and feel mystical potentialities therein. The idea of examining a law, as you examine any other mechanical creation of man, to see that it is logically fashioned for its purpose, stresses and strains calculated, etc., etc., is no more indigenous to their brains than to ours. Besides, they, too, like lawmaking. They, too, no doubt, are solemn, mystical, and verbalists.

The poison in the body politic is not so much the fanatics who, owing to our superstition and our solemnity, are able to enact their prejudices into law, as it is our fundamental American attitude to law itself. If we did not love laws mystically, as children and savages love them, we should not have so many; there would not be the insane march on Washington to get Federal sanction for measures that belong only among municipal ordinances, or State statutes, if they belong anywhere. Laws are to us at once toys and idols. We itch to make them, the more the better; having made them, we must put them in a sacred grove and try to make the tribe worship. Then, looking upon the grinning face of the god, seeing, perhaps, human blood once spilt before him, we come, all in the way of animism, to believe in his mystical existence.

At the same time, since we cannot wholly forget, once out of the grove, that we made him ourselves, from blood, clay, dung, and bark, we do not hesitate, once out of the grove, to disobey him.

Is it not time we discovered what laws are really for, and according to what principles they should be compounded?

AMERICANISM

By FRANK MOORE COLBY

Frank Moore Colby (1865–1925) at the time of his death was editor of "The New International Encyclopædia," a position he had held since 1900. Formerly he had taught history at Amherst, history and economics at Columbia University, and economics at New York University. Among his collections of essays are "Imaginary Obligations" (1904), "Constrained Attitudes" (1910), and "The Margin of Hesitation" (1921).

AFTER all, the crowd certainly likes it — the kind of speech that a Senator once made at a public dinner, which I happen to recall, and if a man wants quick returns from bursts of eloquence, this is the kind of burst he should carry in his manuscript notes. The five hundred diners received it "with great enthusiasm," and he could scarce go on for the "cheers and handclapping." With any crowd it would have been the same. The touch of nature? Not exactly. Only the touch of crowd nature, which rubs off when you are alone. In the mean while what has the man been saying? Why, that something or other is epoch-making; that the situation is intense; that the spirit of Puritanism bids us reach forth, expand, blow up, roar, and, above all, brag that we are God's only this and a heaven-born that, till the word "Americanism" sets the whole world grinning. "The Pacific is the American Ocean. The Gulf is an American Lake. . . . Our flag floats over the Antilles. . . . And when the Stars and Stripes is hauled down in Cuba, let it hang awhile at half-mast in mourning for the people of Cuba abandoned and the duty of the United States deserted. These are epochal facts. The future of the world is in our hands." This is no one man's view. It is crowd language. It is the echo of that lower harmony, that vulgar confluence of egotisms by which we tell the crowd whether it is washed or unwashed, at a New England dinner or at an Australian korroboree. Why call it American? Huxley describes the natives of one of the islands visited by the Rattlesnake as trying to impress the strangers by galloping along the shore, "prancing just as boys do when playing horse." It is not peculiar to American Senators.

"The Puritan," said the Senator, "had the logic of geography,

and we his children must have it, too. . . . All Atlantic and Pacific
canals and the future of Central America so far as affected thereby
are American questions — we cannot permit a concert of powers in
solving them." But since the greater includes the less, why talk of
the future of Central America? It was the future of the world just
now. Are we not going to have the whole thing then — we, God's
onlys and the heaven-sent, and the *Je suis moi's* and the *Egomet
ipse's*? Only a hemisphere after all? Take care or some other Senator will outflap you. There may be a bigger dinner and a bigger
inspiration and a lower barrier of common-sense, and some one who
will know how to take advantage of the collective mental slump.
There is always that danger in these lower appeals. Talk of islands
and isthmuses, and the next man may bid continents. Begin with
planetary systems, not canals. And though we despise it in private,
you are quite apt to find that a herd of us will first endure, then pity,
then hooray.

"There has come a new turn in the world drama," says another
orator. "We have taken the center of the stage. . . . We see the
faces of the nations half sneering, half fearing. . . . The world has
grown intensely conscious of America." This is no new turn. There
never has been a moment when a world was not watching us, when a
continent or two was not amazed by us or a hemisphere provoked,
when an orator was not saying just what Europe thought of us, how
Asia wondered and Africa winked; and that man is no true patriot
who implies that even for an instant we were not the center of the
stage. Nor is it a mere matter of nations. It is a cosmic affair,
with gossip going on in the Zodiac and a rumpus in the Milky Way,
Mars sneering, and Saturn thunderstruck, and an uneasy smile on
the face of the firmament that ill conceals its fear. We hate a cautious patriot who talks like a plum when he feels like a pumpkin.
It is a generous emotion, and why not let it go? In this mood a
world is not enough for us; we bump our heads against the sky.

But the chief danger is the collapse of the emotions when the word
"American" has ceased thrilling through the orator's nose. How
in the world can we keep it up? It is not a solitaire game. None of
us can go on like that all by himself under the stars. The heavens
are too sarcastic. We are soon feeling uncomfortable and hoping
nobody heard. Somebody always does hear. That is the worst of

it. Dickens heard, and he gave us *Martin Chuzzlewit*. A few jeer at it as your true Americanism. A few, who are deadly serious, prophesy the end of all things, inhaling odors from their moral vinaigrette. The rest of us understand the oratorical traditions and know that patriotism is not destroyed by burlesque.

EMPIRE: THE DAYS OF OUR NONAGE ARE OVER[1]

By WALTER LIPPMANN

Walter Lippmann (1889–   ), since his graduation from Harvard in 1909, has become very well known as a writer on political and social subjects. Among his books are "Liberty and the News" (1920), "Public Opinion" (1922), "The Phantom Public" (1925), and "Men of Destiny" (1927). He is now chief editorial writer for the New York "World."

ALL the world thinks of the United States to-day as an empire, except the people of the United States. We shrink from the word "empire," and insist that it should not be used to describe the dominion we exercise from Alaska to the Philippines, from Cuba to Panama, and beyond. We feel that there ought to be some other name for the civilizing work which we do so reluctantly in these backward countries. I think the reluctance is genuine. I feel morally certain that an overwhelming majority of our citizens do not wish to rule other peoples, and that there is no hypocrisy in the pained protest which rises whenever a Latin-American or a European speaks of us as imperialistic. We do not feel ourselves to be imperialists as we understand that word. We are not conscious of any such desire for expansion as the Fascists, for example, proclaim every day. We have learned to think of empires as troublesome and as immoral, and to admit that we have an empire still seems to most Americans like admitting that they have gone out into a wicked world and there lost their political chastity.

Our sensitiveness on this point can be seen by an incident which happened recently in connection with that venerable book of reference, the *Almanach de Gotha*. Here, in this social register of the royal and princely families of Europe, there appears, as of 1924, a list of American "protectorates." They are Cuba, Dominican Republic, Haiti, Liberia, and Panama. Now there can be no doubt that Washington exercises as much real authority in these countries, with

[1] From *Men of Destiny*, by Walter Lippmann. Copyright, 1927, by The Macmillan Company. Reprinted by permission.

the possible exception of Liberia, as London does in many parts of the dependent empire.   Yet the *Almanach de Gotha's* innocent use of the word "protectorates" was immediately protested by Mr. James Brown Scott, Director of the Division of International Law of the Carnegie Endowment for International Peace.   Mr. Scott pointed out, quite accurately, that the United States had never officially admitted the existence of any protectorates, and that Secretaries of State had again and again announced, as Mr. Hughes did in 1923, that "we recognize the equality of the American Republics, their equal rights under the law of nations."

I do not know what the *Almanach de Gotha* is going to do about this, but it is certain that the rest of the world will continue to think of us as an empire.   Foreigners pay little attention to what we say.   They observe what we do.   We on the other hand think of what we feel. And the result is that we go on creating what mankind calls an empire while we continue to believe quite sincerely that it is not an empire because it does not feel to us the way we imagine an empire ought to feel.

What the rest of the world sees is that after we had, in the years from 1803 to 1853, rounded out the territory of continental United States by purchase and by conquest, there was a pause in our expansion; that this was followed by the purchase of Alaska in 1867, the annexation of Hawaii in 1898, the obtaining possession of the Philippines and Porto Rico, and, in a different form, of Cuba as a result of the Spanish War.   From that time on the expansion of American influence in the Caribbean and the West Indies has widened until there is hardly a country in that whole region which has not seen an American intervention.   In an article which was printed in *The New Republic*, Professor Shephard, of Columbia University, has counted the following separate military interventions in the Caribbean between 1898 and 1927.   In Cuba, four; in Panama, five; in the Dominican Republic, five; in Nicaragua, six (the last still in progress); Haiti, one, still in progress; Mexico, two; Honduras, six; Costa Rica, one; Colombia, one.   Scattered all over the Caribbean are American High Commissioners and other officials, working under treaties, loan agreements, and the like.

For all practical purposes, we control the foreign relations of all the Caribbean countries; not one of them could enter into serious relations abroad without our consent. We control their relations with each other, as was shown recently when the State Department thought it an outrage because Mexico recognized one President of Nicaragua when we had recognized another. We exercise the power of life and death over their governments in that no government can survive if we refuse it recognition. We help in many of these countries to decide what they call their elections, and we do not hesitate, as we have done recently in Mexico, to tell them what kind of constitution we think they ought to have.

Whatever we may choose to call it, this is what the world at large calls an empire, or at least an empire in the making. Admitting that the word has an unpleasant connotation, nevertheless it does seem as if the time had come for us to look the whole thing squarely in the face and to stop trying to deceive ourselves. We shall persuade nobody abroad by our words. We shall merely acquire a reputation for hypocrisy while we stumble unconsciously into the cares and the perils of empire. Now an unconscious empire has dangers that may be even greater than a conscious one. There is nothing to be gained by talking about one thing and doing another.

The only effect of this refusal to admit that we are assuming imperial responsibilities is to turn over the management of our empire to business men with a personal share in it, and to our second-rate and least experienced diplomats. We have men in the diplomatic service who have had some experience in Latin-America, but as soon as they have learned enough to be any good they manage to have themselves promoted to a European capital where the plumbing is better. Look at the result. There is no more important post in the State Department to-day than that of the Chief of the Division of Mexican Affairs. It is filled by a gentleman whose name I shall suppress because there is no need to use it. Now note the diplomatic career of this official (as given by *Who's Who*) and see how carefully he has been trained for his responsibilities in regard to Mexico:

Private secretary, American Ambassador to Japan, 1908–09;
Third Secretary, American Embassy at Paris, 1909–10;
With the Division of Latin-American Affairs, Washington, 1910–11;
Secretary of the American Legation, Managua, Chargé d'Affaires, 1911–12;
Lisbon, Secretary of Legation and Chargé d'Affaires, 1912;
Second Secretary of the Embassy, Rio de Janeiro, 1912–14;

Secretary of the Legation, Christiania, February, 1914 (Chargé d'Affaires);

Secretary to the American delegation to the International Conference, Spitzbergen, June, 1914;

Second Secretary of the Embassy, London, 1914–17, First Secretary, 1917–19;

First Secretary of the Legation, The Hague, and Chargé d'Affaires, 1919–20;

Counsellor of the American Embassy at Rome, 1920–24;

And Chief of the Mexican Affairs since 1924.

Here is a trained diplomat as we understand the term, but for what has he been trained? The nearest he ever got to a post in Mexico was to be in Nicaragua in 1911–12, and on the basis of this intensive and intimate knowledge of Mexico, her people and her problems, he acts as adviser on, and interpreter of, dispatches from Mexico for the enlightenment of Secretary Kellogg, who has never had a post in Mexico, and to President Coolidge, who has certainly never had one either. There may be some one in the State Department who knows Mexico intimately and at first hand, but if there is such a person he is not Chief of the Mexican Division.

I have not described this situation in order to cast aspersions upon this official, who may be a useful member of the service. But the situation in which he finds himself is preposterous. It is preposterous that at a critical time the Chief of the Mexican Division should be a man who never had a post in Mexico, and has apparently spent only two years of a busy life, and then fifteen years ago, in any Caribbean country. It is not his fault. It is the fault of a system under which the Caribbean countries, the theater of our empire, are dealt with absent-mindedly, in a left-handed way, without realization of the responsibilities involved.

The refusal to recognize what we are doing in the Caribbean, the persistent use of meaningless, high-sounding generalities about "equality" in lieu of direct discussion of our increasing penetration and control, has prevented the formation of a body of intelligent and disinterested opinion. When something happens in the Caribbean, the only voices heard are those of the oil men, the fruit men, mining men, bankers on one side, and the outraged voices of the Gladstone liberals on the other. The debate is conducted by the hard-boiled and soft-hearted. There is no opinion which is both hard-headed and far-seeing. The effect on policy is bad; the hard-boiled interest works continuously, and the rather amateurish officials in the State Department who are assigned to these duties are unable to cope with it. They do not know enough. They are not strong enough. They have no sufficient incentive to set themselves up against the powerful interests which are telling them what they ought to do. So usually the situation is developed without the check of public criticism until it reaches a climax where marines have to be used. Then the soft-hearted people roll over in bed and wake up. There is a great outcry about imperialism, and the policy of the government becomes confused and vacillating. After a while the soft-hearted clamor subsides, the normal relations are resumed between the hard-boiled interests and the ambitious young diplomats with a career to be made.

There can be no remedy for this until Americans make up their minds to recognize the fact that they are no longer a virginal republic in a wicked world, but they are themselves a world power, and one of the most portentous which has appeared in the history of mankind. When they have let that truth sink in, have digested it, and appraised it, they will cast aside the old phrases which conceal the reality, and as a fully adult nation, they will begin to prepare themselves for the part that their power and their position compel them to play.

POLITICIANS AND THE PRESS
By HENRY F. PRINGLE

Henry F. Pringle (1897–   ) *during his undergraduate days at Cornell University* (*A.B.*, 1919) *had the distinction of being elected to three honorary fraternities — journalistic, debating, and scholastic.   Since his graduation from college, he has done staff work on three New York newspapers — the "Sun," the "Globe," and the "World."   He is the author of two books, "Alfred E. Smith, a Critical Study," and "Big Frogs," "a collection of sketches attempting to analyze Americans whose splashes have resounded."*

I

A MORE or less distinguished British author, having toured America under the auspices of a lecture bureau, was holding a final reception in the smoking-room of the liner that was to take him back to his native shores.   Shortly before the vessel sailed one of the New York newspaper men who cover the departure of ocean liners dropped in for an interview.   What had impressed him most about the United States?   What of prohibition?   What of the American girl?

The Englishman made the answers that departing authors always make under such circumstances.   But then, slightly hesitant as though afraid that it might be a breach of good form, he asked whether he might ask a question.

"Can you tell me," he inquired, "why it is that you Americans seem always to be abusing your politicians and still keep on electing them to office?"

He had, I think, noticed an interesting paradox.   To an increasing extent one hears — on trains, in club lobbies, and at other places where Americans gather — the public men of the country subjected to bitter criticism.   It is widely asserted that most of them are either fools or knaves and that many are both.   Congress is portrayed as a place where a collection of imbeciles assemble all too frequently to harass and bother President Coolidge and Mr. Andrew Mellon.   Even more heated denunciations are directed against State legislative bodies.   These are held to be utterly ludicrous and their members little better than morons.

A chance visitor to this country might logically assume, upon hearing such discourse, that the people had concluded democracy a failure, and that inertia, alone, prevented a revolution and the creation of a monarchy. But certainly he would be puzzled — and this is the most interesting phase of the paradox — were he to examine the country's newspapers for evidence of a dissatisfaction that had seemed general enough to merit reflection in the press. He would find, I venture, little or nothing. Republicans might be liars, but only according to Democratic newspapers. The Democrats might be thieves, but only in the journals supporting the Republican Party. For this there are three possible explanations: first, that the disparaging remarks concerning politicians are limited to a small, if vocal, section of the public; second, that the contempt is shared by all the people, but no one cares enough to take action; third, that the public has small chance to learn the facts because the newspapers do not tell the truth about politics and politicians.

In all three, no doubt, is to be found the complete answer. But the third, the failure of the press to be realistic concerning public men, is by far the most important. Newspaper editors frequently recall with delight and pride that Edmund Burke praised the "Fourth Estate" as greater than the other three estates: the lords temporal, lords spiritual, or the commons. This means, they hold, that the press is more powerful than political parties, mightier than legislatures, even more powerful than the government itself. They like to assure themselves that the press guards the interests of the people, sits in judgment, admonishes, corrects, and advises. Actually, most of the men who write the political news have become mouthpieces (without being paid by them, of course) for politicians whom they view with amusement or contempt.

Any one who has had even the most casual contact with the inside operations of political parties is aware that in no other group are to be found so many timid men, so many greedy for money or for personal advancement, so many whose philosophy of life is to work for themselves without giving a thought to the welfare of the country. Any one who has enjoyed the dubious privilege of witnessing the private lives of public men knows that, by and large, they are nearly illiterate and universally lazy. Is this an exaggeration? Ask any bookseller in Washington whether Congressmen buy books. Examine the type of magazines they read. Glance at the *Congressional Record* for their manner of speaking in public. Drop into the Senate or House office buildings and see how many of these notables are at their desks before eleven o'clock. Check up on the rarity with which either of the legislative bodies convenes at its scheduled hour. And yet these men are treated solemnly and at length in dispatches to newspapers throughout the country. They are permitted to air their views, often anonymously so that they can back out if protests are made by their constituents. Arriving in their home communities, unless these are cities of the size of New York, Chicago, or Boston, they are puffed in the local newspapers, and their speeches to the Chamber of Commerce and to Rotary are greeted with columns of respectful reporting.

All this might be expected in rural districts where a State Senator is viewed as a statesman. But even in the metropolitan dailies the average political story is less reliable, because it is less factual, than almost anything else in the newspaper. Among all those at fault for this, however, the men who actually write the political news are probably the least to blame. Even their superiors, the managing editors, can escape full responsibility. More than anything else, it is the system whereby political news is gathered and published which is at fault. Because of this system the American people have little knowledge of the truth. They are suspicious that all is not well and a few utter loud protests from time to time. They are, though, without leadership and can express their disgust merely by staying away from the polls on election day.

II

American newspapers congratulate themselves, and with reason, on their accuracy. It has long been fashionable, of course, to speak with scorn concerning "just newspaper stories," and to intimate that everything is exaggerated. The tabloids and a few of the more sensational standard newspapers deserve this reproach, it is true. But the majority of the country's newspapers go to infinite expense to verify all details of the stories they print. They often, incredible as it may seem to the laymen, err on the side of conservatism when some big disaster has taken place and refuse, in their early editions, to accept their own reporters' estimates of the dead and injured. An afternoon newspaper, with editions going to press each hour, must occasionally print rumors of what has happened; but these are swiftly replaced by substantiated accounts.

No reputable newspaper, for example, would permit publication of an unverified account of some prominent citizen's death. It would decline to describe an accident by hearsay. Its writers are under strict instructions to keep their own opinions out of their stories in so far as this is humanly possible. But even the most dignified, the most respectable, and the most conservative of our newspapers print political news based on nothing more reliable than gossip. Political writers are permitted to state "on high authority" — a phrase covering any one from the janitor of a district club to the President of the United States — that events of the utmost importance will, or will not, take place. After Mr. Coolidge announced that he did not "choose to run" in 1928, the newspapers continued for weeks to print, "from sources close to the White House," dispatches assuring the nation that he did not mean it. Governor Alfred E. Smith's views on prohibition have been set forth, on similarly nebulous authority, with interpretations both contradictory and ridiculous. One journal, exceedingly friendly to Governor Smith, reached a high point of absurdity during the fall when it ran on its front page a disclosure that "friends of the Governor are disturbed over his growing disinclination to accept the Democratic presidential nomination if it is offered."

What the newspapers do with political writing is, in brief, to dignify rumors and dress them up as though they were facts. This is, obviously, bad journalism, but its evils are even more serious. It permits the politician to send out a "trial balloon," to learn by means of an inspired but anonymous statement the public drift toward a possible policy. If after a day or two he finds that it is meeting with opposition, he is able to issue a formal statement denying that he had ever contemplated anything of the sort. Whereupon, the chances are ten to one, the newspaper will publish this denial. I was once covering a local political fight in New York and was told by a prominent politician that he intended to go over to the insurgent element in the row. He said that I could write a story to that effect as long as I agreed not to reveal my source. This I did, stating that "friends of Commissioner Blank" had been advised of his in-

tentions. The next day the commissioner was summoned to headquarters, soundly lectured, and ordered to stay on the reservation;
whereupon he gave an interview branding as "wholly without
foundation" the rumors concerning his treason. My newspaper
published this interview instead of pointing out the exact facts in the
case. It preferred to protect the politician rather than give its
readers the truth.

Any political writer can give a score of examples of this practice,
limited in no way to ward contests. A presidential candidate
granted an interview some years ago to the correspondent of a hostile
newspaper. It was distinctly understood that anything he might
say was for quotation, and the interview proceeded on that basis.
After the correspondent had returned to his office, he found a message asking him to telephone the candidate.

"Are you going to print my remarks about the tariff?" the nom-
inee asked.

"Why, certainly," answered the correspondent. "We agreed
that I could quote you."

"Well, I've been thinking about it since you left, and it was an
unwise thing for me to say. I don't wish to have it used. If you do,
I'll give out a statement denying that I said it."

And the correspondent, aware of the probability that the newspaper would publish the denial, did as he was told.

What chance, I submit, has the public of learning the truth about
politicians when the vaunted "Fourth Estate" permits itself to be
ordered about like a valet?

III

It is a fundamental thesis of journalism that the news columns are
free from prejudice and that policies are expressed on the editorial
page alone. But I venture to say that not a single newspaper in the
United States consistently follows this ideal. No one will deny, of
course, that it is the right, sometimes the duty, of a newspaper to
declare itself in favor of a particular candidate. It may conscientiously believe that the city, the State, or the Nation can be saved
only by the success of the Republican (or Democratic) ticket, and
may, therefore, excoriate the opposition in its editorials. Unfortunately, though, few journals stop at this point. On the contrary,

they give undue prominence to the speeches of their favorites and ignore, or distort, those of the candidates running against them. As election day approaches, they publish optimistic and purely imaginary accounts of a "swing to our candidate." They send staff writers on long journeys to talk with politicians who are illumined by similar hopes and who utter glowing predictions. The press gets just as silly, in other words, as do campaign managers. These gentlemen, no matter how black the outlook, invariably state on the eve of an election that their candidate will romp into office.

I recall a mayorality campaign in New York in which a well-meaning but ineffective gentleman was running against John F. Hylan. He did not have the ghost of a chance and was well aware of it. His managers were at heart resigned to his defeat and merely went through the motions of staging a campaign. But the anti-Tammany Hall newspaper on which I was working printed each morning a statement that he was "making excellent headway," was "seriously disturbing the Hylan advisers," and "had a fine chance of becoming the next Mayor of New York." He was defeated, as every one knew he would be, by one of the largest majorities in the history of New York municipal elections. But the identical thing happened the next time Hylan ran; and I am fairly sure that this particular journal has not yet learned the impossibility of rising in the air by tugging at its bootstraps.

Obviously, the newspaper reader gets very little reliable information during a campaign. Do his chances improve after the shouting has died away and the successful candidate has been elected? Not very much, I think. Political affiliations are not terminated by the close of a campaign. If a newspaper's pet candidate has been elected, he thereby becomes a man to be supported. His acts are given first-page treatment in the news and are editorially praised. His misdeeds are rarely emphasized, for this would mean a confession that the journal has erred in calling upon its readers to support him. I have known cases in which newspaper editors have stepped, like actors from their parts, out of their pages to take part in political conferences. They have succumbed to an urge to be "Mayor-makers," "Governor-makers," even "President-makers," and they are unwilling to trust merely to the force of their pens. Naturally, having selected their man and having been instrumental in his rise to greatness, the editors adopt a motto of "Our Candidate — In his official life may he always be in the right; but Our Candidate, right or wrong!"

Many a small-town newspaper editor, incidentally, is influenced by the promise of so-called "political advertising." Some of this may consist of campaign announcements, but in the majority of cases this type of advertising is made up of legal notices such as announcements of sheriff's sales, specifications for bids on public contracts, and summaries of the election law. In some counties in various States the party in power may vote to spend large sums, obtained from the taxpayers, in this way. A struggling country editor is likely to "listen to reason" if promised such subsidies.

IV

But all this has failed to explain, in full, the fundamental complaint so often voiced in Pullman cars and club lobbies that American politicians are a scurvy lot no matter what their political affiliations. And it does not entirely explain, either, why no hint of this creeps into the newspaper supposed to mirror life. Some light can be shed, perhaps, by the recital of another incident which occurred in New York newspaper circles.

An important State commission was holding a special conference in a suite at one of the hotels. The matter under consideration was of the utmost importance to the citizens of New York and involved the expenditure of millions of dollars. A group of political writers waited in the lobby for the conference to end in the hope that one of the members would tell them what had gone on. Long after midnight a friendly clerk telephoned from an upper floor that the session had adjourned and that two of the officials were descending in an elevator. In a moment they made their appearance, so intoxicated that they were barely able to stand erect. One of them, made infantile by alcohol, proceeded to slide down the marble banister of the hotel's main staircase. The other stood by applauding. It was apparent that neither was in condition to report on their conference; if, indeed, there was anything to report except the number of bottles of gin consumed. And yet the reporters pressed them with questions, obtained from one a confused remark that "progress had been made," and solemnly wrote articles in which they said that the commission was "on the road to a satisfactory solution of the problem." I was one of the reporters who did so.

On the surface this would seem inexcusable on our part. Here were two State officials who had met to reach a decision in which the public was deeply interested and had spent the night in a drinking bout. Why were they treated respectfully in the newspaper columns next morning and their drunken mutterings translated into a semblance of news? Was it because the reporters feared libel suits? Not entirely; the antics in the lobby had been seen by many persons who could have been called as witnesses. None of us, as far as I know, even considered writing an accurate account. The basic reason for our action was that we all faced the necessity of going to see these men in the future. Had we attempted to give our papers the truth (a course in which we should probably have failed), it would have been impossible for us to have obtained news from this source in the future. More than that, we should have become objects of suspicion and resentment among other politicians, and our usefulness as political writers would have been dissipated.

The illustration is important because it is so typical of the relations between the politicians and the political writers. It is not only the partisan prejudice of his newspaper which keeps the reporter from giving the truth to the public; it is also the power, real or fancied, of the politician to force a friendly attitude. Privately the writer may despise the dishonesty, timidity, and greed of men in public life, but he has persuaded himself that unless he is in their good graces he is likely to return to police-court reporting, a far less genteel branch of journalism. He consequently hesitates about offending them unless, of course, he works for an opposition newspaper. Then he can be critical as long as he limits himself to politics, for this is considered part of the game.

The system has made of the American politician a privileged character, a man whose private life becomes sacrosanct and inviolate unless he is so clumsy as to be drawn into a lawsuit or arrested. Even then, in part because of the influence with court attendants, but chiefly because the reporters are friendly, he often escapes notoriety. I know one high official in a mid-Western community who was involved in a particularly nasty scandal while a member of the State legislature. All the reporters knew about it, yet not one of them published even a paragraph about it. To-day only a few intimates have the slightest notion of the man's past.

It is "common knowledge" — that is to say, one constantly hears comment to the effect — that members of Congress are addicted to violation of the Volstead Act. Every Washington correspondent knows this to be true, and sometimes he writes a humorous but vague story about the "dry legislators who are personally wet." He never mentions the names, however, of the men who vote to uphold Prohibition and then hurry to their offices to inspect the latest bootleg shipment. Liquor was served in the Senate restaurant — brought from the lockers of the honorable members of the Upper House — until a careless waiter dropped a bottle of whiskey on the floor while a score of visitors were present. The American politician could become intoxicated nightly, beat his wife, use snuff, write free verse, or indulge in any other vice, I maintain, with slight danger of exposure. Private citizens and their private lives are legitimate sources of news. But the politician hands out news, or its semblance, and, therefore, the reporters dislike antagonizing him.

It matters very little whether one looks for examples at Washington, at some State capital, or at a city hall; to a large extent it is true at all of them. On the morning when Colonel Charles A. Lindbergh arrived in Mexico City last December, the New York newspapers dwelt at length on the significance of his flight as a bond between Mexico and the United States. One or two of them also printed, in an obscure corner of an inside page, a dispatch from Washington setting forth that while Lindbergh was on his way a daughter of President Calles, chancing to be in Washington, had called at the White House to pay her respects to President Coolidge. She was not permitted to see him, because custom decreed that a foreign citizen must first obtain endorsement from his country's embassy. Some underling at the White House so informed the Mexican President's daughter, and she left after being further told that Mr. Coolidge was "busy having his portrait painted." It would have been interesting to know whether she wrote home about this official snub and what she said.

Here was an example of bureaucracy operating at its worst, yet none of the correspondents covering the White House took the trouble to learn what official had been responsible or to treat it as

anything but a routine matter.   Why?   Because the men assigned
to the White House prefer amicable relations with the attachés and
other attendants.   So it is with the other Government departments.
Washington correspondents share with the rest of mankind, of course,
a fondness for leisure.   The veterans have learned, and soon initiate
new correspondents in the custom, that life is sweeter and easier if
one accepts such news as officialdom desires to give out and worries
as little as possible about anything else.   Some of the correspondents
become virtually special pleaders for the departments that they
cover.   The men detailed to the Senate or the House of Representatives view themselves, after a year or so, almost as members of those
august bodies.   There are, naturally, exceptions, and some of the
Washington correspondents are men with keen, independent, active
minds.   But the critical faculties of many of them have been dulled
by expediency.   It is not only the men who attended the President's
Press Conferences who do what they are told.   Probably seventy-
five per cent of the news that comes from Washington is news that
some politician desires to see in print.   Whether it is true or false,
propaganda or not, is seldom even a matter for idle reflection.

The situation at Washington is paralleled at nearly every State
capital in the land.   Again, the political correspondents are valuable
to the extent that they can obtain news; and the system seems to be
devised to handicap honest, capable reporting.   For years the legislative sessions at Albany, New York, concluded in what were actually drunken debauches.   Pianos were trundled into the Assembly
Chamber and liquor was served on the floor.   So notorious did these
finally become that the correspondents could no longer entirely
ignore them, but their descriptions were greatly softened and spoke
only of "good-natured merry-making as the legislative year ended."

V

The newspapers continue, however, to flatter themselves that it is
their duty to instruct their readers on the political questions of the
day.   Knowing, as their editors must know, that much of their
news is either false or inaccurate, they presume to urge the election
of a particular candidate and the defeat of another.   But there are
signs that the people are beginning to take editorial omniscience less
seriously.   Tammany Hall can win any election in New York City

in the face of united newspaper opposition.   The Kansas City *Star*, a journal of undoubted worth and great prosperity, has seldom been victorious in recent years in its numerous campaigns.

"The public," I heard one political reporter remark a year or so ago, "is getting sick of being told what to do by the papers.   The people buy newspapers, of course, but they get them for the comic strips and the headlines.   When election day comes around, they tell the editorial writers where to get off.   They vote for the other guy."

I do not know whether this is true.   It is, though, self-evident that thousands are becoming cynical about their public servants and that some are learning to look with suspicion upon newspaper political stories.   Partly, I repeat, the newspapers are to blame because of their political affiliations.   Partly it is the system, an outgrowth of years, which causes the political reporter to bow down before the politician, to act as his press agent, to print what he is told to print, to permit his inertia to dull his intellectual curiosity.   The solution lies, as to the first, in the complete divorce of the news from the editorial page.   It ought to be possible for a newspaper to treat all candidates fairly, to judge their campaign orations on the basis of their news value and their conduct in office, after election, on its merits. The cure for the second is not as simple to specify.   Perhaps there will arise some day a managing editor who will study the gathering of political news objectively and realistically.   He may find it necessary to shift his political reporters from post to post, to have his White House correspondent cover the legislature one year and the city hall the year after.

Certainly it is true that in bowing to the American politician the press does not do justice to its own power.   Otherwise it would realize that the politician is impotent without newspaper publicity. The political writers give in to a common trait of the politician, timidity, when they believe themselves in any way dependent upon the friendship of men in public office.   True, a single independent writer might find it difficult to break down the system.   It is quite possible that, working alone, he might find it impossible to obtain the material which his paper wanted and that he would be recalled. But with two or three fellow spirits he could, I am sure, bring the politician to terms in short order.   He could decline to become the confidant of the politician and could serve notice that he intended to write political news just as any other news is written, with fact and not rumor as its basis, with responsibility unclouded by anonymity. The public would swiftly benefit by such a change. It could vote with at least an approximation of the facts regarding a given candidate or issue. It could do more than remain away from the polls and damn all politicians with talk. In time perhaps another American paradox might cease to exist.

THE AMERICAN POLITICAL SYSTEM

AS SEEN BY AN ENGLISH OBSERVER

By HAROLD J. LASKI

Harold J. Laski (1893–   ), *a professor of political science in the University of London, has lectured at Harvard and Yale Universities, and at other colleges in the United States. He is well known in the field of politics and economics through his publications, a few of which are "The Problems of Sovereignty"* (1917), *"A Grammar of Politics"* (1925), *and "Communism"* (1927).

I

NO political system has ever been so vehemently assailed as that of the United States; nor is there any upon which criticism has produced so small an effect. Its large outlines have hardly altered since Bagehot, some sixty years ago, analyzed its deficiencies with a subtlety and penetration which remain unsurpassed. Yet there seem no signs that a foreign observer can detect which indicate any widespread desire for alteration. The constitution as a body of working rules is still, for the average American, too remote from his daily vocation to arouse a profound interest. The very prosperity of America tends to make him belittle their significance. So few politicians have anything like a national significance, so many are politicians because they have failed in other walks of life, that the inhabitant of Main Street is easily tempted to venerate where it seems an extravagant luxury to comprehend.

Yet, if we assume that democratic government is desirable, there is hardly a canon of institutional adequacy against which the American system does not offend. It is desirable that the source of responsibility for governmental error or wrong should be clear and unmistakable; the American system so disperses responsibility that its detection is approximately impossible. It is urgent that the working of institutions should be conducted in the perspective of discussion which educates and clarifies the public mind; but the essential tasks of operation in America are almost wholly concealed from the public view. It is important that the occupants of high office should be chosen upon the basis of ability and experience; yet both the President and his Cabinet are selected by a process which, if it resembles anything, is akin to a dubious lottery. A governmental system, moreover, should be sensitive to the opinion of its constituents, and maximize the opportunity of translating a coherent body of doctrine into statute; yet it seems the purpose of American institutions deliberately to avoid that sensitiveness, on the one hand, and to prevent the making of coherent policy upon the other.

America is the most prosperous of modern states; and its riches conceal from the public view the cost of its institutional inadequacy. It has hardly emerged from planning the development of a continent; and the possibilities of its natural resources have served to obscure the price it may one day have to pay for neglect of the elementary maxims of good government. For the test of a system comes only in times of crisis, and since the attainment of permanent unity no problems of European magnitude have had to be faced. Yet the permanent hold of the Democratic Party upon the South, the deliberate refusal of much that is best in American life to think of a political career, a financial system that, both upon the side of supply and estimate, is a woeful absurdity, the almost total failure to conserve natural resources, the invisible strangle-hold of wealth upon the two great parties — these are only some of the major consequences of the system now in being. America, in fact, is applying eighteenth-century ideas and institutions to the problems of a twentieth-century civilization. Prosperity may postpone the gathering of the harvest; but one day, assuredly, a new generation will reap its fruit.

II

It is worth while to apply these hypotheses to the institutions themselves in detail. The Presidency is the most outstanding, for it has become the most powerful lever of authority there is in the modern world. Yet what is startling about its character is the haphazard way in which its occupant is chosen. An English Prime Minister serves a long apprenticeship before he reaches the pinnacle of a political career. Mr. Gladstone was thirty-five — Disraeli thirty years — in the House of Commons before he was so chosen; both had been for long years essential figures in public life whose qualities had long been tested in the House of Commons. Even Mr. MacDonald and Mr. Baldwin, who arrived at power through accident, had been

members of Parliament for nearly twenty years.   And each was
able to retain office only on the exacting condition of being able
to satisfy in debate a legislative assembly deliberately designed to
maximize the consequence of his mistakes.

The American President is in no such position.   No one knows
who he is to be.   He is only too often the product of a series of accidents in which what is most important is not his possession of quality
or of ideas, but public ignorance about him.   He may well be quite
unknown to the Nation; he may even, like Mr. Roosevelt or President
Coolidge, become President by the act of Heaven instead of by the
choice of the American people.   He has to assume the leadership of
a party without, at least necessarily, being trained to that delicate
function.   He has to influence a legislative assembly where each
chamber is active and powerful; and, at the worst, he may have a
majority in neither, or, at the best, be compelled to purchase acceptance of his policy by shifts and expedients which destroy its
logic or weaken its application.   He has never any assurance that
his will must prevail.   He lacks the exhilarating experience of defending his policy in the full light of day.   He has not grown up in
fellowship with the instruments he has to use; and the knowledge
that a second term is almost certainly the maximum period of leadership does not make for that continuity of allegiance to him upon
which the shaping of a great policy depends.   He has even to gam-
ble in a large degree upon the quality of his cabinet associates; and
since they are rather his servants than his colleagues, he must inevitably bear the burden of their mistakes.   Because, moreover, tradition has made the main embassies the reward of service in his
election, he will be compelled to rely upon a diplomacy largely
amateur in character; no American ambassador in Europe in 1914
had any previous experience of foreign affairs.   He has to accept
the personnel of Congress through which he must seek to work it;
and, even then, he may find that the election in mid-term destroys
the men whom he employs.   Nor is this all.   His period of office is
so short that he has hardly become used to its exercise before he is
driven to think of reëlection; and if he is attracted by this notion, the
price he must pay in complaisance and bargain will be well-nigh
intolerable.   And even if he is successful in forcing a policy upon
Congress, he may well find that the exigencies of the spoils system,

improved though it has been of recent years, fail to give him the instruments which might secure its successful application.

This, at least, is the logic of the system; and it is not an adequate defense of its deficiencies to urge that, despite them, men like Lincoln and Cleveland and Wilson have all been Presidents in the last seventy years. The fact is that any one who studies in detail even the greatest of Presidential careers can hardly but be convinced that the necessary result of its environment is to minimize the best qualities of the occupant. He is fettered where he should be free; he is set apart where he should be in the midst. The absence of a clear organic relation between him and the legislature erodes his power while it destroys legislative responsibility. The rigidity of the system in which he is enclosed, the knowledge that his power is fugitive, the checks and balances which surround him on every hand, these serve only to illustrate the basic thesis that the separation of powers is the confusion of powers. No executive in the world disposes of greater authority; no executive, either, is so deliberately or perversely hampered in its fruitful exercise.

Nor is the position of an American cabinet member so much more attractive. It is only by presidential favor that he attains his office. Service to the party, outstanding ability, long experience in affairs, none of these things give him a prescriptive right to his position. He is a personal nomination of his master. He can make his policy effective only as he convinces the President on the one hand or placates Congress on the other. Resounding success may bring him no credit if President or Congress be jealous; and he has nothing to hope for from the prospect of resignation. Nothing, indeed, in the context of the cabinet has been more significant in recent years than the fact that Colonel House was able to do more than any member of the Cabinet of his time without finding it necessary to assume office. For the work of a cabinet member is too little in the public view to count in any final way. Like a sudden tempest, they are come and gone. To occupy a place gives no lien on the gratitude of the party. The relationship to Congress is too tenuous and indirect to make it easy for them to impinge at all concretely on the public. A few men, like Mr. Hay and Mr. Root, have been significant in modern times; but, in general, neither long experience nor outstanding qualities have been necessary for the tenure of cabinet

office. The requirements of sectionalism, moreover, act as a deter-
rent to possible aspirants; the need to represent the West may check
the ambition of youthful ability in New York or Cleveland long before cabinet office has become an object of conscious desire. The
process of selection is far too haphazard; the prospect offers no such
measure of reasonable certainty as parliamentary systems afford.
The power of the office, moreover, is only dubiously attractive as
against some of the alternative political positions. A senator, for
instance, need never resign in order to express dissent; and where he
differs he can speak from one of the few political platforms in America to which attention is paid. But a cabinet member in retirement
is, with rare exceptions, one of the unburied dead; and it is seldom
that public opinion desires his emergence from the tomb.

Much, doubtless, would be altered if, as so many have desired, the
cabinet member were to speak upon the floor of Congress. But, in
that event, the whole character of the American system would
necessarily change. For the articulation of the Cabinet with the
legislative assembly would compel the development in America of
parliamentary government. To-day it is impossible to assess the
qualities of a good American cabinet official. But if he were to sit
in Congress, even to the limited extent that Chief Justice Taft has
desired,[1] the basis upon which he is selected would have to be completely changed. The ability to speak, the grasp of the subject, the
knowledge of men, the instinct for administration, all these would
become at once essential qualities. An outstanding secretary in
Congress would immediately challenge the position of the President
himself. Collective cabinet responsibility would automatically develop; and the resignation of a secretary whose authority in Congress was recognized would have important consequences upon the
administration and its policy. The habit of debate in the House of
Representatives would be restored, and, with its restoration, there
would be both an increase in the significance of opposition, and a
growth of public interest in the process of politics. A secretary
charged with corruption, like Mr. Daugherty or Mr. Fall, would
have to meet his accusers face to face — a fact which would, at a
stroke, raise the level of political morality in America. Such a development as this, of course, is contrary to the whole tradition of the

[1] *Our Chief Magistrate*, 31–32.

American system; and the possibility of its occurrence is obviously remote if only because, in a period of calm, peoples can rarely be persuaded to prepare themselves for times of storm.   Yet it would be a service if an American statesman of authority were to remind his people how largely the present system was born of accident; had Madison and Jefferson taken a different view of Hamilton, the lines of institutional evolution in America might have moved swiftly toward a neo-parliamentary form.

III

To any critical observer trained in the legislative experience of France and England, the House of Representatives must necessarily seem unworthy of a great people.   It commits every fault against which the canons of political science can utter warning.   The first business of a legislature is to illuminate great principles in debate; but the House has long since ceased so to discuss public questions that the electorate can be persuaded to follow their analysis.   Its essential proceedings should be conducted in the public view; but the main work of the House is done in the dark recesses of committee rooms, whence only rumor and legend emerge for the edification of the press.   A legislature should be so organized that the opponents of government have a clear and full opportunity to make their case against its policy.   But the deliberate purpose of the organization of the House is to reduce opposition to a speechless nullity.   The private member of the House of Commons is already a sufficiently pathetic figure; but he is a giant by the side of the American Representative.   For the rule of residence starts by limiting the political stature of most American Representatives to that of natural parish councillors; while the shortness of the term and the amazing complexities of Congressional procedure mean inevitably that before the Congressman has begun to master his work the grim problem of reëlection confronts him.   His quality, too, necessarily deteriorates under local pressure.   A Congressman cannot attain a perspective about national issues if his constant thought must be about patronage in, and appropriations for, his district.   When he arrives at Washington, there awaits him no creative opportunity.   The chance to sit on a committee with no big issues to debate, the prospect of introducing bills which will never be reported, the opportunity to write speeches that will rarely be delivered — these are not horizons toward which an able man will strain.

The proper commentary upon the system is the simple fact that most Congressmen are unsuccessful lawyers. Even if they stay long in their seats — and the degree of Congressional wastage is startling — the career that awaits them is not a very attractive one. Very occasionally, with McKinley, it is a path to the Presidency, or more frequently, to a senatorship; but, in general, it is a life filled with frustrations. No Congressman has ever exercised the influence over the Nation that Bright or Cobden did in England; nor does he make the impact on public opinion of an eminent educator like Dr. C. W. Eliot or a rich manufacturer like Henry Ford. As a career, indeed, or a source of influence, it is not unfair to describe the House of Representatives as a refuge for the mediocre in national politics.

The Senate is a very different institution. With the Supreme Court, it has been the outstanding success in the American system. Its numbers remain small enough to give individuality to its members and to make possible a debate that is almost always real and not seldom instructive. It has real and coherent authority through its power to ratify treaties and to share with the President in the making of appointments; though the recent decision of the Supreme Court in the Myers case has done something toward rendering ineffective the real value of the appointing power. The members of the Senate have a long enough term to enable them, if they can, to create a sense of their personalities among the electorate. They are thus able, as Congressmen have never been able, to act as the embodiment of ideas. Webster, Calhoun, La Follette, Senator Borah, have all been able, in their very different ways, to make the Senate a platform from which to mold the opinion of the Nation. A Senator, moreover, just because the area of election from which he is drawn is wider, tends to be a more considerable person than a Congressman. He plays, as a rule, a much bigger part in his state; Calhoun and South Carolina, Wisconsin and La Follette, were, for years, almost interchangeable terms. He tends, also, to be a person of real significance in the party. He can shape its destinies in a way hardly open to members of the House.

Not, indeed, that the Senate as an institution is free from grave defects. Its very power — greater than any other legislature possesses — makes it a rival to the President; and it too often yields to the temptation to destroy the coherency of legislation as an exercise in the use of power. Its authority has too often drawn to it men notable either for the wealth they desire to protect or the corrupt State machine they are anxious to preserve. It stands a little stiffly on its dignity; and this too often makes it both debate for the mere joy of debating and legislate without due regard to the facts involved in its measures. It is altogether free from that grave defect which brings the new House of Representatives into being long after public opinion about its character may have changed; but it suffers gravely from the fact that the system of partial renewal — while it makes, of course, for stability — prevents it from being subject to a total expression of popular judgment. Where, therefore, as is frequently the case, it is at odds with the President, the latter has no real opportunity of forcing matters to a decisive issue at the polls. The timetable is always on the Senate's side. And this inevitably means that the Senate is tempted to seek a policy of its own without too close a regard to the wants or needs of the Executive. Because, as a legislature, it never dies, because, also, it shares so largely in the executive power, it tends less to correct the deficiencies of the latter than to absorb its authority. Almost always it will control a weak President; almost always, also, it will destroy the effectiveness of a strong one. It is, by the definition of its place in the institutional scheme, a permanent alternative government to that of the administration; and, of this, it is the necessary consequence that American legislation will rarely be intelligible to those affected by its results.

IV

But the American legislature must be judged less by its internal character than by its external relations. Here, of course, the Fathers proceeded upon assumptions which, in their own day, were judged exigent; and it is difficult to blame them for a construction which Montesquieu and Blackstone had canonized. Yet to-day it is supremely difficult for a foreigner to understand how Americans can remain satisfied with the institutional contact between executive and legislature. Here, once more, the system offends against every reasonable canon of political science. The separation of powers means that both legislature and executive must have fixed terms.

Each lives a life in large part independent of the other, a life, indeed, that may well be conceived in antagonistic terms. Neither, as a result, has an interest in the other sufficient to secure a coherent and responsible policy. The legislature cannot get the executive which it wants; the executive is never sure of a legislature to its liking. The result is to dissipate the energy and impair the efficiency of each. The legislature never has its proper work to perform, which is to make a government to its liking; and the executive can never do its proper work of applying a policy which it fully approves. Each has a certain interest in the failure of the other. A President who always had his way with Congress would completely thwart its personality and purpose. A Congress which trampled on the President would — as the example of Andrew Johnson shows so well — make impossible a logical body of reasonable legislation. If either is to figure successfully in the public view, it must be at the expense of the other. And nothing that either can do will affect the life of the other. Each derives its power independently from the people, and each, whatever its character, must await the fixed period for a refreshment of power. The exigencies of party may, to some extent, mitigate the viciousness of the principle, but it can only obliterate in part the magnitude of the evil.

Nothing so well illustrates this radical defect as the realm of finance. In a parliamentary system, the minister has a plan and he stands or falls by it; if the legislature will not accept his proposals, either it seeks a new government, or he demands a new legislature from the people. Whatever the choice, the result is at least logical and coherent. But in the American system nothing of the kind occurs. The minister makes his proposals; he seeks to placate the chairman of the appropriate committee. But the latter, however well intentioned, will not fully endorse the ministerial plan. He is himself, to begin with, a kind of quasi-minister, with a reputation to make. He has members on his committee who must be placated in turn. The member for Jacksonville thinks that something must be done for his constituents; and the member for Lincoln was promised a new post office. When the measure has been sufficiently mangled in the House, the process will be repeated in the Senate. A thousand competing interests, rarely related to the needs of efficient administration, must be conciliated. What emerges may even, as a total, look not unlike the original proposals of the Executive; but it will be rare to find that the itemized details are the same.   The truth is that for every subject, from finance downward, the United States has at least three ministers; and neither the interest, nor the point of view, of any of them is identical.   And since the Cabinet lacks any collective responsibility, since the party caucus is far too big to give integration to policy, the result is a partial chaos in all that is done. The Presidential system, in brief, makes the executive and the legislature independent at exactly the point where dependence is required; and it secures their inevitable antagonism of interest where public policy requires a unity of interest.   Nor can either, by the fact of independence, bring home responsibility effectively to the other.   The power of punishment is outside in the Nation; and the latter can speak only, not when the event requires, but when the Constitution permits.   But it may then be too late.

Other consequences of importance follow from this separation of Congress from the Executive.   No verdict can be sought from the people at a time when a verdict should be taken; and when the fixed epoch of judgment arrives, events will have done much to obliterate the material upon which a verdict should be rendered.   To an Englishman, for instance, it is literally incredible that no serious penalties should have been visited upon the Republican Party for the scandals of the Harding Administration; but it was of the essence of the American system that when the American people, as here, was wanted, it could not be found.   The result is an inevitable diminution of the popular interest in politics.   The work of government requires a perspective of drama.   The knowledge that grave error will precipitate a catastrophe keeps not only its members and the opposition alert, but also creates an active public opinion outside.   For the latter feels that its influence may be creative.   It may, by its approval or its antagonism, destroy the work in hand.   It inquires into what is being done because it may affect what is being done.   In America, that is only partially the case.   Public opinion is special and interested rather than general and disinterested.   It is a trade which wants a duty on the goods it manufactures, and the road to its wants is not through the channels of opinion, but the avenue of the lobbyist. There is hardly a great subject of general import upon which an agitation in America can hope effectively to influence the government; for the maximum obtuseness on the part of the latter will not advance by one day the period of judgment at the polls.

Experience, in other words, seems to demand that the executive and the legislature should never be rivals for power. If that be the case, the mind of the public is confusion, and its confusion is destructive of its interest. Nor is that all. Their antagonism means that neither can perform its work effectively; each is continually tempted into regions outside its proper competence. A strong executive either reduces Congress to the level of a formless debating society, or is himself reduced by conflict to the position of an angry, if energetic man, declaiming, like Mr. Wilson in 1919, in a vacuum of futility. A weak executive becomes, almost necessarily, the creature of Congress; and there is never sufficient integration of purpose in the latter to make it a desirable master. The main business, indeed, of a legislature cannot be performed under American conditions. For that business is to find a suitable executive which the opposition can criticize, if occasion offers, to the point of defeat. A body of some four hundred and fifty men, like the House of Representatives, or even ninety-six, like the Senate, cannot hope to interfere successfully with the administrative process. The thing is too complex and delicate for anything more than general oversight. Yet it is to this that, under the given conditions, they are perpetually tempted; and the result is that they merely irritate and hamper where they should criticize to clarify. Nor can such a body legislate if it is able to substitute any one's proposals for those submitted to it. Chaos is bound to result if the formal source of legislation is multiple in character. The executive ceases to be responsible because it does not create; and the legislature disavows responsibility because it does not apply. This has been the result of the American system, and increasingly the result in recent years. It is certainly difficult to reconcile its character with the possibility of adequate government.

V

A word is necessary upon what is the outstanding failure in the American federal scheme — the Vice-Presidency. Tradition here has utterly undone the original purpose of the Constitution by reducing the Electoral College to a nullity. The result has been that every Vice-President since the Civil War has been selected for reasons even worse, and more obscure, than those for which a President is chosen.   No Vice-Presidential candidate has ever been nominated with a view to his accession to the Presidency, though this has occurred on five occasions; and in each instance there has either, as with Andrew Johnson and Roosevelt, been a complete reversal of his predecessor's policy, or, as with Chester Arthur, an attitude of complete uncreativeness.   The position, indeed, is utterly anomalous; and no experiment, like that of President Harding with Mr. Coolidge, which seeks to keep the Vice-President in touch with policy, has had any value.   It is bad enough to have Presidents nominated systematically by interested wire-pullers; but it is surely worse to have Vice-Presidents chosen by wire-pullers who are not even interested.   Nothing in the working of the Constitution shows more lamentably the little respect of the system for the quality of men.

That is, indeed, throughout its capital defect.   Granted the premise of the separation of powers, its formal aspects are logical enough.   They are, indeed, politically dubious in the light of historic experience; but, more, they are politically vicious when they operate in the psychological penumbra of Jacksonian democracy. For the essential quality of the system is that it necessarily fails to elevate the temper of public life.   The Presidency, of course, is an office as great as any in the gift of a democracy; but the terms of its conferment are, save by accident, fatal to its being occupied by the man who is fit to exercise its powers.   To be a member of Congress, even to be a Senator, will not often attract the highest talents in the Republic, for the simple reason that the separation of powers insulates the Senator or Representative from reasonable hope of any large and concrete achievement.   The best members of the House of Commons go there because it is the highroad to the Cabinet, and a seat therein means that they put their hands upon a big machine of which the capacity for influence is enormous.   The American legislator lacks almost entirely that prospect; and the American administrator is, on his side, similarly hampered by the knowledge that the machine he is to drive must run along a road largely indicated by others.   There is not enough in such an outlook to attract from men of first quality their whole energy of mind throughout their lives. And it is, indeed, noteworthy that since the Civil War, at least, politics has rarely been the permanent vocation of the outstanding figures of American life.   As with President Wilson, it has been the end of one career; or, as with Mr. Root and Mr. Hughes, it has been an interlude in another.   There is, doubtless, the exceptional instance of Mr. Roosevelt; but it is the general rule that the career of politician as a life-adventure is in America ample enough only to attract the men of routine mediocrity.

And the influence of this, in its turn, upon American social life is notable.   The real leadership of America is rarely found in political circles.   The influence of politics upon the national consciousness, the part played by them in the mind of the average man, is curiously, even pitifully, small.   An American is less instinct with the sense of the State than the citizen of any first-class European power.   He feels less related to, less responsible for, his government.   He is cynical about its activities and its personnel in a way to which only long residence in America can habituate a citizen of Europe.   It affects notably the political speculation of America; there has not been since the Civil War one political philosopher of first-rate eminence in America.   Yet in economics, in metaphysics, in the natural sciences, in jurisprudence, America has been on an equal level with the best of European achievement.   It affects also the press.   American newspapers give a volume of information to which, perhaps, that of only two European journals can compare.   But the comment on that information is, as a general rule, notably inferior to the comment of the European press.   For the latter writes always with the knowledge that the effect it produces on public opinion may well unmake a government.   The power to produce action of a decisive kind is the great motive-force of the finest journalism.   The American journalist has no such power even when the opportunity of a Presidential election is counted in its full force.   Articles which leave men where they were are not likely to be scrutinized with care; and they are, therefore, not likely to be written with care.   There exists always a sense of remoteness between the act and the written word which is fatal to the influence the latter might exercise.

It is worth while, perhaps, to illustrate the small part played in American life by the sense of the political adventure by a concrete example.   One of the acid tests of a political system is its ability to gain the interest of youth simply because, as a career, it demands

a lifetime of service.   The observer who visits the universities of
Europe will find in them a significant body of students already devoted to a political career.   They will find there an active party
life, with its journals, its meetings, its debates.   The politicians themselves naturally look to the universities as an essential recruiting
ground for their future colleagues.   Yet, save in the Presidential
year, there is no such vivid political life in an American college.
The habit of political debate is hardly existent.   The eager disputa-
tion, the desire to take an active part in the conflict in the field, the
desire consciously to adopt a political career, these are unknown.
One cannot meet a body of English trade-unionists without finding
men to whom a political career is an object of ambition; one would
have to search far among the labor-unionists of America to discover
one who consciously desired to be a member of Congress.   Yet, as
Disraeli said, the youth of a nation are the trustees of posterity.   The
future of any system, the quality it will have, depends, in large degree, upon the interest it can awaken in their minds.

It is, of course, true that the power of politics in America to influence or to alter the national life is less than elsewhere.   It is true,
also, that leadership, in the European political sense, has been
notable in industry and law in a significant way; certainly, on the
Bench men like Justice Holmes have given an impetus to creative
action such as a great statesman in Europe contributes to political
effort.   Yet none of this gives to the national life that purposive
integration it is the business of politics to supply.   We have to plan
a modern civilization in terms which necessitate collective habits of
thought; we need then the institutions to give the fullest expression
to those habits.   It is the business of government to-day to preserve
for all citizens the minimum basis of life deemed adequate for men
who would realize in conscious coöperation the eminent worth of
their humanity.   Presidential institutions in America were created
when government had a very different end in view.   Their retention
now serves rather to thwart than to secure the great ideas of which
America was in its origins the sponsor.

IV. BUSINESS

SELFISH BUSINESS [1]

By DURANT DRAKE

Durant Drake (1878–) is at present on the faculty of Vassar College as a professor of philosophy. He has taught at the University of Illinois and, in 1923 and 1924, lectured in German, Swiss, and Italian universities. Among his works on philosophy and ethics are "The Problem of Things in Themselves" (1911), "Problems of Conduct" (1914), "America Faces the Future" (1922), and "The New Morality" (1928).

WHEN MAY BUSINESS BE CALLED SELFISH?

WE do not commonly speak of "corruption," or even of "graft," in business. Yet business in America, as in most countries, is carried on quite frankly and universally for private profit, rather than with an eye to the common good. The difference is that in commerce and industry the principle of individualism, of every man for himself, to increase his personal profits in every way possible within the law, is so completely established, and the ideal of business as a form of public service so generally regarded as utopian, that the politician is frowned upon for his side of the very transactions for which the other side, the business man's side, is held blameless. *Of course* the corporation must provide funds to influence legislation in its favour; that is a part of its "legitimate" expenses. But the politicians who manipulate the legislation are "corrupt"! In short, in spite of high-sounding maxims of Chambers of Commerce and Rotary Clubs, there is less actual disinterestedness in business than in politics. And the harm done to the public welfare by selfish politics is a minor matter compared with the harm done by selfish business.

The plain fact is that the selfishness and stupidity of private business wastes billions of dollars' worth of the national wealth while politics is wasting its millions. Indeed, as the more important part of the graft in politics is a mere by-product of profit-seeking business, we may well consider whether it is not our industrial system rather than our political system which is most in need of reform.

The recent currency of the word "profiteering" is a sign that even the upper classes are becoming uneasy over the morals of business *where it is conspicuously successful.* But the ethics of the profiteers is not different from the ethics of business in general; they have simply had the skill, or luck, to do what practically all the business men are trying and hoping to do — make a lot of money. How many business men whom you know are sacrificing opportunities to make money out of consideration for the happiness of their employees, or of their business rivals, or of their customers, or of posterity?   Some, thank God!   For selfishness is not the only motive that actuates human beings.   But "success" in business means to us making money.   And the desire for success, for the money itself, and the power and pleasure which money can give, is so powerful that it is foolish to expect most men to renounce these things so long as they can get them without punishment, or censure from their fellows.   It may be even harmful to set up idealistic codes for business men, while the laws permit anti-social practices.   For these fine phrases, rehearsed in after-dinner speeches, and accepted with much self-approval, mask from those who give them lip-worship the fact that the actual conduct of their business is actuated by quite other motives, that they are really in business for their pocketbooks.

"Profiteering," at its peaks, has reached astonishing heights.   According to Senate Document No. 259, the earnings of bituminous and lignite coal companies in 1917 averaged around 100 per cent profit on their capital stock.   Relatively few companies got less than 25 per cent, eleven companies got over 1000 per cent, four companies got over 2000 per cent — i.e., profits amounting to more than twenty times the value of their capital stock — in that one year alone. . . . The War years gave opportunities for the diverting of a hitherto unprecedented proportion of the world's income to the pockets of the owners of strategically placed industries.   The United States Steel Corporation, which was doing excellently in 1914 with $23,000,000 in profits, yielded its owners in 1917 $450,000,000 in profits.   The Baldwin Locomotive Company jumped from $350,000 to around $6,000,000 of profits. . . . And so on. . . . It was estimated by careful investigators that the *increased* profits of the corporations of the country amounted to over four billion dollars a year. This means net profits, and did not include the money put back into the business. And these profits resulted only in minor degree from increased production; they resulted primarily from increased *demand*, which permitted the charging of higher prices. . . . Much of this profiteering was in foodstuffs, wearing-apparel, and other necessities of life; so that the higher prices charged directly increased the cost of living for every one. Of course, indirectly, all profits taken by any one raised by so much the cost of living for the rest of us. And the question is, *how much* of a tax are we willing to pay that the owners of industries and commercial concerns may make more money?

Since the War, profits have not been so spectacular. But a new pace was set, new hopes of profit aroused; and the cry, "Hands off business," "Return to normalcy," reflected the eagerness of the "capitalist" class to be free again from the restraints and high taxes which had begun to be imposed. In 1920, we remember that the price of sugar shot up from eight cents a pound to twenty-five cents and more. The sugar-profiteers are said to have made six hundred million dollars in a single year — which amounts to a tax of thirty dollars on every family in the United States. . . . A national bank has just announced that its dividends for the past eighty years have averaged 100 per cent a year. . . . Senator Capper has reported that the consumers are paying fifteen billion dollars more for farm products than the farmers receive. Most of the farmers, indeed, are barely making a living. In ten years the price received by farmers for their wheat rose about 25 per cent; the price of bread rose nearly 100 per cent. A New York baking company has been making over 100 per cent profit in a year. . . . The *Railway Age* reported that when Texas farmers were selling spinach at $5 a ton, Chicago consumers were paying for it fifteen cents a pound, which is $300 a ton. *Some one* was making money!

Mr. Stuart Chase has collected multitudes of facts like the following: Writing inks sell for about $1.25 a quart. The Government Printing Office is able to make its own ink at nine cents a quart. . . . A certain liquid soap is sold at a dollar a gallon; the Chicago Y.M.C.A. makes, for its own use, a better grade for eleven cents a gallon. . . . A certain disinfecting spray was marketed under a brand name for $62 a barrel. When its composition was made known, the price dropped to 47 cents a barrel. . . . And so on. The price which we are paying for the necessities and comforts of life is, in a good many cases, 50 or 100 per cent more than the sum for which these articles could be profitably sold.

The supposed effect of free competition in keeping prices down has ceased to exist in many industries. Price-fixing combinations have run up prices; and even where there is no open collusion, a tacit agreement has maintained a new scale of profits. Not in every field. There are commodities in which, for one reason or other, profiteering has not yet succeeded, and whose price (taking into account the value of money) is lower than before the War. But the accepted principle is to charge "what the traffic will bear," without regard to what would be a "fair" return for capital and management.

The degree of profiteering current goes far beyond the profits declared upon income tax blanks, or the cash dividends paid upon capital stock. Large salaries paid to the insiders consume a considerable share of what is really profits; the American Metal Company, for example, was recently paying about a million dollars a year in salaries to six officers. Many such instances could be given. . . . Profits are often veiled by declaring stock dividends; this permits a really very high percentage of profit to be disguised as a normal dividend upon the greatly enlarged amount of stock. Thus a great deal of the "capital stock" of the more prosperous concerns is nothing but "water," representing no money invested. If lean years come, the investors complain bitterly that they are not receiving a proper return for their money. But the insiders, who foresaw the decline in earnings, probably sold their interest to unsuspecting investors before the decline had gone far. And the stock which has ceased to pay is mostly "water," with no real claim upon society for paying dividends.

The number of people who, when skill and fortune combine to favour them, are in a position to make large profits, either by owning and running a business, or by holding stock in prosperous concerns bought before their prosperity brought up the price of the stock, is considerable. Including those who have hopes of sharing in such profits, a majority of the people who count, that is, who influence public opinion and legislation, come within this class. These people naturally favour unlimited opportunities for profit-making. But they are only a small fraction of the people in the United States. The question is, Is it just that the rest of the people — the millions of employees in business and government, the farmers, the teachers and ministers and other people who have only their salaries to live on — should have their cost of living raised very appreciably in order that certain business men and stockholders may get rich?

WHAT HARM IS BEING DONE TO EMPLOYEES?

Suppose we lay aside the difficult question as to the point at which profit-making becomes in itself unfair to the rest of the community (becomes "profiteering"), and ask *how* these profits are made, and whether the methods of making them are anti-social. In what ways do our money-makers hurt others in their race to make their fortunes?

Well, in the first place, they very commonly hurt their employees; by underpaying them, by failing to remedy dangerous and unsanitary conditions of work, by throwing them out of employment unnecessarily, by hiring children who ought to be in school, and in other ways.

As to the matter of wages, we will merely say that some classes of workers are overpaid, while other groups are scandalously underpaid, depending largely upon the effectiveness with which the different groups are organized. Obviously it is to the immediate financial advantage of employers to pay as little as possible for labour. There have been many heart-breaking cases of owners of industries paying starvation wages at the same time that they were raking off tremendous profits. The situation varies, of course, from industry to industry, from place to place, and from year to year. At present the labouring class in this country is, on the whole, better paid than anywhere else, or than ever before in the history of the world. But we cannot be sure that this relatively fortunate condition will endure. And there are even now many groups of workers who are not getting enough, by the hardest work, to maintain a decent standard of living. *Some* of the profits of business are being made by sweating employees.

Some of the profits are being made at the cost of the health, and even of the lives, of employees. Safety devices, sanitary conditions, cost money; and many of our most prosperous concerns refuse to spend any more than our often very lax laws require for the protection of their workers. Authorities agree that three quarters of the deaths and serious injuries in American industry could be prevented, if the manufacturers so desired, by the use of available methods. Our record in this respect is much worse than that of the civilized countries of Europe.

It is extraordinary how the urge toward profits blinds ordinary respectable people, who think of themselves as "good," and even as "Christian," to the misery which their selfishness entails. For one example: The United States Census mortality statistics recently showed that the death rate from tuberculosis among cotton mill operatives is higher than for all other workers; there is also a very high percentage of deaths from other diseases, owing to conditions of work in the mills, which are to a large extent remediable by the expenditure of capital. But the National Industrial Conference Board, composed of representatives of the American Cotton Manufacturers' Association and of other trades, stirred by protests to investigate this situation, issued a report which whitewashed the cotton manufacturers. They announced the complacent conclusion that "apparently there is no conclusive information as to the health hazards to which cotton mill operators are exposed." . . . And conditions continue as before.

Sometimes the profits of business are increased by shutting down plants and stopping production, that prices may be kept high. That this involves unemployment and an absolute cessation of income for the employees is of no interest to business men who are out to make money. They talk about "overproduction," and lay the blame upon "economic laws." But there is no real overproduction while there are still millions of people in our country (not to speak of the people of other countries) who are undernourished, underclothed, without decent living quarters or the minimum comforts that our productive capacity could give every family. "Overproduction" merely means that the manufacturers expect to make more money by selling fewer goods at a higher price. That they have any responsibility for the happiness of their employees does not enter their heads. The American Woolen Company in a recent year made a 100 per cent profit upon its capital. In the following year it closed some of its mills and operated others on part time, because the price of woollen goods was falling. The owners had already got back all their money invested, several times over. They naturally wanted more. Meanwhile their former employees walked the streets desperately seeking work, the death rate of their children rapidly rose. And thousands of children were staying at home from school because they lacked clothing, which their parents could not afford to buy.

Sometimes children can find work when parents cannot, because they will work for very low wages. The 1920 Census reported over a million children under fourteen years of age as "gainfully employed." And this did not include children in street-trades, in industrial home-work, or in agriculture. A conservative business journal recently estimated the total number of working children at two and a half million. Relatively few of our States give even the protection of an eight-hour day to their working children; and tens of thousands of children are at work for nine and ten hours a day.

There is no need of argument to support the assertion that children should have their time for schooling and outdoor play. It actually *pays* the country as a whole, that they should wait and enter industry later. "For every dollar earned by a child under fourteen, tenfold will be taken from its earning capacity in later years." It would pay the State to *support* these children, giving them their schooling and their playtime, rather than let them stunt their physical and mental growth, impair their vitality, and run the risk of incurring one of the numerous diseases to which child-workers are peculiarly prone. Two or three times as many children as adults are killed or injured in industry, in proportion to the number employed. In Massachusetts in a single recent year twenty thousand children were killed or injured in industrial accidents. The harm done to health, to the minds and morals of the children, by this premature confinement, is beyond computation.

It is not meant that children should do no work at all, but that they should do no work which interferes with their schooling and playtime, which checks their growth, or subjects them to health risks.

But manufacturers, mine-owners, business men, so successfully influence public opinion and legislation that three efforts to control child labour through Federal legislation have proved abortive, and few of the States have been able to pass even fairly adequate laws.

Where good laws have been passed, they are often very poorly enforced. . . . The health, the happiness, the education, the very lives of children (not their own children, but other people's children) are of so little importance in the eyes of those who have a chance to make *profits!*

Few people are consciously cruel. Few are aimlessly cruel. They are led into cruelty because by means of it they can make money. They do not realize the cruelty, because it is the nature of men to idealize their conduct, and to overlook the unhappiness which it causes. And besides, they are caught in a system which they do not see how to change. But looking at our economic order impartially, we see that it does tend, in the nature of the case, to be hard upon the working classes. Hence come strikes, class-strife, socialism, and radical movements of all sorts. . . . On the whole, we gain ground. But only by the hardest sort of effort. And — are we gaining ground fast enough?

WHAT HARM IS BEING DONE TO THE PUBLIC?

Any unnecessary expense in production or distribution is taking so much out of the consumers' pockets. Our money-seeking scramble involves so much waste of effort that the average price of goods is probably at least doubled. In this way the public suffers.

Consider the waste of money and labour in competitive advertising. Each firm with something to sell hopes to get a larger share of business away from its rivals. In some cases more money is spent in the effort to persuade people to buy this or that brand of soap or toothpaste or automobile than it costs to produce the finished article. Mr. Edward Bok, in a recent number of *The Atlantic Monthly*, estimated the total annual outlay for advertising in the United States as $1,284,000,000. Directly or indirectly, the labour power of 600,000 workers is expended, in this struggle of one concern against another, to induce the consumers to buy its goods rather than some one else's. More than half of the output of our printing presses is advertising matter. Of the 2,600,000 tons of newsprint pulp consumed annually in this country, more than 1,500,000 tons is used for advertising. And three quarters of all the matter that goes through the mails is advertising.

Instead of buying our goods according to standard specifications, we buy them for the most part from those who shout the loudest and the most persuasively, with no guarantee that we are getting our money's worth. For the most part we *aren't*. The goods most advertised as superior are often actually inferior to goods less advertised and sold at a lower price. The great bulk of advertising is sheer waste of money, man-power, and the consumer's time. A very little advertising of new and improved products, to call them to the attention of consumers, notices of the current productions at theatres and other places of entertainment, of price reductions (if these are *bona fide*), and other useful information, would be for the benefit of the public. The rest of our colossal advertising activity is the product of our selfish individualism in business, everybody trying to grab the biggest share of the consumers' money, and wasting half of it in the process.

Nor does the harm consist merely in the waste of labour and money. Consumers are persuaded to buy inferior goods, often adulterated or shoddy goods. Chase and Schlinck's *Your Money's Worth*, published in 1927, is full of concrete contemporary examples of the misrepresentation in advertising. Space permits only one short quotation:

We believe that the foregoing evidence indicates only too clearly that there are significant groups of products, if not whole industries, in which the production of sound goods, accurately described, and sold at a fair price, has not been the dominating motive of those in control of the process. We have seen that in the case of refrigerators, lamps, soap and cleaning agents, textiles, furs, weighing scales, paints, heating and cooking devices, varnishes, even loaves of bread [and many other products], there exists an enormous burden of adulteration, bad workmanship, misrepresentation, sharp practice, and even downright bodily danger, which falls back upon the consumer.

Next, consider the waste in competitive business through duplication of plant, of clerks and salesmen, delivery wagons, and so on. The tens of thousands of "drummers" who spend their time trying to persuade the consumers to buy *their* goods rather than their rivals', simply add their salaries and expense accounts to the cost of the goods, without benefiting the public. . . . In many fields there are twice as many factories, mills, mines, shops, as are necessary to meet the public's needs. Newcomers are continually breaking into industries which already have sufficient plant to meet all the demand.

The result is, of course, economic waste, however the newcomer may profit. The waste lies not merely in the partial idleness of plants and clerks, and the unnecessary financial outlay, but in the business failures, of which some fifteen or twenty thousand are reported in an average year.

Let the milk business suffice for an example. An investigation made a few years ago in Washington, D.C., showed that sixty-five dealers supplied the city with duplicate storage, pasteurizing, cooling, and delivery plants. On one city block seventeen milk wagons were counted, serving an average of two or three customers apiece on that block. The result was that the cost of *distributing* milk, including the profits of the various dealers, approximately equalled the cost of *producing* the milk and getting it into the hands of the dealers. . . . Similarly, in New York City a committee of the State legislature stated that "under present conditions it takes almost as many men to bring the dairyman's milk to the consumer as there are dairymen engaged in the production of milk, with all their employees. This is the result of the purely competitive basis upon which the business is handled." Incidentally, this committee found such facts as this: One dealer had expended nearly $200,000 in a single year to stifle competition. Meanwhile the price of milk remained high, and babies of the poor died for lack of it.

Another source of waste in our individualistic industrial order lies in the needless diversification of styles, types, and sizes. The Chamber of Commerce of the United States has estimated that the labour power of some five million people is thus wasted, and the cost of living raised some twenty-five per cent. . . . Still another source of waste lies in the pocketing of ideas, trade secrets, inventions, which are used for the private advantage of the owner, not for the good of the industry as a whole. The most efficient factories, mills, shops, are often as much as two or three, sometimes as much as four or five, times as efficient as the less efficient. If the most efficient machines, methods, practices, were to be utilized by all, production could be more than doubled. A very large part of the failure to use better methods is due, of course, merely to human stupidity. But no effort, naturally, is made by the more efficient producers or distributors to educate their less efficient rivals. On the contrary, many machines are held for the exclusive use of the owners of the patents, many secrets are jealously guarded, that the possessor may make higher profits than his rivals.

An incidental harm done by selfish business is the defiling of our cities by smoke. Most of the smoke which comes from chimneys of factories, heating-plants, etc., is unnecessary, could be prevented by proper devices and proper stoking. It is extremely wasteful. Experts of the University of Pittsburgh, after an exhaustive investigation, stated that in the Pittsburgh district alone four million dollars' worth of coal was being wasted annually in smoke. All sorts of valuable chemicals could be recovered from this waste product. In addition, the loss to the city and its people was continuous and serious. Metals must be painted twice as often in Pittsburgh as in a smoke-free city, and replaced after half the period of time. Stone buildings are disintegrated by smoke. The cost of keeping buildings clean, inside and out, is greatly increased. Collars and shirts must be washed twice as often. Lights must be turned on earlier in the evening. Altogether, it was estimated that the citizens of Pittsburgh were losing ten million dollars a year because of smoke, and the people of the United States some five hundred millions. The cost in health is beyond computation. Smoke shuts off sunshine, irritates the membranes of the eyes, nose, throat, and lungs, and thus causes or aggravates all sorts of diseases. The chances of life are, other things being equal, appreciably less in smoky than in smoke-free cities. . . . But what do the factory-owners care, so long as they are making good profits?

Perhaps the most flagrant cases of selfishness are the cases where valuable goods have been *destroyed*, for fear that they would glut the market and lower the prices so far that profits would fall. High profits come when goods on the market are scarce. Storable goods, like hides, or sugar, may simply be hoarded in quantity — as was done a few years ago when prices of these commodities were boosted to unprecedented heights. But perishable commodities must be put on the market or destroyed. So, a few years ago, shiploads of bananas, brought to the port of New York, were dumped overboard in the Bay, when it was figured that if they were put on the market, the lowered prices for the larger stock would bring lower profits than a higher price for a smaller stock. Meanwhile thousands of poor people in New York City were hungry and undernourished. So, in

1917, when there was a world-shortage of food, potato speculators allowed a part of the potato-crop which they had bought up to rot in the ground, that they might make more money by high prices.

There is another result of selfish business even more serious, in the long run, than any of which we have spoken — the waste of natural resources, which will raise the cost of living for future generations, and perhaps bring the most serious dearth of needed materials. Our oil-supplies are being rapidly squandered, in the most reckless way, scarcely more than ten per cent of the oil available being saved (according to some estimates), the rest being wasted in the scramble for quick profits. What our citizens will do for oil twenty or thirty years from now, and for all the rest of time, no one knows. But in our optimism we trust they will find some substitute; and in our selfishness we do not care. . . . What is true of oil is true of coal and lumber, though not with so startling a percentage of waste. The coal will last some generations yet, and the lumber can be replaced, in time. . . . Meanwhile, the water-power which could be used to save our oil and coal from rapid exhaustion is hardly being tapped. There is more *money*, just now, to be got in oil and coal. "What has posterity done for us, that we should do anything for posterity?"

Our industrial system has much to say for itself. It has called forth a vast deal of energy and inventiveness, it has taught men (in a measure) to coöperate, it has brought into general use a code of honesty (in certain respects), punctuality, orderliness, and steady working-habits. Above all, it is a "going concern"; it works! Any attempt to make sudden and sweeping changes in it would be certain to lead to more or less upset, confusion, and waste of energy in conflict. Using the spectacular development of science and invention of recent decades, and tapping the hitherto unused stores of power latent in coal and oil, it has brought about such a rapid increase of wealth that its shocking wastefulness and selfishness are easily overlooked. So long as it can keep on increasing in efficiency and raising the general standard of living, and so long as it continues to give opportunity to able youths of all classes to get into the game and make their pile, so long it can afford to disregard the grumbling of the "under dogs," the warnings of the relatively few intelligent critics, and the menacing portent of Bolshevism in Russia.

There is no space in this volume to discuss the ideals of the Bolshevists, even if the present writer were competent to do so. But what is clear is, that they come to consider the evils in the "capitalistic" system intolerable. It is of great importance that we should get away from the blind complacency now so dominant, and see these evils as they are, in all their horridness, that we may mend our ways before an ebb in the tide of prosperity brings them into relief as the causes of poverty and misery. . . . But quite apart from the possible future danger of radical or revolutionary movements, we must try, if we love our country, and are zealous for its fair name, if we care for the happiness of our fellows, and of our descendants, so to temper our economic system that it will serve the interests of all, rather than the interests of the few, of coming generations rather than merely of present owners, that it will foster a coöperative spirit rather than that dollar-getting spirit which is, alas! the emblem of American business in the minds of men all over the world.

NEW VARIETIES OF SIN

By EDWARD A. ROSS

Edward A. Ross (1866–   ) has studied at Coe College, at the University of Berlin, and at Johns Hopkins University, and is at present a professor of sociology at the University of Wisconsin. He has written voluminously in the field of sociology, a few of his works being "Honest Dollars" (1896), "Sin and Society" (1907), "Latter Day Sinners and Saints" (1910), and "The Outline of Sociology" (1923).

MODERN sin takes its character from the mutualism of our time. Under our present manner of living how many of my vital interests I must intrust to others! Nowadays the water main is my well, the trolley car my carriage, the banker's safe my old stocking, the policeman's billy my fist. My own eyes and nose and judgment defer to the inspector of food, or drugs, or gas, or factories, or tenements, or insurance companies. I rely upon others to look after my drains, invest my savings, nurse my sick, and teach my children. I let the meat trust butcher my pig, the oil trust mold my candles, the sugar trust boil my sorghum, the coal trust chop my wood, the barbwire company split my rails.

But this spread-out manner of life lays snares for the weak and opens doors for the wicked. Interdependence puts us, as it were, at one another's mercy, and so ushers in a multitude of new forms of wrongdoing.

The sinister opportunities presented in this webbed social life have been seized unhesitatingly, because such treasons have not yet become infamous. The man who picks pockets with a railway rebate, murders with an adulterant instead of a bludgeon, burglarizes with a "rake-off" instead of a jimmy, cheats with a company prospectus instead of a deck of cards, or scuttles his town instead of his ship, does not feel on his brow the brand of a malefactor. The shedder of blood, the oppressor of the widow and the fatherless, long ago became odious, but latter-day treacheries fly no skull-and-crossbones flag at the masthead. The qualities which differentiate them from primitive sin and procure them such indulgence may be clearly defined.

Modern sin is not superficially repulsive. To-day the sacrifice of life incidental to quick success rarely calls for the actual spilling of blood. How decent are the pale slayings of the quack, the adulterator, and the purveyor of polluted water compared with the red slayings of the vulgar bandit or assassin! Even if there is bloodletting, the long-range tentacular nature of modern homicide eliminates all personal collision. What an abyss between the knife-play of brawlers and the law-defying neglect to fence dangerous machinery in a mill or furnish cars with safety couplers! The providing of unsuspecting passengers with "cork" life-preservers secretly loaded with bars of iron to make up for their deficiency in weight of cork is spiritually akin to the treachery of Joab, who, taking Amasa by the beard "to kiss him," smote Amasa "in the fifth rib"; but it wears a very different aspect. The current methods of annexing the property of others are characterized by a pleasing indirectness and refinement. The furtive, apprehensive manner of the till-tapper or the porch-climber would jar disagreeably upon the tax-dodger "swearing off" his property or the city official concealing a "rake-off" in his specifications for a public building. The work of the card-sharp and the thimblerigger shocks a type of man that will not stick at the massive "artistic swindling" of the contemporary promoter. A taint of unworthiness, indeed, always attaches to transactions that force the person into humiliating postures. Your petty parasite or your minor delinquent inspires the contempt that used to be felt for the retailer. The confidence man is to the promoter what the small shopkeeper was to the merchant prince.

Modern sin lacks the familiar tokens of guilt. The stealings and slayings that lurk in the complexities of our social relations are not deeds of the dive, the dark alley, the lonely road, and the midnight hour. They require no nocturnal prowling with muffled step and bated breath, no weapon or offer of violence. Unlike the old-time villain, the latter-day malefactor does not wear a slouch hat and a comforter, breathe forth curses and an odor of gin, go about his nefarious work with clenched teeth and an evil scowl. In the supreme moment his lineaments are not distorted with rage, or lust, or malevolence. One misses the dramatic setting, the time-honored insignia of turpitude. Fagin and Bill Sykes and Simon Legree are vanishing types. Gamester, murderer, body-snatcher, and kidnapper may appeal to a Hogarth, but what challenge finds his pencil in the countenance of the boodler, the savings-bank wrecker, or the ballot box stuffer? Among our criminals of greed one begins to meet the "grand style" of the great criminals of ambition, Macbeth or Richard III. The modern high-power dealer of woe wears immaculate linen, carries a silk hat and a lighted cigar, sins with a calm countenance and a serene soul leagues or months from the evil he causes. Upon his gentlemanly presence the eventual blood and tears do not obtrude themselves.

Modern sins are impersonal. The covenant breaker, the suborned witness, the corrupt judge, the oppressor of the fatherless — the old-fashioned sinner, in short — knows his victim, must hearken, perhaps, to bitter upbraidings. But the tropical belt of sin we are sweeping into is wholly impersonal. Our iniquity is wireless, and we know not whose withers are wrung by it. The hurt passes into that vague mass, the "public," and is there lost to view. Hence it does not take a Borgia to knead "chalk and alum and plaster" into the loaf, seeing one cannot know just who will eat that loaf or what gripe it will give him. The purveyor of spurious life-preservers need not be a Cain. The owner of the rotten tenement house, whose "pull" enables him to ignore the orders of the health department, foredooms babies, it is true, but for all that he is no Herod.

Often there are no victims. If the crazy hulk sent out for "just one more trip" meets with fair weather, all is well. If no fire breaks out in the theatre, the sham "emergency exits" are blameless. The corrupt inspector who O.K.'s low-grade kerosene is chancing it, that is all. Many sins, in fact, simply augment risk. Evil does not dog their footsteps with relentless and heart-shaking certainty. When the catastrophe does come, the sinner salves his conscience by blasphemously calling it an "accident" or an "act of God."

Still more impersonal is sin when the immediate harm touches beneficent institutions rather than individuals, when, following his vein of private profit, the sinner drives a gallery under some pillar upholding our civilization. The blackguarding editor is really undermining the freedom of the press. The policy kings and saloon keepers who get out to the polls the last vote of the vicious and criminal classes are sapping manhood suffrage. Striking engineers who spitefully desert passenger trains in mid-career are jeopardizing the right of a man to work only when he pleases. The real victim of a lynching mob is not the malefactor, but the law-abiding spirit. School-board grafters who blackmail applicants for a teacher's position are stabbing the free public school. The corrupt bosses and "combines" are murdering representative government. The perpetrators of election frauds unwittingly assail the institution of the ballot. Rarely, however, are such transgressions abominated as are offenses against persons.

The grading of sinners according to badness of character goes on the assumption that the wickedest man is the most dangerous. This would be true if men were abreast in their opportunities to do harm. In that case the blackest villain would be the worst scourge of society. But the fact is that the patent ruffian is confined to the social basement, and enjoys few opportunities. He can assault or molest, to be sure; but he cannot betray. Nobody depends on him, so he cannot commit breach of trust — that arch sin of our time. He does not hold in his hand the safety or welfare or money of the public. He is the clinker, not the live coal; vermin, not beast of prey. To-day the villain most in need of curbing is the respectable, exemplary, trusted personage who, strategically placed at the focus of the spider-web of fiduciary relations, is able from his office-chair to pick a thousand pockets, poison a thousand sick, pollute a thousand minds, or imperil a thousand lives. It is the great-scale, high-voltage sinner that needs the shackle. To strike harder at the petty pickpocket than at the prominent and unabashed person who in a large, impressive way sells out his constituents, his followers, his depositors, his stockholders, his policy-holders, his subscribers, or his customers, is to "strain at a gnat and swallow a camel."

No paradox is it, but demonstrable fact, that in a highly articulate society the gravest harms are inflicted, not by the worst men, but by those with virtues enough to boost them into some coign of vantage. The boss who sells out the town and delivers the poor over to filth, disease, and the powers that prey owes his chance to his engaging good-fellowship and big-heartedness. Some of the most dazzling careers of fraud have behind them long and reassuring records of probity, which have served to bait the trap of villainy.

ON THE INDUSTRIAL SCRAP HEAP

By "A WORKER"

"A Worker" gives his own autobiography in the following article.

I AM — or rather was — cheap labor, the kind which is so largely in demand by industrial corporations and many advocates of unrestricted immigration. I am the kind of man that you see from the windows of trains working with a pick and shovel or lifting pig iron into railroad cars. I wear as a usual thing overalls and a blue or khaki flannel shirt, brogans, and underwear and socks according to the state of my pocketbook.

But I always wear them on Sundays. To cheap labor socks and underwear are luxuries, not necessities. Until recently I was a little cog — not perhaps so important as a cog, more like a rivet — in the huge industrial machine. Even as late as May I held my place as a rivet, but since then I have been junked, tossed aside on the industrial scrap heap and, not because my case is unique but because it is entirely typical, I should like to make people understand *how* cheap labor gets scrapped, and what it thinks about scrapping.

My mother died when I was two years old, of consumption and too many babies. My father was even cheaper labor than I have been, so that he was quite unable to bring up a family of five adequately. My earliest recollections are of working — of long days under a fiery sun, struggling with a hoe twice as tall as I. I was eight or nine then. When I was twelve, I went into the coal mines and worked full shifts underground. Black days these were, when the chambers were sometimes full of the voices of the coal and sometimes, in spite of our human activity, silent with a silence more terrifying than even the unhuman voices.

When I was fifteen I came out of the mines and went to sawlogging, which is heavy work even for grown men. The days with the hoe stooped my shoulders and hollowed my chest. The days in the coal filled my lungs with the fine black dust which sooner or later gets nearly every miner. The saw-logging enlarged my heart far beyond its natural size. Of course I did not know what I was doing to myself, but if I had, it would have made no difference. Father was cheap labor, and his boys had to look after themselves. Also none of us was ever properly fed. The reason for this was two-fold. First, we did not have money enough to buy anything but the very cheapest and coarsest food and second, even if we had, we would not have known what proper food consisted of. The food we did have undernourished me and ruined my digestion.

All these things together have landed me on the scrap heap at the ripe age of twenty-six. The doctors say that in time I may not be altogether useless if I take care of myself. But think of it! At twenty-six, when, according to the apostles of labor, I should be going forth as a strong man rejoicing to run a race, I am bent, broken, cast aside. Since I have survived so far, it is quite on the cards that I shall go on living for at least another twenty-six years, though how I am to live or what is to become of my family is as yet unrevealed to me, and it is quite possible that ignorance in this case is bliss.

Since I have been rusting here on the scrap heap, I have had time to think over what I have read, and I have come to certain conclusions, first and foremost of which is this: The industrial system is, economically speaking, wasteful of its human material and, humanely speaking, criminally negligent. If I were an exception instead of being a fair sample of the rule, I would say nothing against the industrial system. If the scrap heap were even a small one, I should still say nothing, but it is large, larger than one would believe, and besides those of us who are actually, so to speak, in residence there, there are others who in another walk of life would be considered too ill to work, but who are working and "doctoring" at the same time, vainly hoping to stave off the scrap heap until some miracle enables them to save enough to keep them from depending on the Charities, Federated, or Associated, or United, as the case may be.

We on the scrap heap do not dread poverty, nor cold in moderation, nor even hunger in moderation. All these things are so much a part of our daily lives that they are as unquestioned as the weather. What we dread is charity. Bread that we do not buy for ourselves but that is bought for us by others. Let me tell you that there is infinitely more joy over a sack of coal gleaned from the railroad track than over a ton donated by one of the many well-meaning societies trying to repair the damage done by the system to which they owe at once their existence and their reason for existing.

To go back, however, to my charges against the industrial system of waste and negligence — still considering myself as a sample, I beg of you to look at me. For eighteen years I have been a producer, but only for the last eight has my production obtained any appreciable value. Now, at the very time when my output should be at its maximum, it is cut off completely. Instead of being a producer I am a consumer — with nothing that I can pay for what I consume. Instead of supporting the system I am a dead weight on its back. Instead of my contributing to it for the next twenty-five or thirty years (and surely a man of twenty-six should be able to look forward to at least twenty-five more years of productiveness), it will in all probability have to contribute to me indirectly. And it serves it right, for it has squandered me. It took my least instead of my most productive years and in so doing it wasted me.

Let me digress a little. In my mind the State and the system are to a certain degree differentiated. Practically all of us are members of both State and system. The difference lies in this. As members of the State we are equal — one man is like another man (theoretically at least). As members of the system we are entirely unequal — our values differ. Just as each citizen is responsible for the well-being of the State, so the State is, or should be, responsible for the well-being of each citizen. If it is not responsible sooner, it will have to be later. If it had been sooner, my value to the State would more than have repaid my cost to the State. As it is, the reverse is the case. Instead of the State's saving me, the system has squandered me and now the State — that is, organized society — will have to look after me with money paid to it by the system.

I am entitled to this help from the State for two reasons: first, because it is the system's fault that I am junk, and second, because part of the money which the system pays to the State should have been paid to me. Had it been paid to me sooner, it would probably have enabled me to avoid the scrap heap. And certainly I would infinitely prefer taking my pay in the form of money justly paid to me for value received than in the form of charity bestowed upon the deserving poor. I believe that both State and system would, in the long run, have found it cheaper.

So much for the economic side of it.   Now for the humane.   I have
already said that I started in working at night.   I had no schooling,
but grew to early manhood physically weakened and mentally untrained.   My pleasures were very few and of the crudest, but such
as they were, they were all I could find.   Not until I met my wife
did I have even the vaguest conception of what a life could hold.   I
knew no books save an occasional Jesse James read to me by my
sister-in-law.   I knew nothing about the theater — not even what it
was.   Underclothes were luxuries.   Newspapers were principally
useful to line shelves.   I had heard of Lincoln and Washington, but
not of Columbus or Shakespeare.   As far as I was aware, Europe
was one of the United States and the United States itself a monarchy.   Hard work, poor meals, an occasional drinking or gambling
spree, and once in a while a revival meeting or a fight made up my
life for years.   After I met my wife came three years of awakening
mind, three years of struggle against industrial depression and increasing ill-health.   Then just when there seemed a chance for
steady work and a little mild prosperity — and by prosperity I mean
enough food of the right kind and enough clothes of any kind — just
when I had learned to appreciate the things that made life worth
living came the scrap heap — not through my fault but through the
negligence of a system that while constantly calling for labor —
cheap labor, pick-and-shovel men, concrete men, pig-iron lifters, etc.,
etc., does not look after the labor it already has, but right and left
squanders it and relegates it to the scrap heap even as I am relegated.
Next I suppose will come the separation of the family.   The State
will send me to some hospital, my babies will go to a nursery, and
my wife back again to work.   This is the portion of cheap labor.

THE DOGMA OF "BUSINESS FIRST"

By STUART CHASE

Stuart Chase (1888–   ) has been a certified public accountant, an experimental worker among the industrial laborers, an accountant on the Federal Trade Commission, and has recently been associated with the Labor Bureau, Inc. His life among the laboring class is recorded in his book, "A Honeymoon Experiment" (1916), and his opinions of industrial America in "The Tragedy of Waste" (1925), and "Your Money's Worth" (1927).

I

ONE hundred and twenty-six years ago my great-great-grandfather was living in a farmhouse with a pitch to its back roof and a great fireplace, ovened and wainscotted, in the town of Newburyport, Massachusetts. He lived in a community that raised the bulk of its own food, built its own houses out of local materials, and spun and wove most of its own clothing. Withal, it was good food, durable and comely clothing, and housing of a unique and lasting beauty. On High Street were the square white houses of the shipbuilders, and out along the country roads were the farmhouses with their well-sweeps and their dipping eaves. And lovely as were the houses of the shipbuilders, lovelier still were ships (soon it was to be clipper ships) which they built. In fact, upon an astonishing amount of the materials which passed through the hands of the men and women of Newburyport, and the other New England towns — upon iron work, pewter, glass, woodwork, textiles, masonry — was stamped an authentic and enduring beauty which all the banalites of the traffic in antiques cannot efface. Reasonably well fed, snugly housed, and with articles to his hand for daily use which now are jealously guarded in museums, my great-great-grandfather lived his life. Anon he hitched up and went over the hills to the town meeting. The steam engine was yet to come, the first textile mill was yet to be built in New England, the industrial revolution was waiting to be born.

A century and a quarter later, after the most stupendous increase in the technical arts which the world has ever seen or is ever likely to see, I look about the place where I live in New York City, and out of the window of that place where the sun never rests, and wonder what, in terms of the life more abundant, the industrial revolution has done for me. How much more rewarding, not only in respect to beauty and the things of the spirit, but in absolute material comfort, is my existence than that of my great-great-grandfather? My housing is drearier and more inconvenient, my food is softer and less succulent, my clothing is uglier and infinitely less durable; the day-by-day pressure of the sights and shadows and odors about me is depressing, and cumulative in its depression.

In the matter of income, my great-great-grandfather was not above the average of his community; quite possibly, as a farmer, he was below it. The joint income of my wife and myself is probably three times the average of the community in which we live. Compare the average householder in New York to-day with the average citizen in Newburyport in 1800, and where does the advantage, in terms of the good life, lie? Look abroad out of these sullen canyons to other cities — Chicago, Pittsburgh, Cleveland, St. Louis, San Francisco, New Orleans — to the suburban cubicles which girdle modern cities, to Main Street, to the farms of the cotton belt and of the tobacco belt, aye, to Newburyport and its outlying farms as they are to-day. What tangible improvements in well-being, beauty, and happiness has a century of unprecedented invention brought to the inhabitants of these places? I ask the question. I know that it has brought some well-being, perhaps a great deal to some people. But, looking into dead walls from my apartment window, I wonder again what are the gifts which Arkwright and Stevenson and Watt have placed in my hands. The amazing thing is that I should wonder at all. There is a machine now which can make plows thirty-two times faster than the blacksmith of Newburyport could ever fashion them, a machine which can make cotton sheeting one hundred and three times faster than my great-great-grandmother could ever spin and weave it, and we have in the energy released by the engines and turbines of America, the labor of three billions of slaves, or nearly thirty servants for every man, woman, and child in the country. Engineers have assured us that technical knowledge is now available, which — if it could be put to work — would banish poverty, double or treble the standard of living, turn ugly cities into noble cities, and by means of giant power and decentralization bring the culture of the town to the countryside.

Why has this not been done? Why do I look out at my blank wall, why are millions infinitely worse housed in slums, why does the tobacco grower of Kentucky abandon the losing struggle against the marching weeds? This is a question not lightly to be answered, a complex and baffling question. But my guess is this. It has not been done because an economy like that of Newburyport, for all its lack of engines, was well within the range of human capacity to administer, being in fact the immemorial economy of self-sustaining groups the world round; but the economy of the machine with its immense distances of transport and its great clots of workers who make no food, and of food growers who make nothing else, has proved to date, except in time of war, to be beyond human administrative capacity. Or better, under the prevailing system of business enterprise, it is held that the machine needs no master with an eye single to the welfare of the group; and whatever potential administrative capacity there may be accordingly never gets a chance to function. The prime charge upon every politician is the welfare of business in terms of monetary profit; only in passing and incidentally may he regard the welfare of the whole community. For it is held as axiomatic that what is good for business is good for everybody; what hurts business, hurts everybody. When Adam Smith spoke of the "invisible hand" which directed this consummation, he little realized that he was founding what has come to be almost a new religion.

> Thus God and Nature formed the general frame
> And bade self-love and social be the same.

The learned Smith and the business men and the politicians may of course be right. Perhaps by scrupulously safe-guarding self-interest and anarchy in business we do secure more in net welfare than we should by any other method. All other methods are, to date, largely a matter of theory because, since the coming of the machine, business anarchy is the only method which has been tried. The Russian experiment is too young to give any sound evidence on either side. But what we may conclude without fear of contradiction is that if business anarchy is the best way to regulate the machine, while it may keep a few more of us alive per acre of crop land, most of us have not gained anything compared with Newburyport, if, indeed, we have not lost. If this is indeed the best way, it is painful to contemplate the results of any other way. Where would a hundred years of coöperation or state socialism or some combination of these two with laissez-faire have landed us? With two-thirds of the families of America now beneath the line of the United States Department of Labor's budget of health and decency, presumably most of us would have long since starved to death had the three billions of power slaves been in any other hands than those of business. Not many of us die of starvation and perhaps, Mr. Coolidge, that is proof enough that yours is the wisest way.

Whatever its ultimate wisdom, anarchy is by definition and by practice wasteful. Nor should business anarchy reflect any exception to this rule. It may not prove unprofitable to take inventory of certain major leakages and losses which are implicit in the going economic structure. Down what blind alleys has technical knowledge gone; what dams have choked and diverted the free flow of invention and discovery; what are the three billions of slaves concerned with that they have not time to destroy these slums, uproot these weeds, build me a decent house in a noble city?

II

The factor which is primarily responsible for the dispersion of energy is, I suppose, the lack of community and regional planning. That the rush of the pioneers to conquer a continent must inevitably be planless is as manifest as is the fact that absence of plan makes for an incredible volume of waste. Cities sprang up on the wrong sites, crops were grown on the wrong soil, factories were built in the wrong places, railways paralleled and choked waterways, forests were butchered to the glory of fire and flood, long hauls displaced short hauls, gas wells blew their billions of cubic feet into the air, pools of unemployed workers began to form, while the machine diluted its output with a tremendous tonnage of ugly, flimsy, shoddy, jerry-built, and generally adulterated products. "Everything turned to profit. The towns had their profitable dirt, their profitable smoke, their profitable slums, their profitable disorder, their profitable ignorance, their profitable despair. The curse of Midas was on this society: on its corporate life, on its common mind, on the decisive and impatient step it had taken from the peasant to the industrial age. For the new town was not a home where man could find beauty, happiness, leisure, learning, religion, the influences that civilize outlook and habit, but a bare and desolate place, without color, air, or laughter, where man, woman, and child worked, ate, and slept. This was to be the lot of the mass of mankind; this the sullen rhythm of their lives. The new factories and the new furnaces were like the Pyramids, telling of man's enslavement rather than of his power, casting their long shadows over the society that took such pride in them." Thus the Hammonds conclude their exhaustive study of the coming of the industrial revolution to England. It was not greatly different in New England or generally in urban America.

Of all the great American cities, only Washington was planned for comfortable living rather than for selling real estate by the front foot. No local region has ever been planned at all and, save for a brief interval during the World War, no budget of national requirements has ever been cast, or the productive capacity to meet these requirements assessed. It is only the sheer fecundity of the machine which has permitted such a sprawling, haphazard growth. If every engine stripped its gears to-morrow, in a few days most of us, in our present geographical location, should begin to starve. In a month we should be dead. Without steam and electricity Newburyport could take no such chances in hurling its people to the economic peripheries, could afford no man power wasted on the shoddy and the jerry-built, could tolerate no excess industrial structure — twice the fields or twice the blacksmith shops or twice the shipways which normal demand called for — nor maintain the luxury of a reserve squadron of unemployed workers. Its economy forced a moderately accurate adaption of production to requirements, and the dependability of the plan is evidenced in the time which still remained, after stark necessities were met, to elaborate and beautify, and stamp upon the output the seal of craftsmanship.

To plan for a continent is a harder task than to plan for a town. During the pioneering decades it was folly to ask for any plan at all. But as the Pacific was reached, some rough appraisal, some conscious attempts to coördination were certainly not beyond human capacity. Regions have been planned from Mesopotamia down. More American cities might have followed Washington — and

Paris. Waterways might have been aided instead of strangled. The people through their Government might have controlled the exploitation of natural resources. As invention and the technical arts expanded, the coördination of national economic life might have become the more competent and accurate. Dreams, yes. But only so was it possible to outdistance Newburyport, only so could the fecundity of the machine create an accelerating reserve of welfare for the whole community. But the religion of private enterprise said no.

Take New York City for example. The congestion of its streets puts a premium on death and injury, and adds enormously in transportation cost to every article the city dweller buys, and to every structure built. I know a building where four hundred bricklayers stand in rows, trowel in hand. Yet so great is the pressure of traffic below them, that never more than a single hour's supply of bricks can be stored in advance — which means a constant stream of trucks delivering hand to mouth. And when the trucks are halted in a traffic jam — as they often are — the masons stand idle. But that idle time goes into the cost of the building. As land values shift, it has become a recognized practice in New York to look on construction as a short-term investment. Thus, instead of lasting its hundred years or so, buildings erected twenty, even ten years ago — perfectly sound buildings many of them — are being torn down and scrapped. New buildings spring up, only to be scrapped, undepreciated, in their turn. Consider the colossal cost, the gigantic waste of such a program. Consider the cost of digging a subway, which, when it is finished, far from relieving congestion, has only accelerated it. Consider the cost of furnishing water, gas, sewage, electricity, telephone service, foodstuffs to a city so badly planned; think of the unbelievable number of bottlenecks through which all these services must pass. Think of the plumbing which has to be renewed on the average every eight years, at a labor cost twice that of the original installation. Yet the technical arts can tell us how to install plumbing which will last a generation. Consider the absurd terminal facilities, the half-loaded milk wagons, the hauls and the cross-hauls, the additional cleaning due to the lack of smoke prevention. Above all, consider the enormous parasitic population of New York: the middlemen, the speculators, the ticket scalpers, the prostitutes, the bootleggers, the dope peddlers, the flunkies, door openers, wash-room dusters; the purveyors of the ultra, the modish, and the snobbish.

In Newburyport there were no parasites, there were no problems of congestion, of subway building, of cross-hauling, of short-term housing investments, of idle bricklayers standing four hundred in a line. There were no seasons of unemployment when half the clothing workers walked the streets. There were no business cycles. There was no importing of bulk foodstuffs over half the world. There were no spirited campaigns, supported by expert psychologists, for the smashing of sales resistance. There was no installment buying. These merry things cost unbelievable sums of money — and what is more to the point than money, they cost *man-power*. What the machine, what the industrial revolution have done in effect is to permit New York City to support a large population of idle, an enormous population of working parasites, and a colossal extra force of useful workers kept busy by the congestion and planlessness of the urban area. No little of the energy of the three billion slaves goes down this trapdoor. The technical knowledge is available to plan cities, to plan regions. Mr. J. Russell Smith alone, one suspects, could tell us how to double living standards. But there is no private profit to be made from such plans. They are proscribed.

III

I am convinced that it is the lack of regional planning which constitutes the main reasons for my failure to gain on my great-great-grandfather in anything like the ratio that productivity per capita gains. Most of the productivity goes into bridging the fissures in the underlying chaos. But this is a large, general and, no doubt, an arguable indictment. It is possible to outline certain other leakages of knowledge more specifically.

Consider for instance the concern of the science of physics, chemistry, and biology with modern warfare. As everybody knows and as corporation income tax returns make quantitatively evident, war is good for business. War has always driven some men mad, but never, until modern science took charge, has there been such a malady as "shell shock." Science as applied to warfare is well on its way to shrivel up the nervous systems of those it does not kill. Gone in battle are the virtues of strength, determination, skill at arms — aye, of courage.   A little man with a leaky heart valve pushes a button somewhere miles away, and the strength and skill and courage go hundreds of feet into the air together with fragments of arms and legs and viscera.   Of the ten million killed and the twenty million wounded in the late crusade for democracy, how many received their hurt in hand-to-hand struggle such as the Romans knew? Probably not one per cent.   The ninety and nine were stricken by the engines of science.

Furthermore, with the development of psychology, the importance of civilian morale in war time is being given its due weight — which means that applied science must not only be directed to the destruction of armies and navies, but to the destruction of the civilian morale that supports them.   Which means the wiping out of cities, the utter terrorizing of general populations, behind the lines.   Competent technicians are at this moment giving their undivided attention to the most efficient means of destroying London, Paris, and Berlin.   Yet when it was recently proposed in Washington that army engineers should design, and army privates should build a bridge across the Potomac, thus salvaging a little of their technical education for the community, the construction industry rallied to a man, and in convention assembled, resolved that the project was an abomination; that construction undertaken for any other end than private profit threatened the whole fabric of the republic.   So the army engineers were happily permitted to go back to their plans for blowing the bottom out of the Suez Canal.

Consider next the extent to which the technical arts have been overborne by quacks bent on the profitable exploitation of new knowledge.   On the skirts of every advance in physics, chemistry, biology, and medicine hangs a well-organized group of astute men of business ready to capitalize with useless and often dangerous drugs and devices the wide publicity which the new discovery has received: vaccines, radiations, glands, salvarsans, vitamines, and even the electron.   Let J. B. S. Haldane, the noted English biologist, state the case: "For every dollar which we can spend on research and publicity together, the food-faking firms have a thousand for advertising 'scientific' foods. . . . The faker is already on the market with radiations to cure rheumatism and make your hair grow.   These are mostly harmless, but probably the sale of X-ray tubes which may cause cancer, will some day be as carefully regulated as that of strychnine. . . . There is no serious reason to believe that any of the rather expensive products of the sex glands now on the market, and often prescribed by doctors, are of any value except as faith cures."

Consider the mauling which science receives at the hands of the high priests of the Nordic saga. In primitive society men who rose to the chieftainship of the tribe looked suspiciously at aspirants from the ranks. So they frequently invited in the royal medicine men to help them hold their power. To-day men of property, of so-called Anglo-Saxon stock, and thus possessing prestige and power, find their possession threatened by radical labor movements, by an incoming horde of shrewd foreigners. They appeal, as always, to the medicine men. But a little difficulty presents itself. The emergence of science has relegated to a twilight zone the gods and myths invoked by the old-time medicine men. Science is on the throne. Softly; what does the commonalty know about science? Only enough not to blow out the gas, and to read scientific supplements in the Sunday newspapers. Good. Science, for the mass of men, is only a new mysticism; a shift from elves in glades to elves in molecules and air waves and germ plasms. And with a zeal which would have distinguished them in the days of the Aztecs, the modern medicine men proceed to "prove by the aid of science" that the Nordics are the anointed race, that present class distinctions are eternal and unchangeable by virtue of the chemistry of the germ plasm, that heredity is everything and environment nothing. In brief, they summon science to support each and every prejudice of the American men of property. Meanwhile, on some of their pronouncements science has come to no conclusion at all, while on the balance the drift of impartial evidence points to diametrically opposite conclusions. More and more, for instance, particularly since the behaviorists began laboratory experiments on new-born babies, it appears that environment as reflected in acquired habits, is the shaping influence on character. But gullible millions swill down this witchcraft, and thus is the new knowledge traduced again.

Consider the predicament in which applied psychology has landed. Psychology is not yet a full-fledged science, but it has made important and far-reaching advances in the past few years. The behaviorists, the psychoanalysts, and the industrial psychologists are laying the basis for profound changes in the technic of group control. Where is this new knowledge being principally utilized at the present time? In the offices of advertising agencies. To-day as never before the man with something to sell knows how to turn into cash three fundamental aspects of human nature: the desire to attract the opposite sex, the desire to exert power over one's neighbors, the desire to get safely and honorably to heaven. In brief, the higher salesmanship has captured applied psychology, horse, foot, and guns. And the very knowledge which might render us significant help is turned against us to create new wants, new desires, new forms of waste. (Some psychologist should write, as he starves, a monograph entitled: "How To Build Up Sales Resistance." No one will read it now, but in a hundred years he will have a statue in the market-place.)

The consumer at large has to-day no standard of reference by which he can determine quality of goods. Only through the painful and wasteful method of trial and error can he hope to separate the shoddy from the sound. The shoddy makers can say as impressive things about their product as the conscientious manufacturer. A certain roofing concern fabricated a great stock in anticipation of Government orders during the war. The stock, after careful test, was rejected as inferior. Nothing daunted, the company, by means of a high-pressure sales campaign, disposed of the whole order to the general public. Yet here and there in well-equipped laboratories an enormous volume of data as to consumer products and their relative values for specific uses is being accumulated. The Bureau of Standards at Washington has been making such tests for years. As a result, the federal government saves a hundred million dollars annually by purchasing materials, not on the stimulation of high-pressure salesmanship, but according to specifications laid down by the Bureau. For building materials, textiles, clothing, soaps, cleansing fluids, lubricants, motors, paper stock, ink, stationery, hardware, leather goods — for nearly every kind of thing which the common citizen uses — the government pays a lower price for a more durable product — a price *below* the usual discount for quantity orders because of the standards and specifications determined by the Bureau.

To date, unfortunately, it has not been the policy of the government to release this knowledge to the country at large. Imagine the tearing of beards in the business world if it should. The Bureau of Standards in its laboratories has found out which makes of textiles stand up and which go to pieces, which paints and varnishes are good and which are bad, which inks keep their color and which do not, what types of filling station pumps invariably give short weight; but so hallowed is the conception of private business that this knowledge has remained locked in government files, serving only government purposes.

"Sure," said an ex-Ford employee, "if I went on tightening up nut number 999 any longer, I'd have become nut number 999 myself." Industrial standardization is one of the mightiest achievements of the new technology, but it is a two-edged sword. Applied with due regard for the human equation, it promises the elimination of untold duplication, confusion, and waste, and a tremendous gain in the general standard of living. Applied only from the point of view of the maximum profit in dollars, it can readily become an unmitigated curse. True to the formula of business *über alles*, it is the latter course which industry has pursued to date. Thirty years ago when Frederick W. Taylor was laying down the principles of Scientific Management, motion study was frankly an experiment. It promised well from the standpoint of increasing output, and nobody knew what it would do to the employee. To-day we do know. Not completely and finally, but psychologists in industry have already developed the general laws governing the effects of rhythm, sound, vision, fatigue. They have estimated that of the million man-years lost annually in America by industrial accidents, a full half of them is preventable. We have a body of knowledge sufficient to fix the limits of factory standardization. Is it applied? It is not. With very little exception it is unutilized, wasted knowledge.

Nor is the standardization of the goods which the factory worker makes in much better state. Obviously, the great values here are maximum standardization in all intermediate processes: standard gauges, measurements, tools, supplies — combined with minimum standardization in those end products where variety adds to the spice of life. As Cornelia Stratton Parker puts it, "I see no reason why the æsthetic spirit of the nation would be degraded if we all used 21-inch sewer pipes instead of some 22-inch, but I don't want to see all women wearing the same hats." These values find little place in the going business structure. There is an appalling lack of standardization in intermediate processes and in end products, like sewer pipes, where standards have only virtue — a lack fostered by trade secrecy and the desire to secure competitive advantages. The United States Chamber of Commerce so far forgets itself as to assess this waste at one-quarter of all industrial effort in America. Meanwhile there is over-standardization in many end products where variety is essential. Standardization is a magnificent technic when rightly used, but in the hands of the business motive it has so far succeeded only in running amuck.

One more item, and our inventory of the perversions of knowledge, while by no means complete, must end. Under the acquisitive organization of industry, society shares in new engineering devices, but only to a degree, and only after a period of maximum obstruction. Chief Clerk Woolard of the United States Patent Office states the case, "There are countless numbers of patents which, if in operation, would much cheapen the articles they could produce, but they are intentionally shelved to prevent competition. Concerns operating under old inventions for which they have expended great sums to erect plants, buy up these new and cheaper methods to prevent competitors from getting hold of them. They then tuck them away in their safes, never to be used."

New inventions may not only be suppressed; they may be presuppressed. A concern may get patents on a whole series of processes in order to tie up the field for the next generation or more. The weighing scale industry is said to have secured advanced patents (by taking them out on some foolish toy) sufficient to close the door to any one else for twenty years. The ultimate social loss of this one case alone has been estimated at a hundred million dollars.

IV

A member of the United States Tariff Commission in a recent book has put the challenge squarely up to us: "The business world knows no waste unless the saving can be accomplished at a profit. What cannot be salvaged at a profit is not waste in the economic sense. As well talk of the waste of atmospheric nitrogen." And there we are.

To release the data of the Bureau of Standards would be alarmingly unprofitable for many corporations. To restrict patent monopolies would stagger the balance sheets of many more. To put the army to building bridges congeals the vitals of the private contractor; to liquidate the blah of advertising would shrink untold dividend checks; to make durable goods would lessen turnover. For every obstruction, every hindrance to the free flow of knowledge has been, so far as may be, capitalized at substantially what the traffic will bear. It earns a profit and is not waste in the business sense. To break its grip and bring technology to the direct relief of the community is treason to business principles and, therefore, unthinkable.

But as the inventory of planlessness and thwarted knowledge unrolls before us it almost moves us to the brink of treason. Why should we bow meekly before a dogma which, measured by its concrete results, has netted us so little in a century and a quarter? Why should we accept as an act of faith the somewhat preposterous theory that a few hundred thousand business men, each working within the high walls of his own back yard with never a look at the world outside, can provide the community at large with more and better food, shelter, and clothing than any one else ever could?

Why dogma at all? Why does it have to be pure individualism versus pure collectivism, or pure coöperation? Why all the blood and tears over the "thin entering wedge?" Governor Smith of New York wants the State to develop the waterpower of the St. Lawrence, which the State owns. Owns, mind you. He is willing to let the distribution of that power remain in the hands of private business. Technically the combination is admirable. The dams and the turbines can be built and operated more economically by the State than by any private company, while distribution can quite possibly be handled more economically by those already skilled in the technic. Yet for this proposal, Governor Smith is held little better than a Bolshevik. Mr. Charles Evans Hughes on behalf of the Petroleum Institute has just petitioned the Government to let oil production go on committing harikari — at the rate of three needlessly wasted barrels for every one reclaimed — because private enterprise must not be interfered with.

On all long-term projects dealing with the exploitation of natural resources, private business simply cannot afford to wait to exploit them systematically and with a minimum of waste. Forests have got to come down, oil fields gush, the cream to be skimmed from coal and minerals, instanter! The principles of profit demand it. Yet whenever and wherever it is proposed that the community handle such exploitation because only the community has the resources and the credit to develop the project according to technically sound principles, the thin opening wedge is brandished, and a thousand editors sniff treason. And so with any fundamental proposal for community planning.

There are doubtless many things that private business can do better and less wastefully than any one else can do them. There are other things which the community through its government can do best. And still other things which coöperative groups within the community can excel in. It does not stand to reason that there is any one divine way of economic behavior for one hundred and sixteen millions of people over three thousand miles of continent. The assumption of high sanctuary by the theory of business anarchy is undoubtedly as much stuff and nonsense as one hundred per cent state socialism.

It must be more than a little of a bore to be a business man dedicated to a lifetime of unrelenting greed. No wonder he and his fellows go into conference, or play golf on the slightest excuse, or take specials to Florida, or wear paper hats, or grow maudlin about Service. There they stand, each in his own trough, a herd across whose backs no statecraft can hurdle. Good, decent citizens mostly, but their dogmas are costing us all that the machine and the industrial arts and the billions of power slaves might have done for us.

And I guess — it may be a wild guess — that until we smash those dogmas Newburyport will continue to hold its own.

PROSPERITY WITHOUT PROFIT

By JESSE RAINSFORD SPRAGUE

Jesse Rainsford Sprague (1872–   ) was in the mercantile business until 1915, in which year he began to devote his time to writing. He has contributed stories, articles, and essays to "Harper's" and "Scribner's" magazines, to "The American Mercury," and to the "Saturday Evening Post."

IT is but a few weeks ago that a number of important British department-store owners came to the United States to study the reasons for American prosperity, and upon their return to London officially reported their findings to the members of their trade. As is so often the case, these reports tended toward self-glorification rather than entire accuracy. It was generally agreed that American department stores have nothing to teach the British. One gentleman made the amazing statement that in many American stores — such is the craze for statistics — fully sixty per cent of the employees do nothing but work upon figures. Another was of the firm opinion that the service in American stores does not compare with that of British stores. Still another gentleman put American business in its place by stating that a department store in Stockholm, Sweden, surpasses anything seen in the United States. All agreed on one thing: that although business in America was brisk, competition was so keen and expenses so high that few enterprises were making money. A phrase they had heard in the United States occurred often in their reports, "Prosperity without Profit."

Astonishing as were most of the findings of these British observers, there is one in which there is a shade of truth. In many American industries there does exist a situation that may rightly be described as prosperity without profit. And where this situation exists it is usually the result, as pointed out by the British business men, of too violent competition and too high selling expenses.

Perhaps for the non-business reader it will be necessary to explain in greater detail the meaning and causes of Prosperity without Profit. Let us assume there are two grocerymen who have shops on opposite corners, each of whom sells fifty dollars' worth of groceries per day.   Of a sudden each resolves that he will double his volume of sales and sell one hundred dollars' worth per day.   The families of the neighborhood really do not require so great an amount of grocer merchandise; and so when the two storekeepers seek to realize their ambitions, intense and costly competition develops. Each grocer attempts to outdo his rival.   Each runs special sales, engages boys to shove printed dodgers under the doors of householders at night, maintains motor-cycle delivery, keeps his store open evenings, sends solicitors to call upon housewives several times each day to learn if anything be needed.

It is possible that by means of such high-pressure activities the families of the neighborhood are made so "grocery conscious" that each merchant actually does realize his heart's desire and attains his volume of one hundred dollars a day.   The chances are the expense of securing this volume is so great that neither earns any money. But the *amour propre* of the merchants is such that neither is willing to admit defeat, and the unprofitable competition continues.   When this occurs the two grocerymen are operating under the condition known as Prosperity without Profit.

Yet this is not all.   The hectic competition thus inaugurated extends to other fields.   The two grocers have contrived to make the families of the neighborhood "grocery conscious."   This means that an undue share of the neighborhood income is spent on groceries; and the neighborhood merchants in other lines seek to protect their interests by similar campaigns of high-pressure salesmanship. Profits are sacrificed all around.   Eventually some unfortunates fall into the hands of the sheriff.   Store clerks lose their positions, and owners of store buildings lose their rents.   There is a small-scale panic in the neighborhood.

This state of affairs may spread from neighborhood to nation-wide proportions if enough business men become so imbued with a desire for expansion that the cost of securing extra volume is disregarded.   It is remarkable how the fetish of greater volume of business has spread during the past few years.   This is strikingly illustrated by an editorial that recently appeared in *Printers' Ink*, a publication which for more than a quarter of a century has been identified with American Big Business.   The editorial in part is as follows:

We know of an institution that attained a startling sales volume last year. This year it has set for itself a quota 25 per cent higher and doubtless will reach it.   Next year another stiff increase will be set up.   This is a description that could be applied literally to hundreds and thousands of other businesses.

Coming from so authoritative a source, the foregoing statement is arresting.   The caption of the editorial is more so.   It is: "Why America is Different."   The writer has set forth in concrete terms what executives with international experience have long known; namely, that European business men do not strive so hard for volume as do their American confrères.   In Europe an enterprise that holds its own from year to year is considered healthy.   With us there is the well-established theory that a business should show an annual increase.

Why should American business men in great numbers set up stiff increases in volume each year?   Certainly it is not because Americans are more grasping than other people.   The always magnificent response of American business men to calls for help from any part of the world would refute this charge if any refutation were needed. Americans like to make money, it is true; but they like to give it away better than most people.   American men, besides, are usually willing to start from scratch and make their own careers.   To depend on influence for business promotion is almost as much discountenanced in the United States as to marry for money.

What reason, then, is there for the intensely competitive spirit that exists in American business if desire for gain is not at the bottom of it?   At the risk of shocking some readers, I am going to offer this explanation: Competition is more intense than in other countries because American business men are more influenced by vanity.

Everything conspires to bring this about.   The present generation in America inherits a condition of easy prosperity such as has never existed before and will probably never exist again.   The hard pioneering work of the country has been finished, but so recently finished that its enormous natural resources are practically intact. Business success comes with almost unbelievable ease in the United States compared with other countries.   In Europe success is so hard to attain that a man cannot afford to have an eye on the grandstand.   With us it is possible for a business man to indulge his *amour propre* and still succeed. Such expressions as, "I'll try any-thing once," or, "I look on my business as a game," are exclusively American.

Examples of easy success in America are so common that to many people no project appears incredible. Recently the Associated Press sent out a story that was printed in many newspapers under the heading, "Will Sing Crime out of Chicago." The text described a group of citizens interested in the music trades who were about to organize a twenty-four-hour campaign of song, during which earnest bands of singers would perform in hotels, churches, and private homes. Under this uplifting influence it was expected that the forces of evil would be put to rout. The gunman, the swindler, the bootlegger would abandon those professions and turn to better things.

This was a typically American attitude born of vanity and easy conditions. It is impossible to conceive of a group of people in London, Berlin, or Paris who would believe crime could be sung out of their communities in twenty-four hours. In the older and poorer countries it is known from hard experience that things are not accomplished so easily.

When a person feels himself financially secure beyond the chance of a reverse it is only natural that he should seek further pleasure through acts intended to impress his fellows. In America there are more people financially secure than in other countries, and hence more actions motivated by vanity. A well-known economist has recently published the statement that vanity has dictated the erection of a large proportion of city skyscrapers during past years. Frequently skyscrapers do not pay savings-bank interest, yet "men who have made fortunes fast put up the biggest, tallest skyscrapers with their surplus money as monuments to themselves and their fortunes." With this statement went the gloomy prediction that "Skyscrapers, as advertisements, are becoming so common that their value is already questionable. With the original reason gone, the vanity element eliminated by competition in this queer form of display, the skyscraper sections of New York and other cities will disappear."

In addition to the natural American temptation toward vanity, it is artificially stimulated by many agencies unknown in other countries. Europe, for example, knows nothing of what we commonly call "success" literature.   This has become so popular a feature with us that many publications make their entire bid for popularity upon the presentation of stories dealing with the spectacular successes of eminent business men.   Salesmanship in one form or another is the quality most frequently stressed.   An example may be drawn from a series of success stories presented by the New York *Sunday World*, one of which concerns itself with the career of Mr. Fred F. French, a nationally known real estate operator and advertiser of the Metropolis.   One of the paragraphs follows:

"The best example for a sales talk is the life of Jesus Christ," continued Mr. French, his eyes alight with vim for the competitive fight.   "He was the best salesman of all time.   He said, 'knock and it shall be opened unto you.'   What He meant was 'keep knocking until the door is opened and if it isn't opened pretty soon kick down the door.'   That's my philosophy too."

One finds it hard to believe this virile expression of an ideal reflects anything more profound than the natural desire to appear before the readers of the *Sunday World* as a dynamic, successful man of business. But its effect is none the less strong; and it is reasonable to believe other executives may be excited by it to more strident methods of salesmanship.

Practically all success literature depends for its appeal on the stimulation of vanity in the reader.   An outstanding example that may be cited is Mr. Bruce Barton's immensely popular book, *The Man Nobody Knows*.   Mr. Barton stimulates salesmanship ambition in his business-men readers by the most subtle flattery.   The Master is depicted as a salesman of surpassing ability.   "Every one of the 'principles of modern salesmanship' on which modern business men so pride themselves is strikingly exemplified in Jesus' talk and work." Jesus knew the art of "putting yourself in step with your prospect." "He picked up twelve men from the bottom ranks of business and forged them into an organization that conquered the world."   Never, perhaps, has a writer hit upon so happy a means of elevating the ego of the business-man reader.   There is a double jog to vanity.   By depicting Jesus as a salesman Mr. Barton not only sets the seal of Divine approval upon salesmanship as an art, but contrives to convey the idea that by salesmanship one grows into the image of the Master.

In the light of such compelling propaganda one does not wonder at the situation described by *Printers' Ink,* wherein "hundreds and thousands" of business executives annually set up increases twenty-five per cent in advance of the previous year. Yet where vanity comes in at the door profits have a habit of flying out at the window. In the preparation of this article I had occasion to interview the head of one of New York's largest banks, and during the interview I was shown a file containing the financial statements of three manufacturing corporations, clients of the institution. None of the corporations had earned an appreciable profit during the preceding year. The largest, doing a business of three millions of dollars, earned precisely $961.

The banker explained the situation as follows: Up to two years ago the corporations, all manufacturing similar lines of goods, paid reasonable dividends. At that time one of the corporations underwent a change in management. The gentleman who assumed its presidency was a vain man who wished to demonstrate his salesmanship powers. The corporation had been doing in round figures two million dollars a year. The new president arbitrarily decreed an annual business of three millions; and to that end set in motion all the machinery at his command. Branch offices were established in various cities where stocks of goods were maintained for quick delivery to merchants. The sales force was doubled. Each salesman was equipped with an automobile to cover his territory more often than was possible by railroad, and each was required to sell a certain volume upon penalty of losing his position. Longer credit terms were extended to merchants as an incentive to buying. In communities where merchants bought too sparingly, competitors were set up in business and financed by the corporation as added outlets for its product.

By these strenuous methods the corporation actually increased its sales during one year from two million dollars to three millions, and to that extent the ambitious president's vanity was satisfied. But the cost of gaining the extra million was so great that practically all profits were eliminated.

Yet that was not all. The corporation's two competitors were also obliged to speed up their selling efforts in order to protect themselves. They also established branch offices, increased the number of their salesmen, and granted longer credit terms. Their profits likewise were dissipated in unnecessary expenses. Three important corporations failed to pay dividends because one man wished to appear before the world as a two-fisted, up-and-coming apostle of efficiency.

If left alone, it is probable that conditions like the foregoing would right themselves, as responsible executives come more and more to realize the futility of over-expensive selling. But success literature is only one of many stimulants to business vanity. Vanity is promoted in many curious ways and from the strangest of motives. No longer ago than June, 1927, a meeting of eminent men took place at Cambridge, Massachusetts, to dedicate the buildings that comprise the George F. Baker Foundation of the Graduate School of Business Administration of Harvard University. These buildings, reported to have cost five millions of dollars, were presented to Harvard by Mr. George F. Baker, the New York banker. President Lowell of Harvard conferred the degree of Master of Business Administration upon a class of more than two hundred graduates, and in so doing used the following words: "By virtue of the authority delegated to me, I testify that you are well trained to enter upon one of the oldest of the arts and the *latest of the professions.*"

This sweeping statement coming from so high a source and conferring the brevet of professional status upon all American business men, was seized upon as an important tribute to American business; and many of those engaged in selling capitalized its splendid stimulation of business vanity. Leading newspapers sought popularity among business readers by quoting President Lowell's phrase upon their front pages and by flattering editorial comment. Scores of similarly optimistic articles have since appeared in the trade press. Retail shopkeepers, even, have found a way to turn the Harvard formalities to account. As these words are written, a leading department store of New York City features in a full-page advertisement the expression, "Business, the latest of the professions," as proof that its bargains are genuine.

It may be assumed that even though Harvard's president made his statement in cold blood he had no other end in view than to encourage more business men to contribute money toward the upbuilding of his institution. Such efforts are a part of the modern university president's job, and by the employment of wholesale flattery Doctor

Lowell merely exhibited keen business acumen. Yet the wisdom of his pronouncement is open to question. There is nothing to indicate that some hundreds of thousands of storekeepers, manufacturers, real estate men, undertakers — all those who buy and sell for a living — have suddenly reached professional status. There is an intrinsic difference between business and the professions. A merchant or a manufacturer sells merchandise. A lawyer or a physician sells personal services. For this reason the professional man cannot push his affairs so freely as can the business man. He is definitely limited in the things he may do for gain. To cite one example: A lawyer or physician must not seek clients through paid advertisements or by sending out solicitors. To do either of these things at once lowers his standing in his community. But a merchant or a manufacturer may quite properly employ both advertising and personal solicitation in the selling of his goods. Few people would wish to see this distinction abolished; yet so long as the distinction exists, business cannot be given the professional status mentioned by President Lowell. Such status predicates restraint; and it is generally admitted that less restraint is practiced by business at the present time than formerly. It is even possible that wholesale flattery of business men may make for still less restraint.

Vanity in business is progressive. We have seen how a single business executive, fired with the desire to demonstrate his powers, may so aggravate competition that an entire industry is reduced to the condition known as Prosperity without Profit. In many lines competition has become so hectic that ordinary salesmanship no longer suffices. Executives drive toward coveted goals of volume by systematic prodding of the vanity instinct in their employees. For this purpose a device known as the "sales contest" has come to be employed during recent years by many important firms and corporations.

The sales contest takes many ingenious forms, but its one object is to create in employees a fighting, he-man, bring-home-the-bacon spirit. The National Cash Register Company of Dayton, Ohio, for example, promotes a contest each month of the year among its twenty-five hundred salesmen in all parts of the United States and Canada. The object of each contest is to prod the individual salesman's vanity. On one recent occasion this event was termed an "aeroplane race"; and in the magazine published by the Company photographs of star salesmen were shown, attired in flying costumes and standing beside their machines ready to burst into flight. At another time the contest was an "automobile race." At the start of the automobile contest this message was sent to every salesman, "Make your plans over the week-end. Then hit Monday morning with a *bang* that will jar the points loose in your territory as they have never been before."

Another nation-wide corporation, the C and D Company, with twenty-five hundred salespeople who sell dresses, hosiery, and underwear throughout the United States, also prods the vanity of its employees by almost continuous contests. A recent event was the hunt of the "Whiffenpoof," a mythical creature described as "anything that keeps a salesman from getting an order." The hunt was under the direction of a salesmanager calling himself "Ram" Rod who divided his force into three camps named Teddy Roosevelt, Buffalo Bill, and Davy Crockett, respectively. Each time a salesperson took an order amounting to five dollars he was credited with the death of one Whiffenpoof. Prizes were offered for the greatest number of kills.

The contest plan has been found so effective as a stimulant to salesmanship vanity that a number of business concerns have been organized to create novel ideas in the way of contests and to sell the products of their inventiveness to various firms and corporations. Among the most successful of these producers of contest plans is the Dartnell Company of Chicago with more than ten thousand subscribing to its regular service. Recently the Dartnell Company produced a special plan for stimulating salesmen which comprised the purchase of certain novelties to be mailed to traveling representatives from week to week. One week, for example, the bagman was sent a miniature feather duster bearing a tag that counseled him to "dust" his territory. Another week he was sent an imitation cannon firecracker with the injunction "Make a Big Noise." One is told that more than twelve hundred firms and corporations purchased the series of novelties and mailed them to their forces of road salesmen.

Originally the contest idea was confined to manufacturers who felt the need of stimulating the *amour propre* of their employees. Of late it has been extended into other fields. The National Surety Company of New York City frequently promotes contests among its representatives throughout the United States and Canada. Recently one of the Company's regional managers, Mr. C. C. Spear, telegraphed from North Carolina that he had made the "largest forgery bond sale ever made in the South," and challenged his brother regional managers to equal his exploit. This incident was seized upon as the basis of a spirited contest, and the following telegram was sent to all regional managers and supervisors by the Company's vice-president:

Speak about the Go-Get-Em Spirit: Spear certainly throws down the gauntlet to other regional managers and surely no red-blooded, two-fisted, fighting regional manager is going to let him get away with any such defy. He is practically thumbing his nose and wiggling his fingers at you. If he falls off his high horse we'll make him literally eat his telegram before a camera in company with the regional manager who gives him the most decisive trimming.

One defect in the employment of flattery as a sales stimulant is the necessity for increasingly stronger potions. In rich New York a mere resort to clubby Business English may create sales; but in communities where life is sustained upon a more austere basis and where ready cash is scarce it is often necessary to supplement the ordinary vanity appeal by almost unbelievable garnishments. Few will deny that sex and vanity are closely allied emotions; and painful as it is to recount it, sex excitation has been authoritatively recommended as a sales stimulant when ordinary means fail.

In the *Merchants' Farm Journal* one reads the success story of a prominent department-store owner of Devil's Lake, North Dakota, and learns how hard-won dollars may be enticed from masculine pockets by skilful exploitation of the female form:

We always had a hard time getting the men customers into the store in large numbers. We sent them invitations to our Easter opening, but few came. So I said to my brother: "We'll have a summer opening. We'll put bathing suits on living models and we'll send personal invitations to the men!" Well, that is one time we had the men at one of our openings.

While the foregoing incident illustrates the desperate state of salesmanship in retail circles, a recent development gives ominous warning that the same deplorable situation may soon exist in the field of

Big Business unless something is done to curb the ambition of executives who demand of their sales forces sensational increases of volume from year to year. Many firms and corporations that formerly depended upon their own salesmanagers to keep the enthusiasm of their forces at white heat now find it necessary to employ inspirational talent from the outside. An entirely new profession has been created through this necessity, and in the pages of many business journals one finds the advertisements of those who, for lack of a better term, may be called revivalists in salesmanship. Among them one notes the name of Mr. W. L. (Bill) Barnhart, whose name, it is stated in his prospectus, is registered as a Trade Mark in the United States Patent Office; and whose lecture, "The Magic Formula of Sales Success," is commended by such organizations as the Advertising-Selling League of Omaha, Nebraska, and the Drexel Institute of Philadelphia. Another, Mr. Willard Scott, advertises to have spoken before more than three hundred gatherings of industrial corporation executives, bankers, chambers of commerce, and college men. Mr. Scott solicits further engagements upon the following testimonial offered by the Adcraft Club of Canton, Ohio: "He made 'em laugh like kooka-burras half full of raisin jack."

From the employment of sex excitation and rollicking laughter as sales stimuli, it is but a step to the exploitation of another intensely human emotion — love of little children. An influential business journal has recently published a success story based upon an interview with the salesmanager of the American Slicing Machine Company of Chicago, in which is explained how that nation-wide organization jolts the vanity of its sales force by linking up the children with the Company's drive for greater volume:

Last fall we offered a turkey at Christmas to every one of our salesmen who beat his quota of sales. To give the contest an added element of human interest we asked each man to appoint a child in his family as mascot, realizing that every one of them would work his head off to make some youngster happy at Christmas. The way these youngsters took hold of the plan was amusing and at times the intensity of their interest was almost pathetic.

The American Slicing Machine Company is not alone in the discovery that children may profitably be used to maintain sales volume. One reads in an influential business publication that a leading soap manufacturing corporation jogs the vanity of little boys and girls at school by providing cards on which they are requested to sign the following pledge:

"Dear Teacher: I promise to wash my face and hands with my little cake of X soap before every meal and before going to bed until it is all used up."

One hesitates to inject a pessimistic note into activities that doubtless furnish much pleasure to ambitious executives, and sometimes do increase sales. But as we have seen, increased sales often mean decreased profits. Illustrating the futility of much of the supersalesmanship that has come into vogue during recent years, Mr. J. F. Lincoln, of the Lincoln Electric Company of Cleveland, says:

The tendency of sales costs to go up fully as rapidly as manufacturing costs have gone down, has been the history of the past ten years. The rate at which sales costs have gone up is stupefying when shown in percentages. In many products thirty-five cents being the only part of his dollar which has anything to do with manufacturing cost and the only part of the dollar which the manufacturer ever sees.

Even in the United States business cannot permanently continue to set up stiff increases without reaching an impasse. An outstanding example is the automobile trade. There is an unusually high rate of failures among retail automobile dealers. In the past most dealers have been obliged to accept certain numbers of cars each month from the manufacturers; and often, when overstocked with cars, a dealer is tempted to make too high an allowance for the second-hand car his customer wishes to trade in. This has become so prevalent that a large proportion of buyers refuse to be influenced toward any particular make of car. A saying in the trade is "A buyer doesn't shop for a car any more. He shops for the biggest allowance on his old car." Where such a situation exists every one in the trade loses. The dealer, perhaps, goes bankrupt. The manufacturer loses through having to secure another dealer. Also, the manufacturer loses in another way; because for every sale that is secured solely on the allowance made for the second-hand car, the manufacturer's advertising is nullified to just that extent. Speaking of these problems, Mr. Alfred P. Sloan, president of the General Motors Corporation, has said:

One of the big troubles of the automobile business is that dealers and manufacturers all have the habit of expecting business every year to be far in excess of that of the previous year.

In line with this statement it is cheering to note that General Motors announces that in the future it will set no arbitrary increases and will adjust its manufacturing to legitimate demand.

Always, just around the corner, is the menace of business depression that invariably follows overselling on a large scale. On this danger an editorial writer in one of the most influential of Big Business journals recently comments:

The prevailing idea in business that a Company must increase its sales each year is the cause of the senseless scramble for volume that is going on in so many industries. It is also one of the causes of rumors that sometimes start a depression. When a sales organization finds it is falling under its previous high-water mark, it is likely to go into a psychological funk. It communicates its pessimism to others. Orders are cancelled, employees are laid off, and the first thing you know there is a depression, although there is really not the slightest reason for it.

If vanity dictates the policies of business to too great an extent a time may come when Prosperity without Profit will shrink into a condition where there is no prosperity and no profit.

V. THE COLLEGE AND EDUCATION

WHAT'S RIGHT WITH THE COLLEGES

BY ARTHUR HOBSON QUINN

Arthur Hobson Quinn (1875–   ) has had a wide experience with college students, having been on the faculty of the University of Pennsylvania since 1894, acting as Dean of the College there from 1912 to 1922. He has written a number of articles for magazines. His histories of the American Drama, the first volume of which was published in 1923 and the second and third, in 1927, cover the period from the beginning of theatrical production in America to the present day, and are well known, as are his other works of a scholarly nature.

IF we are to judge by the amount of criticism printed in the last few years, the colleges and universities of this country are in a bad way. Much of this criticism has the peculiarly fresh and spirited quality which proceeds from the writer's complete detachment from his subject. One efficiency engineer with a delightful disregard of ventilation complains that the class-rooms are not used continuously; and another critic, with more justice, fulminates over the "unit system" which is the root of all evil. But most insistent is the cry that goes up from those who paint the halls of learning as centers of corruption, which must be passed only at the dire peril of the boy who wishes to be exposed for a time to education. According to these critics the college student, like a certain family who did not have the advantages of higher education, learns nothing and forgets nothing. Meanwhile some of the colleges, and all of the universities, are crowded to the doors.

It is not to be supposed that the influx is due to the lurid pictures of college life, or to the destructive criticism so freely offered. There has never been a lack of such destructive criticism. Emerson, who was a product of a régime at Harvard which apparently was free from some of our modern problems, was rather bitter about the matter. "The Good Spirit," he says, "never cared for the colleges." Earlier still, Cooper felt called upon to express himself about Yale, which had expelled him; and still earlier, Franklin was stirred to write an essay upon the results, disappointing to him, of his trusteeship at Pennsylvania. But cannot we proceed from another point of view? Let us acknowledge that things are not perfect by any means, but instead of inveighing against conditions which are apparent even to educational "experts" or to reporters for a newspaper, writing with an eye to sensation, let us see what qualities in the American college are fine and permanent. Then let us attempt to strengthen the forces which have made and preserved these qualities, for one constructive effort is worth a hundred wails over the by-products of college education. We may find that the material is already at hand, needing reshaping rather than destruction.

If there are influences which hinder the full development of these qualities, or if mistakes have been made which must be remedied, let us proceed with a view to fundamentals, and with a conviction that the college is essentially sound. For if it is not essentially sound, it is not worth preserving. And to its worth there is one universal testimony. I have taught for thirty-four years in one liberal arts college, and for ten years as dean of the college, was in a position to talk to hundreds of alumni and students. I have lectured also at the summer sessions of other institutions. In all these contacts, I have never heard one graduate of a course in Arts regret that he had spent four years in college.

In the first place, contrary to the view expressed so vociferously, the alumnus feels that he received quite a generous amount of education. If he has any coherent criticism of the system under which he studied, it is usually a regret that he was allowed to choose so freely for himself. Now this criticism never comes from the alumnus of the seventies or eighties, before the devastating effect of President Eliot's free elective system had become fully apparent throughout the American colleges. In those days the student was taught a group of studies arranged by a number of teachers who knew what was good for him, or thought they did, and more important, who taught him their individual subjects with the knowledge of what he was studying in the other class-rooms, subjects with which they were familiar. This homogeneity, this interrelation of subjects, was the strength of the old-fashioned curriculum, and not the particular subjects which made it up.

This complete homogeneity of the old college course is gone beyond recall. Too many new subjects have forced their way into the curriculum for one student to take them all, and the languages and mathematics have given up the fight for their old preëminence.

But how can we restore the great object of the old-fashioned college, which was not the teaching of Latin and Greek and mathematics, but the *removing of ignorance upon those subjects whose mastery was the touchstone of the education of a gentleman?* Its secondary object, as Marion Crawford has so well put it, was that *thoroughness* in a few subjects which has been at the root of social superiority in all ages. Greek went long ago because it became quite possible for a man to pass through his life and never be confronted with a situation in which ignorance of that language would be an embarrassment. But an ignorance of Latin is a different matter, and the advocates of the "classics" would have been better advised if they had put their strength into saving the one language and had let the other go.

How then are we to remove in four years the greatest amount of ignorance? By charting out the great fields of human knowledge and seeing that the boy or girl does not leave college without having been required to have at least a speaking acquaintance with all of them. First, he must know the language and literature of his native tongue, and must learn to express himself clearly in English. The undergraduates do not object to this requirement, if the English Department is alive to the wisdom of providing guidance in modern British and American literature, especially in the drama. For the undergraduates do talk about books and go to see plays, and many of them are hungry for advice about them. Second, he must have some knowledge of the exact sciences — mathematics, physics, and chemistry. Time is too short to force him into all of them, but he must learn the salutary lesson that two and two always make four. He will accept this group with some hesitancy, but he will become reconciled. Third, he must know something of that other group of subjects, history, philosophy, politics, and economics, in which human relations are made clear to him. Here again, he cannot perhaps be forced into all of them, but there is less objection on his part for he realizes that he cannot take his place among educated men unless he knows at least the vocabulary of these subjects. Fourth, he should be led into the group of the biological sciences, zoölogy, botany, and psychology, where he will learn another important truth, that two and two do not always make four, but sometimes three or five. Fifth, he must be required to continue his study of one ancient language and one modern tongue. But some of you will say, "This is all obvious. Of course he must take these things." *How many American colleges make him take them?* At least, how many make him take them in such correlated groupings as to call to his attention the process through which he is going? How often is it called to his attention that there are these great fields of knowledge and that he cannot afford to be entirely ignorant of any one of them? The ideal would be to make him take all these subjects, but that is impossible — in four years. But he can have a look in at the groups at least, and there is time left for teaching him enough of some one subject to give him a fairly thorough knowledge of it, and still a few hours left for free electives in other fields. Boys and girls will object to some features of this program, but they will send their sons and daughters back to the college that made them take it. One great advantage of such a curriculum, with about two thirds of the students' course required, is that an A.B. can be given for it without blushing, and the absurd compromises of the B.S. and Ph.B. can be quietly dropped by faculties which invented them to meet a supposed demand that really never existed. For the undergraduate respects a curriculum that is given with confidence and based upon experience, especially if he sees on the same campus a school of applied science or a school of commerce in which the course is prescribed.

The point that needs emphasis is that all these subjects are taught now, but that there is still in many quarters an opinion that the undergraduate is competent to select his course for himself. The "arts colleges" have lost prestige because their faculties have not made full use of the material at their disposal, not only in itself but in its interrelations.

The curriculum, of course, is only the framework. What other elements of the American college have filled it with life? Ask any alumnus what he remembers best and he will either recall the names of certain teachers or tell you about the good time he had. There is a difference between the attitude toward the faculty in an alumnus of the eighties and one of the new century. The older men speak of their teachers with more affection; the younger, with more respect. It is not only because the increasing numbers have prevented that personal intercourse which made for affection; it is really because, on the whole, there is more efficient teaching. Part of the time in the eighties or nineties was spent in keeping order. The undergraduate may have loved his preceptors more dearly, but he certainly made life miserable for some of them. Now disorder in the class-room is a thing of the past. The teacher can devote his entire energy to presenting his subject in a proper manner. That he often, owing to large classes, has to make it a dramatic spectacle is true; but in order to do that, he must prepare it more carefully than his predecessor did. Every minute of the hour he is alive, giving his best, fixing his eye on the least interested student and determined to capture him, knowing that if he does so, he has given the rest something worth while.   I prefer to have my son share the teaching of such a man with one or two hundred other students rather than to have him brought into "personal contact" with a less stimulating teacher in a small college with a class of twenty!

That this nice adjustment of a course of study, leading from the more elementary or basic subjects to those which demand more maturity, requires at least four years, should be apparent. The menace of the "junior college" is threatening the very essence of the American college of liberal arts. I wish the glib "experts" who advocate this separation of the lower and upper two years could listen to the conversations that go on in the deans' offices all over this country as that much criticized functionary labors to help the boy who has the disease known as "arts indigestion." It usually comes in the sophomore year, and it makes him wonder what this education is all about. If he meets a sympathetic adviser, he is saved and he is saved because he has two more years in the same place with a continuity that is priceless and which the junior college would destroy.

It is just that continuity which is so vitally needed for the cementing of those friendships which are the second great gift of the college to America. Every college man or woman knows what they are worth, that is, if he or she is worth anything. They are formed in days before distrust becomes a duty, and time or separation can only deepen their hold. When President Coolidge wished to have as his representative in Mexico a man whom he could absolutely trust, he chose his classmate at Amherst. It was not long ago that one of the foremost scholars in America died under circumstances of peculiar distress. He had taught in the East, in the middle West, and in the far West, but among all his friends, those who stood around his coffin and comforted his widow were exclusively members of his class.

Unfortunately as numbers grow, the class is disappearing as a unit in education or in friendship. The fraternity or social club has virtually taken its place in the larger universities, but the result is much the same. Where from fifteen to forty men are initiated into a fraternity at one time, the class delegation within the fraternity takes the place of the small class of the eighties, in the knitting of friendships. The training in responsibility, which was one of the fine things in the earlier college, survives in these later relations. One concrete instance is worth a hundred generalizations. The most difficult problem in fraternity house management is, of course, the question of liquor. All the great national fraternities forbid its members from bringing it into their houses. But the irresponsible alumni bring it in just the same, especially after football games. At one of the houses at a large Eastern university, several of these alumni continued this practice after warnings from the graduate board of trustees of the fraternity chapter which held title to the property. Before the board could act, the undergraduate seniors met and assumed responsibility for putting their house in order. The offending alumni were notified that they could not enter the house again and two of them, who were lodging there, were given one week to leave. Of course the board of trustees supported the boys in their action, but it need hardly be emphasized that the importance of the occurrence lay not so much in the prohibition of liquor as it did in the assumption of responsibility by a group of seniors. The American college has given us nothing more precious than the cultivation of the *esprit de corps,* and it must be preserved by close coöperation between the college authorities and every undergraduate organization that stands for solidarity and for the natural instinct that leads men to form associations. That such coöperation is in active operation is known to every college administrator; but that fraternities, which thirty years ago were indifferent to the scholastic standing of their members, watch now with great care over it, may be news to those who clamor for their abolition.

Is it not time that the public conception of so-called "college life" should begin to square with the facts? The old idea that a boy went to an isolated spot for four years and then "commenced life" persists still in the minds of those unacquainted with the changes that have been brought about in American education. The boy who enters a university has been already in close contact with life and he remains in even more vital relation to it during his residence. Parents are gradually awaking to the fact that the best way to prevent their sons from dissipating is to provide them with something else to occupy their minds. The automobile has placed the country college and the city university pretty much on the same basis, as far as opportunity to waste time or spend it profitably is concerned. The undergraduate, of course, is under none of the delusions which agitate the critics of the colleges. He knows he is like any other boy from eighteen to twenty-two except that he is being furnished with standards that are higher than those of his brother who proceeds earlier to the practical atmosphere of a bank or an insurance company. He is usually kept too busy by his course of study to neglect it, for the room is needed urgently for those who will work. Notwithstanding the current delusion, he does not seek "snap courses," because they are usually hard to find. What he absolutely refuses to suffer is boredom, even at the price of ease. In short he is a keen young person, who is eager for the right kind of guidance, and while he overemphasizes his "activities" and his various societies and "hats" and "keys" — that is only human.

Education — friendship — and the devotion to something beside himself. These are what the American college has given and will continue to give if the "expert" is not allowed to crush its first two formative years back into the precocious maturity of the high school and drag its last two, even more precious in their development, up into the professional atmosphere of the graduate school. It may be an illusion that we have been educating men to a point where they can think clearly, can see into the heart of a problem, can preserve the distinction between what is important and what is unimportant, and who can be liberal to all sincere opinions, whether these agree with their own or not. If this be a dream, it is at least a noble dream.

But it is not a dream — it is a practical reality. The essential qualities of the four-year college were not built upon the shifting sands of mere temporary utility, nor has it proceeded along the by-roads of pedagogical science, whose paths are marked by the mile-

stones of mistake.   Its progress has been upon the broad highroad of
the human understanding, reaching back, as it always has done, to
the fountains of knowledge, and leading forward, as it must continue
to do, into the realities of life.   We believe in this form of education
not only because we see the minds of boys and girls kindle every day
as they are brought into contact with the mental and spiritual inheritance of the race, but also because the graduates in unending proces-
sion tell us of their successes, won with the weapons the college has
given them.   And we believe in it most heartily because we know
that when the days come in which a man is his own best companion,
he will realize how priceless are those resources which no one can
take from him but himself.

It is for us never to lose courage no matter how closely the college
seems to be invested by its enemies, for if we can hold the citadel long
enough, we shall win at last.   Or if we do not survive to witness the
return of sanity to educational discussion, at least the victors we have
trained will find our bodies by the wall.

THE BUSINESS OF EDUCATION

By LUDWIG LEWISOHN

*Ludwig Lewisohn (1882–   ) has taught at the University of Wis-
consin and at Ohio State University, and was, for a time, dramatic editor of "The Nation." He was born in Germany, coming to America
with his parents when he was eight years old.   He has written an
autobiography, "Upstream" (1922), several novels, "Don Juan"
(1923), and "The Island Within" (1928), has translated and edited
the works of Gerhardt Hauptmann, and has written extensive critical
works on the modern drama and Continental literatures.*

I APPLIED myself to the business of education.   To what we, in
America, call the higher education of the most democratic type.
For the university of Central City is a state institution.   It is coedu-
cational.   There are between five and six thousand students and a
faculty of nearly five hundred.   The university is divided into eight
chief colleges to all but one of which — the college of medicine — a
graduation certificate from a high school admits the student.   In a
word, any boy or girl in the State who has completed a high-school
course may go to Central City and learn anything within the whole
realm of human knowledge which may seem most effective in developing the individual.   These state universities represent a handsome idea.   If the teaching were not propaganda, if the teachers
were not slaves. . . . Yet from these universities fiery things may one
day come.   Not now.   Let me remember.

I stroll on the campus in spring as I have done many times.   The
students are not disturbed by my approach, for they stand in no
particular awe of their professors.   Those that know me go on with
their conversation, simply including me in it if I stop.   They know
that my attitude is always comradely.   I watch their faces.   There is
not a vicious face on the campus.   I try to recall one among the
hundreds of students I have taught.   I cannot.   Dull faces, vacant
faces.   Not one that expresses any corruption of heart and mind.
I look about me again and watch for one face that betrays a troubled
soul, a yearning of the mind, the touch of any flame.   There is none.
How many such faces have I seen in classroom or campus?   I count
them: one, two, three — well, four.   I must except the handful of

Russian Jews. Thought and emotion are their birthright. But my young Americans? Many of the girls are dainty and comely. The peasant is obliterated here in a single generation. The boys have bright and cheery faces — rather more flattened and less salient, upon the whole, than the girls'. A little coarser in modelling and tinting. But all, all incurably trivial. I listen to their talk. It is of games, parties, examinations. Never of the contents of the tests. But of the practical fact that they have to be faced. Who has ever heard an eager argument among these students on any of the subjects — art, religion, economics, sex — that are supposed to employ the minds of men? Who has ever seen them keen about anything except (symbolically speaking) football and fudge? It is, as a matter of fact, considered rather bad form among them to show any stirring of the mind. It is considered "high-brow," queer, that is to say — different, personal and hence, by a subtle and quite mad implication consoling to stupidity and emptiness — undemocratic.

A Continental would ask: Why do they go to the university? In Central City comparatively few went for social reasons. An extraordinary proportion of the students earn their maintenance wholly or in part. They and their parents make real sacrifices in the cause of education. I found few of those young men and women really slack and trifling. There was practically no disciplinary problem. The students came to the classroom to learn something. I have seen both French and German friends speechless before that contradiction. But gradually I fought my way to its true meaning which is this: To the "average, intelligent American" education, for which he is willing to deny himself and pay taxes, means — skill, information — at most, accomplishment. Skill and knowledge with which to conquer the world of matter. It does not mean to him an inner change — the putting on of a new man, a new criterion of truth, new tastes, and other values. The things he wants at the university are finer and more flexible tools for the economic war which he calls liberty. And like tools or weapons they are external to him and are dropped when the classroom period or the working day are over. He then merges himself again into the great level of the democratic mass from which he strives to be distinguished only by the possession of those sharper tools. By his outlook upon life, his distinction of taste, his finer palate for truth he would hesitate to be differentiated from his fellows.   He would seem to himself in danger of being a "high-brow" and a snob.   Occasionally I used to hear a gifted student, alive to the deeper meaning of the humanities, passionately disclaim the values he had himself attained, in a blind terror of non-conformity.   And I heard students say, not once or twice: "But the majority is of another opinion; I'm probably wrong."

Our students, then, came to the university not to find truth, but to be engineers or farmers, doctors or teachers.   They did not want to be different men and women.   It is in conformity with this popular purpose that the elective system of studies has been pushed back from the college into the high school and that state universities have been compelled, by actual legislation in some cases, to admit high-school graduates simply by virtue of a definite amount of study without distinction of content or quality.   The recent introduction of psychological tests, when it is not, as in certain private universities of the East, a weapon against radicals and Jews, can be made to function in precisely the same way.   And I do not say that, given the aim, the system is not practical.   If the aim of education is merely to gain rough, useful tools for striving with the world of matter, and to gain them rapidly — the system works.   I suppose that these state universities do turn out very fair engineers and farmers and veterinarians.   But when their job leaves these men free they are but little different from people who have not gone to college.   They go to foolish plays, read silly magazines, and fight for every poisonous fallacy in politics, religion, and conduct.   A professor of geology in the university of Central City was publicly converted by Billy Sunday. The fact that he was not thereupon privately "fired," that he was still thought capable of teaching his science, symbolized the situation in its naked horror.

One or two of my colleagues and I were wont, in our interpretation of literature and thought, to speak freely in the classroom of those deep and serious matters concerning which it befits men and women to think all their lives.   A few students — a very few — followed our leading.   A number, also small, offered a sullen resistance.   The majority considered us interesting, stimulating, a little quaint, and regarded these lectures as pleasant exercitations which had no contact with reality.   A student, for example, would take advanced courses in philosophy and literature, and return, with no sense of discrepancy, to the formularies of a third-rate conventicle. Another, a girl with a face full of intelligence and vivid sweetness, "majored" in French literature. She knew the language well and had read widely. But Montaigne and Anatole France never spoke to her. Her real interest was in Y.W.C.A. work and she was anxious to become a missionary. Her one desire was to save the followers of Buddha through the doctrines of the Fifth Street Baptist Church.

This phenomenon was a recurrent one. So let me repeat: Our people do not believe in education at all — if education means a liberation of the mind or a heightened consciousness of the historic culture of mankind. Philosophy and morals are taken care of by the Fifth Street Baptist Church. College is to fit you to do things — build bridges, cure diseases, teach French. It is not supposed to help you to be.

Convictions on all ultimate questions our students brought with them ready-made or continued deliberately to draw from sources other than ourselves. And these convictions constitute the most rigid and the palest inner culture objectively. I know it almost tangibly. For years I read it in the eyes of my students, and noted it in all their reactions, bruised myself daily against its dull and vicious edges. If I understood this ethos rightly, it holds that the aim and end of life is happiness in terms of blameless prosperity. It very sincerely distrusts intensity or distinction of mind and carelessness of material success. These things make for error and do not make for prosperity. It does not believe in virtue — *virtus*, power, the creative instinct in the intellectual or moral world — but wholly in such negative commandments as will contribute to honest material well-being. You must not drink fermented liquors, you must not criticize your neighbor harshly, you must not — except in business where the contrary is the supreme law — act selfishly; you must not doubt that America has achieved an unexampled freedom nor that the majority is right — "they say: 'the majority rules'" — and hence you must shun non-conformity to the fundamental beliefs of the majority as undemocratic and un-American. Also as un-Christian. For the Churches have substituted prohibition for saintliness and a state of economic competition in which blamelessness achieves prosperity for the kingdom of God.

How, it will be asked, can such convictions — so humdrum, so middle-aged, so unheroic — armor as with steel the impassioned spirit of youth? Alas, youth in Central City had no rebellions or curiosities or yearnings. Young things there were not wild things. Adolescents neither wrote verse nor broke idols. A thoughtful physician assured me that nine tenths of those young Americans with their untroubled eyes and steady gaze were undersexed. And I found a weighty confirmation in this: it was practically impossible, in studying literature, to get an emotional response. Those students had no emotional experience. Their inner lives were supremely poverty-stricken. Nothing in them cried out. In addition, their morality is one of restraint and negation. So that whatever feeble sparks of personality might smoulder here and there are smothered by the morals and beliefs of the mass-life. Thus personality itself came to seem almost wicked and propriety synonymous with goodness. If they could live so quietly in a moral world which seemed to have no contact with reality, it was because reality in them had little sharpness or insistence. They had become what home and church and school wanted them to be. The ideal of conformity, of colorlessness, of taking the world to be a tame and shop-keeping sort of affair had been achieved. . . .

Democracy was — was it not? — to set the individual free, to make room in the world for all types of personality, to make life comradely, vivid, flexible? My students had one positive instinct. It was quiet and it never became cruel. But it was unbreakable: the instinct of intolerance. They were quietly intolerant of all qualitative distinctions — even in themselves. I said to a class of seniors: "High-brow is usually a term applied by ignorant people to those whose finer qualities and insights they should seek to emulate." My class laughed in its pleasant, courteous way. An hour later in the library I witnessed this scene. A blond, tousle-headed lad, my chief comfort during a certain year, was trying to sell copies of a magazine which, with the help of the Russian Jewish students, he had tentatively established. The magazine was crude enough. But it was alive. There was verse in it, unrhythmed and gawky, but hopeful, and prose with some close thinking in it and a social outlook and a breath of the future. My friend Jim smiled at me and shouted: "Buy the second number of *The Torch*!" One of my seniors passed, the daughter of a federal judge. She shook her smooth,

comely head with a self-satisfied little grin: "Too high-brow for me!"
There was an inimitable characteristic little upward inflection on
the last word. She bought *The Sly-Cat* — the students' comic
paper — you may be sure, and laughed over its unspeakable inani-
ties. It was natural, you say. The act — yes. But the spirit of the
act! She refused *The Torch* with self-righteous triumph and read
The Sly-Cat with a solid sense of doing the right thing — because it
was the ordinary thing. She had made a fetish of commonness —
except in the matter of money and clothes and motor-cars. So had
they all....

OXFORD AS I SEE IT

By STEPHEN LEACOCK

Stephen Leacock (1869–   ) is best known as a humorist, although as head of the Department of Political Science at McGill University, Montreal, and as a lecturer and writer in political economy, he is widely recognized in the scholastic field.   Among his collections of essays are "Literary Lapses" (1909), "Nonsense Novels" (1911), "Essays and Literary Studies" (1916), and "My Discovery of England" (1922).

MY private station being that of a university professor, I was naturally deeply interested in the system of education in England.   I was therefore led to make a special visit to Oxford and to submit the place to a searching scrutiny.   Arriving one afternoon at four o'clock, I stayed at the Mitre Hotel and did not leave until eleven o'clock next morning.   The whole of this time, except for one hour spent in addressing the undergraduates, was devoted to a close and eager study of the great university.   When I add to this that I had already visited Oxford in 1907 and spent a Sunday at All Souls with Colonel L. S. Amery, it will be seen at once that my views on Oxford are based upon observations extending over fourteen years.

At any rate I can at least claim that my acquaintance with the British university is just as good a basis for reflection and judgment as that of the numerous English critics who come to our side of the water.   I have known a famous English author to arrive at Harvard University in the morning, have lunch with President Lowell, and then write a whole chapter on the Excellence of Higher Education in America.   I have known another one to come to Harvard, have lunch with President Lowell, and do an entire book on the Decline of Serious Study in America.   Or take the case of my own university. I remember Mr. Rudyard Kipling coming to McGill and saying in his address to the undergraduates at 2.30 P.M., "You have here a great institution."   But how could he have gathered this information?   As far as I know he spent the entire morning with Sir Andrew Macphail in his house beside the campus, smoking cigarettes.   When I add that he distinctly refused to visit the Palæontologic Museum, that he saw nothing of our new hydraulic apparatus, or of our classes in Domestic Science, his judgment that we had here a great institution seems a little bit superficial. I can only put beside it, to redeem it in some measure, the hasty and ill-formed judgment expressed by Lord Milner, "McGill is a noble university": and the rash and indiscreet expression of the Prince of Wales, when we gave him an LL.D. degree, "McGill has a glorious future."

To my mind these unthinking judgments about our great college do harm, and I determined, therefore, that anything that I said about Oxford should be the result of the actual observation and real study based upon a bona fide residence in the Mitre Hotel.

On the strength of this basis of experience I am prepared to make the following positive and emphatic statements. Oxford is a noble university. It has a great past. It is at present the greatest university in the world: and it is quite possible that it has a great future. Oxford trains scholars of the real type better than any other place in the world. Its methods are antiquated. It despises science. Its lectures are rotten. It has professors who never teach and students who never learn. It has no order, no arrangement, no system. Its curriculum is unintelligible. It has no president. It has no state legislature to tell it how to teach, and yet — it gets there. Whether we like it or not, Oxford gives something to its students, a life and a mode of thought, which in America as yet we can emulate but not equal.

If anybody doubts this let him go and take a room at the Mitre Hotel (ten and six for a wainscoted bedroom, period of Charles I) and study the place for himself.

These singular results achieved at Oxford are all the more surprising when one considers the distressing conditions under which the students work. The lack of an adequate building-fund compels them to go on working in the same old buildings which they have had for centuries. The buildings at Brasenose College have not been renewed since the year 1525. In New College and Magdalen the students are still housed in the old buildings erected in the sixteenth century. At Christ Church I was shown a kitchen which had been built at the expense of Cardinal Wolsey in 1527. Incredible though it may seem, they have no other place to cook in than this and are compelled to use it to-day. On the day when I saw this kitchen, four cooks were busy roasting an ox whole for the students' lunch: this at least is what I presumed they were doing from the size of the fire-place used, but it may not have been an ox; perhaps it was a cow. On a huge table, twelve feet by six and made of slabs of wood five inches thick, two other cooks were rolling out a game pie. I estimated it as measuring three feet across. In this rude way, unchanged since the time of Henry VIII, the unhappy Oxford students are fed. I could not help contrasting it with the cosy little boarding houses on Cottage Grove Avenue where I used to eat when I was a student at Chicago, or the charming little basement dining-rooms of the students' boarding houses in Toronto. But then, of course, Henry VIII never lived in Toronto.

The same lack of a building-fund necessitates the Oxford students' living in the identical old boarding houses they had in the sixteenth and seventeenth centuries. Technically they are called "quadrangles," "closes," and "rooms"; but I am so broken in to the usage of my student days that I can't help calling them boarding houses. In many of these the old stairway has been worn down by the feet of ten generations of students: the windows have little latticed panes: there are old names carved here and there upon the stone, and a thick growth of ivy covers the walls. The boarding house at St. John's College dates from 1509, the one at Christ Church from the same period. A few hundred thousand pounds would suffice to replace these old buildings with neat steel and brick structures like the normal school at Schenectady, N.Y., or the Peel Street High School at Montreal. But nothing is done. A movement was indeed attempted last autumn towards removing the ivy from the walls, but the result was unsatisfactory and they are putting it back. Any one could have told them beforehand that the mere removal of the ivy would not brighten Oxford up, unless at the same time one cleared the stones of the old inscriptions, put in steel fire-escapes, and in fact brought the boarding houses up to date.

But Henry VIII being dead, nothing was done. Yet in spite of its dilapidated buildings and its lack of fire-escapes, ventilation, sanitation, and up-to-date kitchen facilities, I persist in my assertion that I believe that Oxford, in its way, is the greatest university in the world. I am aware that this is an extreme statement and needs explanation. Oxford is much smaller in numbers, for example, than the State University of Minnesota, and is much poorer. It has, or had till yesterday, fewer students than the University of Toronto. To mention Oxford beside the 26,000 students of Columbia University sounds ridiculous.   In point of money, the $39,000,000 endowment of the University of Chicago, and the $35,000,000 one of Columbia, and the $43,000,000 of Harvard seem to leave Oxford nowhere.   Yet the peculiar thing is that it is not nowhere.   By some queer process of its own it seems to get there every time.   It was therefore of the very greatest interest to me, as a profound scholar, to try to investigate just how this peculiar excellence of Oxford arises.

It can hardly be due to anything in the curriculum or program of studies.   Indeed, to any one accustomed to the best models of a university curriculum as it flourishes in the United States and Canada, the program of studies is frankly quite laughable.   There is less Applied Science in the place than would be found with us in a theological college.   Hardly a single professor at Oxford would recognize a dynamo if he met it in broad daylight.   The Oxford student learns nothing of chemistry, physics, heat, plumbing, electric wiring, gas-fitting or the use of a blow-torch.   Any American college student can run a motor-car, take a gasoline engine to pieces, fix a washer on a kitchen tap, mend a broken electric bell, and give an expert opinion on what has gone wrong with the furnace.   It is these things indeed which stamp him as a college man, and occasion a very pardonable pride in the minds of his parents.   But in all these things the Oxford student is the merest amateur.

This is bad enough.   But after all one might say this is only the mechanical side of education.   True: but one searches in vain in the Oxford curriculum for any adequate recognition of the higher and more cultured studies.   Strange though it seems to us on this side of the Atlantic, there are no courses at Oxford in Housekeeping, or in Salesmanship, or in Advertising, or on Comparative Religion, or on the influence of the Press.   There are no lectures whatever on Human Behaviour, on Altruism, on Egotism, or on the Play of Wild Animals.   Apparently, the Oxford student does not learn these things.   This cuts him off from a great deal of the larger culture of our side of the Atlantic.   "What are you studying this year?"   I once asked a fourth year student at one of our great colleges.   "I am electing Salesmanship and Religion," he answered.   Here was a young man whose training was destined inevitably to turn him into a moral business man: either that or nothing. At Oxford Salesmanship is not taught and Religion takes the feeble form of the New Testament. The more one looks at these things the more amazing it becomes that Oxford can produce any results at all.

The effect of the comparison is heightened by the peculiar position occupied at Oxford by the professors' lectures. In the colleges of Canada and the United States the lectures are supposed to be a really necessary and useful part of the student's training. Again and again I have heard the graduates of my own college assert that they had got as much, or nearly as much, out of the lectures at college as out of athletics or the Greek letter society or the Banjo and Mandolin Club. In short, with us the lectures form a real part of the college life. At Oxford it is not so. The lectures, I understand, are given and may even be taken. But they are quite worthless and are not supposed to have anything much to do with the development of the student's mind. "The lectures here," said a Canadian student to me, "are punk." I appealed to another student to know if this was so. "I don't know whether I'd call them exactly punk," he answered, "but they're certainly rotten." Other judgments were that the lectures were of no importance: that nobody took them: that they don't matter: that you can take them if you like: that they do you no harm.

It appears further that the professors themselves are not keen on their lectures. If the lectures are called for they give them; if not, the professor's feelings are not hurt. He merely waits and rests his brain until in some later year the students call for his lectures. There are men at Oxford who have rested their brains this way for over thirty years: the accumulated brain power thus dammed up is said to be colossal.

I understand that the key to this mystery is found in the operations of the person called the tutor. It is from him, or rather with him, that the students learn all that they know: one and all are agreed on that. Yet it is a little odd to know just how he does it. "We go over to his rooms," said one student, "and he just lights a pipe and talks to us." "We sit round with him," said another, "and he simply smokes and goes over our exercises with us." From this and other evidence I gather that what an Oxford tutor does is to get a little group of students together and smoke at them. Men who have been systematically smoked at for four years turn into ripe scholars. If anybody doubts this, let him go to Oxford and he can see the thing actually in operation. A well-smoked man speaks and writes English with a grace that can be acquired in no other way.

In what was said above, I seem to have been directing criticism against the Oxford professors as such: but I have no intention of doing so. For the Oxford professor and his whole manner of being I have nothing but a profound respect. There is indeed the greatest difference between the modern up-to-date American idea of a professor and the English type. But even with us in older days, in the bygone time when such people as Henry Wadsworth Longfellow were professors, one found the English idea; a professor was supposed to be a venerable kind of person, with snow-white whiskers reaching to his stomach. He was expected to moon around the campus oblivious of the world around him. If you nodded to him he failed to see you. Of money he knew nothing; of business, far less. He was, as his trustees were proud to say of him, "a child."

On the other hand he contained within him a reservoir of learning of such depth as to be practically bottomless. None of this learning was supposed to be of any material or commercial benefit to anybody. Its use was in saving the soul and enlarging the mind.

At the head of such a group of professors was one whose beard was even whiter and longer, whose absence of mind was even still greater, and whose knowledge of money, business, and practical affairs was below zero. Him they made the president.

All this is changed in America. A university professor is now a busy, hustling person, approximating as closely to a business man as he can do it. It is on the business man that he models himself. He has a little place that he calls his "office," with a typewriter machine and a stenographer. Here he sits and dictates letters, beginning after the best business models, "in re yours of the eighth ult., would say, etc., etc." He writes these letters to students, to his fellow professors, to the president, indeed to any people who will let him write to them. The number of letters that he writes each month is duly counted and set to his credit. If he writes enough he will get a reputation as an "executive," and big things may happen to him. He may even be asked to step out of the college and take a post as an "executive" in a soap company or an advertising firm. The man, in short, is a "hustler," an "advertiser" whose highest aim is to be a "live-wire." If he is not, he will presently be dismissed, or, to use the business term, be "let go," by a board of trustees who are themselves hustlers and live-wires. As to the professor's soul, he no longer needs to think of it as being handed over along with all the others to a Board of Censors.

The American professor deals with his students according to his lights. It is his business to chase them along over a prescribed ground at a prescribed pace like a flock of sheep. They all go humping together over the hurdles with the professor chasing them with a set of "tests" and "recitations," "marks" and "attendances," the whole apparatus obviously copied from the time-clock of the business man's factory. This process is what is called "showing results." The pace set is necessarily that of the slowest, and thus results in what I have heard Mr. Edward Beatty describe as the "convoy system of education."

In my own opinion, reached after fifty-two years of profound reflection, this system contains in itself the seeds of destruction. It puts a premium on dulness and a penalty on genius. It circumscribes that latitude of mind which is the real spirit of learning. If we persist in it we shall presently find that true learning will fly away from our universities and will take rest wherever some individual and enquiring mind can mark out its path for itself.

Now the principal reason why I am led to admire Oxford is that the place is little touched as yet by the measuring of "results," and by this passion for visible and provable "efficiency." The whole system at Oxford is such as to put a premium on genius and to let mediocrity and dulness go their way. On the dull student Oxford, after a proper lapse of time, confers a degree which means nothing more than that he lived and breathed at Oxford and kept out of jail. This for many students is as much as society can expect. But for the gifted student Oxford offers great opportunities. There is no question of his hanging back till the last sheep has jumped over the fence. He need wait for no one. He may move forward as fast as he likes, following the bent of his genius. If he has in him any ability beyond that of the common herd, his tutor, interested in his studies, will smoke at him until he kindles him into a flame. For the tutor's soul is not harassed by herding dull students, with dismissal hanging by a thread over his head in the class room. The American professor has no time to be interested in a clever student. He has time to be interested in his "department," his letter-writing, his executive work, and his organizing ability and his hope of promotion to a soap factory. But with that his mind is exhausted. The student of genius merely means to him a student who gives no trouble, who passes all his "tests," and is present at all his "recitations." Such a student also, if he can be trained to be a hustler and an advertiser, will undoubtedly "make good." But beyond that the professor does not think of him. The everlasting principle of equality has inserted itself in a place where it has no right to be, and where inequality is the breath of life.

American or Canadian college trustees would be horrified at the notion of professors who apparently do not work, give few or no lectures and draw their pay merely for existing. Yet these are really the only kind of professors worth having — I mean, men who can be trusted with a vague general mission in life, with a salary guaranteed at least till their death, and a sphere of duties entrusted solely to their own consciences and the promptings of their own desires. Such men are rare, but a single one of them, when found, is worth ten "executives" and a dozen "organizers."

The excellence of Oxford, then, as I see it, lies in the peculiar vagueness of the organization of its work. It starts from the assumption that the professor is a really learned man whose sole interest lies in his own sphere: and that a student, or at least the only student with whom the university cares to reckon seriously, is a young man who desires to know. This is an ancient mediæval attitude long since buried in more up-to-date places under successive strata of compulsory education, state teaching, the democratization of knowledge and the substitution of the shadow for the substance, and the casket for the gem. No doubt, in newer places the thing has got to be so. Higher education in America flourishes chiefly as a qualification for entrance into a money-making profession, and not as a thing in itself. But in Oxford one can still see the surviving outline of a nobler type of structure and a higher inspiration.

I do not mean to say, however, that my judgment of Oxford is one undiluted stream of praise. In one respect at least I think that Ox-

ford has fallen away from the high ideals of the Middle Ages.   I refer
to the fact that it admits women students to its studies.   In the Middle Ages women were regarded with a peculiar chivalry long since
lost.   It was taken for granted that their brains were too delicately
poised to allow them to learn anything.   It was presumed that their
minds were so exquisitely hung that intellectual effort might disturb
them.   The present age has gone to the other extreme: and this is
seen nowhere more than in the crowding of women into colleges
originally designed for men.   Oxford, I regret to find, has not stood
out against this change.

To a profound scholar like myself, the presence of these young
women, many of them most attractive, flittering up and down the
streets of Oxford in their caps and gowns, is very distressing.

Who is to blame for this and how they first got in I do not know.
But I understand that they first of all built a private college of their
own close to Oxford, and then edged themselves in foot by foot.   If
this is so they only followed up the precedent of the recognized
method in use in America.   When an American college is established, the women go and build a college of their own overlooking
the grounds.   Then they put on becoming caps and gowns and stand
and look over the fence at the college athletics.   The male undergraduates, who were originally and by nature a hardy lot, were not
easily disturbed.   But inevitably some of the senior trustees fell in
love with the first year girls and became convinced that co-education
was a noble cause.   American statistics show that between 1880 and
1900 the number of trustees and senior professors who married girl
undergraduates or who wanted to do so reached a percentage of — I
forget the exact percentage; it was either a hundred or a little over.

I don't know just what happened at Oxford but presumably something of the sort took place.   In any case the women are now all
over the place.   They attend the college lectures, they row in a boat,
and they perambulate the High Street.   They are even offering a
serious competition against the men.   Last year they carried off the
ping-pong championship and took the chancellor's prize for needle-
work, while in music, cooking, and millinery the men are said to be
nowhere.

There is no doubt that unless Oxford puts the women out while
there is yet time, they will overrun the whole university.   What this

means to the progress of learning few can tell and those who know are afraid to say.

Cambridge University, I am glad to see, still sets its face sternly against this innovation. I am reluctant to count any superiority in the University of Cambridge. Having twice visited Oxford, having made the place a subject of profound study for many hours at a time, having twice addressed its undergraduates, and having stayed at the Mitre Hotel, I consider myself an Oxford man. But I must admit that Cambridge has chosen the wiser part.

Last autumn, while I was in London on my voyage of discovery, a vote was taken at Cambridge to see if the women, who have already a private college nearby, should be admitted to the university. They were triumphantly shut out; and as a fit and proper sign of enthusiasm the undergraduates went over in a body and knocked down the gates of the women's college. I know that it is a terrible thing to say that any one approved of this. All the London papers came out with headings that read — ARE OUR UNDERGRADUATES TURNING INTO BABOONS? and so on. The *Manchester Guardian* draped its pages in black and even the London *Morning Post* was afraid to take bold ground in the matter. But I do know also that there was a great deal of secret chuckling and jubilation in the London clubs. Nothing was expressed openly. The men of England have been too terrorized by the women for that. But in safe corners of the club, out of earshot of the waiters and away from casual strangers, little groups of elderly men chuckled quietly together. "Knocked down their gates, eh?" said the wicked old men to one another, and then whispered guiltily behind an uplifted hand, "Serve 'em right." Nobody dared to say anything outside. If they had some one would have got up and asked a question in the House of Commons. When this is done all England falls flat upon its face.

But for my part when I heard of the Cambridge vote, I felt as Lord Chatham did when he said in parliament, "Sir, I rejoice that America has resisted." For I have long harbored views of my own upon the higher education of women. In these days, however, it requires no little hardihood to utter a single word of criticism against it. It is like throwing half a brick through the glass roof of a conservatory. It is bound to make trouble. Let me hasten, therefore, to say that I believe most heartily in the higher education of women; in fact, the higher the better. The only question to my mind is: What is "higher education" and how do you get it? With which goes the secondary enquiry, What is a woman and is she just the same as a man? I know that it sounds a terrible thing to say in these days, but I don't believe she is.

Let me say also that when I speak of co-education I speak of what I know. I was co-educated myself some thirty-five years ago, at the very beginning of the thing. I learned my Greek alongside of a bevy of beauty on the opposite benches that mashed up the irregular verbs for us very badly. Incidentally, those girls are all married long since, and all the Greek they know now you could put under a thimble. But of that presently.

I have had further experience as well. I spent three years in the graduate school of Chicago, where co-educational girls were as thick as autumn leaves — and some thicker. And as a college professor at McGill University in Montreal, I have taught mingled classes of men and women for twenty years.

On the basis of which experience I say with assurance that the thing is a mistake and has nothing to recommend it but its relative cheapness. Let me emphasize this last point and have done with it. Co-education is of course a great economy. To teach ten men and ten women in a single class of twenty costs only half as much as to teach two classes. Where economy must rule, then, the thing has got to be. But where the discussion turns not on what is cheapest, but on what is best, then the case is entirely different.

The fundamental trouble is that men and women are different creatures, with different minds and different aptitudes and different paths in life. There is no need to raise here the question of which is superior and which is inferior (though I think, the Lord help me, I know the answer to that too). The point lies in the fact that they are different.

But the mad passion for equality has masked this obvious fact. When women began to demand, quite rightly, a share in higher education, they took for granted that they wanted the same curriculum as the men. They never stopped to ask whether their aptitudes were not in various directions higher and better than those of the men, and whether it might not be better for their sex to cultivate the things which were best suited to their minds. Let me be more explicit. In all that goes with physical and mathematical science, women, on the average, are far below the standard of men. There are, of course, exceptions. But they prove nothing. It is no use to quote to me the case of some brilliant girl who stood first in physics at Cornell. That's nothing. There is an elephant in the zoo that can count up to ten, yet I refuse to reckon myself his inferior.

Tabulated results spread over years, and the actual experience of those who teach show that in the whole domain of mathematics and physics women are outclassed. At McGill the girls of our first year have wept over their failures in elementary physics these twenty-five years. It is time that some one dried their tears and took away the subject.

But, in any case, examination tests are never the whole story. To those who know, a written examination is far from being a true criterion of capacity. It demands too much of mere memory, imitativeness, and the insidious willingness to absorb other people's ideas. Parrots and crows would do admirably in examinations. Indeed, the colleges are full of them.

But take, on the other hand, all that goes with the æsthetic side of education, with imaginative literature and the cult of beauty. Here women are, or at least ought to be, the superiors of men. Women were in primitive times the first story-tellers. They are still so at the cradle side. The original college woman was the witch, with her incantations and her prophecies and the glow of her bright imagination, and if brutal men of duller brains had not burned it out of her, she would be incanting still. To my thinking, we need more witches in the colleges and less physics.

I have seen such young witches myself — if I may keep the word: I like it — in colleges such as Wellesley in Massachusetts and Bryn Mawr in Pennsylvania, where there isn't a man alllowed within the three-mile limit. To my mind, they do infinitely better thus by themselves. They are freer, less restrained. They discuss things openly in their classes; they lift up their voices, and they speak, whereas a girl in such a place as McGill, with men all about her, sits for four years as silent as a frog full of shot.

But there is a deeper trouble still. The careers of the men and women who go to college together are necessarily different, and the preparation is all aimed at the man's career. The men are going to be lawyers, doctors, engineers, business men, and politicians. And the women are not.

There is no use pretending about it. It may sound an awful thing to say, but the women are going to be married. That is, and always has been, their career; and, what is more, they know it; and even at college, while they are studying algebra and political economy, they have their eye on it sideways all the time. The plain fact is that, after a girl has spent four years of her time and a great deal of her parents' money in equipping herself for a career that she is never going to have, the wretched creature goes and gets married, and in a few years she has forgotten which is the hypotenuse of a right-angled triangle, and she doesn't care. She has much better things to think of.

At this point some one will shriek: "But surely, even for marriage, isn't it right that a girl should have a college education?" To which I hasten to answer: most assuredly. I freely admit that a girl who knows algebra, or once knew it, is a far more charming companion and a nobler wife and mother than a girl who doesn't know x from y. But the point is this: Does the higher education that fits a man to be a lawyer also fit a person to be a wife and mother? Or, in other words, is a lawyer a wife and mother? I say he is not. Granted that a girl is to spend four years in time and four thousand dollars in money in going to college, why train her for a career that she is never going to adopt? Why not give her an education that will have a meaning and a harmony with the real life that she is to follow?

For example, suppose that during her four years every girl lucky enough to get a higher education spent at least six months of it in the training and discipline of a hospital as a nurse. There is more education and character making in that than in a whole bucketful of algebra.

But no, the woman insists on snatching her share of an education designed by Erasmus or William of Wykeham or William of Occam for the creation of scholars and lawyers; and when later on in her home there is a sudden sickness or accident, and the life or death of those nearest to her hangs upon skill and knowledge and a trained fortitude in emergency, she must needs send in all haste for a hired woman to fill the place that she herself has never learned to occupy.

But I am not here trying to elaborate a whole curriculum. I am only trying to indicate that higher education for the man is one thing, for the woman another. Nor do I deny the fact that women have got to earn their living. Their higher education must enable them to do that. They cannot all marry on their graduation day. But that is no great matter. No scheme of education that any one is likely to devise will fail in this respect.

The positions that they hold as teachers or civil servants they would fill all the better if their education were fitted to their wants.

Some few, a small minority, really and truly "have a career" — husbandless and childless — in which the sacrifice is great and the honor to them, perhaps, all the higher. And others no doubt dream of a career in which a husband and a group of blossoming children are carried as an appendage to a busy life at the bar or on the platform. But all such are the mere minority, so small as to make no difference to the general argument.

But there — I have written quite enough to make plenty of trouble except perhaps at Cambridge University. So I return with relief to my general study of Oxford. Viewing the situation as a whole, I am led then to the conclusion that there must be something in the life of Oxford itself that makes for higher learning. Smoked at by his tutor, fed in Henry VIII's kitchen, and sleeping in a tangle of ivy, the student evidently gets something not easily obtained in America. And the more I reflect on the matter the more I am convinced that it is the sleeping in the ivy that does it. How different it is from student life as I remember it!

When I was a student at the University of Toronto thirty years ago, I lived — from start to finish — in seventeen different boarding houses. As far as I am aware these houses have not, or not yet, been marked with tablets. But they are still to be found in the vicinity of McCaul and Darcy, and St. Patrick Streets. Any one who doubts the truth of what I have to say may go and look at them.

I was not alone in the nomadic life that I led. There were hundreds of us drifting about in this fashion from one melancholy habitation to another. We lived as a rule two or three in a house, sometimes alone. We dined in the basement. We always had beef, done up in some way after it was dead, and there were always soda biscuits on the table. They used to have a brand of soda biscuits in those days in the Toronto boarding houses that I have not seen since.

They were better than dog biscuits but with not so much snap. My contemporaries will all remember them. A great many of the leading barristers and professional men of Toronto were fed on them.

In the life we led we had practically no opportunities for association on a large scale, no common rooms, no reading rooms, nothing. We never saw the magazines — personally I didn't even know the names of them. The only interchange of ideas we ever got was by going over to the Caer Howell Hotel on University Avenue and interchanging them there.

I mention these melancholy details not for their own sake but merely to emphasize the point that when I speak of students' dormitories, and the larger life which they offer, I speak of what I know.

If we had had at Toronto, when I was a student, the kind of dormitories and dormitory life that they have at Oxford, I don't think I would ever have graduated. I'd have been there still. The trouble is that the universities on our Continent are only just waking up to the idea of what a university should mean. They were, very largely, instituted and organized with the idea that a university was a place where young men were sent to absorb the contents of books and to listen to lectures in the class rooms. The student was pictured as a pallid creature, burning what was called the "midnight oil," his wan face bent over his desk. If you wanted to do something for him you gave him a book: if you wanted to do something really large on his behalf you gave him a whole basketful of them. If you wanted to go still further and be a benefactor to the college at large, you endowed a competitive scholarship and set two or more pallid students working themselves to death to get it.

The real thing for the student is the life and environment that surrounds him. All that he really learns he learns, in a sense, by the active operation of his own intellect and not as the passive recipient of lectures. And for this active operation what he really needs most is the continued and intimate contact with his fellows. Students must live together and eat together, talk and smoke together. Experience shows that that is how their minds really grow. And they must live together in a rational and comfortable way. They must eat in a big dining room or hall, with oak beams across the ceiling, and the stained glass in the windows, and with a shield or tablet here or there upon the wall, to remind them between times of the men who went before them and left a name worthy of the memory of the college. If a student is to get from his college what it ought to give him, a college dormitory, with the life in common that it brings, is his absolute right. A university that fails to give it to him is cheating him.

If I were founding a university — and I say it with all the seriousness of which I am capable — I would found first a smoking room; then when I had a little more money in hand I would found a dormitory; then after that, or more probably with it, a decent reading room and a library. After that, if I still had money over that I couldn't use, I would hire a professor and get some text books.

This chapter has sounded in the most part like a continuous eulogy of Oxford with but little in favor of our American colleges. I turn therefore with pleasure to the more congenial task of showing what is wrong with Oxford and with the English university system generally, and the aspect in which our American universities far excel the British.

The point is that Henry VIII is dead. The English are so proud of what Henry VIII and the benefactors of earlier centuries did for the universities that they forget the present. There is little or nothing in England to compare with the magnificent generosity of individuals, provinces and states, which is building up the colleges of the United States and Canada. There used to be. But by some strange confusion of thought the English people admire the noble gifts of Cardinal Wolsey and Henry VIII and Queen Margaret, and do not realize that the Carnegies and Rockefellers and the William Macdonalds are the Cardinal Wolseys of to-day. The University of Chicago was founded upon oil. McGill University rests largely on a basis of tobacco. In America the world of commerce and business levies on itself a noble tribute in favor of the higher learning. In England, with a few conspicuous exceptions, such as that at Bristol, there is little of the sort. The feudal families are content with what their remote ancestors have done: they do not try to emulate it in any great degree.

In the long run this must count. Of all the various reforms that are talked of at Oxford, and of all the imitations of American methods that are suggested, the only one worth while, to my thinking, is to capture a few millionaires, give them honorary degrees at a million pounds sterling apiece, and tell them to imagine that they are Henry the Eighth.   I give Oxford warning that if this is not done the place will not last another two centuries.

THE COMEDY OF LEADERSHIP
By CHRISTIAN GAUSS

Christian Gauss (1878–), Dean of the College at Princeton University, is well-known as a lecturer, editor, and writer. Since graduating from the University of Michigan in 1898, he has given much time to study, both in this country and abroad, and has been a teacher of Romance languages, first at his alma mater, later at Lehigh University, and finally at Princeton. He is the author of: "Through College on Nothing a Year" (1915), "Why We Went to War" (1918), and has compiled, translated, or edited numerous other volumes.

IN history, certain misleading phrases, like certain misguided individuals, have done incalculable harm. "The king can do no wrong" was such a phrase. The notion of natural rights as typified in "The world owes me a living" belongs in the same dismal category. They forestall investigation. Man's indolent habit grants such phrases long life. You do not need to pursue a tantalizing line of thought farther after you have found one. Once such a phrase has clicked into the receptive mind, it is hard to dislodge it. An aphorism may be untrue, but it is always labor-saving. It economizes effort, for it is difficult with legitimate arguments to convince a persistent, hard-headed opponent, while it is easy, especially in the presence of a crowd, to knock him down with a slogan. It is worth our while in this connection to examine some of these catchwords which have recently become popular in our discussions of higher education.

Not very long ago one of our largest American universities sent out a questionnaire to about one hundred and fifty colleges in an effort to determine what qualifications, if any, besides previous intellectual training, they were demanding of candidates for entrance. Most of these colleges were not attempting to restrict enrollment, yet fifty of them replied that men were admitted not only on the basis of their knowledge of so-called entrance subjects but that qualities of leadership also were required.

When an American professor is called upon to recommend a candidate for one of the Rhodes scholarships at Oxford, he is requested to testify not only to the candidate's scholarship and to his manly qualities but also to his possession of these same qualities of leadership. I confess I have always been somewhat embarrassed by this opposition which is being set up in the colleges between their good scholars and their leaders. It used to be assumed that a man who stood at the head of his class was a leader. Thirty or forty years ago we did not embarrass a lad by calling him this big name, but we expected most from the men who, in college, had learned most about physics or chemistry or Latin or mathematics or medicine or law. If a student had done this, we thought he was qualified to take his place in the world. Now we expect something quite different, and in addition to or in default of scholarly aptitude the colleges are accepting something else as just as good, or possibly a little better.

It is quite proper that we should require of candidates for higher education something more than mere book learning. President Little, of the University of Michigan, made it plain not very long ago that in his opinion the man who had received an education from the state owed something to the state in return. Public education, an education obtained at the expense of the public, like public office, is a public trust. No criminal is so dangerous as an educated criminal. It is for this reason that from time immemorial colleges have demanded of candidates for admission a certificate of good character. In these piping times of ours we are, however, setting up another hurdle. We are requiring in addition evidence of leadership.

There is an initial difficulty about all this, but then the course of true education never did run smooth. When the prospective freshman knocks at the gate it is a simple matter for the college to discover whether he knows any Latin or algebra or English or history. The college sets him an examination and reads the answers. In most cases they tell the story. A certificate from the principal of the school from which the boy comes will on this score also provide reliable testimony. Character and leadership are, however, more difficult to discover. It is an open secret to all college officials that every candidate has a character. He can in any case bring a written one. Everybody's son, when his parent is seeking admission for him, has a good character. Almost every school graduate, according to his head master or principal, has at least a passable one, or else of course the school would not have granted him its diploma.

Character is something which you must discover after the applicant has entered college. What the director of admissions does not know will not hurt the candidate. It is occasionally regrettable that the college did not know in time how unformed the character of their applicant was. They might have done something to improve it instead of later having to dismiss him as hopeless. I have never yet found a college reprobate who had to be dismissed for serious delinquency who had not been able to bring a thoroughly creditable certificate of character — often one signed by a clergyman.

Now no one will deny that qualities of leadership also are an asset. They are, however, at sixteen or eighteen equally difficult to discover. You cannot ask an applicant point-blank, "Are you a leader?" He is usually a modest chap and would be embarrassed. His parents, when forced to testify, feel no such embarrassment. They often answer the question even if it is not put to them, and they all answer it in precisely the same way. Every mother's son is a leader. Where the applicant is called upon to give references, he almost never names his own friends and school classmates who know him well, but older friends of his parents who do not. They know only the family. Usually it is a minister, a prominent business man, or an alumnus.

After reading thousands of such testimonials, directors of admission and entrance committees have on almost unanimous testimony sadly reached the conclusion that the son of everybody's friend is also a leader. This is gratifying to our American pride, but hardly useful in a selective process. Where the writer of such a letter leaves any possibility of doubt, it is usually because he admits — by implication — that he does not know the applicant. In such cases he concentrates upon the candidate's father and leaves no doubt that the father is a leader in his community.

The attempt to determine aptitude for college on the basis of qualities of leadership has, on the whole, not been a success. Leaders at the age of sixteen have become altogether too common. They are a drug on the academic market. But many of the colleges are unwilling to let well enough alone, and they are insisting not only that their youthful candidates be leaders when they enter college but they have been telling these same young men that it is the primary purpose of the college to develop these qualities of leadership still farther and so make them irresistible.

A revolt which took place in one of the smaller colleges of the East is still fresh in the minds of many. Some of the undergraduates went out on strike. They were insisting that certain restraints be removed and that responsibilities which had always rested upon the faculty be devolved upon the students. There was even talk of their deciding what subjects should be taught and who should teach them. When, some time after the hubbub, I met the very able president of this college I was astonished to find how coolly he took all this.

"You know," he explained, rather in sorrow than in anger, "it is all our own fault. We have brought this upon ourselves. We have been telling young men and boys for so many years, at every high school and college commencement, 'You are the hope of the future, the leaders of the nation,' that they are beginning to take us at our word. They wish to exercise those talents for leadership which we have so excessively attributed to them."

A comparison of the statements made by the founders of some of our oldest American colleges with the statements of some of their recent successors will indicate quite clearly the change which has come over this country in its attitude toward the function of higher education. The preamble to the charter of Harvard College, bearing the date May 31, 1650, reads:

Whereas, through the good hand of God, many well-devoted persons have been, and daily are, moved and stirred up to give and bestow sundry gifts . . . for the advancement of all good literature, arts, and sciences in Harvard College . . . and all other necessary provisions that may conduce to the education of the English and Indian youth of this country in knowledge and godliness.

Yale was founded in 1701 when the general assembly of the colony granted a charter for the foundation of a collegiate school whose purpose was to prepare young men for service "in Church & Civil State."

At William and Mary the same ends were in view. Princeton had been founded, so the old document of 1748 tells us, "For the Benefit of the Inhabitants of the said province" and because "of the great Necessity of coming into some Method for encouraging and promoting a learned Education of our Youth in New Jersey."

The Dartmouth charter of 1769 makes it plain that the founders were concerned

For the education and instruction of youths of the Indian tribes in this land in reading, writing, and all parts of learning, which shall appear necessary and expedient, for civilizing and christianizing the children of pagans, as well as in all liberal arts and sciences, and also of English youths, and any others.

It will be found that the word "leadership" is strikingly absent from these sober, old-fashioned documents; yet in those days the percentage of the population that went to the colleges was severely restricted by the conditions of pioneer life. I do not believe that the phrase will be found in the acts creating the older state universities. It is different in many of the colleges of recent foundation. All must now have a college training. The prospectus of a women's college in the South tells us:

In order to meet the needs of the present day every young woman should, if possible, receive a thorough education.

A struggling college in the Central South prints the following statement of its educational ideals:

We therefore favor the policy of selecting carefully all students, this selection to be made on the basis of moral character, intellectual fitness and preparation, qualities of leadership.

A statement by the president of a recently founded college in the far Northwest carries us into the heart of the new dispensation:

The study of many catalogs will reveal the fact that certain courses and requirements are considered fundamental to the accomplishment of the task of higher education in preparing leadership.

In a Central Western college catalogue we find:

A great educational program is necessary for any people who would contribute their part in leadership and power.

In the Middle West also this rich promise is held out, and a college there not only "offers a most unique opportunity for the development of community leadership" but it conducts seminar courses in "Christian leadership" as well. It would be monotonous to multiply such quotations which would merely ring in the changes on this newfangled word now heard on all sides in academic circles.

At an educational convention not very long ago I enjoyed the privilege of sitting beside a man long recognized as a distinguished figure in higher education in this country. The word "leadership" had been used in some of the discussions. He was profoundly discouraged and I tried feebly to cheer him, but he closed the conversation with the remark: "We have inflated higher education in this country to such a point that it is an almost worthless currency. The first thing we must do is to deflate it and put it back upon a sound-money basis."

My elderly friend dated from an earlier time and he evidently had been unable to adjust himself to present conditions. It is probable that he was more pessimistic than the situation warrants. But it is only fair to him to say that he was not thinking primarily of the wastage of hard-earned dollars and cents.

The sums of money involved in higher education are, to be sure, considerable. The endowments contributed for this purpose in the United States amount to $1,000,000,000, and the physical plants of the universities are worth as much more. Outside of what is paid for board and room, the annual cost of conducting these institutions amounts to $300,000,000. It is perfectly proper therefore to ask the question: "Are we getting our money's worth?" And men in the business of education should be prepared to answer it.

Personally, I do not believe that the sums spent for higher education in this country are too large. They are not too large, for instance, if we use as a basis of comparison the sums spent annually for naval or military purposes. I believe all reasonable men, however, are convinced that all these sums are not spent as wisely as might be. However that may stand, before the process of financial deflation and readjustment can begin we must eliminate from contemporary discussion of higher education some of these bulging phrases.

First of all, we should recognize frankly that the percentage of our population to which we are attempting to give higher education is immensely larger than it is in the most highly civilized and educationally best organized European countries. In 1925, Great Britain, with a population of 43,000,000, had about 46,000 men enrolled in its institutions of higher learning. Germany, with 63,000,000, had 68,000 such students. France, with 40,000,000 in 1924, had 53,000 aspirants to higher education. At the same time in the United States, with 117,000,000, we had 664,266; that is, with a population twice that of Germany, which has always been keenly interested in scholarship, we in this country had ten times as many college students.

It is true that as compared with Europe we are exceedingly prosperous. Financially speaking, more of our young men and women can afford to spend four years in college. But the financial status of a young man or of his family should not be the only condition which determines his matriculation. In a democracy it should be possible for any boy to go to college no matter how poor or how rich. Whether poor or rich, he should be allowed to go, however, only in case higher education of this type will be good for him and good for the community at large.

Two years ago a distinguished European scientist and professor spent some months in our country making a survey of our colleges and universities. He was deeply impressed. Before he left he stated his conclusions on American higher education as follows:

> In your country you teach everything, even those things which involve almost no theory and are largely matters of experience and practice. In some of your colleges I found that you teach cement mixing, the packing of eggs and fruit, ice-cream making, sewing and dressmaking. You even teach teaching, and have great schools of education or pedagogy. You have the best equipped and most magnificent newspaper offices in the world. From my personal experience, I know also that you have the most enterprising newspaper men, yet you teach journalism in the colleges.
>
> In one respect, I cannot understand the logic of your position. Here in America you had developed in the school of experience and without formal courses the ablest business men and captains of industry in the world. You were not satisfied. Now you have added to your colleges great schools of business and commerce. You are more idealistic than we are. You have a more naïve faith in education than we have in Europe.

For the time being let us merely note that here again a distinguished European observer has tagged us with the adjective "idealistic." He did not necessarily intend it as a compliment. Shall we take it as such?

What our European critic told us about our educating for business is probably true also of our newer notion of education for leadership. We were blessed by excellent leaders in this country before the colleges ever dreamed of making it their business to prepare them. Washington was such a leader, and so was Lincoln. The majority of our great American artists — painters like George Inness and

Winslow Homer — had not enjoyed the possibly doubtful benefit, in their case, of academic training. It has been possible for men like Mark Twain, Walt Whitman, and Sherwood Anderson to succeed even in literature without it, just as it has been possible for the Wright brothers, for Henry Ford, and Edison to achieve a quite reasonable degree of success in invention and industry. In the days of our prosperity, however, we are trying to make an essentially difficult process easier, and we enregiment our young men for leadership by enrolling them in the colleges.

"Come to us," the college says to the eager lad, "and we will make you a leader. You will have four years of college life thrown in."

Is it any wonder that more than 700,000 of them are now in the colleges and that too large a percentage are disappointed and unhappy failures? We have overdone it. We have made it all too easy and promising. President Angell, of Yale, put the case very forcibly before the superintendents of schools in his address before the National Education Association at its recent meeting in Boston:

> The whole political-educational conception under which we are working is too largely that a college or university education is open at little or no cost to any one of moderate capacity and still more moderate powers of application. There is little or no sense of privilege about it and practically no sense of obligation. Merely to multiply the number of college-trained youths who go back into the community with no vivid feeling of duty to capitalize for the benefit of the commonwealth the training they have received is quite as likely to prove a curse as a blessing for the state.

In the meantime the movement to found more and more junior colleges proceeds unabated, while the older institutions attempt to stem the tide by processes of selective admission. To ask for qualities of leadership does not, however, seem to have helped. The colleges which have tried it are beginning to develop a healthy skepticism.

Some months ago I stopped in to visit a friend who is the dean of a college which several years ago was forced to restrict its enrollment rather drastically. It, too, had insisted that its youthful applicants possess qualities of leadership. It was plain to me that I was intruding upon one of his busier days. The benches in front of his office were crowded with unhappy young men. A number of them were particularly well set up — good football or crew material. Some of them would have made excellent cowboys, ranchers, or mounted policemen, but their disconsolate faces were those of the academically damned. All hope had left them.

My friend apologized for being so busy and explained that the college had just ended its mid-year examinations a week before.

"You see, I am calling in my failures. I am dismissing my leaders." He smiled sadly when he said this. I smiled, too, though I believe I was not expected to, for he continued earnestly: "You know, it is no laughing matter. Some of our greatest leaders are our poorest students."

The significance of this remark will be evident to any one who ponders the question: Who are the leaders at the age of sixteen? It will be even plainer if he will begin a little lower in the scale and ask: Who are the leaders at five and six?

One of the directors of a great educational foundation threw an unexpected light on this subject for me in a recent conversation. During the summer months he had been living in a cottage on the seashore and commuting to his office. Every morning and evening he met the daughter of his neighbor. She was a blue-eyed, bright-faced child, still so young that her hair had not yet been bobbed, but hung loose above her shoulders. One night on his return he met her with her hair plaited into two hard straw-colored, blue-ribboned little pigtails. She apparently expected some comment, and he complimented her upon her grown-up appearance.

"Yes," she answered proudly, "I'm five years old. My brother's seven, and what's more, he wears suspenders."

Evidently to age five an added two years, with their necessary accouterments, means a great deal.

A boy's perspective changes, to be sure, as he passes into his teens; but to the lad of fourteen his classmate of sixteen still possesses a very considerable advantage, particularly if he is big and strong and proficient in athletics. The older boys in school are for this reason most likely to be the leaders.

Now these oldest members of any class are very often those least proficient in their studies. That is why they have fallen behind. But in a community of American youth, the boy who carries himself well, who is a good pitcher, fullback, or hurdler, will be more looked up to by his fellows than the younger student who spends most of his time over his books and leads his class in Latin or algebra.

I believe it is fair to say that the class officers in freshman classes in college are chosen in overwhelming majority from the members of the football squad. This is neither vicious nor unnatural, but it results often in the situation to which my unhappy colleague had called attention. Even if we did succeed in obtaining those regarded as leaders in the high schools, we should not necessarily be getting the candidates best suited to profit by higher education.

I am not attempting to lay down here what the proper qualifications for admission to college should be. I do not believe that they should be exclusively scholastic. There should be evidence, if a man is to be educated at the expense of others, that such education will redound to the benefit of his fellows. What I wish to show here is that the colleges at present are suffering from an overemphasis upon the idea of leadership, and that a man of twenty-two who goes back to his community with an exaggerated confidence in his ability as a leader will be of very little use to himself and of none to the community.

I believe that some of the problems in the colleges to-day are the result of this overemphasis. Youth has ever been eager and enthusiastic, and therefore restless. They have always found it difficult even in the very good old times to be entirely at ease and happy under the instruction of their elders in the cage of a college. This restlessness has increased with the promulgation of the notion of leadership by the colleges themselves. Occasionally it results in unhappiness. I am sure many college officials have been nonplused by amusing if regrettable misunderstandings like one in which I became involved not many weeks ago.

An undergraduate, a junior in college, a fair but not a brilliant student, hard-working, possibly a shade too solemn for one so young, used to drop in to see me in the late afternoons. He had discussed with me previously college problems in general and some of his own difficulties with his work. He came in to see me the other day, and I thought this visit would be somewhat on the same order.

He threw me off completely by asking me pointblank, "Do you think a father should send his son to college?"

That was where I lost him. I did not catch his drift, and so I spoiled it all by asking, "Whose son are you thinking of?"

"Of course," he answered, in a hurt but matter-of-fact way, "I was thinking of my own son — when I have one."

My mistake lay in forgetting that nowadays, with all this pressure, a lad of eighteen is often no longer a boy. At the pace we are going he has sometimes already become an expectant parent. My young friend was really in deep trouble. Sensitive, shy, serious, he was really excellent college material, yet he was beginning to be convinced that he was a failure. With only a year and a half still to go, his rigorous honesty would not allow him to believe that he was in any sense a leader.

As is often the case with the troubles of boys in college, his difficulty came from his home. He had been made to feel his responsibilities too heavily ever to be a good fellow or popular. His mother was forever inquiring as to whether he had been elected to this or that. It was not enough for her that he was behaving himself admirably and spending more time than usual upon his work. She had wanted him to make a good club. I am sure she would have increased his allowance if he had been elected manager of the band or member of the banjo club or the Nightriders. She wanted him to be a leader. He knew he was not, and under the pressure of scant recognition from more buoyantly spirited undergraduates and the continuing disappointments and implied reproaches at home, he wished to throw up the academic sponge and hand in his resignation.

Fortunately, however, most undergraduates of the present are thicker-skinned. Upon such the everlasting talk of leadership at high-school and college commencements makes little impression. There is so much nonsense in the air nowadays that they have established a toleration to it. They can resist a good deal of it, even where it comes, as in this case, from above. They often have more common sense than their elders. They know that a leader is one who has followers. The 2,000, 5,000, or 10,000 men in any one college cannot all be leaders. Only the straggling faculty would be left to follow them. Even this country, which has less than 30,000 names in *Who's Who*, cannot make a place for the 700,000 reputed leaders now in the colleges, and where would we be if all these leaders ever started to march in different directions?

At a critical period in the history of higher education in America, when we were not quite certain of what the aim of the college should be, we invented the labor-saving but mischievous phrase "education for leadership." It is, of course, of the highest importance that in a democracy there should be men of sterling character to whom their fellows will look for guidance, but such character and such leadership are and must always be the by-products of useful and devoted lives.

A boy who gives himself whole-heartedly to the round of his daily duties with the idea of performing them as well as he possibly can will develop those qualities of manliness, persistence, and loyalty which are the basis of character. On the other hand, a boy who is too much concerned with developing his talents for leadership often regards his humdrum work in college or later in the office as secondary, and neglects the immediate and sometimes uninviting task before him. The young man in college who, regardless of what his fellows may think of him, devotes himself to the study of chemistry with the intention of penetrating the mysteries of Nature will, after very many long years, perhaps when he is fifty, be recognized by other chemists as a leader. He may become a leader only if he forgets all about leadership and tries merely to make of himself a good chemist. So it will be with any man who earnestly studies English or mathematics or medicine, or any other subject for its own sake.

With regard to leadership, it is strikingly true that he who loses his life shall save it. We have put the cart before the horse and must unhitch and start over again. We must begin the necessary process of deflating higher education. One of our first steps, if we are to get back upon a sound-money basis, will be to get rid of this unfortunate and often pernicious nonsense about leadership.

THE CO-EDS: GOD BLESS THEM!

By BERNARD De VOTO

*Bernard De Voto (1897–   ) received his A.B. from Harvard in 1920.
He served as an officer in the United States Army in 1917 and 1918, and
was, from 1922 to 1927, on the faculty of Northwestern University. He
is now a writer. Besides his contributions to many magazines, he has
written three novels, the last, "The House of Sun-Goes-Down," being
published in 1928. He has produced, too, a history, "The Taming
of the Frontier" (1925), and a textbook, "The Writer's Handbook"
(1927), other writers collaborating in both these works.*

NOT long ago a man with whom I had roomed at college came
to visit me and during his stay expressed a desire to observe me
perform as a teacher. The motive that prompted him was no doubt
malicious, but it was quite forgotten before he had sat through his
first class. For he and I had gone to one of those monastic Eastern
colleges where few women ever get past the visitors' gallery at the
commons, and now for the first time he was seeing co-education. I
expected him to say something appropriate about the lecture I delivered, for I had talked about Coleridge, and Professor Lowes's book
was hot from the press; but he seemed to have forgotten that I had
been any part of the hour's diversion. As we strolled across the
campus, he tried vigorously to reduce to order the confusion that his
experience had brought him.

The first coherent idea that he voiced was, "Good Lord! I was
expecting a college, not a sample room. That front row! It looked
like the hosiery window at a spring opening or the finale of a Vanities
first act. What do you teach 'em, dancing?"

A moment later, "Educational patter from the little ash-blonde:
'Does a poet know what he is writing or does he just tap the subconscious?' That's what happens when you expose a predestinate
chocolate-dipper to Psych A."

And then, "How can a man teach with a roomful of beautiful girls
listening to him? Do you expect the men to keep their minds on
Coleridge? And you can't be ass enough to want girls who look like
that to handicap themselves with an education."

Later still he settled matters to his satisfaction. "Don't tell me you even try to teach 'em anything. You've got a living to make, and you merely elect to make it talking about Coleridge to a chorus of ravishing girls who all their life long will continue to associate Coleridge with henna and *Narcisse Noir,* and who merely use your classroom as a convenient place to pry luncheon-dates out of susceptible males. It's an old delusion that you can educate women. You're not fool enough to think that even one of that ballet has any idea that Coleridge wrote poetry, or what poetry is, or gives a damn, anyway. Sure! I saw 'em putting down pages of notes. You'll give them A when they come back to you on the final."

It was all very amusing. It reminded me forcibly of the day, some five years before, when I faced my first co-educational class. The offer of the position had reached me on a desert ranch, where I was working for my board and where even the pittance the Dean offered me seemed munificent. I traveled two thousand miles and bolted from the train-shed directly to a room containing thirty-five freshmen who were waiting to be told what to do for their first college assignment. I was on the rostrum before I fully realized that Atlantis was, after all, a co-educational university; and the sight of "that front row," crammed with new fall creations and shiny with French-nude stockings, appalled me. For the moment I wished myself back in the Idaho desert, untempted by an instructor's salary fully half as large as a milkman's, eating mutton three times a day, and rejoicing in the only beard I have ever owned. I was not long from that Eastern college, you see, and I knew all about the higher education of women. I knew that Middle-Western universities were contemptible from the point of view of scholarship (the knowledge had been confirmed by my being hired to teach at one). I knew that girls went to such places primarily to find husbands who didn't live in the old home town. I knew, furthermore, that women didn't belong to the class of *educabilia,* which included in fact only a distressingly small percentage of males. And I knew, finally, that most women didn't pretend to take education seriously and that the few who did were not only æsthetic atrocities, but also the most saddening numskulls to be encountered anywhere by a vigorous mind.

To be sure, several of the graduate schools of my own university admitted women; and there was a regulation whereby students of a neighboring women's college might very occasionally enter an under-

graduate course.   That I had been in a philosophy course which one
of these rare specimens attended probably contributed to my idea of
her sex's mentality.   She was so homely that we called her "The
Pure Reason," and she was eternally interrupting the professor's
lecture, no matter what it concerned, with the stern question, "Is
that reconcilable with Kant?"   She was miserable whenever his
language descended to intelligibility, and her distress at his mild,
unworldly witticisms so saddened him that he gave them up altogether.

I could not see, after a desperate glance, anything corresponding
to "The Pure Reason" in my first class.   Quite the contrary.   There
were fully as many men as women in that class, but I was not aware
of them.   I could see only women, and they were all staggeringly
beautiful.   It could not be possible that such stunning girls would
even pretend to take an interest in intellectual matters.   They were
undoubtedly a frivolous and giddy crew who would ogle me out of
passing grades and coax me into letting them go free of assignments,
and chatter and make up their faces during my most solemn flights.
The room seemed oppressive with femininity, and I was quite sure
that such an atmosphere, however favorable it might be to nature's
designs for the perpetuation of the race, was frost and blight and
mildew to that orderly discipline of the mind which I considered
education.

Well, one learns, and I wonder now that in the moment of shock
I did not recall the empirical fact that nine tenths of the truly wise
people I had known were women.   Even if I had, at that stage I
should doubtless have contended that wisdom was something apart
from education, some derivative from the nebulous function which
is called intuition.

Before long, however, I began to realize that not all my pupils
were beautiful, and with that first discrimination began a series of
readjustments which quite reversed most of my preconceptions.
The whole point of this article, which is a recantation, is my discovery that the greater part of the education which the modern
college manages to achieve, in the intervals between endowment
campaigns, football championships, and psychological survey, is
appropriated by the very sex who presumably do not belong to the
educabilia at all.

The women, these scatterbrained co-eds, are better material for education than the men and readier at acquiring it, and are also the chief hope for the preservation of the values which were long declared to be the ideals of liberal education.

Here I must make one or two stipulations. It must be understood that I speak entirely in generalizations, having no space to take account of exceptions, and that I generalize about the average student, not the exceptional one. To judge the colleges on the basis of the superior student — two per cent of the enrollment — would be foolish, and to attempt a differentiation between superior men and superior women would be more foolish still. Above a certain level of intelligence there seems to be little fundamental difference between the sexes, so far as their work in college is concerned. The tendencies with which I am now concerned are those of the mass, the undistinguished young folk who are the backbone of the colleges; and I am speaking of the tendency, not of any given individual who may oppose it. It must also be understood that I am generalizing from my own experience. I have checked it so far as possible by the experience of others, but without much finality on either side. A publicly expressed opinion on this subject is rare, since it exposes one to the headlines and editorials of the press, the recriminations of a dean who is harassed by officious associations, and an avalanche of letters from the nation's cranks. It is easier to get a privately expressed opinion but it is also more likely to be conditioned by the accidents of the week. The Kappa Alpha weeper may have cried Professor Smith out of a passing mark for a sister half an hour before he defies the whole University Club to find him one co-ed who ever did a lick of work. Or Professor Smith may have married his brightest senior and so wedded an idea that the co-eds, as a sex, comprise the upper three fourths of the intellectual scale, to the complete exclusion of the men.

The first observation is that the old debate is over, and the old problem of what aim a college education should have, if not solved, is at least settled forevermore. Even ten years ago the battle between the humanists on the one hand and the vocationalists on the other was still vigorous. Its outcome though unmistakable was not yet achieved, and the dwindling but vigorous defenders of liberal education showed no signs of panic. To-day, after ten years that have telescoped a century of evolution and have left the American colleges completely bewildered, hardly even the tradition survives. Not eight colleges in the country even pretend to champion the old ideals or to adapt them to post-war problems; and of those that do pretend, the loudest-voiced has done more to injure the cause than any dozen of its most Rotarian rivals.

By and large, the American college is now a training-school. It is engaged in preparing its students for their vocations. It is a feeder for the professional schools, on the one hand, and for business, on the other. Primarily it provides training for salesmanship. In the mass, young men come to college to learn how to sell. In the mass, they are not interested in the kind of education that is generally called liberal — or humanistic or cultural or intellectual. The man who comes to college to-day is not there to grow in wisdom, or to invite the truth to make him free, to realize his fullest intellectual possibilities, to learn the best that has been said and thought, or to fit himself to any other of the mottoes carved above his college gates. He is there to get through the prerequisites of a professional school or of business. In either case he is righteously intolerant of all flapdoodle whatsoever that does not contribute directly to the foreseen end. Anything which undertakes to make him more efficient he will embrace with as much enthusiasm as he has left over from "activities" which are the organized hokum of college life. Anything else — be it anthropology or zoölogy or any elective in between — he will resent and actively condemn. He'll be damned if he's got time to waste on wisdom — or knowledge — or truth and beauty — or cultural development — or individuality — or any of the other matters with which the colleges used to be concerned.

One who speaks to the college man of a different kind of education meets not the derision his opponents might have cast on him before the War, but an incomprehension, a complete failure to understand his language that is a thousand times more conclusive. Such an outcome was inevitable from the moment that the higher education became democratic, and its original momentum dates from the establishment of State-supported universities. But whereas, in spite of its democratic power, the really powerful authorities were opposed to the development as late as 1917, those same authorities have been since then its most enthusiastic leaders. Where the ideals of liberal education still survive they are cherished by aging and solitary men who can never head an educational body or sit on a president's throne. The administrations have gone over wholly to the popular cause. Recently the President of one of our largest universities said flatly to his faculty, "The students are our customers and we must give them what they want." His language was more forthright than that of most of his peers, who adopt the terminology of Service, but unquestionably he expressed the philosophy of most of them. With this policy in the throne-room the faculties in general whoop up the process. Ask any college teacher which departments have their budgets ratified without a murmur of complaint. Ask any department-head what courses he must stress to the trustees who guard the purse-strings. Ask any one what the dominant ideas of his campus are and what professors are picked for the key-positions in the faculty committees. The colleges have gone out to give the student what he wants. And what he wants may be defined as courses that are thought to provide training in efficient salesmanship.

This is, however, education from the point of view of men. The women — those lovely co-eds whose stockings so disturbed my friend — are another matter. In the mass, they see no need to prepare themselves for law or dentistry and feel no call to become expert at selling. Their lives still have room for the qualities that education once dealt with. They have time for wisdom — and knowledge — and truth and beauty — and cultural development — and individuality. That is why they are so significant for the future if society has any use for liberal education and expects the colleges to have anything to do with it.

The canons of liberal education — if I correctly interpret its champions — may be summarized as receptiveness to new ideas, freedom from prejudice or other emotional bias, insistence on factual or logical demonstration of everything presented as truth, ability to distinguish between appearance and reality developed somewhat beyond the naïve faith of the uneducated, refusal to accept authority or tradition as final, and skepticism of the fads, propagandas, and panaceas that may be called the patent medicines of the mind. To abbreviate some centuries of definition still further,

the liberally educated man is supposed to possess an intelligently dis-
criminating mind.   The avenues by which this desirable possession
may be acquired need not be scrutinized here.   It suffices to remember what attributes have been considered the desiderata of liberal
education and to estimate their relative distribution between the
sexes in the colleges of to-day.

According to ancient theory, women's judgment is swayed by
emotional considerations to a far greater extent than that of men.
The daily routine in the colleges quite controverts the theory.   It is
the men, for instance, who die for dear old Rutgers.   Here at Atlantis we have just emerged from a period of athletic failure which has
given me an excellent chance to observe the passions in their natural
state.   I have seen many men in tears because the football employees
of Utopia, that university of poltroons, had walloped our own; but I
have never seen a co-ed leaving the stadium other than dry-eyed.
The bales of themes that have rolled in upon me demanding a sterner
athletic policy, bigger salaries for bigger fullbacks, in order to vin-
dicate Atlantis as the best college in the world, have been without
exception the work of men.   The idea that the worth of a college is
to be judged by the success of its football team is a man's idea.   So
is the idea that Atlantis is the best college in the world.   A man is
not satisfied, it seems, unless he can assure himself and the world at
large that the college he attends is clearly superior to all others: a
co-ed does not bother her mind with such infantile rationalizations.

As with football and world-leadership, so with the other functions
of the college.   Some years ago a newspaper, during a dearth of excitement, discovered the foul taproot of Bolshevism and the dead
hand of Lenin (its own phrases) in an Epworth League at Atlantis.
The organization that promptly had itself photographed kissing the
Stars and Stripes, to prove Atlantis free of that moral plague, was a
fraternity, not a sorority.   The parade of patriotic youth carrying
posters that damned all Bolshevists to the American Legion was
entirely male.   Male, too, were the petitions praying the President
to redeem Atlantis before the world by expelling the Epworth
League — they originated and circulated among the fraternities.
So jingoism widens out: the co-eds think, the men throb.   It is not
enough that Atlantis is the world's-champion university with the
loveliest campus and the most modern gadgets from the school of

education.   America, as the nation that is graced by Atlantis, must necessarily be immaculate, inimitable, and in all ways supreme.

Every year passionate organizations in the colleges pass hundreds of resolutions condemning the un-American conduct of some hapless professor who has suggested that the English plan of government is better than the American plan, that the Germans have a better civic policy, that the French eat better cooking, that a Japanese has thus far done the best research in this or that, that a Portuguese preceded a native Bostonian in sailing round Africa, or that the Mona Lisa is clearly superior to a fire-insurance calendar.   Every one who knows the colleges will recognize the phenomenon as one of the weariest bores of campus life.   How many of these resolutions come from co-ed organizations?   I have yet to observe one.   It was a man, I remember, who refused to find any literary value in the Old Testament — obviously there couldn't be, he said, for it was written by a bunch of kikes.

In my survey of contemporary literature I deal perforce with much fiction and poetry of the day that, in method, is Freudian, and with much that is behavioristic.   In general, the men are antagonistic to it.   They object to both Freud and the behaviorists, partly on the ground that they are new, but mostly on the ground that they are unpleasant.   The young male is affronted by the public discussion of sex-motives though he is a whale at discussing them in private, and he is much more deeply affronted by behaviorism.   Consequently, he does not consider whether they are true, but merely loathes them. Now this is proverbially a feminine response, and it exhibits with admirable clarity one of the crucial functions of intelligence.   The person who says, for instance, "I'd hate to think that Freud is right" betrays an essentially ignorant attitude of mind; the seeker after truth has nothing to do with liking or hating and the only intelligent question is, Is Freud right?   But this ignorant, or proverbially feminine, response in my advanced class is confined to the men.   The dispassionate point of view is invariably that of the co-eds.   They do not unthinkingly accept the new literature.   They welcome it as an interesting phenomenon, something to be analyzed and appraised without preconceptions.   That, I submit, is the intelligent, the educated attitude.

Perhaps a few examples are relevant.   It was a man who rejected

Elmer Gantry because it must be bad art since Sinclair Lewis could not possibly be sincere in such a biased and contemptible book.   The tangle of fallacies displayed by this earnest senior was the kind traditionally ascribed to the feminine mind which cannot think impersonally; yet it was a co-ed who in class informed him that a man who differed from him was not necessarily insincere, asked him what an author's sincerity had to do with his art, and criticized *Elmer Gantry* from an intelligent point of view.   It was another man who in amazement and disgust pronounced Mr. Anderson's *Winesburg, Ohio* an utterly untrue book, the phantasm of a diseased mind.   It was a co-ed who checked off on her fingers the analogues of Anderson's characters whom she had observed in her own home town and named a number of Russian and French novelists who, though respectable in her opponent's eyes, used precisely the same method. It was a man who called Katherine Mansfield "nasty-minded" and found no moral teaching in her work: it was a co-ed who put him in his place.   Finally, after we had read *Ulysses* it was the men who pretended to understand it and, without pretense, condemned it utterly — but the co-eds who admitted that they could not understand it but found occasional passages of magnificent prose and tentatively accepted the method as valid.

This, however, is all literary criticism.   I am, perhaps, betrayed by the limitations of my subject?   Not if I correctly observe the adventures of my colleagues.   Is the campus stirred by a protest against the atheistical teachings of the zoölogy department?   Then the howl is sure to be traced to some embryo revivalist from the Red-Flannels Belt — some one whose sister is not in the least appalled. Does the Dean have to listen for some hours to complaints against Mr. Dash of the history department, who has suggested that economic considerations somewhat influenced the wisdom of the Fathers in 1787, and so is patently subsidized from Leningrad?   Then the complainant is Bill Juicy, the pride of Sigma Sigma, who would die the death rather than hear Hamilton traduced.   At that very moment Alice Apple, with whom Bill has a heavy date to-night, is writing a report for Mr. Dash's class and adding in a postscript that Mr. Dash must be wrong about Jefferson, for Alice cannot believe that even Jefferson could be so consistently high minded as Mr. Dash maintains.   Or the large class files out of University Hall where Mr. Circle has been lecturing on Watson's theory of conditioned response. Bill Juicy lights a cigarette and ponders the lecture briefly. It's all a bunch of hooey, for if Watson is right then Bill can't think for himself. And that, in the face of Sigma Sigma's united stand for compulsory military training, is absurd. Bill dismisses Watson — whom he will thereafter associate with a brand of shock-absorbers — and goes to the fraternity house to find out whom to vote for in the class elections. But Alice, who also lights a cigarette as soon as she is screened from the Dean of Women, is also pondering. If Watson can establish his thesis; if those experiments Circle talks about are exhaustive, then — well, it's going to chase Mr. Dot of the Ethics course and Mr. Starr of the Social Progress course into a corner they'll never escape from. H'm — it rather knocks old Dot's idea of the Moral Will into a cocked hat.

In various courses I have taught the wide expanse of English literature from Chaucer to James Joyce, but, apart from the tittering bromides of Polonius, I have found only one sentiment that appealed irresistibly to the male students in the class. That is the declaration in which Pope plumbed the depths of Bolingbroke and dredged up the assurance that whatever is, is right. It is the hoariest and most awesome conviction of the Babbitt mind, and its acceptance by the college youth of to-day is a broadly farcical commentary on our times. Here, I realize, I run counter to the shibboleths of the newspapers, which intermittently grow hydrophobic over a rebellious generation. It would be delightful and encouraging if the newspapers were right, but they are not. The wave of revolution that Mr. Coolidge discerned from afar when Vice-President never broke among our classic halls. How should salesmen-to-be revolt against anything? If whatever is, isn't right to the last electron, then the future is unsure and efficiency is imperilled. It must be right, and the bozo that says it isn't must be extinguished with the full police power of undergraduate taboos. There need be no apprehension about college men among those shadowy personages who are assumed to be interested in the preservation of the established order, for college men are sound to the core. Beside the conservatism of a fraternity, a Directors' meeting of United States Steel would have a pronounced Bolshevistic tinge. A caucus of the Republican Old

Guard is distinctly radical in comparison with the men of a normal American college. They are not only instinctively reactionary, but even consciously so — and with an unctuousness that would appall the editor of the *Wall Street Journal*.

I have just said that this condition is farcical, and to my low, pedagogical mind, which studies the American scene without rancor, it is precisely that. But from another point of view it is pitiful and, indeed, tragic. For youth is the gallant season when the milk bill is of less consequence than certain spears and the glory of dashing oneself against them. Youth satisfied with anything is youth curdled with the hope of selling bonds. There is a time for the slaying of dragons and the pursuit of Utopias. I must maintain, even, that a fair share of revolutionary thought is essential for the full development of intelligence; for soil is made fruitful by plowing, and dynamite in deep-blast charges is acknowledged to be the best means of breaking up the clods and setting free the chemistry of creation. Ideally, college should give young minds four years of splendid intoxication. Made drunk with the freedom of ideas, college students should charge destructively against all the institutions of a faulty world and all the conventions of a silly one. I need not say that they do not.

My courses in advanced composition are an outlet for the ideas of the students who take them. In five years I have had a number of dissenters. I have had themes that inveighed against war and against marriage, themes that advocated an immediate proletarian revolution in the United States, themes that spoke highly of free-love or anarchy or communism, compulsory education in birth-control or the unionization of the farmers, military despotism or the creation of American soviets. One might focus on these themes — the work of some fifteen or twenty persons — and feel gratefully sure that all was well with the colleges, that such bright if momentary enthusiasms were evidence that college youth remained generous and undiscouraged. I might not dissent from such a judgment, but I must add that of the fifteen or twenty only one was a man.

I do not mean to suggest that the co-eds as a group are radical, but only that the college radical is more apt to appear among them. And I do insist that, as a group, they are more liberal than the men, less terrified by the prospect of social or intellectual change, and less suspicious of novelty. They seem to take for granted that in whatever is there must be, *ipso facto*, a great deal of nonsense. They are willing to examine what is proposed in place of it. The men merely set up a yell for the police or what, intellectually, corresponds to the police.

Above all, they are interested. The college man lives up to the type that has been created for him by the humorous magazines in that he seems perpetually bored. His is not the boredom of cynicism, not even of the callow cynicism of the cartoons, but the boredom that is usually called Philistine. Show him that the principles of Mr. Blank's course in "Business Psychology" will enable him hereafter to close a sale, and he will cast off his lethargy and dig; but through courses in the Greek thought of the Fourth Century or the social institutions of Medieval Spain he wanders somnolent and pathetic, a weary, grumbling low-brow who has been cruelly betrayed into registering for what rumor held to be a snap course. The excitements and the ecstasies of the intellectual life are not for him. He has no hunger for those impractical, breathless, dizzying wisdoms that add stature to the soul. But the co-eds, whether self-consciously or not, are really interested in living by the higher centers of the brain. Education retains, for them, something of its old adventurousness; and, for them, there is still some delight to be had in the pursuit of intellectual ends which can never, by any conceivable means, be turned into commissions. The sex is proverbially curious — and curiosity is no poor synonym for intelligence. And no doubt another proverbial attribute, stubbornness, is responsible for the other virtue that remains to be dealt with. Skepticism seems to be indispensable for education, but the college man neither possesses it nor respects its possession in others. He relies on the commercial honesty of the institution that accepts his tuition: surely no professor would accept money for saying something that was not true. A text-book cannot lie, and a professor will not. Logic, evidence, experimentation, and verification are all very well, no doubt, but an uneconomic waste of time. In a pinch, I would undertake to convince a class of men nearly anything, merely by repeating many times that it was so because I said it was so. One does not teach women that way. One painstakingly examines all the facts, goes over the evidence, caulks the seams of one's logic, and in every way prepares oneself for intelligent opposition. It may be the devilish obstinacy of the sex. No doubt it is, but also, whatever its place in the ultimate synthesis of wisdom, it is the beginning of knowledge.

All this narrows down to one very simple thing. Democracy has swamped the colleges and, under its impetus, college men tend more and more to reverse evolution and to develop from heterogeneity to homogeneity. They tend to become a type, and, our civilization providing the mold, the type is that of the salesman. The attributes that distinguish it are shrewdness, craftiness, alertness, high-pressure affability and, above all, efficiency. There seems to me little reason to believe that the tendency will change in any way. I have not, indeed, any reason to believe that for the Republic any change is desirable. The mass-production of salesmen, we may be sure, will not and cannot stop. But, at least, there is one force that moves counter to this one. The co-eds, in general, develop into individuals; and, in general, they oppose and dissent from the trend of college education. I do not pretend to say whether their opposition is conscious or merely instinctive, nor can I hazard any prophecy about its possible influence on our national life. But if, hereafter, our colleges are to preserve any of the spirit that was lovely and admirable in their past, I am disposed to believe that the co-eds, those irresponsible and overdressed young nitwits, will save it unassisted.

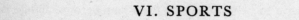

VI. SPORTS

THE GREAT SPORTS MYTH

By JOHN R. TUNIS

John Robert Tunis (1889–) is a professional sports writer as well as a former member of the Harvard track and tennis teams. With F. R. L. Crawford he won the doubles championship at Worthing, England, in 1926, and, with C. F. Aeschliman, that of Monte Carlo in 1925. At present, besides being a frequent contributor of stories and articles to American magazines, he is American sports correspondent for Canadian, English, and French periodicals. His book, "Sports, Heroics, and Hysterics," was published in 1928.

I

I HAVE an English friend who, some thirty years ago, was champion of a little golf club situated on the Sussex Downs between Hove and Worthing. During the Boer War, in which he served as a subaltern, he lost his left arm, which incapacitated him for golf. With zeal he turned to tennis, developed a good game and in a few years became, despite his handicap, one of the best players in the local club. When the World War arrived he somehow wangled a commission for himself and, leading a battalion into action on the Somme, lost his right leg. My last meeting with him took place several winters ago at a British Lawn Tennis and Croquet Club on the French Riviera. He had learned croquet and was by then a low-handicap player, pressing the club champion closely.

That man, I submit, is a sportsman. He knows the thrill of real sport, of playing, not for championships, for titles, for cash, for publicity, for medals, for applause, but simply for the love of playing. Everyone knows this thrill who has felt a golf ball soar from his club and watched it bound down the middle of the course, two hundred and fifty yards ahead; who has finished a long, tense rally at tennis with a passing shot that cuts the sideline and leaves a helpless adversary shaking his head in admiration at the net; who has followed two Airedales jumping and leaping through country uplands on a mellow, crisp afternoon in the fall. A long cross-country walk with a dog, three close sets of tennis, a foursome on a day when the course is uncrowded and the sun shines high above — this is sport, real sport, the expression of the sporting spirit at its best. On these occasions one tastes the full flavor of the game, one finds that complete and satisfying relaxation of mind and body which to the work-weary brain is such perfect solace. In this informal and unorganized sport one finds not only the game but the player at his best. Umpires? Referees? Officials? The need of them does not exist. Implicitly one trusts one's opponent because one trusts oneself; impossible to question the score, impossible to hesitate as to whether a shot did or did not touch the line. All that is finest in sport can be found — is found — in such friendly encounters upon golf links and tennis courts.

But of late years a strange and curious fiction appears to have grown up regarding sport, whereby the effects of such friendly sport are improperly attributed to those highly organized athletic competitions that take place each year from January to December.

Let us grant that sport between individuals is a working laboratory for the building of character. Let us admit freely that the health of nations is being improved by friendly outdoor games. By all means let us give thanks and sing praises for the opportunities afforded by such sports to get out into the open air and freshen ourselves for the burdens of life that grow daily more exhausting. But let us not confound the precious informality of individual sport with the huge, widely advertised sporting contests with which we are being inundated from year's end to year's end.

This fiction I call the Great Sports Myth. It is a fiction sustained and built up by the large class of people now financially interested in sport. There are the news gatherers and the sports functionaries for the daily press; in their very natural efforts to glorify their trade, they have preached unceasingly the notion that all the values to be found in informal athletic games are present as well in the huge, organized, sporting spectacles. There is the paid instructor, the football or baseball or track coach, the trainer or association head who, after all, can hardly be blamed if he attempts to depict his efforts as a cross between those of a religious revivalist and of a social service uplifter. These gentry — the newsgatherer, and the new professional sports uplifter — tell us that competitive sport, as well as informal, unorganized sport, is health-giving, character-building, brain-making. They imply, more or less directly, that its exponents are heroes, possessed of none but the highest moral qualities; tem-

pered and steeled in the great, white heat of competition; purified
and made holy by their devotion to intercollegiate and international
sport. Thanks to them — and to others not entirely disinterested
— there has grown up in the public mind an exaggerated and sentimental notion of the moral value of great, competitive, sport
spectacles.

The sports writers are required to regard the whole sporting panorama with an almost religious seriousness. It is their job; their
bread and butter. Hardly one dares publicly to question the sanctity of organized competitive athletics. One who should dare to
suggest that our idols of the sporting world have feet of clay might
find himself in serious trouble when next he went out upon a story.
If he intimates that this or that sport has become a vast and complicated business, he will get short shift should he ever visit its Association headquarters. What more natural, therefore, than that every
one so employed should further embroider that delightful fiction,
the Great Sports Myth? Hence the annual appeal to rally to the
defense of the Davis Cup is as solemn as if our national life hung in
the balance. And the amount of space given by the press to the
college football system is proof of the hold the Great Sports Myth
has upon us. On the evening before the Harvard-Yale game at
Cambridge, even as sedate a newspaper as the Boston *Transcript*
devotes no less than four pages to the conflict; special writers, sporting writers, feature writers, editors, and their more humble confrères,
treat the morrow's match as earnestly and sententiously as they do
the forecasts of a Presidential election upon Election Eve.

II

The manner in which the American public is fostered and fed upon
the Great Sports Myth is not only amazing; for anyone who gets an
opportunity to peek behind the scenes it is one of the most discon-
certing signs of the times. For the sporting heroes of the nation are
its gods. From day to day, from month to month, from year to year,
we are deluged with a torrent of words about these Galahads of sport;
the amateur football players of the colleges, and the "shamateur"
golf or tennis players, who often take a hand in exalting their own
personalities through the medium of the press. In the winter months
we are treated to columns of "dope" about these supermen, of chatter

and gossip about their every movement. In the early spring the star of sport moves eastward; for six weeks we are regaled, via the Atlantic cables, with the feats of Mr. Tilden, Mr. Hagen, Miss Wills, or Mrs. Mallory, in the French and British tennis and golf championships. By July the travelers are back again in their native haunts — not infrequently with hard words to say about conditions and competitors across the sea — and then the deluge of sporting bunk begins in earnest. The channel swimmers are busy explaining why channels are so broad and trainers so thick. In August come the big aquatic events, the yachting and motor boat races; in early September, the matches for the Davis Cup. Almost every fall we have a "major league" prize fight. October brings colds, coal bills, and the World's Series, with its front page cavortings of Home-run Kings and Strike-out Emperors. And as the sporting year draws to an end in late November, the nation goes completely daft over intercollegiate football. Except for the imposing lists of All-American teams — composed by gentlemen who have perhaps seen in action some three hundred of the thirty thousand football players of the United States — we have a rest in December. And we need it!

Man has always, I suppose, been a worshiper. Doubtless he always will be. We Americans do not seem to take to religious prophets. We have no Queen Marie, nor even a Mussolini, to raise upon a pedestal. Consequently we turn hopefully to the world of sports. There we find the material to satisfy our lust for hero worship; there we discover the true gods of the nation. Messrs. Hagen, Tunney, Tilden, Jones, Ruth, Cohen, Dempsey — these become the idols of America's masculine population, young and old. And why not? After all, we ask ourselves, are they not athletes? Have they not been cleansed (and so sanctified) in the great white heat of competition, upon the links or the gridiron, the court or the diamond? That competitive sport — any kind of competitive sport from squash tennis to prize fighting — makes for nobility of character, such is the first commandment of the American sporting public. This, in fact, is the foundation of the Great Sports Myth.

III

Yet, in plain truth, highly organized competitive sports are not character-building; on the contrary, after a good deal of assistance at and some competition in them, I am convinced that the reverse is true. So far are they from building character that, in my opinion, continuous and excessive participation in competitive sports tends to destroy it. Under the terrific stress of striving for victory, victory, victory, all sorts of unpleasant traits are brought out and strengthened. Too frequently the player's worst side is magnified; his self-control is broken down much more than it is built up. I know this is heresy. I realize that the contrary is preached from every side. (Most fervently, however, the preachers are sports writers, football coaches, or others who have some other direct and personal interest in the furtherance of the Great Sports Myth.) I am aware that the participants in American sports are all supposed to be little short of demigods. Yet if football, for instance, is the noble, elevating and character-building sport it is supposed to be why, I wonder, is it necessary to station an umpire, a field judge, a head linesman, and half a dozen assistants to follow the play at a distance of a few yards and to watch zealously every one of the twenty-two contestants in order that no heads and no rules may be simultaneously broken?

"NERVE–TENSED STALWARTS KEYED UP FOR SUPREME EFFORT OF SEASON."

So ran the headline of a pre-game football story in a big New York daily last fall. Anyone who has seen the average athletic contest at close range will testify to the accuracy of this characterization. Instead of being in sound mental and physical condition when they go out on the links, the gridiron, or the river, our gods are actually in a state of nerves which often leads them to do things otherwise incomprehensible. The plain truth is that the intensive strain of modern competition and the glare of publicity created by the press, the movies, and the radio, wear down and destroy the nerve tissue of the average competitor. How else can one explain the petulant outburst and the no less petulant actions of Mr. Walter Hagen on his return from his trip to England after having failed to win their golfing title some years ago? Or the performances of Mr. Tilden upon the court? Off the court, Mr. Tilden, as his friends will testify, is a charming and urbane gentleman. Once he gets into combat, however, he becomes, in his zest for victory — a zest that every champion

in competitive sport must have or perish — something totally unlike
his normal self.   He will turn and glare at any linesman who dares
give a decision against his judgment; before the thousands in the
stands he will demand the removal of the offender; he will request
"lets" at crucial moments, object when new balls are thrown out, in
short do things he would never do were he not so intensely concen-
trated on winning.

Nor would it be just to Mr. Tilden to single him out for criticism.
Those who saw the Davis Cup Challenge Round in 1914, will remember the childish behavior of the man who is considered by many
the greatest tennis player of all time, Mr. Norman Everard Brookes.
After the third set of his match with Mr. R. N. Williams (which was
won by the American, 10–8) the crowd, anticipating a victory for the
United States, rose — as was but natural — in loud and vociferous
cheering.   Mr. Brookes promptly clapped his hands to his ears and
kept them there as long as the cheering went on.

Any one who has spent a winter in the south of France during the
reign of the late Queen of French tennis, Mademoiselle Suzanne
Lenglen, will testify to her strenuous efforts to avoid defeat by remaining out of tournaments in which she seemed likely to be beaten.
In 1926, during the visit of Miss Helen Wills to the Riviera, her attempts to avoid the American were so amusing that a famous Parisian
daily ran an article entitled, "Tennis ou Cache-Cache?"   (Tennis or
Hide and Seek?)   This, mind you, is not the conduct of youngsters
new to competitive sport; it is the conduct of champions and super-
champions.   Concentrating as they must to win, they hardly know
what they are doing or saying.   For the time being, they become
self-hypnotized.   Follow them around the sport circle from week to
week, and from year to year, and you will, I am sure, lose any illusion you may have about the uplifting effect of present-day competitive sport.

The popular belief is that sport teaches self-control, that it shows
us how to accept not only victory but defeat with a graceful and sincere smile.   If you are a believer in the Great Sports Myth, I wish
you might visit the locker-rooms and dressing-quarters of our club-
houses and athletic buildings and mingle with our champions before
and after their contests.

"He beat the gun, that's why he copped."

"I was interfered with in the last quarter, on that forward pass, or I'd have scored a touchdown."

"I'll beat that big stiff or burst a blood vessel."

"That decision in the third set cost me the match — sure the ball was on the line, I saw it."

"This man Smith has always been against us; we'll have to see he doesn't get a chance to referee any of the 'varsity games again."

These — with embellishments unprintable — are the sort of things you hear on the inside at every big sporting contest.   You may, perhaps, imagine this to be an exaggeration.   Get someone who has umpired a match between Mr. Tilden and Mr. Richards to tell you how they addressed each other as they shook hands across the net after a tense, five-set battle!   It is no accident that Mr. Robert T. Jones is almost the only champion in any branch of sport who is genuinely popular with those who play against him and, therefore, see him under the stress of modern competition.   The strain at the top is too great for most men.

Curiously enough, although the majority of our sporting heroes are magnified and worshiped, Mr. Jones seems to have had something less than the breaks from the gentry of the sporting press.   This doubtless came about because these devotees of the Great Sports Myth have created a charming fable about Mr. Jones which exactly fitted into their ideas about the character-building benefits of competitive sport.   Mr. Jones as a youngster, they aver, was a perfectly terrible chap.   When he first took up golf he threw his clubs about. He broke them up whenever he missed a six-foot putt.   He swore. He cursed.   Really, he was a perfectly terrible fellow!   But behold the influence of the game!   Now a more charming young sportsman it would be hard to find.   Due, of course, the inference is, to the soul-saving and character-forming effects of sport.

A lovely fiction.   But untrue.   Yet I have never seen this untruth refuted in an American newspaper; to do so would tend to destroy the Great Sports Myth.   However, to an English reporter, about a year ago in London, Mr. Jones vouchsafed the following:

I've read newspaper comments in which I am told that I not only won the British championship at St. Andrews but conquered myself as well.   What is it all about?   Have I ever been a bunch of fireworks?   I played my first championship when I was fourteen years old, and I am twenty-five now.   In all that time I have made a fool of myself only twice, once at the Red Cross tournament in Boston in 1915, when I was fifteen years old, and once at the British open championship at St. Andrews when I was nineteen. Is that being worse than anyone else? Chick Evans can throw a club away in the midst of a championship and nobody minds. Why pick on me?

The only break I ever made at home was in Boston ten years ago. I've played right along since then. Where's the sense of throwing Boston at me now? Of course it's nice to have people say nice things about you, but honestly, when New York papers make me out such a glowing example of moral discipline I don't know what to make of it.

Poor Mr. Jones. Of all our athletic stars, he is most surely the one who deserves a fair break and yet, thanks to the obsession of sporting writers and their devotion to the Great Sports Myth, he has received a bad one. There is a moral in this for those who have the time and patience to discover it.

IV

Yet another tenet of the Great Sports Myth is the time-worn belief that international competition in sports strengthens the bonds between nations and between individuals. It usually does nothing of the sort! Surely, if football players from two of the largest universities in the United States indulge in fisticuffs before eighty thousand spectators in their big test of the season, there is little chance for a general kissing-match at an international sporting reunion such as the Olympic games!

When these games approach and one hears the usual platitudes about the great good they do in international relations and the benefits they confer upon humanity at large, I am minded of a small paragraph which was culled from the *Auto*, the great Parisian sporting newspaper. Translated exactly, it reads:

M. Moneton, the referee of the match between the Racing Club de Calais and the Stade Roubaisienne, thanks the members of the Racing Club de Calais team for saving his life directly after the match.

Not every sporting contest ends in a free fight as this one presumably did, but there is far more hard feeling generated by sport than is usually admitted by the adherents of the Great Sports Myth. When the Irish Rugby team played France last winter, the crowd got out of hand and rushed for the referee, the Captain of a Scottish team twenty-five years ago. He managed to escape to the dressing-room whence, as the mob stood outside howling for his blood, he was eventually escorted from the grounds under police protection.

You never hear much about such things? Certainly not. The sporting writers do not dwell upon them for very obvious reasons. The sort of thing they prefer to play up can be illustrated by an article which appeared several years ago in the *Princeton Alumni Weekly* entitled, "The Sublimation of War." The writer's argument was to the effect that if all nations were "sport loving and dominated by the true instincts of sport," war would be completely eradicated. The Sublimation of War! We had a taste of it several months later when the break came between Harvard and Princeton.

Dignified in front-page headlines by the sonorous title, "SEVERANCE OF ATHLETIC RELATIONS," this episode reflected credit upon neither of the universities nor upon their followers. According to the tenets of the Great Sports Myth, Princeton and Harvard undergraduates should have been loyal friends and good fellows both on the field and in the stands. Such, as the saying goes, was not the case. Trouble began early in 1922 when one after another of the best Harvard players were taken from the gridiron in the Princeton game with various injuries which removed them from the "sublimating" effects of sport for the rest of the season. Murmurs of rough play were heard at Cambridge; they continued, in increasing volume, as Princeton went on defeating Harvard by overwhelming scores. The climax was reached in the season of 1926 when, the day before the game, the Harvard *Lampoon* appeared with a disgraceful attack upon Princeton and her supporters. The game which followed was a sorry spectacle; hisses and groans arose from both sides of the field and, in their comments during the following week, even the most ardent devotees of the Great Sports Myth, in writing for the press, agreed that such an affair was neither stimulating nor worth repeating. After the game the undergraduates of the two universities regarded one another much as did Germans and Americans in 1918. With all the solemnity of a nation rupturing diplomatic relations with a powerful neighbor, Princeton "broke with Harvard," as the newspapers screamed in headlines from their front pages.

Recriminations, insinuations, rhetorical attacks, and counterattacks ensued; the press carried columns and pages of the effect of this break upon the world of sport — and not a soul who commented on the fracas appeared to see the amusing side of the whole affair. Sport, the healer of relationships between nations; sport, the promoter of good feeling and good comradeship; sport, that brings forth all that is best and noblest in human nature, was producing — what? Gouged noses, broken ankles, bad feeling, cursing, and reviling in the sanctity of dressing-rooms; coarse accusations and cheap humor in the publications of a great university. If sport cannot do better than this among representatives of two of the principal American colleges, how can it be expected to unite Gaul and Teuton, Arab and Scandinavian, black man and white, as it is popularly supposed to do by those who prate glibly about peoples "dominated by the true instincts of sport."

Such breaks in relations between our universities, are not, it appears, uncommon in intercollegiate football. The facts are not generally known; but almost every large college in the country has, at some time in its history, broken with some great rival. Thus the Army and Navy broke between 1893 and 1899; now they are at it again. Harvard and Yale broke between 1894 and 1897. Pennsylvania and Lafayette broke between 1900 and 1903. Princeton and Harvard, after breaking between 1897 and 1912, broke again in 1926 until some future date unknown, thereby bidding fair to establish a National Intercollegiate Breaking record for all time. At the present moment the list of colleges is a fairly large one; should it increase materially it would seem that our universities might have difficulty in completing their schedules. Thus Princeton, having broken with Pennsylvania years ago, has now broken with Harvard; the Army has broken with Syracuse; Columbia has broken with New York University; and the Navy has broken with the Army. These are some of the breaks publicly announced. Others are being kept under cover.

Now, if our highly organized sports taught as much of mutual understanding, generosity, and forbearance as their advocates claim they do, there might be some excuse for the elevation of sport into a kind of national religion. Yet why is it that the United States, by common acclaim the greatest sporting nation in the world, is so sensitive to criticism, so open to flattery? In point of fact, what the fetish of competitive sport inculcates in us most successfully is the desire to win. Not at any cost? Certainly not! There are far too many linesmen, referees, umpires, field judges, and minor officials to permit of that sort of thing.   But our gods are all winners: it is Tunney, Hagen, Jones, Miss Wills, not Mrs. Mallory, Johnston, or Ouimet who are worshiped and glorified.   It is the champion, not the way in which the championship is won or lost, that attracts the plaudits of the mob whose creed is the Great Sports Myth.   The King can do no wrong.   And the King (pro tem) is always the man at the top of the pile.

Moreover, by thus elevating our athletic heroes to peaks of prominence, by prying into their private lives, by following them incessantly in the columns of the daily press, by demanding of them victories and yet more victories, we force them to lose all sense of proportion — if indeed they ever had any.   For it is a debatable question whether any one with a sense of proportion — or a sense of humor, which comes to much the same thing — could so far lose himself in this sporting miasma as to become a champion.   Judging by their remarks in public, one is forced to conclude that many, if not all, of our sporting gods are muscle bound between the ears.

PIGSKIN PREFERRED

By ROBERT LITTELL

Robert Littell (1896–   ), the son of Philip Littell, journalist and critic, has already achieved distinction of his own as a writer.   He is dramatic critic on the "New York Evening Post," and a contributing editor to "The New Republic."   "Read America First" (1926) is a collection of his published essays.

Harvard Athletic Authorities have installed a dozen electric lights so that the football team may carry on practice work at any hour. . . . Now Harvard will have no excuse for losing because of lack of twenty-four-hour facilities.
— *Daily News.*

EDUCATION, as the above item (which is not of our invention) will testify, is advancing by leaps and bounds.   This is one of the biggest bounds ever made.   In fact, while our day remains only twenty-four hours long, no further bound in this direction is possible.

This courageous innovation ought not to be surprising.   For Harvard is one of the most progressive universities in the country. And not alone in athletics.   In scholarship also she — "she," for like excursion boats, colleges are feminine — she has distinguished herself by recognition of the long neglected subject of business.   As compared with Latin, Greek, and the Renaissance and plane (not solid) ornithology, the study of business is a tender plant, and must be watered if it is not to perish in all but a few enthusiastic garrets.   The President, and good fellows, and overseers and superintendents and foremen of Harvard were wise to see this obscure condition clearly, and courageous to remedy it.   In action, their courage exceeded their wisdom, and they have constructed a mechanism so vast, and a financial reservoir of proportions so oceanic, that the tender plant is in more danger of being drowned than not watered.   However, let us not be pessimistic.   Some if not all business will sprout sturdily in spite of this golden cloudburst, and there seems no small doubt that among the lost arts revived will be those of giving short change, punching time-clocks, dressing windows, reading ticker-tapes and compiling sucker lists.

Football, like business, is seldom pursued for its own sake.   As a prominent half-back once said: "I don't run back punts for my health." It is not for amusement that the Harvard squad charges and blocks and tackles all afternoon, and it is not for sheer love of sport that they are now getting ready to grind through signal practice by artificial light. In fact, all this practice is mighty hard work, ever so much harder work than brain work. There is a malicious popular belief that football players are not naturally inclined toward brain work. This is unfair: football players have merely chosen the sterner course. Many more fail at this course than at brain courses. Only a few men each year, out of the dozens of candidates, win their letter. It is much more difficult to earn an H than an A.B. All honor, then, to those who aim at one letter rather than two. An A.B. can be obtained nowadays without burning the midnight oil. But an H requires hours and hours of midnight electricity. Never, in the history of all education, has there been so arduous a night school.

It is quite proper that football should be taken seriously. In the past it was often considered a sport, and it was played for fun in a slapdash, unprofessional manner by young men who enjoyed the exercise. This race of dilettantes is now extinct, and has given place to a more conscientious generation which realizes the true function of football in any well-conducted alma mater. For alma mater flourishes by victory on the gridiron, and droops after defeat. No alma mater can withstand prolonged unsuccess at football. The reverberations of humiliation in the Stadium or the Bowl are far-reaching. Attendance in classes on Egyptology, Cryptology and the Italian drama drops off. Scholarship standards quiver and collapse. Bright young men in middle western high schools hear from afar the dismal thunder of defeat and go elsewhere. Graduates and alumni (they are not identical) storm and sulk in the suburbs, write angry letters, tear up checks and send their sons to the University of Nebraska. The loss of these checks is more serious than the loss of the sons. There are always plenty of sons, but checks are more ephemeral, and subject to seasonal influences. The autumn season, with its toll of games lost or won, profoundly affects the writing of checks. And checks build universities, while young men merely inhabit them.

A graduate is one who is proud of his alma mater. An alumnus is one who is ashamed of her when she begins to lose football games.

An alumnus writes more checks than a graduate, and is in every way a sterner man. He makes certain demands, and he stands by to see that the goods are delivered. He is a realist. He knows the value of professors and instructors, and rightly assigns to them a very minor rôle in the educational process. He sees to it that these learned cogs are paid strictly according to their services. He reserves his real enthusiasm for the football coach, and makes sure that the salary for that position will attract the kind of man who can win games and keep his desk clear.

But the alumnus, for all his hardheadedness, has yet to go the whole hog. He is still dealing in half measures. The desperate resolve of the football authorities at Harvard to perfect their team by putting electric lights on the field ought to spur the alumnus to equally rigorous action. His path is clear: football must be rescued from the paralyzing limbo between amateurishness and professionalism. Much as he might sigh for the old days, it is obviously too late to regain for the game a lost amateur standing. The present status is impossible. Onward, then, to a business basis. The players must of course remain amateurs, but the game should be professionalized. This happy device would at once save honor and avoid paying salaries to the players. A stock company should obviously be floated, with the alumni subscribing for the shares. Only a few graduates would be allowed to participate, as their loyalty to the team is somewhat open to question. But since graduates are almost universally poorer men than alumni, perhaps it would not be necessary to make this humiliating discrimination against them.

The details of such a scheme we leave to men plainly more qualified than ourselves. We confess, with no little hesitation and fear, that our own mentality is more of the graduate type than the alumnus. This means, for one thing, that we cherish the pale remains of some anxiety about educational matters in the old sense. And we should therefore like to be allowed to put in a timid plea that some of the profits of the Stadium Common, or Bowl Bonds, or Pigskin Preferred, which under the reign of a competent coach would be considerable, be paid in to the University for strictly educational purposes. We do not go so far as to suggest that a professor's salary be raised, out of these profits, to a figure so near that of the football coach as to give grounds for any serious jealousy or competition. It would be safer to avoid this issue by endowing, with the Pigskin dividends, a few erudite courses in allied subjects, such as Greek games 2a, or Discus 13, or Checkers among the Early Christians, which would, by partaking at once of the nature of sport and learning, endanger neither. These courses, it goes without saying, could only be given in the year following football victories. Defeat, particularly over a period of years, would diminish profits, or even wipe them out, and if the alumni stockholders in Pigskin Preferred passed a dividend or two, Discus 13 could no longer be thrown.

After this sensible reorganization, of course the electric lights on the practice field would burn forever. In this era of competition, no Harvard football team, once having inaugurated them, could give them up. In fact, these artificial lights would be rapidly copied by rival colleges, and would in a few years be looked back upon as only the first step in a sort of football armament race. The plain electric light bulbs would give way to infra-red rays, which are known to induce that super-normal adrenal activity which marks the difference between a mediocre line-plunger and an All-American full-back. Music is a notorious aid to drop-kicking, and for many years the psychological laboratories could compete in discovering just which tunes produced most field goals. Gradually the exactions of the larger Football would stimulate every science, every research department, would draw a little useful contribution from every course taught in the University. Football law, football hygiene, the drama of football, football ballistics, football histology, the æsthetics of football — there is no area of human knowledge in which the football could not make at least a first down.

But let every bit of research, every signing of contract with coaches, every advanced secret practice, every cutting of the Pigskin melon, be performed by electric light. Too much daylight isn't good for the game — or business — of football.

OUR CHANGING SPORTS PAGE

By WILLIAM O. McGEEHAN

*William O. McGeehan (1879–   ) has all his life been associated
with newspapers and the outdoors.   As a mere sideline he served in both
the Spanish-American and World Wars.   He began his real work as a
reporter in San Francisco where he also served as city editor.   From
1915 to 1920 he was sports editor on the "New York Tribune," and
then held the same position on the "Herald" until 1922.   At present he
is with the "New York Herald-Tribune."*

IN something less than a quarter of a century the sport department
of an American newspaper has developed from a column of type
to four and five pages daily, with a special section of its own on
Sunday.   Taking the press as a mirror of the life of the times and a
gauge as to the importance of current events, there certainly has
been a change in the national attitude toward sport.

The charge has been made that the interest in sport, amateur and
professional, has been stimulated artificially by the American newspapers.   Of this charge I hold that the newspapers are entirely
guiltless.   As far as the newspapers are concerned, there is no revenue
through the stimulation of interest in sports, for this branch of the
news brings little or no advertising.   In expanding the sport pages
the newspapers have merely responded to an insistent demand from
their readers.

Up to about six years ago the New York dailies were standing on a
limit of two pages for sports pages.   At that time I was sports editor
of the *New York Herald*.   One summer evening I made some estimates as to space requirements and went with them to the managing
editor.   There were two crucial baseball series, a championship
prize-fight, some important golf and tennis, a big day at the race-
track, and some other events.

"I do not see how all of this can be kept in two pages," I said.

"Well, then, let us have three sports pages," said the managing
editor.   "It will come eventually, so why not now?"

So it was the *Herald*, I am convinced, that started this daring innovation, the same *Herald* which, under the elder Bennett, chronicled
the opening of a race-meet with this brief notice: "There will be

horse-racing at Sheepshead Bay to-day, and the same crowds of blacklegs and gamblers that frequent such places may be expected out in full force."

The newspapers have not led the change in attitude toward the various sports. They have followed it, and how strangely that attitude has changed toward those various sports!

I can remember the time when a man who was addicted to the strange, imported game of golf would sneak through devious and unfrequented ways to the links and slink behind a tree when the derisive passers-by would pass in buggies. To-day, a competent authority tells me, there are three million golf-players in the United States and recruits are flocking to the army every day.

Bobby Jones, twice winner of the British Open, when he returned to his native Atlanta, was given a greeting fully as effusive as that tendered the late John L. Sullivan by the joyous citizens of Boston when he returned to his native city, heavyweight champion of the world. Taste in the matter of popular idols certainly has changed.

Gentlemen with large sums invested in baseball-parks and professional baseball franchises have come to view the encroachments of this imported game of golf upon what they consider their preserves with no little alarm and considerable indignation. Baseball, of course, is our own national game, just a little older than the Civil War, and should be conserved for patriotic as well as business reasons.

When golf first invaded the United States the "sand-lots" were filled with juvenile baseball-players who hardly would waste the time from their games to deride the self-conscious golfers. But the business of caddying attracted many of these youngsters from baseball, because it was highly lucrative, and the youngsters soon began to develop an interest in golf. Gene Sarazen is an example of a golfer who might have been a baseball-player if the occupation of caddy had not been open to him.

Here is a thought that will increase the alarm of the baseball magnates. The fact that there are three million golfers in the United States means that there are close to half a million boys who are caddying rather than playing the national game. And this is cause for alarm, for it means not only that this material from which professional baseball-players might be developed is being diverted from the national game but also it means a decrease in the number of baseball fans in the coming generation.

To be a baseball fan one must have played the game to some extent at some time or other. To anybody who has not played the game it is quite incomprehensible, just as incomprehensible as it would be to an Englishman or as incomprehensible as cricket is to the American. Therefore it will be seen that the recent drives of baseball magnates to sustain the interest in the national game in the members of the younger generation are not altogether altruistic.

As yet there has been no indication of a decrease of interest in baseball. Despite a few baseball scandals the magnates report bigger crowds for the season of 1927 than in the year preceding. In fact, the attendance at baseball games for the last quarter of a century has increased steadily, with allowance, of course, being made for the "war years." As far as is known, then, golf has not diverted the patrons of the national game from the baseball-parks. Perhaps it never will, and the increasing number of golfers indicates only that the interest in sport is increasing all along the line and that no sport ever will take the "fans" away from another sport.

The American game of intercollegiate football is still younger than the national game of baseball, and, judging from the annual changes in the rules, still in the making. The shift in the popular attitude toward this game is remarkable. The "college-boy" athlete was looked upon with utter contempt by the rugged followers of baseball when the game which started in an impromptu contest between Princeton and Rutgers was taken up by the other colleges.

The collegiate football-player with the "chrysanthemum" haircut used to be an object of considerable derision until it finally dawned upon the sport-follower who knew not his campus and who had no alma mater to guide him that intercollegiate football was far from a gentle sport. Even this did not reconcile the non-collegian. He still regarded the college boys as queer persons indulging in disorganized assault and mayhem.

The change in the view-point has been steady but swift. I was checking up the matter of attendance at the various sports a while ago, and I made the startling discovery that intercollegiate football in season draws more spectators than the national pastime. This is all the more remarkable when you consider that the big-league baseball season stretches over a regular period of about one hundred and fifty-four days, while the colleges are limited to a playing-season that does not exceed ten games.

It was a football game that drew the second largest number of paid admissions for a sporting event or any other event last year, the Army-Navy game at Soldiers' Field in Chicago. It is my firm conviction that if the enclosure had been big enough to hold a crowd twice or three times that size there would have been no difficulty in drawing that crowd.

There are certain football "classics" for which, of late years, there have been five applications for every ticket sold and where the "general public" has to be excluded because those affiliated in some way with the colleges concerned fill the stadium. The Yale Bowl at New Haven, the most commodious football field in the country, barely can accommodate a fifth of those who would like to see a Yale-Harvard game.

Once in this bowl I saw seventy thousand people sit for two hours in a driving storm of rain and sleet during the progress of a game between these two universities. Less than one thousand left the bowl before the referee's whistle ended the battle in the mud.

It is easy enough to understand the increased attendance at prize-fights and the gathering of one hundred and seventy thousand men and women spending approximately three million dollars to see one ten-round struggle between heavyweights. Popular opinion once forced this game into the position of a fugitive sport.

Not so long ago prize-fights had to be held in comparative secret, in barns, on bits of turf hidden from the authorities, while the spectators connived to evade the authorities bent upon preventing these breaches of the peace and dignity of the various States. The interest always was there, but the number of spectators with the means, the hardihood, and the determination to see the prize-fight through was limited.

With the advent of Mr. Tex Rickard all of these inhibitions were removed. It seemed that he was able to make it not only respectable to see a prize-fight but the "smart thing." He knew that the desire always was there, and that the "sport-followers" of to-day were not even slightly changed from the crowds at the Roman arena.

I can remember, when California housed nearly all of the big prize-fights, that there were grave debates upon the subject of admitting women to prize-fights. Mr. Rickard has been pointing with pride for some time that ladies whose names are in the social register are regular patrons at his bouts and that they demand the best of "ringside seats" for the big bouts. It requires something of a very serious nature, for instance, to make Miss Ethel Barrymore miss a heavyweight championship, and I remember meeting a lady of no little social prominence in her own private car, which she had parked at Shelby, Montana, while she waited the clang of the gong for the Dempsey-Gibbons bout. She was taking her two young sons to the ringside with her.

Not so many years ago you would have to wait for *The Police Gazette* to come out before you got all of the really interesting details of one of these big fights. Now you will get columns upon columns of it from your favorite newspaper. I recall at the Dempsey-Willard fight in Toledo which took place only a few months after the end of the war marvelling for a few seconds at the sense of values.

The typewriters and the telegraph-instruments were clicking. Airplanes outside the arena were tuning up, ready to rush photographs to various parts of the country. I remarked to Mr. Grantland Rice, who sat near me: "There will be about ten thousand times as much written about this as there was about the battle of the Marne." After which I proceeded in the work of contributing seven thousand words to the surplus chronicles of the minor battle.

There was a time, and not so long ago, when tennis was classed as essentially a "sissy's game." Now it is apparent that the supposedly robust and virile game of baseball is as child's play by comparison. It has become so that even a prize-fighter in training may play tennis without the slightest suspicion that he must be slightly effeminate.

The general public has become more intimately acquainted with this game through such personalities as Larned, Wilding, McLoughlin, Johnston, and Tilden, and they realize now that it is one of the most strenuous forms of athletics in the catalogue. The development in the interest in women's tennis is marked. Last year, when the battle between Mlle. Suzanne Lenglen and Miss Helen Wills at Wimbledon seemed assured, there was quite as much interest in this country and in France as there was in the heavyweight championship fight between Jack Dempsey and Georges Carpentier. The missionary work done by the great tennis-players has made a sceptical general public acquainted intimately with one of the most beautiful of all games, and the popular respect for a great tennis-player increases steadily.

The change in women in sport— and I do not mean as lookers-on — is the most startling. Consider first the costume and the style of the pre-May Sutton Bundy women tennis-players and compare them with the Willses, the Mallorys, and the Lenglens. Certainly you will find a different type of woman athlete.

Perhaps the most striking figure of the new woman in athletics is that of Gertrude Ederle, who swam the English Channel in faster time than any of the men who swam it before her. She startled and puzzled France from the moment she entered the country.

When the French customs officers arrived to look over her baggage they found her muffled in a white sweater and holding a medicine-ball under her arm. This puzzled them particularly. She could not explain its use to them and that it was her custom to toss it about while she was in training. The more she tried to make its use clear the greater their bewilderment, and when, to illustrate, she tossed it playfully at one of them both fled, making remarks about mad Americans of both sexes.

Before she conquered the Channel her first instructor, Mr. I. de B. Handley, told me confidently that she would not only swim the Channel but that she would break all of the records of all the men in doing it. When I saw her training like a young prize-fighter on the coast near Gris Nez I was just as confident as Mr. Handley that this was an athletic field or element in which at least one woman would excel.

And yet it has been only a matter of twelve years since women really began to swim. They could not swim in the old-fashioned bathing-suits which the conventions required for women, with the long skirts imprisoning their limbs and the water-logged stockings impeding their movements. When Gertrude Ederle took to the water at Gris Nez she wore a thin pair of tights, a light brassière — and a coating of grease.

There are many who regarded the feat of Gertrude Ederle as the most magnificent gesture of feminism. Yet I do not regard her as anything of a superwoman, for the same Women's Swimming Club, with its little tank where she was developed into this magnificent athlete, is developing many more like her. They are planning now to send out a fifteen-year-old girl in an attempt to break not only Gertrude Ederle's record but the records of all of the men swimmers who have conquered that angry stretch of water that lies between Gris Nez and Dover.

The athletic girl once was regarded as unmaidenly, unwomanly, or a freak. Now she is not merely accepted but she is taken for granted, which is the highest tribute that could be paid to her accomplishment. In view of the comparatively recent developments, I have come to the conclusion that the time is coming when the non-athletic girl may be regarded as freakish and unusual. This certainly is not a matter to view with alarm.

But as to the overwhelming general increase of interest in sports in the United States there are many indications of an increasing pessimism. The Association of American College Professors last year deplored the false sense of values in the colleges as illustrated by the ever-increasing interest in intercollegiate football. There has been much discussion of the evil of exalting the gladiatorial spirit at the expense of the intellectual side.

The prize-fights which are attracting bigger and bigger gatherings of both men and women are denounced by some as being brutal and appealing to the lowest instincts and almost at the same time as being indifferent bouts between young business men who are defrauding the public under pretense of furnishing them with bloodshed and brutality. There is pessimism because Babe Ruth, the maker of home runs, is being paid only a little less than the President of the United States.

From the serious-minded business men who have not yet become addicts of the game of golf there are complaints and grumblings about the time that is being wasted on the links. Perhaps this complaint will throw some light on the increased interest in sports of all sorts. The nation has the time and the money for indulgence in sport. Not only that, but energy that used to be burned entirely in the mere business of living has been loosed through the improvement in living conditions and the labor-saving machinery. This energy must find an outlet and it does, an outlet that is comparatively a joyous one measured with the manner in which it used to be taken up.

The nation's attitude toward sport has changed, because it has been given the time to consider the various sports without the old harassments.   And the people, approaching them and viewing them in that happy frame of mind, find that some of the sports are better than others but that all of them are good.

GAS AND THE GAMES

By GEORGE S. BROOKS

George S. Brooks (1895–   ) left the University of Rochester in 1917 and joined the United States Army, serving in France during the World War. Upon his discharge from the army, he became a free-lance writer, a dramatist, and a newspaper man, finally becoming, in 1925, managing editor of "McClure's Magazine." He has, of course, contributed to many magazines, and is the author of several books, among them "James Durand: Able Seaman" (1926) and "Spread Eagle" (1927).

MORE profound blah has been scribbled and spoken about the significance of our national vogue for sports than upon almost any topic, including Fundamentalism, Freud, the League of Nations, and the hot weather. Every after-dinner orator, conducting drives for college or Y.M.C.A. gymnasium funds, has pointed with pride and fountain pen to our outdoor enthusiasms as a convincing proof of racial and social vigor.

It has made good advertising copy, excellent publicity material for the press-agents for automobile manufacturers and for Spalding, Reach, and others who make tennis-rackets and golf-balls.

"Gas and the games" has become the motto of these United States. It has replaced "E Pluribus Unum," "A penny saved," "To hell with the public," "Rum, Romanism, and Rebellion," "He kept us out of war," "Normalcy," "The full dinner-pail," "The hardcider candidate," "I want to see a phonograph in every American home," "54–40 or fight," "It floats," and other honored slogans for which men have dared their all. While the Spirit of St. Louis flew to Paris, the spirit of America went by subway to the Yankee Stadium to pay $27.50 each for a ringside seat at a mediocre if not a fixed fight.

Contrary to the opinions of professional and amateur sport-promoters, the writer contends it is doubtful if the tremendous furor over motors and sports proves anything — except that our civilization has reached a highly artificial state, and that most of our citizens are bored with their jobs.

Certainly the judgment of comparative values has become

warped. The head-lines of to-day, recounting, as this is written, Babe Ruth's thirty-third home run of the season, will scarcely be perpetuated by historians. About the time that one and one-half millions of our fellow citizens lined the sidewalks from the Battery to Central Park to cheer for Gertrude Ederle, a modest, unassuming chemist came to town. He was unheralded by the Vienna papers when he left, he was unnoticed by our metropolitan dailies when he arrived.

He came to this country to work in a research laboratory for seventy-five dollars a week. And he had been invited to continue his research here, because his discoveries of the secrets of cell growth and cell change may lead to the conquest of cancer, drug addiction, and tuberculosis. Cheering multitudes have not disturbed his work, although six surgeons gave him a table-d'hôte dinner at a second-rate club.

John Smith, driving to his golf club in his Whosis Eight sedan, is quite properly more interested in Bobby Jones's putting and the mystery of Detroit — Will Henry put steam heat and bath in his new model?

The figures in the *World Almanac*, which represent the nation's expenditure for baseball, gas, football, tires, tennis, new cars, golf, old cars, poker chips, rebuilt cars, and for Work or Street "On Bridge," contain so many ciphers that [they pass the comprehension of the salaried man. From the Summer White House come Republican boasts about the number of automobiles in Kansas. Those figures, say national committeemen, demonstrate the flood of Coolidge prosperity in the corn belt; the same statistics for New York City are quoted by the Rockefeller Institute to show that 73.95 per cent of our citizens are leading purer lives; and, to this reporter's way of thinking, they prove only that no evidences of birth-control have been observed in the Ford factories.

Henry Ford himself, having apologized his way back into Abraham's bosom, is now running neck and neck with Tex Rickard, Harvey Firestone, Cash and Carry Pyle, Mr. Rolls-Royce, and Gene Tunney as popular candidates for the Nobel Prize as outstanding benefactors of mankind. It in no way diminishes the regard in which they are held by the public if one mentions that their service to humanity has been paid for at astonishingly high rates.

A most casual study of the relationship of sports to the life-cycles of various civilizations seems to show that twice in a nation's history are sports the subject of considerable popular interest.

The first period is during the primitive, pioneer days when the overflowing of strength, vigor, and skill leads to competitive contests in the village square, in the walled fortress, on the deck of a flatboat as it drifts down the Mississippi, on the heights above the field of Marathon just before the wrestlers were summoned to charge the invading host.

These were the "tournaments" of the Middle Ages, or, more exactly, the tournaments had their beginnings in such friendly contests; friendly, although they often led to death. Such were the games upon the sand that Homer and Livy described. The hatchet-throwing of the boys in New England pioneer times, Lincoln's broad-jumping contests on a summer afternoon, the baseball games behind the Northern lines during the Civil War, were all examples of these primitive high spirits.

But this is not the athletic interest which shouts: "Gas and the games"; "Bread and the circus." The paid athlete and the interest in athletics on a wholesale scale have been, in other ages, contemporaneous with an economic or political development that gathered the power of the state into the hands of one man or one group.

The athlete's golden age, in Greece and Rome, followed the establishment of dictatorships. One may fancy the haughty Romans of the equestrian order, stripped of their last real authority, pitching horseshoes in the Forum for lack of treaties to debate. Augustus Cæsar must have developed some fine golfers when he took the few remaining responsibilities of government off the venerable shoulders of the senators who, from Augustus's time on, appeared in public only to satisfy the pageant-love of the crowd.

Then, since it was manifestly pleasanter to sit in the shade and watch a Gallic champion horseshoe-pitcher matched against the Sicilian champion than to pitch horseshoes oneself, the paid athletes became a feature of Roman life. After that it was only a question of shrewd promotion by the Pyles and Rickards until the great gladiatorial spectacles were presented to thunderous applause in the Colosseum.

Athenian philosophers, restrained by an imperial injunction which enjoined them from thinking aloud lest they disturb the political foundations of the nation, doubtless took to betting on Marathon runs, javelin-casts, hammer-throws, and Hellespont swimmers. Sculptors and painters immortalized the winners of the game, for the same reason that a contemporary sculptor modelled Ty Cobb. He thought the statue would be easy to sell in Detroit.

One might say that the world has seen three great conquests, each bringing in its train, along with the political inactivity which followed a concentration of governmental power, a tremendous interest in athletics.

The first of these was the military conquest, the political supremacy of Rome, built over the bodies of her legionaries. And as the ruling power passed from free men to senate, from senate to triumvirate, and later was vested solely in the emperor, there was little for the leisure classes, both upper and lower, to busy themselves about, except professional entertainments. Among these, sports became the most popular.

Upon the collapse of this military power rose the spiritual. Rome ruled again, but this time through the church. Over Roman paved roads marched the new conquerors, sackcloth-clad monks. Before them crumbled princeling and city-state, for all men paid their tribute again to Rome. And as the church, through its temporal and secular princes, gained the ascendancy, the people, serfs and nobles, lost their last vestige of governmental power. They cried out for jousts and tournaments. It was little enough to ask to be entertained.

Even when a reformation threatened, actual readjustments of political institutions were not possible until a shrewd Venetian banker discovered that power, comparable to that once held by the Cæsars and the church, could be bought with money; and that money, put out at interest instead of usury, could breed money, while preserving the principal. The bankers followed the popes as the popes had succeeded the Cæsars.

Devotion to sport in our day may be said again to have followed a concentration of power — in this present instance, the concentration of money.

Comparatively young men can remember when each store along each Main Street was a separate, competitive business, whose details occupied the life and the thoughts of its owner. John Curran or John Donovan (and their experience is quoted, for it happened that they survived the business transformation of this quarter-century) began the retailing of tobacco when a dealer bought carefully and shrewdly of Connecticut and Havana and Manila leaf, hogsheads of choice Burley, which he treated and seasoned for the trade. His business day was a succession of guesses to hit the buying and selling market, to please the public taste.

In corner stores such as those that have replaced their shops a youth of twenty-five now makes change and, reading his instructions from the New York office which arrive each morning, boosts Corn Husk Cigarettes or Burdock Leaf Plug "as per instructions of the 26th inst."

All up and down Main Street, as the chain stores increase from tobacco to hosiery shops, from knitted goods to shoes, and drugs, and books, and furs, and suits, and coats, thinking executives have been replaced by routine clerks, directed and dominated from a central office.

Nor should one suppose that these conditions apply only to the retail-business field. The local foundry is now owned and directed from another city. The shoe-factory, where an owner once labored with adverse markets and perverse cutters, is now administered by wire and letter from Boston. The resident executive, whatever his title may be, has only to worry if the postman should not arrive.

You need not infer that these figure-head managers receive less for their routine duties than the owner-manager of the 1900's. There is no particular scarcity of money. So long as capital is not frightened or rendered coy by injudicious exposure of personal initiative, the managers are very comfortable. They usually have money to spend for anything that will entertain them.

But the ritual of business permits no innovations. That ritual is now set in the directors' meetings in New York as surely as the pope in Rome fixes the order of service for the mass.

It may be that the pope himself cannot now change a word or syllable of the collect. And perhaps the directors of the Amalgamated Cork-Screw and Bottle-Opener Company, Inc., also would be powerless, should they face the necessity of revising the Merchandising Plan No. 1 as set down by Jones I, the Cork-Screw and Bottle-Opener king.

As the cities fill with routine workers, whose each day is a monotony of repetition, so fast does the desire for motor, movies, and sports increase. The car makes possible a variety of scene; the movie and the games give a blessed oblivion to the realities of the standardized job. For capital desires obedience instead of originality, and young men afflicted with intelligence have to exist as best they may. Initiative is as misplaced in modern affairs as in the army.

In other words, golf is not an "instinctive seeking after health in God's great outdoors," as a romantically minded advertising writer for clubs and balls puts it. Motor tours to the national parks are no newly awakened yearning after nature. The canonization of a swimmer, a fighter, an outfielder, a quarter-back is not entirely a universal tribute to a properly developed body.

Business and occupation become duller as the central control increases. Motoring, motion-pictures, camping out, playing or watching games are merely an escape from the circumscribed routine of factory, store, or office.

Nearly two generations of compulsory education, a multiplicity of colleges, universities, and educational endowments, a mass of publications and books and free libraries, one hundred and fifty years of self-government, the refining influence of the radio, the educational ditto of the cinema, the best efforts of the best minds in Washington, and the Anti-Saloon League have succeeded in educating us to the point where a dull, questionably manœuvred non-championship "boxing bout" draws more than one million dollars at the gate.

Last week, in the Breakfast Club, the writer heard a very intelligent and successful metropolitan editor admonishing a young college graduate who was "going into journalism." The youngster was quite happily unconscious that he will call his profession "a job of hustling news" inside of twelve months.

"See if they won't let you break into the sports department," advised the editor. "It's the only editorial department that pays anything nowadays. And the sports writers are the only ones who have a personal following."

It is obvious that the monotony of existence is more oppressive in the smaller cities than in rural or metropolitan districts. And it is the people in the cities who are the real devotees of "gas and the games." The farmer, gambling with prices, weather, and labor, has no need for an athletic safety-valve and his pleasure automobile is really a business machine which takes him quickly to the grocery-store. In New York or Chicago and the half-dozen of the larger urban communities there is always a kaleidoscopic pageant which seems to be all-sufficient for a great part of the population that makes it. The group becomes a perpetual Narcissus, always entranced at watching its own image.

But in those cities where driving one's own car to work is still a possibility, golf-players, the Sunday drivers, the tennis, fight, foot-ball, baseball fans flourish and multiply. As mankind and woman-kind, they are divided into two parts. The cleavage is sharp and distinct. The botanical name of the first group is *Americanus sub-urbanitus*. It grows luxuriantly and its habitat is just outside the one, two, three, or four mile circle whose centre is the court-house steps. The second or opposing group has for its habitat the space within the one, two, three, or four mile circle, and naturalists call it *Americanus apartment-housitus*.

The suburbanites do their own cooking. The apartment-dwellers buy cooked food from restaurant or delicatessen-store. Both complain of the incompetence and scarcity of maids and both cliques have indigestion.

The suburban citizen owns his own car, or will as soon as the last three payments are made. The apartment habitant calls a taxi. And, as in their attitudes toward automobiles, which one drives and one hires, so do they differ in their relationship to sports. In a broad sense the apartment clique hires its sport. From its ranks are drawn the inveterate patrons of the professional paid athlete, whether he be playing as a college, amateur, or admittedly commercial star. They take their sport, as the great Bismarck took his beer, sitting down.

The suburbanite, if bred true, holds loudly that one must play the game oneself if one is to derive benefit therefrom. So he wastes away over tennis for exercise, toils over his golf for social and busi-ness reasons — or to wear funny-looking stockings, one never knows which. He makes a great point of keeping himself "fit." He usu-ally dies a few years sooner than his apartment-house cousin who violated every rule of health and common sense.

Sporting enthusiasms mean that business, like society, is as dull as was English country life in the days of Tom Jones.   No parodies on popular songs sung at semiannual "salesmen's banquets" or "let's-sell-a-hundred-million-dingeses conventions" can make it anything else.

If this be heresy, make the most of it.

VII. SCIENCE

THE CHANGING MIND OF MAN

By EDWIN E. SLOSSON

Edwin Emery Slosson (1865–) is director of Science Service, Washington, D.C., an institution founded to spread scientific knowledge in a popular manner. He has been professor of chemistry at the University of Wyoming, and literary editor of "The Independent." Among his better-known books are "Creative Chemistry" (1919), "Chats on Science" (1923), and "Keeping Up with Science."

WHEN this weary old World got to the end of Chapter XIX of his history, he turned over the page with a yawn and the wish that he would find Chapter XX more exciting than the *fin de siècle* stuff he had been reading. He found it so.

The real dividing line between the two eras is not the century mark, but August 1, 1914. If any book written after that date is the same as though it had been written before we may safely say that it has little relation to actual life. It is not merely in trivial externalities such as the use of Petrograd or Leningrad instead of St. Petersburg but an indefinable though easily detectable alteration of spirit. In more than one novel appearing shortly after 1914 it was possible to tell just how far the author had got when he opened the morning paper and saw that war was declared. We of the present generation used to be amused at our parents because they dated every event in their lives as "before the war" or "after." But we have fallen into the same habit.

What an effect the Civil War had upon American literature is more readily realized by an outsider than by one of us. It is not merely that the struggle against slavery brought out the best of our poetry and prose, but that the great conflict is still furnishing our writers with motives and plots. A few years before the War when I was on a Pacific steamer, I got to talking with a young New Zealander about American literature. "I have stopped reading American novels," he said. "They are all the same and I know the formula. Virginia mansion — southern girl — northern lover — southern rival — Fort Sumter fired upon — war — wounded — she saves him — he saves her — peace and wedding bells."

Of course I denied the slander on American literature, but I could not help thinking of it the other night when I dropped into a motion picture show and found them reeling off this same old plot. Now if sixty years after the Civil War is over its incidents are still the staple of our stories, we may imagine how long literature will be concerned with the Great War.

There was at first manifest as a reaction from the long strain upon our sympathies a disposition to ignore not only the War but whatever else is repugnant in life. This feeling gave rise to an ostrich-literature of astonishing extent and variety. The movement in its best forms may be what William James called it, "the religion of healthy-mindedness"; in its worst forms it is hardly more than a callous hedonism. A single Mark Tapley is a blessing to the community, but when everybody tries to look on the bright side of things all at once, there is apt to be a jam, and toes are likely to get stepped on. Some one has defined a pessimist as "one who has been living in the society of optimists." It was natural that an overdose of the gladiola books should plunge us later into Schopenhauerean gloom. If we do much whistling to keep our courage up we are likely to get down in the mouth.

Now we are in the midst of a reaction from the war enthusiasm. Ex-service men write novels and plays exposing the seamy side of life in the trenches. Pessimism is a dominant note among conquerors and conquered, alike victims of the great catastrophe.

Anatole France said: "Europe is ill, dying. It is Europe that is now the sick man of the world. And peace has not brought its balm."

In France Professor Demangeon of the Sorbonne writes of *Le Déclin de l'Europe*, published in the United States under the title of *America and the Race for World Dominion*. He sees the center of gravity of international politics removed from Europe and the hegemony of the world passing into the hands of Asiatic and American peoples. In England, Webb's *Collapse of Capitalism*, and Dean Inge's *England*, in our own country, Stoddard's *Revolt Against Civilization* must be regarded as symptomatic, though they may be considered unsound. Professor Santayana, in his *Character and Opinion in the United States*, suggests that: "Civilization is perhaps approaching one of those long winters that overtake it from time to time. A flood of barbarism from below may soon level all the fair works of our Christian ancestors, as another flood two thousand years ago leveled those of the ancients."

In Germany Oswald Spengler has produced a book which in scope of scholarship and eloquence of style reminds one of Schopenhauer, Hegel, and Hartmann. It is *Der Untergang des Abendlandes*, "The Downfall of Western Europe"; a comparative morphology of world history, in two large volumes. That it struck the tone of the times is shown by the fact that it figured in the list of best sellers in Germany and America and has already engendered a young library of Spenglerian philosophy. Spengler claims to have discovered the universal formula for the development and decline of political institutions, art, science, religion, and philosophy. He shows the courage of his convictions in daring to project his curve into the future and lay out a course of events. According to Spengler's theory Europe passed from the stage of Culture to that of Civilization in 1800, and has before it the stage of Cæsarism (2000 to 2200) manifested by increasing naturalism in political forms; decomposition of folk organisms into amorphous masses of men; their reabsorption in an empire gradually assuming the character of primitive despotism. The final state (after 2200) is "Egyptianism, Mandarinism, Byzantinism"; torpidity and dissolution of the imperial mechanism; the booty of younger peoples or foreign robbers; slow relapse into the state of early man.

Whether or not we believe with Spengler that political life and philosophic thought move in cycles, it is evident that there is in history an alternation of periods of integration and disintegration, of unification and dissolution, of synthesis and analysis.

The political and intellectual worlds are, like the physical world, balanced between centrifugal and centripetal forces and they sway alternately to either side. The nineteenth century was an epoch of aggregation, of the drawing together of nations into empires and of like-minded groups of different nationalities into world-wide organizations. In the twentieth century the opposite tendency obviously prevails. The great empires are split up into little, isolated, jealous, and antagonistic nationalities. Probably none of us — perhaps no future generation — will live to see as much international intercourse and individual freedom of movement as we saw in 1914. While engineering is reducing the national barriers that have held peoples apart, while railroads and radios are short-circuiting time and space and, as we say, "making the world smaller," the artificial barriers of national boundaries, tariff walls, divergent speech, and hostile attitude are being erected or resurrected.

It is an era of secession, of separation, when the desire for self-determination may overcome the instinct for self-preservation and the lure of self-interest. Languages are being resolved into their constituent dialects and obsolescent tongues revived to serve as a basis for further subdivision. The Ukrainian, Irish, Finnish, Latvian, Lithuanian, Norwegian, Slovak, and Hebrew languages are ardently cultivated, but the advocates of Esperanto and Ido are now rarely heard. Race prejudices are encouraged and systematically cultivated. Sectarian distinctions are being emphasized.

The partition of the common world is naturally followed by the partition of the common mind. The Balkanization of Europe results necessarily in the Balkanization of the mentality. The new map of Europe looks like a patch-work crazyquilt, and doubtless our brains seen under the proper rays would look the same. We are living in an era of speeding up and splitting up. The general trend of the times is toward particularization in politics, science, art, and philosophy.

In literature we have shorter stories and shorter paragraphs, shorter sentences and shorter words. A volume of fiction is usually made up of a chain of short stories. We might call it the catenary type of fiction as distinguished from the reticulate form of the last century.

In painting we see the stipple, the pointillist, the separately discernible brush-strokes. In a futuristic portrait arms, legs, ears, and eyes are scattered over the canvas as though it were a battlefield.

In the most popular form of art to-day, the motion picture, each scene lasts but a thirtieth of a second, and an act of over thirty-five seconds is considered long and tedious. In the movie drama only fifteen minutes may elapse between the introduction of the man and the maid to one another at the beginning and the close-up of the close-up of the couple at the close.

In education specialization has been carried to the extreme, and the field of scholarship is parceled out in private claims like the map of an oil field in a boom.

Nature study in its modern form is characterized by the recognition of individuality in animals and plants. The old idea of evolution was a long, slow accumulation of minute differences, no sudden breaks. The new theory is evolution by jerks. Darwin's favorite was *Natura non fecit saltum,* "Nature never makes a jump." The Mendelist keeps nature on the jump all the time.

In physics we have the jerk theory of energy taking the place of the old continuum. The ether is abrogated by edict of Einstein. He denies the possibility of simultaneity and has given us the conception of local time, as well as space. The ultimate indivisible unit of matter that the Greek named the "atom" proves to be divisible. It should henceforth be deprived of its alpha privative and be called the "tom." The elusive electrons, though thousands of times smaller than the atom and moving with almost the speed of light, can be caught and counted as individuals.

In philosophy we may trace the same trend in the dominance of pluralism over monism and of pragmatism over universalism.

It would be highly improbable that all these tendencies should be disconnected. We must assume that they are all characteristic of the man's mental mood in the present time, though what may be their common cause we may be able to discover.

I must not be understood as meaning that I object to all these movements. That would be as erroneous as it would be futile. Some of them I like and some I do not like, but that makes no difference to anybody but myself. The same tendency that is an advance in science and philosophy may be a retrogression in art or literature.

What makes our age different from all the preceding and invalidates the deductions from history is the possession of inanimate power. Man is drawing upon the accumulated capital of the millions of years prior to his advent. In his use of coal and oil he is lighting his houses and running his machines with the sunshine of the Carboniferous Era. Science has given each of us, every man, woman, and child in America, if the apportionment were equal, a train of twenty slaves to wait upon him night and day.

What this acquisition of inanimate energy might mean for the advancement of civilization we can hardly conceive, for of late it has been largely used for the destruction of civilization.

We have now come to realize that what is done by an engine depends as much on the character of the engineer as on the power of the machine. Our horse-power per capita has risen to an unprecedented height. But has our mind-power per capita increased with it in proportion? If not, this new-found force may prove dangerous to us. The question on which the future depends is whether men can muster up among them enough mentality and morality to manage the stupendous powers which applied science has recently placed in their hands. Once upon a time, long before the oldest of us was born, before any man was born for that matter — I refer to the Jurassic Era — the ruling race was composed of creatures much larger and more powerful than we are. There were giants on the earth in those days, gigantic saurians which when they stood up on their hind legs would tower up four times as tall as a man. But their cranial cavity was smaller than ours. The Jurassic saurians had grown too big for their brains; so they perished.

Now the addition of machine power to the natural strength of man is equivalent to adding stronger arms and longer legs, more skillful hands and sharper senses. It increases his physical capacity but does not directly enlarge his mental ability. It endows him with a giant's strength but does not teach him how to use it.

Among the horrid fancies that haunted the head of Samuel Butler of Erewhon was a nightmare of a coming age when the machines that man has made for his service should rise in Spartacan revolt and enslave man. This skit of Butler's on "The Mechanical Creation" is brought to mind by recent events.

The last few years have made it manifest that in our civilization the mechanical forces have got ahead of the moral forces. Man is mounted on a bigger horse than he can ride. Making war was an efficient process; making peace is — not. The chemist did his bit with amazing, even alarming, proficiency. The diplomat fell down on his job. The physical sciences have evidently been developed so far beyond the political science as to constitute a menace to civilization. The modern man, like the Arabian fisherman, has liberated from the bottle genii that he does not know how to control.

The late War revealed to the horror of the world the possibilities for destruction that science has placed in the hands of mortal man. Unless he has undergone a moral reformation, of which there is no apparent sign, he is not likely to be deterred from using them by a paper prohibition. The Prince of the Power of the Air will be the ruling spirit in the next war — if there is a next war. It is now possible to send an airplane, with or without a pilot, by day or night, over the enemy's country to sprinkle the ground with a liquid so deadly that a whiff inhaled or a few drops touching the skin will cause death. There is no need for fine sighting and mathematical calculations such as the artillery man requires; no need to know where the enemy is. The airships of self-propelled projectiles will simply move over the land, as a farmer's potato-bug sprinkler goes over a field, and a certain strip of territory, say a mile wide and a hundred miles long, will be instantaneously depopulated and will remain uninhabitable for days to come. In the next war there will be no frontiers, no entrenched line, no exempt cities, no distinction between combatant and non-combatant. Fortifications will be futile, for the wall that will withstand a forty-two centimeter projectile is easily penetrable to a molecule of poison gas. On sea the revolution will be quite as complete. There will be no need to sink ships in the next war, for the reason that it is not worth while shooting a riderless cavalry horse.

Can we say that man has reached a moral and mental maturity so that he can be safely entrusted with such dangerous weapons? We cannot take them from him as we can take a revolver from a child. But it is clear that unless man can learn how to make proper use of his new-found knowledge he is likely to destroy himself. Science has endowed man with the power of a superman, but his mind remains human, all too human. He is like a pauper come into a fortune, a laborer who has been put into the position of boss of the shop, a private promoted to command the regiment, a slave made the master of slaves. Man has had no training for such responsibilities as have now been thrust upon him. This new command of time and space, this mastery of unknown forces, this apparition of new perils, this entrance into untried fields, all these are too much for man of to-day. He secretly shrinks and openly blusters. He alternately cowers and brags. He lacks confidence in himself and therefore he suspects others. He is afraid of the dark. He is afraid of his shadow, for that is dark. He shudders with ancient fears. The modern man is suffering from shell shock. He has all the various symptoms. Those who stayed at home are often worse than those that went over there. The victorious nations show the same symptoms as the defeated.

The causeless suspicions, the sudden hatreds, the erratic actions, the intolerance of opposing opinion, the unwillingness to face facts, the return to primitive modes of thought, the alternations of despair and dissipation, the substitution of emotionalism for rationality, the revival of superstition — such are the stigmata of hysteria and such are the characteristics of our time.

In mental diseases where the conscious will relaxes and the more recent centers of thought decay, the patient relapses into a sort of second childhood, using baby-talk, drawing the crude pictures that he made when first he took pencil in hand and reverting consciously to the unconscious voices of infancy. We see the same symptoms in society to-day.

An uprush of infantilism from the unconscious mind of the human race is dragging the modern world back to the superstitions, obscurantism, formalism, gargoylism, and parochialism of the Dark Ages.

Our most advanced artists take as their teachers the most backward savages surviving on the earth. Formerly ambitious young painters went to Greece or Rome to study. Now they journey to Tahiti or the Congo. If a modernist art gallery should be preserved for several thousand years, the archeologist of that day studying the style would unhesitatingly assign it to a period prior to, and more primitive than, the Upper Paleolithic when the Cro-Magnon man depicted the mammoth and the reindeer on the walls of the caves of Altamira, twenty-five thousand years ago.

Modern literature, especially poetry, shows marked reversion to infantile types, in the breaking up of the logical sentence into disconnected fragments, in the appearance of nouns without verbs and adjectives without nouns, in the shortened paragraphs, in the ejaculatory style, in the over-ruling of sense by sound, in the repetitions almost reaching the point of echolalia.

In music the same reversion to the childhood of the race is apparent. The tom-tom sets the pace for modern progress, and the primitive piper calls the tune to which we dance.

The movement toward medievalism in art, religion, industrial organization, and social forms is gaining strength under the leadership of such brilliant writers as Gilbert K. Chesterton. It seems as if man, with his eyes half opened, resents the light. "Pull down the curtain," he shouts to the scientist, "or I'll pitch you out of the window." Then he rolls over and pulls the cover over his head to get another nice long sleep such as he had from A.D. 300 to A.D. 1200.

The world, like a child at Christmas, is willing to receive the material gifts of science but refuses its moral lessons. The world will accept from the hands of science, railroads and radios, soft raiment and foreign foods, airplanes and submarines, but turns a deaf ear when science would talk of peace, efficiency, economy, foresight, and the frank facing of facts.

It was commonly supposed that the fight for evolution and the higher criticism of the Bible which has absorbed so large a part of the intellectual activity of the nineteenth century had been virtually won by the beginning of the twentieth, but we see now a strong movement against both.

We became accustomed to the censorship and the mass suppression of unpopular opinions during the War, and the disposition to use such legal and illegal means for the repression of undesirable views has been growing ever since. The most remarkable feature of the situation is that there is almost universal acquiescence in the restriction of the rights of free speech and propaganda for which our ancestors fought and suffered martyrdom.

Along with the suspicion of science and scholarship comes a distrust and dislike of modern civilization, which is built on a scientific foundation. People are looking back with longing eyes to a presumed primitive paradisial period, or forward to a rural Utopia, to an Edenic or Arcadian life. Some would have us take to the woods; some to the South Seas. "Back to Nature" is the theme of poets, romancers, and even preachers. In India Mahatma Gandhi heads a powerful movement for the elimination of machine power and its products. In Germany the multiform *Wandervogel* movement shows a tendency to revert to prehistoric sun-worship and to discard the costumes and customs of civilized life.

The revival of the worship of the heathen earth-goddess, Magna Mater, began in an inoffensive fashion in the literature of the latter part of the eighteenth century and has since infected all classes and countries. It is now securely enthroned in the two strongholds that

were erected against it, church and school. The neo-pagan poet
Swinburne, who wrote:

> Thou hast conquered, O pale Galilean;
> The world has grown gray from thy breath,

was premature in his despair. He might better have written:

> Thou hast conquered, O rosy Rousseau;
> The world has grown gay from thy breath.

Those who say "God made the country but the devil made the
city" are reading history backward. The word "pagan" means
literally "countryman" (*paganus*). "Civilization" is by self-definition
a product of the city dweller (*civis*). Our modern nature-lovers are
trying to rob the Creator of credit for the highest products of creative activity, those manifested by man. They would make a scape-
goat of God and drive him out of the town into the desert. But God
is not in the thunder or whirlwind, but in the voice, the artificial
creation of man. It is only by overcoming nature that man can
rise.

The cult of naturalism is now dominant everywhere. The call of
the wild is drowning out the appeal of civilization. "Back to barbarism!" is the slogan of the hour. Sink into savagery. Praise the
country and denounce the city. Admire cliffs but make fun of skyscrapers. Extol forests and despise laboratories. Exalt the physical
and ignore the intellectual. Spend $500,000 on a new gymnasium
and let the old library go to ruin. Abolish compulsory Latin and
establish compulsory swimming. Patronize football and neglect
debating. Up with the soldier and down with the savant. Promote
pugilism and suppress pacifism. Jazz your music and cube your
painting. Roughcast your walls, corrode your bricks, deckle your
book-edges, wormhole your furniture, coarsen your fabrics, and de-
form your pottery. Condemn everything new and worship everything old. Regenerate obsolescent languages, restore antiquated
spelling, adopt medieval costumes, revive ancient rituals, inflame
traditional animosities, resurrect forgotten realms, reërect overthrown barriers. Cultivate the primitive virtues of personal bravery
and clan loyalty. Reprove and repress the Christian virtues of
kindliness and universal sympathy.

Some of the signs of the times I have enumerated are good things in themselves, some are trifles of no consequence, but they all hang together and a floating straw shows the current of a river as well as a log. A change in taste is often the precursor of a shift of the trend of human affairs. The dominant tendency of the times is undoubtedly downward and backward, and the advance of science has not yet availed to check it.

It is a reactionary spirit, antagonistic to progress and destructive to civilization. Science and Christianity are at one in abhorring the natural man and calling upon the civilized man to fight and subdue him. The conquest of nature, not the imitation of nature, is the whole duty of man.

We should "move upward, working out the brute, and let the ape and tiger die." Our sins are mostly survivals. Like the vermiform appendix they are vestigial organs, needing excision. It is those who believe in perpetuating the pugnacious propensities of the lower animals and man in his lower stages who are responsible for these years of war and the consequent anarchy. Modern literature is tainted throughout by that most pestilential heresy, zoölatry. From the child's primer to the sociological treatise, animals and insects are held up for our admiration and imitation.

The back-to-nature movement is more psychological than actual. Hundreds of books appear annually in favor of country life, and the only volume in opposition is the decennial census report. For in spite of the eloquent advocates of rurality the cities continue to grow. Thousands of men are forced to labor in dark coal mines in order that they may read the praises of God's own sunshine. Thousands of editors, artists, and nature-writers live in the world's largest city all the year round in order that they may depict its horrors and hardships and urge others to flee to the freedom of the country.

I have often seen and admired the editor of some metropolitan garden magazine, sticking bravely at his desk in the hottest days of summer and pursuing his studies late at night in the roof garden or the winter garden. Others may take his advice and take to the woods but he, like Casabianca, still stands upon the burning deck of the mammoth metropolis. Such heroism inspires like unselfishness. The youths and maidens of our villages and farms, reading in these journals how much more happily situated they are, near to Nature's heart, are seized with compassion for the unfortunate urbanite and rush into the largest city within reach in order to leave more room in the country for the over-crowded city dwellers.

I have referred to the reversion of primitive modes of thought and expression, the blind worship of Nature, meaning by that the sub-human or sub-civilized.

Along with the increasing admiration for the natural comes an increasing belief in the supernatural. The modern believer is disposed to repudiate the Saints and prophets and to pin his faith on Sir Oliver Lodge and Eusapia Palladino. Amulets are again in fashion. The ouija board rivals the typewriter in the production of literature. Astrology has more adherents than lived in ancient Egypt and Babylon. Palmistry is more studied than botany. Rosicrucianism has had a renaissance. The old Roman method of divination has been revived and the apparatus, consisting of a ball on the end of a thread, is being sold for two dollars to determine the sex of a chicken from the egg. The magic wand, the divining rod, is used now to find water and gold and lost articles. A mint of money has been made out of those who were willing to believe that the disease, sex, religion, and race of a distant patient could be determined from the electronic oscillations of a drop of ink or blood. Rain-making, one of the earliest of the magic arts, is to-day a profitable profession. Speaking with tongues, which Paul tried to eradicate from the church of Corinth, is a growing practice in certain of our sects. As David Starr Jordan says: "War lifted the lid on society, and secret actions and beliefs held in the dark now dance openly on every green."

Witchcraft has appeared again in our courts. In a recent French trial evidence was brought forward in court to prove that the accused had killed people by sticking pins into their wax figures. Satan-worship has become a cult, and the Black Mass is celebrated in Paris. That Lord Carnarvon was the victim of Tut-Ankh-Amen's curse is commonly believed. Bleeding images appear in Ireland and weeping virgins in France. Necromancy, or communion with the spirits of the dead, is the fashionable faith of the hour. Sir Conan Doyle, doctor and detective, published photographs of fairies. The Great War was most prolific in miracles. Volumes have been written on the visions and legends of this War. St. George and St. Jeanne d'Arc made up their ancient quarrel and fought on the same side, as numerous witnesses attest. The angels of Mons formed the theme of many a sermon and learned article, and the fact that the vision was traced back to a short story by Arthur Machen in a London daily did not shake faith in it. The eighty thousand Russian soldiers who were transported from Archangel to Scotland and down through England to France were seen by many people en route. One lady who reported seeing them in a railway station said she knew they were Russians because "they wore their cossacks." It seems this legend originated in the fact that the supply of Russian eggs was cut off when Petrograd was blockaded, and so the exporter telegraphed to the London house "eighty thousand Russians shipped via Archangel."

Against witchcraft and necromancy State and Church fought for hundreds of years by all the means in their power. It must not be assumed that the warfare against witches was altogether irrational and unjustified. There was really never any such thing as witchcraft, but there have always been witches. Some of them were harmless; some of them were harmful. A malignant old woman who was believed and believed herself to have the power to inflict injury on her neighbors by her curses and conjurations was undeniably a nuisance to the community. There were two ways the community might have adopted to get rid of the nuisance; one was to punish witches, and the other was not to believe in them. The latter course was impracticable in most communities until recent times; so the former was generally adopted. The same penalty was imposed for catching a hare or cutting down a tree; that is to say, death. But killing off witches did not eliminate the belief in witchcraft. On the contrary it gave it judicial confirmation. So the laws against witchcraft have been abrogated or allowed to fall into innocuous desuetude.

The last prosecution under the witchcraft law in England took place in 1904, when Sir Alfred Harmsworth, editor of the *Daily Mail*, instituted proceedings against Professor and Madame Keiro, palmists and crystal gazers. The jury found them guilty of both fortunetelling and of obtaining money under false pretenses, but the judge only took into consideration the latter count and suspended sentence at that. Instead of burning witches we advertise them. The general atmosphere is becoming so foggy with superstition that we may expect a revival of witchcraft mania and persecution to break out at any time even in our own enlightened land. The death of

Mr. Bryan at the close of his fight against evolution at Dayton, Tennessee, is ascribed by many of his adherents to "mental assassination" by his opponents all over the country.

One of the changes that we must frankly face is the rebellion against the code of morals on which our civilization is based. Formerly those who broke with the Church were careful to declare that they acted in the interests of a purer religion and a higher morality. Those who denied the divinity of Christ were loud in their profession of admiration for the teachings of Jesus. Now, however, we must recognize that a large and increasing class of people in every country not only violate the standards of Christian ethics, but explicitly repudiate them. Violence is advocated as a necessity of the class struggle and even as a desirable thing in itself. Murder is taught as a fine art; the opium dream of De Quincey has become a reality. The destruction of property, the smashing of machines, the damaging of products, the ruination of business, are urged as a sacred duty. Handbooks on the theory and practice of sabotage are published. Work is neglected, not merely from natural laziness, but from conscientious causes. The violation of contract, the breaking of promises, is regarded as the highest ethics. Hatred is diligently cultivated. Licentiousness is openly advocated. Altruism is denied as undesirable or impossible. Sympathy is denounced as a symptom of weakness and degeneracy. Charity is considered as a double injury; it curses him that gives and him that takes. Thrift and industry are classed as vices instead of virtues. Cursing is commended; drunkenness is defended; family quarrels are encouraged; and wife-beating is advocated by popular writers of the day.

Such sentiments in one form or another crop up in current literature so frequently and in such varied forms that it is vain to try to suppress them by any sort of censorship. If it were possible to crush out the Bolsheviki in Russia, the syndicalists of France, the anarchists of Italy, the Nietzscheans of Germany, and the I.W.W. of America, there would still persist this spirit of denial of the established principles of ethics. It is not merely anti-Christian; it is clearly anti-moral, for it is a challenge to all that has been regarded as the code of morality throughout the recorded history of the human race. The code of Hammurabi of Babylon, the maxims of Ptah-Hotep of Egypt, and the laws of Moses show that essentially the same fundamental principles of right and justice were held then as now.   In the seven thousand years since, few persons have questioned them though many have disregarded them.   The new thing is that now we hear them openly and emphatically denied and denounced.   We can only hope that the advocates of the new immorality may be as unsuccessful as the preachers of the old morality in persuading the people to follow their injunctions.

SCIENCE AND THE FAITH OF THE MODERN

By EDWIN GRANT CONKLIN

*Edwin Grant Conklin (1863–   ) is a professor of biology at Prince-
ton University, and is interested in the manner in which science applies
to evolution, heredity, and education. Perhaps his best-known work is
"The Direction of Human Evolution" (1921).*

A BOOK was published in this country two years ago bearing
the striking title *Science Remaking the World*. Fourteen well-
known scholars contributed chapters on subjects ranging all the way
from electrons to evolution, from industries to food, medicine, and
public health, all showing how man is gaining control over his environment.   But science is remaking the world in much more fundamental ways than in these practical and material respects.   It is
remaking not only the outer world in which we live, but also the
inner world of our thoughts and ideals.   It has brought about the
greatest intellectual revolution in human history, a revolution that
concerns the origin, nature, and destiny of man himself — and
thoughtful men everywhere are inquiring what the results are
likely to be.

Many distinguished authors, scientists, philosophers, and theologians have attempted recently to analyze present tendencies and to
forecast the future, with results that range all the way from ecstatic
visions of optimists to the dismal lucubrations of pessimists.   Apostles
of sweetness and light and eternal progress have been more than
matched by the "Gloomy Dean"; Haldane and Thomson have been
answered by Russell and Schiller.   Ancient mythologies have been
revived in the titles of modern Sibylline Books that set forth the
future of mankind as symbolized by Dædalus, Icarus, Tantalus, and
Prometheus.

Many advocates of the old philosophy and theology of supernaturalism and tradition attribute the present disturbed state of the
world to science, which they say has been undermining the old
foundations of the social order, and they call upon all men everywhere to repent and to return to the old faith.   On the other hand,

many advocates of science and the new knowledge maintain that for persons of mature minds, the old, naïve faith of childhood and of the childhood age of the race is gone, and gone forever, and that the only hope for the progress of mankind lies in more knowledge, newer and better faith, and not in a return to old beliefs.

Let us briefly compare some aspects of the old faith and the new knowledge and then inquire what is the duty of forward-looking men in this age of intellectual, social, and religious unrest.

The old cosmogony, philosophy, and theology sought comfort, satisfaction, and inspiration rather than unwelcome truth.   It magnified man by making him the climax and goal of all creation.   It placed the earth, man's home, at the center of the universe.   The sun, moon, and stars were created to give light to the earth.   All things were made to minister to man's welfare.   Man himself was created in the image of God, perfect and immortal.   By his first disobedience he fell from his high estate and

> Brought death into the world and all our woe.

But the promise was given that ultimately evil should perish and good should triumph.   The great Drama of Humanity ran from Paradise Lost to Paradise Regained, from initial perfection to final perfection.

In this old philosophy and theology supernaturalism was universal; there was no proper conception of nature and of natural law. The earth was peopled not only with godlike men but also with manlike gods, angels, spirits, witches, demons.   Some supernatural being was responsible for every phenomenon.   The movements of sun and stars, the return of the seasons, wind and rain, lightning and rainbow, volcanoes and earthquakes, plagues and pestilences, were willed by some supernatural being.   All nature was the expression of wills, big or little, good or bad.

The old ethics was based primarily on the will of God, supernaturally revealed in code or book, and to this certain rules were added from time to time by Church or State under divine guidance. Right was what God approved, wrong was what He forbade, and if ever doubts arose with regard to these there were not lacking those who would interpret the will of God.   Man himself was a free moral agent.   No bonds of heredity or necessity rested on his mind or soul.

He was the architect of his own character, the arbiter of his own destiny. All good was the result of good will, all evil of evil will, and good would be rewarded and evil punished either in this life or in an eternal life of bliss or torment.

There was enormous satisfaction in this view of the universe and of man. It not only glorified man, explained evil, and promised redemption, but it was a great stimulus to efforts for betterment and a source of high ideals and aspirations, and undoubtedly its commands and sanctions worked powerfully to preserve the ethical code. Furthermore, there was admirable directness and positiveness in the old ethics regarding right and wrong, truth and error, freedom and responsibility, rewards and punishments. There was no hazy middle ground between these, no relativity of truth or right or duty to confuse the mind. Things were absolutely true or false, completely right or wrong. This old faith with its specific commandments was especially well suited to immature minds. In the childhood of the individual and of the race there is need of authority and obedience before it is possible to appeal to reason. Childhood is predominantly the age of obedience, adolescence of imitation and example, maturity of reason and judgment. The results of permitting children to grow up as their nature and judgments dictate are perilous for the children and annoying to the neighbors. One such harassed neighbor asked the mother of some children of nature how she expected them to become civilized, and she said, "Oh, we are relying on the germ-plasm"; upon which the unscientific neighbor eagerly asked: "Where do you get it?"

Heredity, or the germ-plasm, determines only the capacities and potentialities of any organism. In every individual there are many capacities that remain undeveloped because of the lack of stimuli suitable to call them forth. These inherited potentialities are both good and bad, social and antisocial, and it is the purpose of education to develop the former and to suppress the latter. In the heredity of every human being there are many alternative personalities. Education is chiefly habit formation, and good education consists in the formation of good habits of body, mind, and morals. It is the duty of parents and teachers to guide children in this respect, to replace unreason by reason, selfishness by unselfishness, and antisocial habits by social ones. To trust to germ-plasm is to forget that heredity furnishes capacities for evil as well as for good, and to disregard the universal experience of mankind.

Society is compelled to repress many of the primordial reactions and instincts of the natural man.   Our whole culture rests upon the suppression of antisocial impulses and the cultivation of social and moral reactions.   If such reactions are to be built into character and become "second nature," they must be cultivated early, preferably in the home, and ethical teaching must be clearcut and authoritative.   The old ethics, when wisely inculcated, was admirably suited to this purpose.   It did develop men and women of high moral character, and to a large extent it forms the foundation of our present social systems.

Contrast with this older philosophy, theology, and ethics the newer revelations of science.   The man of scientific mind seeks truth rather than comfort or satisfaction.   He would follow evidence wherever it leads, confident that even unwelcome truth is better than cherished error, that the permanent welfare of the human race depends upon "the increase and diffusion of knowledge among men," and that truth alone can make us free.   Science is not an esoteric cult and scientific methods are not mysterious or magical processes.   Huxley once defined science as trained and organized common sense, and scientific methods of inquiry are only the careful and accurate methods that are used by intelligent people everywhere in the affairs of every-day life.   These methods consist in observation, comparison, analysis, and generalization.   Every sensible person uses these methods in his business or profession, and in his judgments of men, policies, and institutions.   It is only in its greater accuracy that the scientific method differs from those in universal use.   It is true that no scientific observation, comparison, analysis, or generalization is ever complete or perfect; it is true that in science, as well as in all affairs of life, we deal with probabilities of a higher or lower order rather than with certainties; it is true that all generalizations are theories rather than facts and that all scientific knowledge is relative and not absolute.   But in spite of these limitations, no other method of inquiry has been found as reliable as the scientific method.

It would seem incredible, were it not an actual fact, that any one should object to the use of such methods of inquiry regarding the origin and nature of man, society, government, ethics, religion, the

Bible, or anything else; but, alas! there are thousands, if not millions, of people in this country, some of them educated and intelligent with respect to things with which they have had experience, who refuse to apply common-sense methods of inquiry to such subjects, who characterize those who do this as atheists, blasphemers, dishonest scoundrels, and who denounce science and scientists for laying impious hands on sacred things which must never be studied by the methods of common sense.

To those who refuse to apply scientific methods of inquiry to the study of man and society, cosmogony and theology, ethics and religion, but who base their whole conception of these upon ancient traditions or unreasoning emotions, science has no message; they neither understand the language nor appreciate the methods of science.   But to the increasing number of those who recognize that man, society, and human institutions are proper subjects of scientific investigation, and who also realize that neither authority, tradition, nor prejudice is a safe guide in the search for truth, the question may well arise as to what effect the scientific study of these subjects will have on human ideals, aspirations, and conduct.   Accordingly, these remarks are addressed to those only who accept the methods and results of science in their application to man but who are concerned that mankind shall grow not only wiser but also better as the ages pass.

The methods and results of science have shaken to their foundations the old cosmogony and philosophy.   It is now universally recognized that the earth is not the center of the universe, but a mere dot in a mediocre solar system whirling through immeasurable space.   Man is only one of some millions of species of living things on the earth, and although in mind and soul he is the paragon of animals, it is becoming increasingly certain that the traditional views regarding his supernatural creation and divine perfection are no longer tenable.   On the contrary, the sciences of geology, biology, psychology, sociology, and anthropology are furnishing an ever-increasing amount of evidence that the body, mind, and society of man are products of evolution.   The old philosophy of universal supernaturalism is giving place to a philosophy of universal naturalism; everything that has been scientifically analyzed is found to be natural — that is, orderly, lawful, causal — and many men of science claim that "nature is everything that is." Belief in an anthropomorphic God, a big man in the skies who made us little men in His own image, established society, ethics, and religion by His commands, and governs the world as a human autocrat, is rapidly yielding place to more idealistic conceptions.

It appears probable that the universe and man are subject to immutable natural laws; that causality is universal in the living, as well as in the lifeless world; that the entire man, body, mind, and soul, develops from a germ and is the product of heredity and environment; that will itself is no exception to universal causality, since it is merely a link in the chain of cause and effect, being itself the effect of preceding causes and the cause of succeeding effects; that freedom is the result of intelligence acting as cause; that intelligence is the capacity of consciously profiting by experience; that instincts and emotions are causally related to body functions; that society, ethics, and even religion are based primarily on instincts, emotions, reaction patterns, and ductless glands.

Some of these conclusions are tentative and may be modified by further research, but there can be no doubt as to the general trend of the scientific study of man and his activities. These conclusions, or others of a similar nature, are now accepted by most of the recent investigators in human biology, psychology, and sociology. The application of science and the scientific method of observation and experiment to human behavior has revealed much concerning the physiology of mind as well as the hidden springs of action, the unconscious complexes that determine our constitutional hopes and fears, our prevailing loves and hates, our delusions and failures, and "the sin which doth so easily beset us." Recent studies indicate that there is also a physiology of ethics, and that our conceptions of right and wrong, of good and bad, are associated with particular body functions, reaction patterns, and instincts. In short, man himself, in all of his manifold complexities and activities, is a part of Nature.

These studies and conclusions have raised serious apprehensions on the part of many friends of science and violent opposition on the part of some adherents of the old order, who hold that the guesses of "science falsely so called" are destroying the foundations of religion, ethics, and all that is most valuable in human life. On the other hand, many Christian scientists who have been convinced by the evidence of the essential truth of these new discoveries, are equally certain that truth and goodness and beauty, faith and hope and love, reverence and aspirations and ideals are just as real and as desirable as they ever were, and that religion and ethics remain secure whether the old traditions stand or not.

There can be no doubt that science has given us grander conceptions of the universe than were ever dreamed of in former times. Contrast the old cosmogony with the revelations of modern astronomy, physics, and geology; the old conception of the creation of the universe in six literal days with our present conceptions of the immensity and eternity of natural processes; the old views of the special creation by a supernatural Workman of every one of a million different species of animals and plants, beasts of prey and their victims, parasites and pests, with the scientific view that animals and plants and the universe itself are the results of an immensely long process of evolution!

Even in its revelations concerning man, science is giving us not only truer but also grander views than the old ones. There is sublimity in the conception of man as the climax of vast ages of evolution, as the highest and best product of this eternal process, as the promise of something better still to be. The evolution of man from lower forms of life is not degrading but inspiring. Nature and human history love to proclaim the fact that a humble origin does not preclude a glorious destiny. "The real dignity of man consists not in his origin, but in what he is and in what he may become."

So far as the substitution of natural law for chance or caprice is concerned it has been a great gain not only in our conceptions of the world but also with regard to our inmost selves, for it means order instead of chaos, understanding in place of confusion. If all our activities are the results of natural causation, it means that the will is not absolutely free, but practical people have always known that freedom is relative and not absolute; that we are partly free and partly bound. We know that we are able to inhibit many reactions, instincts, and forms of behavior and to choose between alternatives that are offered. But this does not mean that such freedom is uncaused activity; on the contrary, science shows that it is the result of internal causes, such as physiological states, conflicting stimuli, the remembered results of past experience or education, all of which are themselves the results of preceding causes. Conscious will is not "a little deity encapsuled in the brain" but intelligence acting as cause, while intelligence in turn is the capacity of consciously profiting by experience.

But however we may explain that which we call *freedom*, it is plain that for practical purposes it exists, though in varying degrees in different persons or in the same person at different times, and that it entails a corresponding degree of *responsibility*. The universality of natural law does not destroy ethics nor the basis of ethics; on the contrary, it places morality upon a natural, causal, understandable basis. Furthermore, it leads to a more rational view of human behavior and to a more sympathetic attitude toward the criminal or the offender. As long as men regarded non-ethical conduct as the result of absolutely free will, or of an evil spirit within man, it was logical enough to exorcise the demon by torture and in general to "make the punishment fit the crime" rather than make it fit the criminal. But an understanding of the fact that non-ethical conduct is causal rather than capricious and is the result of natural rather than supernatural causation leads society to look for and to correct these causes rather than to seek vengeance or retribution. Indeed, the only justification for punishment of any kind is the correction of the offender or the protection of society; there is no longer any place in civilized society or in a rational theology for retributive or expiatory punishment.

A study of human history and pre-history shows that there has been a wonderful development of ethics and of religion. There is no satisfactory evidence that these were handed down from heaven in perfect form, but there is abundant evidence that they, in common with all other things, have been evolving and that this process has not yet come to an end. Much of the ethics and religion of the Old Testament was condemned by Christ and would not be tolerated in civilized society to-day. Some of the ethical codes and religious practices current to-day will probably be considered barbarous in times to come.

Variations and mutations are the materials of the evolutionary process and they occur in all possible directions; some of them are progressive, many are retrogressive, but only those that are fit survive. The present is apparently a period of great social, ethical, and religious mutations, and many of these are certainly retrogressive; but let us hope that the decent instincts and the common sense of mankind will see to it that these retrogressive mutations do not survive.

Whatever the ultimate basis of ethics may be, whether divine commands, intuitions and instincts, utility or pleasure, the content remains essentially the same: however much codes and practices may change, our ideals and instincts remain much the same from age to age. Whether written on tables of stone or on the tables of our hearts, the "cardinal virtues" are still virtues and the "deadly sins" are still sins. The deepest instincts of human nature cry out for justice, truth, beauty, sympathy. Ethics that is based on pleasures of the highest and most enduring sort, on pleasures of the rational mind, the better instincts, refined senses, is not different from the ethics of the divine command to "lay up for yourselves treasures in heaven." These are "the enduring satisfactions of life." The new ethics of science does not essentially differ in content from the old ethics of revelation, and the commandments of a God within are no less binding than those of a God without.

Nevertheless, the decline of faith in the supernatural origin of man and of ethics, the decreasing fear of hell or hope of heaven, and the increased freedom of thought and action brought about by science and education have led, in some instances, to a general weakening of the ethical code. When increasing freedom carries with it an increasing sense of responsibility and duty it never endangers progress, but when liberty degenerates into license it marks the beginning of social and moral decay. Freedom is one of the principal goals of human endeavor, but the best use man can make of his freedom is to place limitations upon it. We can be safely freed from external restraints only in so far as we replace these by internal inhibitions.

Partly as a result of this increased freedom from the old restraints, but largely as one of the terrible aftermaths of the World War, lawlessness, immorality, and selfishness seem to be more than usually evident throughout the world to-day. The war gave social sanction to murder, arson, and theft; it unchained the wild beasts in men that long had been restrained; it glorified acts which in times of peace would have been abhorred; and it is no wonder that we are now reaping the whirlwind. Grafters in high office and bandits in high-powered cars are preying on society. Lawlessness and selfishness are widespread. Social solidarity has diminished; races and nations are suspicious or antagonistic; many political parties, churches, labor-unions, social classes are split up into warring factions. Jealousy, suspicion, intolerance, hate, and war are preached from some pulpits and from many platforms and presses. The war that we fondly hoped was to end wars, has apparently only ended peace.

The new freedom which recently has come to women, and which is in the main a progressive change, has led to some bizarre views in these later days. Some of its radical advocates are demanding that it shall mean freedom from all sex distinctions and restraints, except such as are purely personal and voluntary — freedom from marriage and reproduction and the care of children; abolition of the family with its cares and responsibilities; state subsidies for such women as are willing to be mothers and state infantoria for the rearing of all children. Less extreme and therefore more dangerous tendencies are seen in the acceptance of pleasure as the sole basis of ethics and the interpretation of the ethics of pleasure as the satisfaction of animal appetites for food, drink, and sex. The reaction from undue sex repression has led to the opposite extreme of sex exploitation. Obscene literature and plays are not only tolerated but justified and patronized by many leaders of public opinion. In several universities student publications have been suppressed recently by the authorities because of indecency or blasphemy. Free love, trial marriage, easy divorce are widely preached and practised. We vigorously condemn and forbid polygamy in Utah but easily condone worse practices nearer home. The question of the old catechism, "What is the chief end of man?" is now answered by multitudes of people: "To glorify pleasure and enjoy it while it lasts." They say frankly: "I have but one life to live and I propose to get the most pleasure possible out of it. Why should I think of social progress or of posterity? What has posterity done for me? Let us eat, drink, and be merry — for to-morrow we die." Yes, persons who live as mere animals die as the beast dieth; they deserve no immortality on earth or anywhere else. Whether we believe in religion or not, our better instincts revolt against such ethics. We are more than brutes and cannot be satisfied with the pleasures of brutes. We may not accept the old ethics of supernaturalism and tradition, but we cannot adopt the ethics of pigs and hyenas.

What is the remedy for this condition? Fundamentalists think that science in general, biology in particular, and the theory of human evolution most of all, are responsible. They would, therefore, prescribe by law that the latter may not be taught in tax-supported institutions. But if state legislatures are to decide that evolution shall not be taught, they should also eliminate the teaching of all subjects which furnish evidences of the truth of evolution; they should forbid the teaching of morphology, physiology, ecology, paleontology, genetics, comparative medicine, comparative psychology, and sociology. Indeed, there are few subjects that are now studied and taught by comparative and genetic methods that should not be banned. If the farmers of Tennessee and Kentucky can decide what may be taught in biology, they can also decide what may be taught in mathematics, as indeed one sufferer from interminable decimals proposed when he introduced a bill to fix by law the ratio of the circumference to the diameter of a circle at exactly 3.

I have been assured by persons who are very orthodox in faith but very heterodox in spelling and grammar, that "Evolution is all rot"; that it is "leprocy" (sic); that "the heads of evolutionists are full of mud" (their own, of course, being full of "monkey"); and that "God hath chosen the fools of this world to confound the wise," leaving it in doubt as to who is which. Mr. Bryan's characterization of scientists as "dishonest scoundrels" shows the same unrestrained emotionalism as the antivivisectionists show when they call animal experimenters "inhuman fiends." Antievolution, antivivisection, antivaccination, and antiscience are all the outgrowths of extreme emotionalism, recklessness in handling facts, and an utter ignorance of the value of scientific evidence.

Fundamentalism, if logical, would demand the abolition of the teaching of all science and scientific methods, for science in general and not merely the theory of evolution is responsible for the loss of faith in the old traditions. It is folly to attempt to promote education and science and at the same time to forbid the teaching of the principal methods and results of science. The only sensible course would be to abolish altogether the teaching of science and scientific methods and to return to ecclesiasticism. The Church once told scientists what they could think and teach, and now state legislatures propose to do it.   Such methods of resisting change have always failed in the past and are foredoomed to failure now.

The real problem that confronts us, and it is a great problem, is *Counter* how to adjust religion to science, faith to knowledge, ideality to reality, for adjustment in the reverse direction will never happen. Facts cannot be eliminated by ideals and it is too late in the history of the world to attempt to refute the findings of science by sentimental objections or supposed theological difficulties.   If science makes mistakes, science must furnish the cure; it can never be done by church councils, state legislatures, nor even by popular vote.

The only possible remedy for the present deplorable condition is not less but more and better science and education; science that recognizes that the search for truth is not the whole of life, that both scientific reality and religious ideality are necessary to normal, happy, useful living.   We must keep our feet on the ground of fact and science, but lift our heads into the atmosphere of ideals.   "To the solid ground of Nature trusts the mind that builds for aye." Education from the earliest years must teach love rather than hate, human brotherhood rather than war, service rather than selfishness; it must develop good habits of body and mind; it must instil reverence, not only for truth but also for beauty and righteousness.

"Where there is no vision, the people perish."   Man cannot live by bread alone; he must have ideals and aspirations, faith and hope and love.   In short, he must have a religion.   The world never needed a religion of high ideals and aspirations more than it needs it now.   But the old religion of literalism and of slavish regard to the authority of church or book, while well suited to some minds, cannot serve the needs of those who have breathed the air of science. Must all such be deprived of the benefits of a religion which they need and be forced into a false position of antagonism to religion as a whole because they cannot accept all the literalism, infantilism, and incidentalism of so-called fundamentalism?   The fundamentalists, rather than the scientists, are helping to make this an irreligious age.

Science has destroyed many old traditions but it has not destroyed the foundations of ethics or religion.   In some respects it has contributed greatly to these foundations:

1. The universality of natural law has not destroyed faith in God,

though it has modified many primitive conceptions of deity. This is a universe of ends as well as of means, of teleology as well as of mechanism. Mechanism is universal but so also is finalism. It is incredible that the system and order of nature, the evolution of matter and worlds and life, of man and consciousness and spiritual ideals are all the results of chance. The greatest exponents of evolution, such as Darwin, Huxley, Asa Gray, and Weismann, have maintained that there is evidence of some governance and plan in Nature. This is the fundamental article of all religious faith. If there is no purpose in the universe, or in evolution, or in man, then indeed there is no God and no good. But if there is purpose in nature and in human life, it is only the imperfection of our mental vision that leads us sometimes to cry in despair: "Vanitas vanitatum, all is vanity." No one can furnish scientific proof of the existence or nature of God, but atheism leads to pessimism and despair, while theism leads to faith and hope. "By their fruits ye shall know them."

2. Science leaves us faith in the worth and dignity of man. In spite of weakness and imperfection, man is the highest product of a billion years of evolution. We are still children in the morning of time, but we are attaining reason, freedom, spirituality. The ethics of mankind is not the ethics of the jungle or the barnyard. In the new dispensation men will no longer be restrained from evil by fear of hell or hope of heaven, but by their decent instincts and their high ideals. When love of truth, beauty, goodness, of wife, children, humanity, dies in us our doom will be sealed. But it will not die in all men; the long-past course of progressive evolution proves that it will live on, somewhere and somehow.

3. Science leaves us hope for the future. Present conditions often seem desperate; pessimists tell us that society is disintegrating, that there will never be a League of Nations, that wars will never cease, that the human race is degenerating, and that our civilization is going the way of ancient Egypt, Assyria, Greece, and Rome. But though nations have risen and fallen, and cultures have waxed and waned, the major movements of human history have been forward. After civilization had once been attained, it never completely disappeared from the earth. The torch of culture was handed on from Egypt to Greece and from Greece to Rome, and from all of these to

us. One often hears of lost arts and civilizations of the past, but the best elements of any culture are immortal.

The test of biological variations and mutations is whether they lead to increasing fitness, and the test of all social and moral mutations and revolutions, such as those of to-day, is whether they lead to increasing perfection and progress. The great principle of the survival of the fit has guided evolution from amœba to man, from tropisms and reflexes to intelligence and consciousness, from solitary individuals to social organizations, from instincts to ethics, and this great principle will not be abrogated to-day or to-morrow. It is the "power, not ourselves, that makes for righteousness." Man can consciously hasten or hinder this process, but he cannot permanently destroy it. He can refuse to take part in it and can choose to be eliminated, but the past course of evolution for millions of years indicates that somewhere and somehow this process will go on.

The evolutionist is an incorrigible optimist; he reviews a billion years of evolution in the past and looks forward to perhaps another billion years of evolution in the future. He knows that evolution has not always been progressive; that there have been many eddies and back currents, and that the main current has sometimes meandered in many directions; and yet he knows that, on the whole, it has moved forward. Through all the ages evolution has been leading toward the wider intellectual horizons, the broader social outlooks, the more invigorating moral atmosphere of the great sea of truth.

What progress in body, mind, and society; what inventions, institutions, even relations with other worlds, the future may hold in store, it hath not entered into the heart of man to conceive. What does it matter if some men refuse to join this great march onward, what does it matter if even our species should become extinct if only it give place to a better species! Our deepest instincts are for growth; the joy of life is progress. Only this would make immortality endurable. Human progress depends upon the increase and diffusion among men of both knowledge and ethics, reality and ideality, science and religion. Now for the first time in the history of life on this planet, a species can consciously and rationally take part in its own evolution. To us the inestimable privilege is given to coöperate in this greatest work of time, to have part in the triumphs of future ages. What other aim is so worthy of high endeavor and great endowment?

SCIENCE AND MODERN LIFE

By ROBERT ANDREWS MILLIKAN

Robert Andrews Millikan (1868–   ) received his formal education at Oberlin College and Columbia University, and later studied in Germany. His scientific career has been a brilliant one, evidenced by his receiving the Nobel Prize in 1923 for his research in connection with the electron. He was a teacher of physics in the University of Chicago from 1896 to 1921, and is now director of the Laboratory of Physics, California Institute of Technology. He has written several authoritative textbooks, as well as numerous scientific articles of semi-popular nature.

I

LAST summer it was my lot to be called out of my laboratory to attend in rapid succession (1) a meeting of the Committee on Intellectual Coöperation of the League of Nations at Geneva, a body called into being for the sake of assisting in laying better foundations for international good will and understanding than have heretofore existed; (2) the annual meeting of the British Association for the Advancement of Science at Leeds, one of the most important of the Old World's scientific bodies, whose meetings have marked the milestones of scientific progress; and (3) the International Congress of Physics held at Como and at Rome in commemoration of the hundredth anniversary of the death of Alessandro Volta, the discoverer of current electricity, and thus, in a certain sense, the initiator of this amazing electrical century — suitable errands to inspire reflections on the place of science in modern life. I should like to present them in the form of a few pictures.

As we sped, a thousand persons, across the Atlantic in an oil-burning ship in which even the modern stoker — whose "hard fate" has often been held up as a symbol of the evils of our "mechanical age" — has now a comfortable and an interesting job, for he simply and quietly guides the expenditure of hundreds of thousands of man-power represented in the energy of separated hydrogen and oxygen and carbon atoms rushing eagerly together to fulfill their predetermined destiny, and merely incidentally in so doing sending the ship racing across the Atlantic — in the face of that situation, could I, or could any one not completely blind to the significance of modern life, fail to reflect somewhat as follows?   If Cicero, or Pericles, or any man of any preceding civilization, had been sent on a similar errand, had he had any power at all except the winds, it would have been the man-power furnished to the triremes by the straining sinews of hundreds of human slaves chained to their oars, slaves to be simply cast aside into the sea, if they weakened or gave out, and then replaced by other slaves!   Could any man fail to reflect that our scientific civilization is the first one in history which has not been built on just such human slavery, the first which offers the hope, at least, and a hope already partially realized, of relieving mankind forever from the worst of the physical bondage with which all civilizations have heretofore enchained him, whether it be the slavery represented by Millet's man with the hoe — a dumb beastlike broken-backed agricultural drudge — or the slavery at the galley pictured in *Ben-Hur*, or the slavery of the pyramid builders referred to in the books of Moses?

Or again, could any one who stood with me at the base of the column of Trajan, matchless relic and symbol of the unequaled magnificence of Rome, fail to muse first that ancient man in the immensity and daring of his undertakings, in the grandeur of his conceptions, in the beauty and skill of his workmanship, in his whole intellectual equipment, was fully our equal if not our superior?   For we shall leave no monuments like his.   But could he also fail to reflect that ancient man built these monuments solely through the unlimited control of enforced human labor, while we not only have freed that slave, but have made him the master and director of the giant but insensible Titans of the lower world?   We call them now by the unromantic names Coal and Oil.   It is our triumph over these that has given to him freedom and opportunity.   This is one side of the picture of science and the modern world, a side that can be presented with a thousand variants, but all having the same inspiring significance.

Another picture.   In a comfortable English home out in the country in North England a small group is seated, sipping after-dinner coffee, enjoying conversation, and interrupting it now and then to listen to something particularly fine that is coming in over the radio.   The technique of the reproduction is superb, but no more so than that with which we are familiar in our American homes, for the whole broadcasting idea, as well as the main part of its technical development, is American in its origins. But the program that is on the air in England is incomparably superior to anything to be heard here, for the English Government has taken over completely the control of the radio. It collects from each owner of a receiving set twelve shillings a year, and then, with the large funds thus obtained — for there are many radio fans in England as in America — it provides the radio-land public of England with the largest return in education and in entertainment for eight mills a night ever provided, I suspect, anywhere in the history of the world. For it employs only high-class speakers, musicians, and entertainers of all sorts, so that the whole British nation is now being given educational advantages of the finest possible sort through the radio, at less than a cent a family a night, collected only from those who wish to take advantage of them.

Nor is it merely the subject matter of the radio programs that is commendable. The value of giving the whole British public the opportunity to hear the English language used, in intonations and otherwise, as cultured people are wont to use it, is altogether inestimable. And, sitting there in the North of England, we had but to turn the dial to the wave length used by Berlin and we heard an equally authoritative use of the German language, and I envisaged a whole population, or as many of it as wished, learning a new language, easily and correctly, instead of through the stupidities of grammar, as we now go at it. What a stimulant to the imagination! What possibilities are here, only just beginning to be realized, for public education, for the enrichment of the life of the country dweller, as well as the city resident, solely because of such an influence as this of modern physics upon modern life.

II

Religious Science

Now turn to another picture which presents the other side of the story. Sir Arthur Keith, the foremost British anthropologist, is now the president of the British Association. The Leeds meeting represented the fiftieth anniversary of the meeting at which Darwin's then new theory of evolution had been first vigorously debated. Sir Arthur took last summer, as the subject of his presidential address, "Darwin's Theory of Man's Descent As It Stands To-day." He showed that fifty years of fossil study had given extraordinary confirmation to the general outline of the evolutionary conception, had placed it, indeed, upon well-nigh impregnable foundations.

The following Sunday the Bishop of Ripon preached upon science and modern life. He thought we were gaining new scientific knowledge, and acquiring control of stupendous new forces, faster than we were developing our abilities to control ourselves, faster than we were exhibiting capacity to be entrusted with these new forces, and hence he suggested that science as a whole take a ten-year holiday.

When, the next day, the newspaper men, who had had as good a story out of the whole incident as our newspapers got out of the Scopes trial, pressed the Bishop to define more sharply just what he meant by a ten-year scientific holiday, he was reported to have said that he thought the workers in medicine and in public health ought not to stop, since then the germs of disease might steal a march on us, and unavoidable suffering be thereby caused. He had had in mind, rather, a vacation for physics and chemistry and the parts of biology not associated with the improvement of health and the alleviation of suffering.

The Bishop's explanation is of value as throwing an illuminating side light upon the sort of emotionalism and misunderstanding that is represented in much of the present public antagonism to our scientific progress. The question which the Bishop raises is proper enough, but the conclusion is altogether incorrect. For, first, physics and chemistry cannot take a holiday without turning off the power on all the other sciences that depend upon them, for biological science is at bottom only one of the applications of physics and chemistry; and, second, physics, chemistry, and genetics are, in fact, the great, constructive sciences which alone stand between mankind and its dire fate foreseen by Malthus. The palliative sciences, such as the Bishop mentioned, are indeed worthy of support, but without the fundamental sciences they only hasten and make inevitable the horrors of that day.

The incident is presented because it is illustrative of a widespread attitude as to the danger of flooding the world with too much knowledge. The fear of knowledge is quite as old as the Garden of Eden. Prometheus was chained to a rock and had his liver torn out by a vulture because he had dared to steal knowledge from the gods and bring it down to men. The story of Faust, which permeates literature up to within a hundred years, is evidence of the widespread, age-long belief in the liaison between the man of knowledge and the powers of darkness. It will persist so long as superstition, as distinct from reverence, lasts.

But there is a real question, not to be thus easily disposed of, which the Bishop's sermon puts before the man of science. It is this. "Am I myself a broadly enough educated man to distinguish, when I am engaged in the work of reconstruction, between the truth of the past and the error of the past, and not to pull them both down together? Am I sufficiently familiar with what the past has learned, and what it therefore actually has to teach, and am I enough of a statesman not to remove any brick from the structure of man's progress until I see how to replace it by a better one?" I am sorry to be obliged to admit that some of us scientists will have to answer that question in the negative. Such justification as there may be for the public's distrust of science is due chiefly to the misrepresentation of science by some of its uneducated devotees. For men without any real understanding are of course to be found in all the walks of life.

This problem, however, is not at all peculiar to science. In fact, the most wantonly destructive forces in modern life, and the most sordidly commercial, are not in general found in the field of science, nor having anything to do with it. It is literature and art, much more than science, which have been the prey of those influences through which the chief menace to our civilization comes. After the law of gravitation, or the principle of conservation of energy, has been once discovered and established, physics understands quite well that its future progress must be made in conformity with these laws, at least that Einstein must include Newton, and it succeeds fairly well in keeping its levitators and its inventors of devices for realizing perpetual motion, under suitable detention, or restraint, somewhere. But society has as yet developed no protection against its perpetual-motion cranks — the devotees of the new, regardless of the true — in the fields of literature and art, and that despite the fact that sculpture has had its Phidias and literature its Shakespeare just as truly as physics has had its Newton or biology its Pasteur.

I grant that in literature and art, and in nonscientific fields generally, it is more difficult than in science to know what has been found to be truth and what error, that in many cases we do not yet know; nevertheless there are even here certain broad lines of established truth recognized by thoughtful people everywhere. For example, the race long ago learned that unbridled license in the individual is incompatible with social progress, that civilization, which is orderly group life, will perish and the race go back to the jungle unless the sense of social responsibility can be kept universally alive. And yet to-day literature is infested here and there with unbridled license, with emotional, destructive, oversexed, neurotic influences, the product of men who either are incompetent to think anything through to its consequences or else belong to that not inconsiderable group who protest that they are not in the least interested in social consequences anyway, men who, in their own words, are merely desirous of "expressing themselves." Such men are, in fact, nothing but the perpetual-motion cranks of literature and of art. It is from this direction, not from the direction of science, that the chief menaces to our civilization are now coming.

But, despite this situation, I should hesitate to suggest that all writers and all artists be given a holiday. This is an age of specialization, and properly so, and some evils from our specialization are to be expected. Our job is to minimize them and to find counter-irritants for them. I am not altogether discouraged even when I find a humanist of the better sort who is only half educated.

Let this incident illustrate. Not long ago I heard a certain British literary man of magnificent craftsmanship and fine influence in his own field declare that he saw no values in our modern "mechanical age." Further, this same man recently visited a plant where the very foundations of our modern civilization are being laid. A ton of earth lies underneath a mountain. Scattered through that ton in infinitesimal grains is just two dollars' worth of copper. That ton of earth is being dug out of its resting place, transported to the mill miles away, the infinitesimal particles of copper miraculously picked out by invisible chemical forces, then deposited in great sheets by the equally invisible physical forces of the electric current, then shipped three thousand miles and again refined, then drawn into wire to transport the formerly wasted energy of a waterfall — and all these operations from the buried ton of Arizona dirt to refined copper in New York done at a cost of less than two dollars, for there was no more value there.

This amazing achievement not only did not interest this humanist, but he complained about disfiguring the desert by electrical transmission lines. Unbelievable blindness — a soul without a spark of imagination, else it would have seen the hundred thousand powerful, prancing horses which are speeding along each of those wires, transforming the desert into a garden, making it possible for him and his kind to live and work without standing on the bowed backs of human slaves as his prototype has always done in ages past. Seen in this rôle, that humanist was neither humanist nor philosopher, for he was not really interested in humanity. In this picture it is the scientist who is the real humanist. Nevertheless, the Bishop of Ripon was right enough in distrusting the wisdom, and sometimes even the morality, of individual scientists, and of individual humanists, too. But the remedy is certainly not to "give science a holiday." That is both impossible and foolish. It is rather to reconstruct and extend our educational processes so as to make broader-gauge and better-educated scientists and humanists alike. There is no other remedy.

III

To the Soul

But, says some one, these pictures so far deal only with the superficial aspects of life. What has science to say to him whose soul is hungry, to him who cries, "Man shall not live by bread alone"? Has it anything more than a dry crust to offer him? The response is instant and unambiguous. Within the past half century, as a direct result of the findings of modern science, there has developed an evolutionary philosophy — an evolutionary religion, too, if you will — which has given a new emotional basis to life, the most inspiring and the most forward-looking that the world has thus far seen. For, first, the findings of physics, chemistry, and astronomy have within twenty-five years brought to light a universe of extraordinary and unexpected orderliness, and of the wondrous beauty and harmony that go with order. It is the same story whether one looks out upon the island universes brought to light by modern astronomy, and located definitely, some of them, a million light years away, or whether he looks down into the molecular world of chemistry, or through it to the electronic world of physics, or peers even inside the unbelievably small nucleus of the atoms. Also, in the organic world, the sciences of geology, paleontology, and biology have revealed, still more wonderfully, an orderly development from lower up to higher forms, from smaller up to larger capacities — a development which can be definitely seen to have been going on for millions upon millions of years and which therefore gives promise of going on for ages yet to be.

> A fire-mist and a planet,
> A crystal and a cell,
> A jellyfish and a saurian,
> And caves where the cavemen dwell;
> Then a sense of law and beauty,
> And a face turned from the clod —
> Some call it Evolution,
> And others call it God.

That sort of sentiment is the gift of modern science to the world.

And there is one further finding of modern science which has a tremendous inspirational appeal. It is the discovery of the vital part which we ourselves are playing in this evolutionary process. For man himself has within two hundred years discovered new forces with the aid of which he is now consciously and very rapidly making over both his physical and his biological environment. The Volta Centenary, a symbol of our electrical age, was representative of the one, the stamping out of yellow fever is an illustration of the other. And if the biologist is right that the biological evolution of the human organism is going on so slowly that man himself is not now endowed with capacities appreciably different from those which he brought with him into the period of recorded history, then since, within this period, the forward strides that he has made in his control over his environment, in the development of his civilization, have been stupendous and unquestionable, it follows that this progress has been due, not to the betterment of his stock, but rather primarily to the passing on of the accumulated knowledge of the race to the generations following after. The great instruments of progress for mankind are then research — the discovery of new knowledge — and education — the passing on of the store of accumulated wisdom to our followers. This puts the immediate destinies of the race or of our section of the race, or of our section of our country, largely in our own hands.   This spirit and this conviction are the gift of modern science to the world.   Is it, then, too much to say that modern science has remade philosophy and revivified religion?

IV

The next picture brings into the foreground what I regard as the most important contribution of science to modern life.   The scene is laid in Geneva; the occasion, a meeting of the Council of the League of Nations.   The speaker is Nansen, the tall, white-haired, rugged-faced, heavily mustached Norwegian explorer, now directing the tamed and controlled energies of his fierce viking blood to trying to find a solution to the tragic situation of the Armenians, a situation to which heretofore there has been no solution except extermination. After four years of effort he brings in a discouraging report, and thinks the League of Nations must write down "the record of its first failure."   He requests the Council to strike the Armenian matter from its program, promising, however, to keep at it himself and to try through other agencies to find a solution.   Then Briand of France speaks.   Quietly he begs Nansen not yet to despair of the League's assistance.   He is sure some solution can be found, and promises that his country, in financial straits though it be, will not be lacking in lending its assistance.   The representatives of other nations follow in similar vein, the problem is retained on the Council's program, and the conviction is at least fortified that with the right kind of attack a solution may yet be found to an age-old difficulty — that extermination is not the only answer to race rivalry.

With the right sort of attack!   What is it that the League of Nations as a whole is trying to do?   It is trying for the first time in human history to use the objective mode of approach to international difficulties, in the conviction that there is some better solution than the arbitrament of war.   But whence has come that conviction?   Without the growth of modern science it certainly would have been slower in coming.   Perhaps it would not have come at all. In the days of the jungle, war *was* probably the best solution — at least it was the only solution.   It was Nature's way of enabling the fittest to survive, and we are not so far past the days of the jungle yet. Within fifty years as great an historian as Eduard Meyer and as great a humanist as John Ruskin have lauded war as the finest developer of a people. But it has been quite recently demonstrated that war is no longer, in general, the best way to enable the fittest to survive. The Great War profited no one. It injured all the main participants. Modern science has created a new world in which the old rules no longer work.

New occasions teach new duties; Time makes ancient good uncouth;
They must upward still and onward, who would keep abreast of Truth.

Alfred Nobel was perhaps not far from right when he thought that he had taken the main step to the abolition of war by the invention of nitroglycerine. He has, I suspect, exerted a larger influence in that direction than have all the sentimental pacificist organizations that have ever existed. For sentimental pacificism is, after all, but a return to the method of the jungle. It is in the jungle that emotionalism alone determines conduct, and wherever that is true no other than the law of the jungle is possible. For the emotion of hate is sure sooner or later to follow on the emotion of love, and then there is a spring for the throat. It is altogether obvious that the only quality which really distinguishes man from the brutes is his reason. You may call that an unsafe guide, but he has absolutely no other unless he is to turn his face back toward the jungle from which he has come. There is no sort of alternative except to set up in international matters, precisely as we have already done in intercommunity and interstate affairs, some sort of organization for making studies by the objective method of international difficulties and finding other solutions.

But what exactly do I mean by the objective method? Somebody has said that "what we call the process of reasoning is merely the process of rearranging one's prejudices," and we admit the truth of this assertion when we say, as we so often do, "Oh, yes, I understand that is the excuse, but what is, after all, the reason?" Indeed, there is no question that a large part of what we call reasoning is in fact simply the rearranging of prejudices. In so far, for example, as we are Republicans, or Democrats, or Presbyterians, or Catholics, or Mohammedans, or prohibitionists, because our fathers bore those brands — and many of us will be admitted by our acquaintances, at least, to have no other real grounds for our labels — our so-called reasonings on these subjects certainly consist in nothing more than the rearrangement of our prejudices. The lawyer who takes a case first, and develops his argument later, is obviously only rearranging his preconceptions.

If, however, one wishes to obtain a clear idea of what the objective method is, he has only to become acquainted with the way in which all problems are attacked in the analytical sciences. In physics, for example, the procedure in problem solving is always first to collect the facts — namely, to make the observations with complete honesty and complete disregard of all theories and all presuppositions, and then to analyze the data to see what conclusions follow necessarily from them, or what interpretations are consistent with them. This method, while not confined at all to the physical sciences, is nevertheless commonly known as the scientific method in recognition of the fact that it has had its fullest development and its most conspicuous use in the sciences. Indeed, I regard the development and spread of this method as the most important contribution of science to life, for it represents the only hope of the race of ultimately getting out of the jungle. The method can in no way be acquired and understood so well by the study of the analytical sciences, and hence an education which has left out these sciences has, in my judgment, lost the most vital element in all education.

Nor is that merely the individual judgment of a prejudiced scientist, as the following quotation from one of our most prominent humanists, a member of the faculty of Harvard University, shows:

It is the glory of pure science and of mathematics that these subjects train men in orderly and objective thinking as no other subjects can. Here are fields of study in which loose or crooked thought leads inevitably to demonstrable error, to error which cannot be glossed over or concealed. Here are branches of knowledge in which there is no confusion between right and wrong, between *post hocs* and *propter hocs*, between the mere coincidences and the consequences of a cause. When you have finished with a problem in any of the exact sciences you are either right or wrong, and you know it. That is why we call them exact sciences, to distinguish them from philosophy, sociology, economics, and the other social sciences, in which the difference between truth and error is still, in most cases, a matter of individual opinion. Many years ago physics was known as "natural philosophy"; it was merely a body of speculative ideas concerning the mechanics of nature. It became an exact science by developing an inductive methodology, which makes all the difference between science and guesswork.

Some years ago, in the Harvard Law School, we thought it worth while to inquire into the educational antecedents of the student body, with a view to ascertaining whether there was any relation between success in the study of law and the previous collegiate training of these young men. In the Harvard Law School there are more than a thousand students, all of them college graduates, drawn from every section of the country. Nearly all of them have specialized, during their undergraduate years, in some single subject or group of subjects — languages, history, science, philosophy, economics, mathematics, and so on. Offhand one would probably say that the young man who had devoted most of his attention to the study of history, government, and economics while in college would be gaining the best preparation for the study of law — for these are the subjects which in their content come nearest to the law; but that is not what we found. On the contrary the results of this inquiry showed that the young men who had specialized in ancient languages, in the exact sciences, and especially in mathematics, were on the whole better equipped for the study of law, and were making higher rank in it, than were those who had devoted their energies to subjects more closely akin.

But can education, even in the sciences, do the work fast enough to prevent the catastrophe feared by the Bishop of Ripon? Can we learn to control our emotions and impulses and our new-found powers, to take the long view, and to do the rational thing instead of the emotional, or the vicious, thing with the enormous forces given to us by science? Can we alter human nature?

Perhaps the following is a partial answer: twenty-five years ago if any one had asked you or me or any body of men, however intelligent, whether human nature could be so altered in a reasonable time as to make it safe to entrust practically every grown man in California and part of the women and children with a thirty-horsepower locomotive which they might drive at will through the crowded cities, and race at express-train speed over the country roads of California, the answer would certainly have been a decided negative. Nobody on earth, I suspect, would have thought such a result possible. And yet that is precisely what has happened. It is true we have accidents, too many of them by far. There is still much to improve, and yet the risk is so small that we never think of it when we enter an automobile. I marvel at the success of it every time I drive in city streets. I glory in it when I see the new race of men the taxi business has created in a city like London. Contrast the clear-eyed, sober, skillful, intelligent-looking London taxi-driver of to-day with the red-nosed wreck of a human being who used to be the London cabby of a quarter century ago, and see what responsibility and power do in altering human nature.

Also the picture which modern science has unfolded of the age-long history of the biological organism is one in which it is seen adapting itself with marvelous success to changes in external conditions. That we, too, at our end of this evolutionary scale, have inherited this adaptability was one of the most striking lessons of the late war, in which we settled down to the endurance of what we thought intolerable conditions with amazing rapidity.

V

If, then, there be any notes of optimism in modern life, one of them is certainly the note played by modern science. If there be any escape from Malthusianism — the world's greatest problem — science alone can provide it. It is clearly the development of science and its application to modern life that have made possible the support in Great Britain to-day of forty million people, when a hundred and fifty years ago Benjamin Franklin called England over-populated with eight millions, and when Robert Fulton a little later, in a prophetic mood, saw England holding sometime "a population of ten million souls." Perhaps this population has to-day gone too far, but the check is being applied. In both England and Sweden to-day the birth rate is less than it is in France. With the creative power of physical science, and the application of intelligence to the findings of biological science, even this problem of population can be faced with a good measure of hope. An international union for its continuous study was formed last summer at Geneva. That is the objective way to begin to attack it.

Finally, can science save our civilization from the fate that has befallen its predecessors, the Sumerian, the Egyptian, the Greek, the Roman, and the others that have risen and then declined? Are the Keyserlings, the Spenglers, and the other prophets of decay and death to be regarded as real prophets?

The answer is, of course, a secret of the gods, but that these "prophets" are "multiplying words without knowledge" it is easy to show. For our modern civilization rests upon an altogether new sort of foundation. These older civilizations have rested upon the discovery of new fields of knowledge or of art — fields which the discoverers have indeed cultivated with such extraordinary skill that they have been able to reach a state of perfection in them that succeeding generations have often been unable to excel. Witness the sepulchral art of the Egyptians, and the perfection of such principles of architecture as they knew how to use; witness the sculpture, the painting, the esthetic and the purely intellectual life of the Greeks — an accomplishment so great as to inspire an outstanding modern artist to say that there has been no new principle discovered in either sculpture or painting since the age of Pericles; witness the principles of government and of social order discovered by the Romans, or the arch in architecture, altogether Roman, but reaching perhaps its perfection in the Romanesque and the Gothic of a few centuries later; witness the discovery of the principles of music in central and southern Europe in the Middle Ages, and the perfection that art attained within two or three centuries. And let us remember, too, that humanity for all time is the inheritor of these achievements. This is the truth of the past which it is our opportunity and our duty to pass on to our children.

But our modern world is distinctive not for the discovery of new modes of expression or new fields of knowledge, though it has opened up enough of these, but for the discovery of the very idea of progress, for the discovery of the method by which progress comes about, and for inspiring the world with confidence in the values of that method. So long as the world can be kept thus inspired, it is difficult to see how a relapse to another dark age can take place.

Even if the biological evolution of the human race should not continue — though why should what has been going on for millions of years have come to an end just now? — yet the process by which progress has been made within historic times can scarcely fail to be continuously operative. This process is the discovery of new knowledge by each generation and the transmission to the following generation of the accumulated accomplishment of the past — the discovery of new truth and the passing on of old truth.

The importance of both elements in this process has not been realized in the past, and dark ages have come. But the means for the spread of knowledge, for its preservation and transmission, the facilities for universal education and inspiration, the time for leisure, and the opportunity for thought for everybody — all these have been so extended by modern science, and are capable of such further extension, that no prophecy of decline can possibly have any scientific foundation. Even arguing solely by the method of extrapolation from the past, modern science has shown that the ups and downs on the curve of history are superposed upon a curve whose general trend is upward, and it has therefore brought forth a certain amount of justification for the faith that it will continue to be upward. In the last analysis, humanity has but one supreme problem, the problem of kindling the torch of enlightened creative effort, here and there and everywhere, and of passing on for the enrichment of the lives of future generations the truth already discovered — in two words, the problem of research and education.

VIII. RELIGION

RELIGION AND THE YOUNGER GENERATION

By JAMES BISSETT PRATT

James Bissett Pratt (1875–   ) has studied at a multitude of colleges, including Williams, Harvard, Columbia, and the University of Berlin, and at times when he was not thus engaged has taught philosophy. At present he is a professor at Williams College. He has also spent much time studying the native religions in India, Japan, China, and Siam. Some of his more important books are: "The Psychology of Religious Belief" (1907), "India and its Faiths" (1915), and "Matter and Spirit" (1922).

THERE can, I think, be little question as to the truth of the general impression that something has happened to the religion of our young people. They do not believe what their predecessors believed; they do not express the feelings their predecessors felt and expressed; they do not act as their predecessors acted. Most important of all, they are not interested in the religious things that interested the older generation. Their grandfathers believed the Creed; their fathers a little doubted the Creed; they have never read it. I purposely put the matter in exaggerated form, but as a bare outline of the general impression many people are getting from what they regard as "typical" representatives of the rising generation, this will fairly serve.

This impression is probably due chiefly to the attitude of some of our young people towards the churches. Thus *The Congregationalist* tells us: "The vast majority of [college] students are not interested in the church. They have no sense of the importance of the church. They have relegated the church beyond the horizon of their interests." And in another connection the same periodical speaks of the "coldly critical and even contemptuous attitude towards Christianity" shown by many young men and women in contrast to the "fervent faith and consecrated spirit" of "their fathers and mothers." The more extreme representatives of these so-called typical young people go to church neither to pray nor to scoff; if they can help it they simply do not go. If they go they are well behaved but inwardly bored. An unusual preacher can catch and hold their attention, but few there be that can. Nor is there any rule by which the trick can certainly be done. If the minister preaches down to them, they are quick to discover the fact and despise him for it. If he discusses politics, they think he had best stick to his last. If he expounds theology, they hurriedly close their ears. And if he speaks of the inner things of the spirit, they fail to understand the terms he uses.

Of course, many do still fervently go to church as their fathers went, and eagerly listen to the sermon as their fathers listened, and inwardly feel as their fathers felt; but I have in mind that large portion of the younger generation — whether a minority or a majority I know not — which is developing an attitude towards religion seldom met with thirty or forty years ago, and which therefore sets the tone for the general impression that the observer inevitably forms. These young people are as far removed from heresy as from orthodoxy. The rampant atheism of the Thomas Paine-Colonel Ingersoll variety, which so tortured our pious mothers and grandmothers, is as little characteristic of the young men and women of whom I write as is the orthodox dogmatism which Paine and Ingersoll attacked. If you ask them whether they are orthodox or heterodox, they may hardly know what you mean, and they certainly will wonder that you should care.

Year by year this contrast with the past becomes more marked — as, I think, every college teacher, every one who is brought into contact with the development of thoughtful young men and women, must note. For nearly twenty years I have been giving a course on the history of religions. I remember with what hesitancy and with what precaution, in the first years of my teaching, I turned from China, India, and Persia, and approached the religion of the Old Testament. The transition had to be made with all the sympathetic skill I could muster; and never a year went by but some of my students came to me after sleepless nights, wearied with inner struggle, sometimes with indignant voices, to talk out, after class, the implications involved in the Higher Criticism and in the attempt to deal with the Hebrew religion in the same historical light as we had studied Hinduism and Buddhism. All this is changed now.

The inspiration of the Scriptures does not interest young people. Neither do the Scriptures. It is not safe to take for granted any knowledge of Old Testament or New.   Many a college student to-day, I feel sure, would fail to find anything funny in Tom Sawyer's predicament when before the assembled Sunday School he was asked to name the first two Disciples, and answered David and Goliath.   When Mark Twain wrote his earlier books, Hebrew kings and prophets, Christian apostles and martyrs were familiar acquaintances of elementary-school children.   Many of our recent college graduates know as little of them as they do of Greek mythology.   Not long ago one of the students in the course on the history of religions which I have mentioned informed me (on paper) that the ancient Hebrews were fairly moral considering their time, "though of course they did not have our Ten Commandments."

The youth of every age have probably been looked upon somewhat askance by their elders as radical or irreligious.   Yet it is certainly true that not often has the change in religious attitude from one generation to another been so great as has the change that we are observing to-day.   A large proportion of our young men and women not only do not know what they believe on religious and cosmic matters, but in an unusual degree have little care to come to any conclusion.   They feel much less need of a creed or of any definite form of faith than most youthful generations have felt.   They have probably less respect for authority than any of their predecessors have had since the Renaissance.   They are, I think, very fine young people, with many noble ideals which they serve with considerable fidelity, but they have notably less sense than had their ancestors of any supernatural sanction for their morality.   Their outlook is peculiarly objective.

Conditions vary, of course, from place to place, and I am told that in the Middle West there has been much less falling off of interest in church and religion than in the East.   I may, moreover, have exaggerated the situation in the East — in fact, for purposes of emphasis I have consciously done so.   Nevertheless, most observers, I believe, would agree in the main with what I have said.   Agreement, however, would end here, and would turn into rank disagreement on the question whether the change that has come about in the attitude of young people towards religion is a sign of degeneration or of progress.   One type of mind can see in it nothing that is good.   Mrs. Gerould, for example, thinks the morals of the younger generation are in a bad way, and attributes their degenerate condition to the loss of religion. Religion for her, moreover, means belief in God and an authoritative moral code based on that belief. She declares that to the weakening of religion in this sense are due "the vulgarity of our manners and the laxity of our morals."

Somewhat to my surprise, I found the opposite point of view to be the prevalent one among both the clergymen and the educators with whom I have discussed the matter. They admit the changed attitude of the younger generation towards religion, but most of them insist that there is much more of gain than of loss in the change. The old-fashioned college prayer-meeting has indeed been given up; but its place has been taken by the Forum or the Good Government Club or the night school. Students no longer painfully analyze and expose their inner life in fervid (or hypocritical) "experience meetings"; but they spend evenings teaching English or arithmetic to newly arrived immigrants, or their Saturday afternoons directing a Boys' Club, or they study social conditions with a view to the betterment of society and the prevention of evil. They talk less about saving their souls, but they far outstrip their predecessors in actual social service. One college professor, writing to me of the changed attitude of the young, comments, "All this is not a matter for sadness but rather for satisfaction. They are mentally a far more wholesome lot than our narrow-minded, prejudiced fathers were." Another educator, the president of a college in New York State, in a recent letter, puts it thus: "The day when the leaders in the prayer-meetings copied in the examination room seems fortunately past. There is more honor and more sincerity, while I admit there is less evidence of a formal attitude towards religion." Much the same opinion was frequently expressed — and apparently with the adhesion of nearly all present — at the symposium on religious conditions recently held by the college faculties of Western Massachusetts. The general verdict seemed to be that while the lower fifty per cent of our college students are somewhat bewildered on moral questions, the upper fifty per cent are notably more efficient and aggressive in the cause of genuine righteousness and in devotion to truly Christian ideals, than were the upper fifty per cent of students in the same colleges twenty-five years ago.

Between views as diverse as these two types — the pessimistic and the optimistic, we may term them — there is obviously more than a difference in evaluation. The disagreement as to the goodness or badness of our young people's religious attitude is based in part upon a disagreement as to the facts. The younger generation are very nearly devoid of religion, hold the pessimists. The younger generation are at heart as religious as the old, insist the optimists; their change of creed, their loss of interest in the church, their lack of respect for authority, and their ignorance of the Bible are merely *forms*, merely superficial matters and of no vital importance. So far as this divergence of opinion is due to disagreement as to what the word *religion* should be taken to mean, the dispute is hardly worth our consideration. In fact there is, I think, no important disagreement between the pessimists and the optimists as to how the word religion should be interpreted. Both sides, I fancy, would agree that religion means something more than morality or social service, something more also than creed; that it has to do with man's cosmic as well as his human relations, and that it involves his emotions and his conduct as well as his belief. But the question really at issue is by no means verbal, and it goes much deeper than this. It is this: Have the younger generation, in throwing aside (or in being deprived of) some of the traditional "forms" of religion, lost anything of solid and vital importance, anything that is essential to or helpful for the values of life? I use both the phrases *essential to* and *helpful for* the values of life because the two are by no means identical and both must be considered. The double question is plainly, in the last analysis, one of psychology.

Are the traditional forms of religion which the young seem to have laid aside, essential to the values of life? And, first of all, are they essential to religion? On this question there can be little doubt that the position of the optimists is unshakable. Religion and also life can get on — can continue to exist — without these forms, because both life and religion are deeper and more fundamental than any forms of expression or means of cultivation can be. The young people of our day are doubtless by nature just as religious as any of the older generations. It will not do, indeed, to say that man has a religious instinct; yet it will be very near the truth to assert that man is instinctively religious, and that, therefore, no surrender of traditional creeds and institutions can deprive him of religion. Given a being endowed, as man is, with the emotions of awe and reverence, with the sentiment of love, with curiosity intensified by reason into an incipiently metaphysical or cosmic sense — given such a being, you are bound to find emerging in his consciousness that attitude towards the Determiner of Destiny which is, psychologically considered, what we mean by religion.   The forms which our traditional Christianity has developed are, therefore, by no means essential to religion, and the fact that the younger generation make less use of them than did their predecessors by no means proves that they are irreligious.   Without religion, in fact, they cannot long be.   Before their race is run they must and will, by the very foundation principles of human nature, work out some sort of attitude — or many varied attitudes — towards the Determiner of Destiny.

If, however, both life and religion can get on without the traditional forms of expression and cultivation which past generations have made use of, it does not necessarily follow that they can get on *just as well*, or that these ancient rites can be dropped without genuine loss to the values of life.   Here, in fact, is the real heart of the question.   And if we are to discuss it intelligently, our first effort should plainly be to define more clearly than we have yet done what these "traditional forms" of religion are.   I am not sure that I can tell all that should be included under this term, but the main part of its meaning will, I think, be summed up under the following four heads: a definite faith; a revered and familiar sacred book; a religious sanction for morality; a systematic and deliberate cultivation of the spiritual life, both public and private — through institutional activities, and through prayer, reading, and contemplation.   Both optimists and pessimists will, I think, agree that the present generation of young people make less use of these four things than have their predecessors for many a century.   Are these four things such genuine helps to the religious life that a partial loss of them means a partial loss in the contribution which religion is able to make to life's values?

First of all, then, let us ask whether a fairly definite religious faith is of any real utility.   There is no doubt that its value has been tremendously overestimated and overstated throughout all the religious centuries.   We know to-day that for a large proportion of mankind, it is possible to get on very comfortably throughout a

large part of life without a definite stand on metaphysical and religious questions. Yet a consideration of both history and psychology makes it unquestionable that religious faith brings hope and consolation in the hours of anxiety and anguish, furnishes a background
of peace and confidence and poise to all life, adds a peculiar impetus
to the inner forces of both individual and collective activity, and acts
as a unifying power, knitting together into one organic body millions
of otherwise separate or even antagonistic individuals; and that
nothing has as yet been found which will fully take its place and perform equally well these functions.

The religious faith need not, of course, be extensive or susceptible
of exact definition. To contribute to life the things I have mentioned it need not be formulated into a creed. Nor need it be accepted in any dogmatic fashion or regarded as in any way final. But
if it is to have much value, it must be at least a tentative and working
program, and it must be at least sufficiently inclusive and sufficiently
definite to give its possessor a general point of view as to the nature of
the universe and the place and destiny of man. Such a working
faith cannot fail to be of service; and he who goes through life without anything of the sort must either live upon the surface of things,
blind to the deeper problems of the world, or must face the pro-
fundities with a minimum of confidence and courage.

A revered and familiar sacred text contributes much less to life
than does a religious faith, and its value has been very greatly exaggerated. Doubtless the Bible was a real help to the Hebrews and
the Puritans of old; but we do not know just how well they might
have done with some substitute for it, and we do know the pernicious
extremes to which reverence for its letter has often been carried.
There can be little question, however, that every great religion has
owed much of its beneficent power to the sacredness of its texts; and
that the inner lives of Christians, especially of Protestant Christians,
have been peculiarly enriched by the nobler passages of the Bible
that have been and are still their familiar and most revered possessions and the constant companions of their pilgrimage. But not
every one realizes the extent to which this contribution which the
Bible is able to make is due to the fact that its passages were first
learned and loved *in early childhood and as sacred words*. Met with for
the first time at a later age, they could never have this power.

Treated as purely secular writing, they could never have this power. The inner hold that the Bible has had over the souls of men has been due to the fact that, with its own inherent nobility, it has come into the life of the impressionable child or youth and has borne the seal of the community's reverence.

Men can get on without the Bible. They can live good and religious lives without it, or without any sacred book. The man who does not know the Bible, or whose acquaintance with it has begun in unimpressionable middle age, will probably never know that he is missing anything. But it will still be true that he lacks one of the chief aids to quiet confidence and active inspiration which for nineteen centuries Christians have possessed, and for which he has no adequate substitute.

One of the solid advantages which Christians once derived from a definite faith and a sacred text was a religious sanction for the moral life. That this was a very real help can hardly be questioned; for the thing I am thinking of was not merely the Criminal Law of a "magnified nonnatural man." The phrase "religious sanction for morality," to be sure, usually brings to mind supernatural reward and punishment, Heaven and Hell. All the Christian generations before our own have lived and died with the moral stimulus of a belief in future supernatural punishments for the bad and rewards for the good. How far Hell was a help in the moral life need not be discussed here. For whatever may have been true of it in the past, we have seen Hell burn out. It has become for most Protestants a dead issue — a kind of extinct volcano. But this negative sort of sanction was by far the less important contribution that religion had to make towards noble living. Indeed no very lovely flower of morality ever grew out of fear of hell-fire or desire for heavenly reward. The religious and truly Christian sanction of the finer morality has always been, and is to-day, the desire to be a worker together with God in some great world purpose, the longing so to share in the life and work of Christ as to be able to say with St. Paul, "I live, yet not I but Christ liveth in me." One can be a moral person without such a religious impetus. The exceptional man can, in fact, without any religious sanction, be an enthusiastic leader in great human causes, a devoted, self-sacrificing servant and lover of his kind. But for the ordinary man, the belief in the divine approval of the moral life, the sense of some connection between human causes and cosmic purposes, the identification of devotion to humanity with devotion to Christ, the beloved Master — for the ordinary man these things bring a reinforcement to the moral life which he can hardly do without, unless he is to fall back into very ordinary morality indeed.

Religion, then, is a real aid in the cultivation of the moral life. But not only the moral life is susceptible of cultivation. The same is true of the spiritual life as a whole, in the large sense of the word. To say this is only to assert that the life of the spirit is a psychological entity and that it is subject to psychological conditions and the laws of growth. That it is worth cultivating is the testimony not only of Christianity but of all the great religions. Each of the great religions, as is well known, has developed systematic methods to this end which have been practised with success by millions of adherents. The methods peculiarly characteristic of Christianity may be described, as I have already indicated, as twofold in character — public or collective and private or individual. By collective methods for the nurture of the spiritual life I mean, of course, the various forms of public or communal worship and religious activity; and by individual methods, such things as the reading of religious literature, whether found in the Bible or elsewhere, private prayer, and the occasional or systematic devotion of a few minutes now and then to the contemplation of universal and eternal themes, the taking stock of one's own moral gains and losses, the deliberate turning of one's thought away from the practical and pressing details and interests of the immediate, the practice of waiting and listening and of tuning one's soul to the larger harmonies.

Those who have never tried any of these things sometimes testify that they are absurd. So far as I know, all those who have systematically pursued them testify that they are immeasurably worth while. And I speak not of the mystics, though it might well be to the point to do so. I refer merely to those thousands of simple Christians, many of whom we have all known — the mothers of most people of middle age, for example — who have found the "daily strength for daily needs" in a few moments of prayer or the perusal of a Psalm. In our enthusiasm for social service and efficient activity and objective results I think we often forget how much of strength and poise the more spiritual and truly efficient members of the Christian world have regularly drawn from the deliberate and more or less systematic cultivation of the spiritual life. The experience of the race has shown these methods to be rich in results and productive of unmeasured values; and an attempt on the part of civilized humanity to dispense with these and all other aids towards fostering the spiritual life, on the theory that the spiritual life can fully take care of itself, needing no culture, or that the spiritual life is not worth cultivating, would be an experiment in human living which to me at least is not a theme for pleasant contemplation. It would mean turning away from the inner and deeper aspects of life, specializing in the objective, specializing in bread and butter, and neglecting the empirical fact to which all historical and psychological study of man's religions bears testimony, that man, if he is to be fully man, cannot live by bread alone.

Accordingly, while I by no means concur in the opinion of the pessimists expressed by writers like Mrs. Gerould, and while I consider the present younger generation in many ways superior to any of their predecessors, I cannot agree with the roseate views, or share in the sanguine hopes, of those I have called the optimists. The situation which we face is a serious one. Our young people are admirable as well as lovable; but admittedly they have cultivated to a smaller degree than their forbears for some centuries the "traditional forms" of the religious life. The lack of these "traditional forms" will not make them unhappy or bad or irreligious; but unless remedied it can hardly fail to some extent to impoverish their lives and to make of them less complete, less fully rounded, less joyous human beings than they would otherwise be.

What are the causes that have brought about these changes in the religious life of the young? Some people tell us it is the war. Others assure us that the war has done all sorts of fine things for religion. My own view is that the war has had very little influence one way or another. Some slight and passing influence, of course, it has had. Most notably, perhaps, it has increased interest in the question of a future life and thus attracted attention to man's destiny, his nature, and his relations to the universe. Thus, it has temporarily increased the religious faith of a number of people and has deepened the thought of many more. On the other hand, it has shaken the faith of quite as many by making the conception of an overruling Providence increasingly difficult and adding to

> . . . the heavy and the weary weight
> Of all this unintelligible world.

"If there be a God, how can He permit all this useless slaughter, this domination of brute force?" Something like this was the burden of millions of soldier souls in the trenches and of aching mother hearts at home. Indirectly, the war caused a large influx of wealth in certain portions of American and English society, and an undreamed rise of pay among the working people, and this acted on many of them as sudden prosperity often acts, in destroying all conscious need of religion and in focusing attention upon the variety of exciting and pleasant things that this world had to offer. The total effect of the war upon religion was, I think, certainly bad rather than good; but this total effect was slight and passing. The religious changes that we find going on or already accomplished are too profound to be accounted for by wars or rumors of wars; and in fact the process of change was already far advanced long before 1914.

The immediate cause of the religious changes that we have been considering is to be found rather in the influence of home training and of society as a whole upon the developing minds of the present younger generation. This goes without saying, and indeed tells us but little. The young people of this, as of every other period, have taken what they have been given; and if they differ from their elders, it is because they have had a different "bringing up." But why has their "bringing up" been less religious than that of their parents? Their parents — I write of people of forty or over — were brought up with great religious care. Obviously, something has happened in the last forty years that has so influenced the parents of our present young people as to make it almost impossible for them to give their children the sort of religious training which they themselves had. We must remember, moreover, that children are brought up not only by their parents but by the whole community in which they live. School, church, their comrades, newspapers, books, magazines, the conversations of their elders which they overhear, these and many other sources help to form their point of view; and the general movements of thought in their community can no more be kept from their growing minds than can the circumambient air. These general movements of thought, of course, influence parents quite as much as children, and in fact influence the children at first through their parents. Thus it has come about that forces tending towards the neglect of the traditional religious forms of expression and cultivation act doubly upon the young.

It is no easy thing (as every parent knows who has tried it) to ground one's children in a familiar knowledge of the Bible, to see to it that they say their prayers every night, to send them regularly to Sunday School, to make sure that they have their lessons, to *take* them later on to church every Sunday, to talk over the sermon with them, to keep up the custom of family Bible reading and perhaps of family prayers and of grace at meals, and to attend to the many other details which parents and grandparents used to attend to in bringing up *their* children in the knowledge and admonition of the Lord. To do this in such a way as to make it count requires the steady and persistent effort of the will throughout long years with no let-up or vacation or moral holiday. This is not the sort of thing that is done merely by the force of habit or inertia. Our fathers kept it up because of the steady impetus of a living religious conviction which held their unwavering attention. When this conviction is weakened and the attention is repeatedly diverted from what conviction is left, the steady and wearisome exertion of will comes to be out of the question. The result is both negative and positive. Negatively, the child lacks in his impressive years that careful and thorough religious training which in preceding generations was so common; and positively, he drinks in (without any one intending that he should do so) his parents' indifferent attitude.

To make our question as to the causes of the present religious conditions more fundamental, we must therefore ask what has happened in the last half-century to weaken the religious convictions of middle-aged parents and other grown-up people, and to divert attention from them. Plainly a good many things have happened in the last fifty years that have influenced the religious life. The most important of these may, I think, be included under one or another of the following topics: the steady and rapid growth of the naturalistic point of view; the waning of the ancient authorities in matters of belief and conduct, and indeed of respect for authority in general; and, lastly, the great increase and growing complexity of practical concerns and secular interests and "diversions."

Of these three I suppose the first is the most fundamental and important. I have called it the extension of the naturalistic point of view rather than the rise of Darwinism or any other single intellectual movement, for Darwinism, great as its influence has been, is only one part of a much larger movement, which took its rise with Galileo — or was it with Democritus, or Thales? — and whose end is not yet. Its cumulative effect has been not simply to make us regard the account of Creation in Genesis as a myth and to weaken the Argument from Design; it has accustomed us to regard the cosmos as a whole and all that in it is, man's spirit included, as subject to the laws of science; and these laws of science we easily interpret to mean the laws of mechanism.

The tendency is to go far beyond anything that science itself would justify and to take for granted a naturalistic philosophy which, once fully understood, is seen to be quite incompatible with any view of the world which Christianity or any other religion has ever taught. There is nothing in the teachings of science that is inconsistent with liberal Christianity — or, for that matter, with liberal Buddhism or liberal Hinduism. But the custom of thinking in the categories of natural science has had the effect upon the popular mind of making it forget all other categories and thus by a gradual and unobserved process of bringing it to take for granted that all other categories are impossible; while upon a large number of trained and influential thinkers it has had the similar effect of inducing them to build up deliberately a carefully constructed monistic hypothesis framed with the express purpose of interpreting all reality under one formula, and thus of banishing from the world all spiritual influence, or, what amounts to the same thing, retaining the spiritual only to reinterpret it into the mechanical and material. This naturalistic tendency in contemporary thought is advancing with rapid strides and under many names. Materialism, Pragmatism (in its extreme form), Neo-Realism, Behaviorism, are all branches of the movement. Its monistic aspect, moreover, has a great attraction for certain minds, and under the guise of Objective or Absolute Idealism it has misled many of the religious leaders of our times, who have thus, all unconsciously, been decoyed into the camp of Naturalism, without seeing whither their steps inevitably must lead.

The influence of all this upon religious faith has been enormous, and the only wonder is that its effect has not been more destructive than we find it to be. The naturalistic attack upon religion, in fact, has been the more insidious because of the great value of the scientific mode of thinking under whose banner so much of its advance has been made. It is most desirable that the scientific point of view should become common property, that it should rescue us from the many harmful superstitions and false conclusions which it has replaced. The conception of the universal sway of evolution in all living forms has been one of the most fruitful, even one of the most inspiring, revelations of our time. It is not surprising, therefore, that these great values of modern science, once appropriated by a naturalistic philosophy and wrongly identified with its own teaching, should make for it a winning hand, and by imposing upon many minds, both untrained and trained, should make the Christian view of the world appear to be what the upholders of Naturalism brand it as being, "mediæval," "superstitious," and "outgrown."

Another of the influences that have helped to weaken the traditional forms of the religious life is the waning of the older religious authorities — the rise of the Higher Criticism and the loss of the older faith in the inerrancy of the Scriptures. But this is only a part of the general decay of respect for authority whether in Bible or Church or Prophet, and of the general growth of independent thought. This liberal movement as a whole has certainly been a gain to the human spirit. It has freed us from servitude to the letter and has put faith upon a much more spiritual and truly Christian foundation. We would not, if we could, go back to the old days of unthinking faith and unscientific creed, and we could not if we would. Yet if we would see clearly, we must not blink the fact that one of the effects of this emancipation of the human mind has been to weaken incalculably the foundations of religious faith for millions of Christians before anything very substantial could be given them in place of what has been taken away. Tell it not in Gath, publish it not in the streets of Askelon, but we may as well confess to each other that the glowing promises which we of the liberal movement made to ourselves twenty years ago of a rationalized and newly vitalized

Christian faith which should fill the masses with a more spiritual religion and take the place of their old bondage to the letter, have not been fulfilled. The bondage to the letter is rapidly going, but the new spiritual faith is not spreading with anything like the same rapidity.

Besides, our modern world is so full of a number of things that most men's religion, whether of the old or of the new type, plays a much less important part in life than religion formerly played. We have so much to do that there is no time for cultivating the spiritual side of our natures. We cannot read our Bibles because we must read the newspapers. We cannot spend five minutes in quiet contemplation because of the meeting of the Forum or of the Wednesday Morning Club. We cannot go to church because Sunday morning is the only time we have for getting even with our correspondence. The world is very much more complicated and very much more interesting than it used to be. And I cannot help wondering, too, whether the religion which the churches give us is not, on the whole, rather less interesting than it used to be. I have no statistics, and I doubt whether statistics on the subject are at all possible; but I have the general impression that the brains of the country are not trooping into the pulpit as they once did, and that the sermons which we hear to-day are not all that sermons once were. Lyman Abbott was asked some years ago why so few people went to church; to which he replied that the wonder to him was why so many people went.

What, then, is the prospect for the future? Not altogether dark, I think. For, as has been pointed out, religion is too fundamental to human nature ever to be lost. Our young people are truly religious at bottom; and while they do not seem to be spending much of their time remembering their Creator in the days of their youth, the days are ahead of them in which the exigencies of life will inevitably thrust upon their attention the eternal problems and bring them more and more into some religious attitude. There are a few vague signs, moreover, in the community at large, of a new sense of the need of religion. How far this is shared by the younger members I do not know, but there is little doubt that, if it grows to any noticeable extent, they cannot be uninfluenced by it. Young people are more sensitive than the rest of us to social pressure and to the convictions of society, and if the community as a whole becomes convinced of the need of religion, they will share the conviction. That there is such a growing and conscious need of religion I am not sure; but from the expressions of all sorts of people, from assertions that one finds making an obvious effect upon audiences, from opinions one sees expressed in the newspapers and in popular magazines, one gathers that such a tendency is on foot. A somewhat significant indication, for example, of the sort of thing I mean is the growing popularity of Francis Thompson's great poem, "The Hound of Heaven," and the unmistakably deep impression it makes upon readers and audiences when quoted. The sentiment of the poem seems to be echoed in many hearts. Many seem to have "fled Him down the nights and down the days," and to have heard the

> . . . Voice that beat
> More instant than the Feet —
> "All things betray thee, who betrayest Me."

Apparently the exhortation "One world at a time" has been tried by a good many people and found deceptive. It may be that one world at a time is not enough for man. It may be, as religion has always taught, that man is the kind of being that needs two.

The younger generation have already launched upon their course, and we older ones can do little for them now. They must work out their own salvation with diligence. That Christendom will ever return to the old creeds and to the old attitude to the letter of Scripture is out of the question — our Fundamentalist friends may as well make up their minds to that once for all. New forms of faith, new attitudes towards the Determiner of Destiny must be worked out, must grow by a continuous process out of the old. And I do not think these new forms will be the work of any one or two or three religious geniuses. The days of the founders of new religions and of the great reformers of the old are probably over. The social group as a whole must feel its way together and work out its new solutions. The task must be performed collectively. This, of course, will be done under the guidance of its leaders; but these leaders will be many and will work in collaboration with one another. It follows that Christendom will very likely never again have the unity of belief that once it had. But this independence and divergence of individual thinking need not prevent a very real religious unity. The new faiths thus achieved must be in harmony with science; though, if they are to contribute much to the life of the spirit, they can hardly be in servile subjection to a naturalist philosophy.   But, as I have pointed out before, there is nothing in the science of to-day — and not likely will there be anything in the science of to-morrow — incompatible with a truly religious faith, nor with a reverent attitude towards and an intimate use of the great scriptures of the Old and New Testaments.   Nor is the time ever likely to come when the cosmic view of things and the sense of loyalty to great religious leaders will not be of immeasurable potential assistance in the moral life to those wise enough to use them.   And, finally, the spiritual life of man will always be capable of intense cultivation, by the old methods and doubtless by new and as yet unguessed ones, for all those who realize that it is worth the effort required.

What the present younger generation and their successors will do with religion, it is for them to decide.   They may do with it what they will.   I do not feel that our generation — I speak as one of the older ones — have done quite our full duty by the young people; but perhaps nothing better could have been expected.   At any rate, the tiller is slipping rapidly from our hands.   We can do little now but impress upon our younger friends the enormous issues at stake — at stake for them and for their successors — and the genuine value of some of the things which in the lightness of youth they tend to minimize.   Let them remember that religion is a pearl of great price; that the spiritual life, though it can never be killed out of the race, is a tender plant which gives its fairest flowers only after careful culture; that liberty is not the only thing whose price is eternal vigilance.

HOW IT ALL BEGAN [1]

By LEWIS BROWNE

*In 1902 Lewis Browne (1897–   ) came from London, his birth-
place, to the United States. After taking an A.B. at the University of
Cincinnati, he attended the Hebrew Union College Rabbinical Seminary
and Yale University, and became in 1920 rabbi of Temple Israel at
Waterbury, Connecticut. Later, to get material on comparative religion, he traveled much in Russia and the Orient. Since 1926 he has
resigned all rabbinical work to devote himself to writing. His principal
books are "Stranger Than Fiction" (1925), "The Story of the Jews"
(1926), "This Believing World" (1926), and "That Man Heine"
(1927).*

I

FINALLY, we come to the creation of the great gods. Just as the
tribal chieftain in time became a king, so the tribal fetish in time
became a god. It was a natural evolution. The wild spirit once
thought to dwell in a tree or hill was first conjured into a portable
fetish, so that the wandering tribesmen might enjoy its protection
wherever they moved. (Readers of the Bible will remember how
that spirit of Jehovah — or more properly, Yahveh — dwelling in
Mount Sinai, was transferred to a portable "ark" which the primitive
Hebrews carried with them on their wanderings.) Later on, when
such shepherd wanderers settled down and became farmers, their
nomad spirit sometimes settled down with them. (The old "ark" of
the bedouin Hebrews was given a resting-place at last in the temple
at Jerusalem.) This did not always occur, however, for the mortality rate among deities was exceedingly high during the transition
period from pastoral to agricultural life. And even the spirits that
did manage to survive, came through completely altered in character.
Their functions henceforth were new ones, and often their names
were new, too. Only tell tale little atavisms in the ritual remained
to betray their nomadic origin.

But even the lives of the deities surviving that great transition still
remained precarious. Indeed, if anything, the mortality rate

---

[1] From *This Believing World*, by Lewis Browne. Copyright, 1926, by The Mac
millan Company. Reprinted by permission.

among them then increased. For now came greater changes than ever before occurred among men, and consequently greater changes had to occur among the gods. Tribes fused. The task of resisting invasions, or of building irrigation dams, compelled many clans to merge, and their customs, myths, and gods had to merge, too. Gods appeared on the scene who were obviously composites, with composite names and composite rituals. And as the population increased, and certain villages grew to be towns, city-states, nations, and finally empires, the jurisdiction of these composite gods grew also. They began to gobble up the little gods of the tributary lands, and thus in time became the almost undisputed lords of millions of worshippers.

Many centuries still had to run their course before any one could imagine a deity who was the One God of the Universe. Men still continued to be polytheists, believing in many gods. They might pay homage only to one, the god of their own particular tribe. They might consider him the mightiest god of all and picture him, as did the Hindus in their grotesque idols, as having arms that reached everywhere and eyes that saw all. But they never denied the existence of other gods sustaining similar relations to other tribes.

Significantly, however, even the mightiest god could not strike so much terror in the heart of civilized man as the rudest idol did in the heart of the savage. Time had dealt hard with fear. Man was still far from able to control his universe, but at least he showed signs of beginning to cope with it. And as a result the "powers" of the universe became less terrifying. Man began to say they were his allies and partners, and if he exalted them extravagantly he did so largely in order to exalt himself. The gods of the nations became simply the divine leaders of the nations, the heavenly kings.

II

The idea that the gods were heavenly kings had at least one implication of tremendous importance. Earthly kings were naturally expected to see to the enforcement of the laws of the nation. It was their task to see to it that crime was detected and that criminals were punished. But always certain crimes occurred that could not be detected, just as ever and again some criminals escaped without punishment. Particularly was this so in the newly swollen cities, where policing in the form of neighborly prying was no longer possible. In those new capitals, with their milling, thronging, turbulent populations, morality seemed to have no chance. The taboos which had been strictly kept in the compact little clan came to be transgressed in the cities almost with impunity. For a while the breakdown of society seemed inevitable.

But the idea that the gods were heavenly kings saved the day. By the logic of analogy it was reasoned that as earthly kings punished crime that was detectable, so heavenly kings punished that which was *un*detectable. So there really was no chance of avoiding justice ultimately. Neither might nor cunning was of any avail, for even though one escaped the judgement of the earthly king, there was another, the inevitable and inexorable judgement of the god, still to face. The god in the sky saw all and knew all. Not a taboo or a law existed but he was concerned with its enforcement. (Indeed, he was the actual author of all taboos and laws — at least so it was soon said.) So there was no chance for the transgressor — he could never escape.

And thus was born the idea of sin. Crime, which was really an offense against society, came to be thought of principally as a sin against the god. And because often no one could put his finger on the punishment visited upon the offender by the god, the idea of conscience arose. The god, it came to be believed, punished the wicked in secret ways, sending evil spirits into them to gnaw at their souls and give them no rest. And when it was seen that many of the wicked seemed quite untroubled by evil consciences, quite unperturbed by secret punishments, then the idea of future suffering was advanced. It was claimed that, even though some of the wicked went scot free in this world, in the next they would not be nearly so fortunate. No, indeed! After death they would get even more than their just due, roasting in flames — according to the dwellers in torrid lands — or freezing in ice-floes — according to the inhabitants of arctic regions.

The actual course of development out of which were evolved these ideas of sin, conscience, and post-mortem retribution, was, to be sure, not nearly so simple as is made out here. For centuries man fumbled about to lay hold of these ideas, blundering off into the most pathetic errors, and beating his way back only with the horridest pain. But finally the great task was accomplished, and morality, at the cost of being religionized, was preserved.

It was no small price to pay. Religion proved in time rather too effective a preservative. It sheltered too extensively and indiscriminately, keeping alive not merely the morals necessary to the life of society, but also every scrap of ancient ritual and savage taboo. Religion developed a tendency to hold on to everything with equal tenacity, allowing no difference between the slightest rite and the gravest law. Or if it did admit any difference, its verdict was usually in favor of the rite. Priestly teachers were inclined to tell the people that ritual, the proper treatment to be accorded the gods, was decidedly more important than ethics, the proper treatment to be accorded to mere men. What was more injurious, they often taught that all offenses, both against rite and right, could be atoned for in but one way: by sacrifice. Justice, they declared, could always be tempered, and the guilty might perhaps even go scot free, if only enough rams and fatlings were offered the heavenly judge.

That teaching, naturally enough, proved in time a gigantic obstacle in the path of civilization. Indeed, the whole career of religion among civilized folk is in a measure the story of the struggle to remove that obstacle. In essence it is the story of prophet warring on priest; of him who would moralize religion wrestling with him who had ritualized morals.

III

But though religion may have exacted a high price for its saving of morality, still — *it did save it.* That is something many people are inclined to forget. They are accustomed to dwell only on the evils, on the thwartings and frustrations, which certain forms of religion in later days brought upon civilization. But it is well to remember that, had it not been for religion and its underlying faith, there would not have been any civilization to frustrate. Civilization is but another name for man's increasing victory over fear — and the first phases of that victory were attained almost solely through religion. Religion was the boot-strap by which man raised himself out of savagery. Or, to return to a metaphor we have already used, it was the bank of reeds to which man clung as often as the dark waters of fear threatened to flood over him.   In a very real sense it was his salvation.

It was the salvation of society, too.   Not merely did religion make it possible for one man to live by himself, but even more did it make it possible for two men to live together.   Even the beginnings of society would have been rendered impossible by man's innate fear simply of the dead — let alone of the living — had religion not come into high standing in the world.   At the sight of death, the natural reaction of the savage was flight.   Instinctively he wanted to burn the whole village in which the corpse lay, and run!   And at first probably he did follow that instinct, and for centuries no camp ever lasted more than a few weeks or months. . . . But then was born the idea of burial rites to placate the spirits of the dead, religious rites that firmly rooted the survivors to the place where the dead were buried. Religion found a way to rob death of a little of its ghastly frightfulness.   Villages were now actually created around graves, instead of being burnt down over them.   Man, once so terrified by the ghosts that he fled at the least suspicion of their presence, now dared to go right up to them and implore their aid.   Ancestor-worship arose.   Tribes often depended for their solidarity upon the sole bond of supposed descent from a common ancestor.   Failing that, the tie that served to hold them together was a common ritual.   Ceremonies at birth, puberty, marriage, and death were the things that bound those clansmen into a compact group.   The same was true of the annual festivals.   And thus, by and with religion, the living together of men was made possible.

More than that: by and with religion the living together of men was made not merely possible, but also desirable.   Religion clothed and adorned the cold nakedness of primitive existence with shreds and patches of beauty.   All that grace and color which transmutes mere existence into Life — in a word, all Art — may truly be said to have arisen out of religion.   Sculpture had its origin in idol-making, architecture in temple-building, poetry in prayer-writing, music in psalm-singing, and dancing in the seasonal worship of the gods.

It may seem to us incredibly rude, this conglomeration of terrors and hopes, of clutchings and gropings, of stupidities and yearnings, which for want of a better name we call Primitive Religion.   But for all that it was holy — for it saved mankind.

CONCLUSIONS OF A MAN GONE TO THE DEVIL

By HERBERT ASBURY

Herbert Asbury (1891–   ) received all his formal education in the schools and colleges of Farmington, Missouri.   Since 1910 he has been doing newspaper work, with the exception of the time spent in the United States Army during the World War.   Besides contributing articles of a general nature to magazines, he has written a number of detective stories, and a mystery and horror novel, "The Devil of Pei Ling," which appeared in 1927.   "Up From Methodism," the story of his boyhood, was published in 1927, and "The Gangs of Old New York," a history of early gangsters of that city, in 1928.

IF there is anything in religious inheritance, or in the influence of a religious environment, I should be, if not an actual Pastor of a flock, at least one of the most devout of the faithful, a snooping Brother concerned only with good works.   But instead of carrying on the work of my forefathers, I find myself full of contempt for the Church, and disgust for the forms of religion.   To me such things are silly; I cannot understand how grown people can believe in them, or how they can repress their giggles as they listen to the ministerial platitudes and perform such mummeries as are the rule in all churches.

Never since the night of my "conversion" have I gone into a church to worship.   I have frequently entered such dens of righteousness, but my visits, except for a few that I made soon after Brother McConnell's revival meeting to please my father and mother, have been on newspaper assignment or out of curiosity.   I have inquired into the doctrine of almost every sect that has adherents in America, but in none of them have I been able to find any sign of a true and beneficent God.   I can see only groups of sanctimonious, self-seeking Little Jack Horners chasing about poking their fingers into some one else's pie, and then shouting gleefully: "Look at me, God!   Look what I found!   Ooooh!   Ain't it nice and smutty?"   They cannot practice their religion without prancing and cavorting before the public eye; they are constantly showing off.   They are not so much concerned with the glory of God as with the glory of the front page.   And what time they are not whirling giddily in such imbecilities, they are engaged in disgusting squabbles among themselves as to who shall have the local agency for purveying religion; they want to copyright salvation in the name of their particular sect.

On all sides we hear that religion is the greatest thing in the world and that mankind's chief need is more of it. But it is my conviction that mankind would be infinitely better off with less of it, and probably best off with none of it. Nothing has ever caused more trouble. The whole history of religion is a record of war, murder, torture, rape, massacre, distrust, hypocrisy, anguish, persecution, and continual and unseemingly bickering; it is a rare church that has not been the scene of disorderly brawls. It has divided towns and nations into bitter factions; it has turned brother against sister and father against son; it has blighted romances; it is a prime cause of insanity; there is hardly anything harmful to the human race that it has not done as it pursues its meddlesome, intolerant way down the ages. Its followers proclaim loudly that their particular belief is synonymous with love, and bawl threats and epithets against any one who denies it; but in truth religion comes more nearly to being synonymous with hatred and revenge, with each sect praying to God to grant it special privileges and to damn the others.

I have never at any time regretted my complete withdrawal from all forms of religion and churchly ceremony. During many years of my childhood, while mental and physical habits were forming, these things kept me in constant terror; I was horrified by the thought of the awful things that God was preparing to do to me; I was fearful and miserable lest I give birth to an idea that was not perfectly righteous and in keeping with His commands as laid down by His agents. The Bible, which I necessarily interpreted in the light of what I had been taught, caused me more nightmares than any other book I have ever read, and I was vastly more alarmed by the tales of the fires of Hell related to me by the Preachers and the Brothers and Sisters than I was in later life by the thunder of German artillery or the crackle of machine-gun bullets.

Since I left Farmington I have been near death many times, both as a soldier in France and from the natural illnesses incident to civil life. At least three times I have been told that I had but a few hours to live. Yet even then I did not feel the need of a religion, nor for a preacher or a priest to pray over me to a God that neither of us knew, and perform ceremonies founded on pagan rites. How can an intelligent God pay any attention to a last-minute deathbed repentance that is so obviously the result of fear and nothing else? The religionist expects God to wash all his sins off the slate merely because, when he is about to die, he says he is sorry. If there be a God, cannot He look into such a shrunken little soul and see that there is nothing in it but a fear of death and a horror of the unknown?

I am not an atheist, because for all I know to the contrary there may be a God, or any number of Gods, but to me the God worshipped by my forefathers and by the religionists of to-day is a cruel, preposterous creation conceived by a people who felt the need of chastisement. He is a celestial traffic cop, hounded by whimpering weaklings who beseech Him to tell them they are on the right road, and yet keep trying to show Him which way traffic should go. In the Christian and Jewish conceptions of the Heavenly Father I can see nothing that is fit for a civilized man to worship; indeed, the nearer a man approaches civilization and intelligence, the less need there is for him to worship anything. Conversely, it is the stupid, illiterate man, knowing neither how to read nor how to think, who is most often the religious fanatic. He understands nothing and is afraid of everything; he goes through life as a small boy goes past a graveyard at night, whistling to keep up his courage. He requires religion and its twin, superstition, to give him strength to contemplate the wonders of the sunset and the falling rain.

For my part, I simply refuse to worry about God. If there is a God, I hope that I may in time find favor in His sight and obtain my share of the spiritual loot; there is nothing that I can do about it. And if there is no God, there is nothing I can do about that, either. I profess neither knowledge nor theory about the Supreme Being and the heavenly wonders; knowing nothing, I believe nothing, and believing nothing, I am prepared to believe anything, asking only reasonably correct information and authentic signs. These I fail to find in selfish prayers, constant squabbling over the wishes of the Lord and the building of magnificent temples within sight and hearing of ramshackle tenements of the poor. I do not believe that I shall ever find them, for

> Wherefore and whence we are ye cannot know,
> Nor where life springs, nor whither life doth go.

Without religion I thoroughly enjoy the business of living.   I am oppressed by no dreadful taboos, and I am without fear; I set myself no standards save those of ordinary respect, decent consideration of the rights and privileges of others, and the observance of the laws of the land except Prohibition.   To my own satisfaction, at least, I have proved that religion and the Church are not at all necessary to a full and happy life.   And if I am thus a sinner and my chance of ultimate salvation forfeit, then the fault lies at the door of those fanatics whose method of teaching religion to a child was, and is, to hammer it into his head by constant threats of terrible punishment, by drawing torturing word pictures of Hell, by describing God as a vicious, vindictive old man, by scolding and tormenting and laying down taboos until the poor child's brain whirls in an agony of fright and misery.   I know of no better way to salute them than to refer them to certain words of their own savior, to be found in the thirty-fourth verse of the twenty-third chapter of the Book of Saint Luke.

If I ever have a son, which now seems unlikely, his boyhood will be quite different from my own.   For him Sunday shall be a day of rest and pleasure; there shall be no taboos, and no attendance upon church and Sunday school, unless their performances are more interesting than other available entertainment.   They now rank just below the moving pictures, and are therefore last.   I shall bring my son in contact with the sacred books of the Christians, the Jews, the Buddhists and of all the other religions as rapidly as he is able to comprehend them, and he shall be permitted to choose his own religion if he decides that a religion is necessary to his happiness and peace of mind.   But if he shows any signs of becoming a preacher, priest or rabbi, or even a Brother, I shall whale Hell out of him.   I am that intolerant.

WILL SCIENCE DISPLACE GOD?

By HARRY EMERSON FOSDICK

Harry Emerson Fosdick (1878–   ) is one of the most widely known American theologians. He attended Colgate University, Union Theological Seminary, and Columbia, and has in recent years received honorary degrees from a number of distinguished colleges. Since entering the Baptist ministry in 1903, he has been active as the pastor of various churches, as a teacher in Union Theological Seminary, and as a lecturer and writer. Among his books are: "The Manhood of the Master" (1913), "The Meaning of Prayer" (1915), "The Meaning of Faith" (1917), "Christianity and Progress" (1922), and "Adventurous Religion" (1926).

IN one of our American colleges founded long ago in piety and faith for the furtherance of the Gospel, a professor recently made a "Senior Chapel Address" frankly skeptical of God and immortality, the key-note of which was sounded in the words, "God becomes progressively less essential to the running of the universe." There is occasion for thought along many lines, not only for religious people but for all our citizenship, in this suggestive spectacle of an American college chapel founded for the worship of God thus transformed into a platform for denying him. But behind all other questions lies the basic issue which the professor raises. He thinks that modern science is making God increasingly unnecessary.

That is the nub of the whole matter in the age-long conflict between science and religion. That way of stating the issue — not that science theoretically disproves God, but that science progressively makes him "less essential" — correctly focuses the problem. Religious people, fretted by fear of modern views of the world, have comforted themselves with the assurance that science cannot disprove God. Of course it cannot! They have assuaged their grief, mourning the loss of old theologies, by the conviction that, as new telescopes do not destroy the ancient stars, so new ways of viewing God's operations do not negative the Ancient of Days himself. Of course not! But that is not the ultimate issue in the conflict between science and religion. The professor has that matter correctly put. What modern science is doing for multitudes of people, as anybody who watches American life can see, is not to disprove God's theoretical existence, but to make him "progressively less essential."

Although its applications and its consequences are innumerable, the reason for this can be briefly stated.   Throughout man's history in the past and among the great majority of people to-day, religion has been and is a way of getting things that human beings want. From rain out of heaven to good health on earth, men have sought the desires of their hearts at the altars of their gods.   Closely associated in its early history with magic — the search for some spell or incantation, some Aladdin's lamp which would make the unseen powers subject to the user — religion has always provided for its devotees methods of worship, forms of ritual, secrets of prayer, or spiritual relationships with God guaranteed to gain for the faithful the benefits they have sought.   In every realm of human want and craving, men thus have used religious methods to achieve their aims and, whether they desired good crops, large families, relief from pestilence, or success in war, have conceived themselves as dependent on the favor of heaven.   And now comes science, which also is a method of getting what human beings want.   That is its most important character.   As a theoretical influence it is powerful enough; as a practical influence it is overwhelming.   It does provide an astoundingly successful method of getting what men want.

Here is the crucial point of competition between science and religion.   In realm after realm where religion has been offering its methods for satisfying men's desires, science comes with a new method which works with obvious and enormous consequence. Quietly, but inevitably, man's reliance for the fulfilling of his needs slips over from religion to science.   Not many men stop to argue against religion — they may even continue to believe it with considerable fervor — but they have less and less practical use for it. The things they daily want are no longer obtained that way.   From providing light and locomotion, or stamping out typhus and yellow fever, to the unsnarling of mental difficulty by applied psychology, men turn to another method for their help.   God is not disproved; he is displaced.   The old picture of a bifurcated universe, where a supernatural order overlies a natural order and occasionally in miraculous interference invades it, becomes incredible.   Creation is all of one piece, a seamless garment.   And if, now, in this indivisible and law-abiding world we can get what we want by learning laws and fulfilling conditions, why is it not true, as the professor said, that "God becomes progressively less essential to the running of the universe"?

It is the more important to visualize this matter clearly and deal with it candidly because the conflict between science and religion is so seldom conceived and faced in terms of this central problem. From the first, an instinctive fear of science has characterized organized religion, as it manifestly characterizes a great deal of American Christianity to-day. That fear is justified and the peril real, but it does not lie in the quarter where it is popularly located.

That modern science is neither the science of the Bible nor the traditional science of the churches, that the ancient Book represents an ancient cosmology no longer tenable, so that the Bible cannot any more be used as a court of appeal on any scientific question whatsoever, became apparent long ago. The point of danger has been commonly supposed to lie there. Genesis versus astronomy, Genesis versus geology, Genesis versus evolution — such have been the major conflicts between the churches and the scientists. But such contentions, large as they have bulked in noise and rancor, are child's play compared with this other, central, devastating consequence which science is silently but surely working in popular religion. Science to-day is religion's overwhelmingly successful competitor in showing men how to get what they want.

This shift of reliance from religious to scientific methods for achieving human aims is so obvious that any man's daily life is a constant illustration of it, and in particular it grows vivid to one who travels in lands where memorials of old religions stand beside the achievements of new science. This would have been a famine year in Egypt in the olden time; so low a Nile would have meant starvation to myriads. One stands amid the ruins of Karnak and reconstructs in imagination the rituals, sacrifices, prayers offered before Amon-Re seeking for help in such a famished year. But no one went to Karnak this year for fear of starving, or to any Coptic church or Moslem mosque or Protestant chapel. Men have gotten what they wanted through another kind of structure altogether — the dam at Assuan.

This sort of thing, indefinitely repeated in areas where man's most immediate and clamorous needs lie, constitutes the critical effect of science on religion. It does not so much controvert religion as crowd it out. The historians are saying that it was malaria that sapped the energy of ancient Greece and drained her human resources. For centuries folk must have prayed against their mysterious enemy, sacrificed to the gods, and consulted oracles. From the days of the Dorians to the Christian churches in Corinth and the Moslem mosques that succeeded them, they tried by religious means to stave off their stealthy foe. But when a few months ago the Near East Relief took over old Greek army barracks at Corinth, put two thousand refugee children into them and straightway had twelve hundred cases of malaria, it was an American trained nurse who went into the community and despite apathy, ignorance, piety, and prejudice, cleaned up the whole countryside so that no one need have malaria there again.

Reduplicate that sort of thing interminably and the consequence is clear: we rely more and more on scientific methods for getting what we want. Travelers among primitive people must remark how deeply and constantly religious they are, so that no hour of the day is free from religious motive. Of course they are thus uninterruptedly religious. They would better be. Religion is the chief way they know of being sure of everything they want, from children to crops, from good health to good hunting. But with us many an area where only religious methods once were known for meeting human needs now is occupied by science, and the mastery of law-abiding forces, which science already has conferred, puts into our hands a power that makes trivial all the Aladdin's lamps magicians ever dreamed. A clever statistician recently has figured that in the mechanical appliances used in the United States in 1919 there was a force equal to over a billion horse-power, and that with a hundred odd million people to be served and each unit of horse-power equal to ten of man-power, every inhabitant of the United States, man, woman, and child, had on the average as good as fifty human slaves now working for him. There is no limit to the possibilities of that procedure, men think. We can in time have what we want.

Where, then, does God come in? Learn the laws, master the law-abiding forces — that seems to an ever-increasing number the only way to achieve our aims. It holds as true of mind as of matter, as true of morals as of mind. Whether in improving our crops, healing our diseases, educating our children, building our characters, or providing international substitutes for war, always we must learn the laws and fulfil the conditions, and when we do that the consequences will arrive. Such is the scientific method which everywhere wins out as the competitor of traditional religion in meeting human needs. And the upshot is that religion seems ever less necessary: "God becomes progressively less essential."

It is a tragic pity that, with this crucial problem facing religion in its relationship with science, anybody should be wasting time over foregone conclusions like evolution. For this far-more-central matter must be faced, and it can be faced triumphantly.

In the first place, science may be a competitor of religion conceived as a means of getting what we want, but it is not on that account a competitor of the kind of religion that the great souls of the race have known. Religion at its best never has been merely or chiefly a means of serving man's selfish purposes; it has rather faced men with a Purpose greater than their own which it was their business unselfishly to serve. The real prophets of the spirit have not so much relied on their religion for dole as they have been called by their religion to devotion. They have found religion's meaning, less in getting gifts from it, than in making their lives a gift to it. Religion, as Professor Royce of Harvard kept insisting, is at heart loyalty — loyalty to the highest that we know. The prayer of primitive religion and of a lamentable amount of traditional and current religion is "My will be done," and the sooner science breaks up that king of sacramental magic, pulverizes that vain reliance on supernatural sleight-of-hand, the better. Real faith will not thereby be touched; that has another sort of prayer altogether: "Not my will, but thine, be done." Any man who in this morally loose and selfish time undertakes to show that that prayer, translated into life, is less necessary than it used to be has a task on his hands. The generation is sick for lack of it. Our prevalent doctrine of moral anarchy — let yourself go; do what you please; indulge any passing, passionate whim — is a sorry, ruinous substitute for it. God as a benign charity organization that we can impose upon — let science smash up that idea! But God as the Goal of all our living, whose will is righteousness and whose service is freedom — he does not become "progressively less essential." He becomes progressively more essential, and unless we can recover him and learn anew loyalty to the Highest in scorn of consequence, our modern society, like that other group of bedeviled swine, is likely yet to plunge down a steep place into the sea.

Whenever any man discovers something greater than himself and in self-forgetting service gives his life to it, there religion has struck in its roots. There is such a thing as the "religion of science," where men at all costs and hazards live for the love of truth. Knowing, as I do, some churchmen formally religious but really undevoted to anything greater than themselves, and some scientists formally irreligious but devoted with all their hearts to the love of light, I have no doubt what the judgment of the Most High would be. He who faithfully serves the More-than-self has, in so far, found religion. So there is a religion of art in which men give their lives to beauty, as Ghiberti spent laborious years upon the bronze doors of the Florentine Baptistery that Michelangelo called the Gates of Paradise; and there is a religion of human service where men count others better than themselves and live for the sake of generations yet unborn. The Over-Soul appears to men in many forms and claims allegiance. When, however, man ceases this fragmentary splitting of his ideal world — truth here, beauty there, love yonder — and sees that God *is* love, truth, beauty, and that he who dwells in these and lives for them is dwelling in God and God in him as the New Testament says, he has found religion crowned and consummated. What is there in our modern knowledge that has disparaged this spirit of devotion to the Highest or made it less necessary? What is there that can possibly take the place of it?

There is nothing peculiarly modern about this idea of religion as loyalty; it is at least as old as Gethsemane, as old as the prison house of Socrates, and the great hours of the Hebrew prophets. It has challenged conscience many a century in those who have thought it needful "to obey God rather than men." Religion may have started with selfish magic but it did not flower out there. It flowered out in a Cross where one died that other men might live abundantly. When that spirit takes modern form, it turns up in folk like Doctor Barlow, a missionary who deliberately swallowed the germs of a Chinese pestilence and then went to Johns Hopkins that by the study of the results the plague, whose nature had been unknown, might be combated. Science is no competitor of that kind of Christianity; that kind of Christianity uses science and all its powers in the service of its God.

It strikes an interested observer of this present generation's life that nothing has happened to make that spirit less necessary than it used to be. It strikes one that there are some things which a college professor might better say to our youth than that God is becoming less essential.

This impression is deepened by another fact. Though the mechanical equivalent of fifty human slaves be serving each of us in the United States, and though that be multiplied as many times as imagination can conceive, by no such scientific mastery of power alone can our deepest needs be met. Religion is, in part, like science, a way of satisfying human wants, but there are wants that science cannot satisfy. The idea that the scientific method by itself can so fulfil the life of man that a new psalm sometime will be written beginning, "Science is my shepherd; I shall not want," and ending, "my cup runneth over," is not borne out by the actual effects of modern knowledge on many of its devotees. Consider this picture of creation drawn by one of them:

In the visible world the Milky Way is a tiny fragment. Within the solar system is an infinitesimal speck, and of this speck our planet is a microscopic dot. On this dot tiny lumps of impure carbon and water crawl about for a few years, until they dissolve into the elements of which they are compounded.

Call that, if you will, a *reductio ad absurdum* of blank skepticism, yet anybody who is acquainted with our colleges knows students who are in that pit or on the verge of it or scattered all up and down the road that leads to it. A purposeless physico-chemical mechanism which accidentally came from nowhere and is headed nowhere, which cannot be banked on for moral solvency, and to which we have no more ultimate significance than the flowers have to the weather — that is the scientific universe without religion. Something that man deeply needs is obviously left out of such a world-view. There are human wants, profound and clamorous, which that picture cannot supply.

While it is true therefore, that there are areas where traditional religion and modern science meet in cutthroat competition and where the winning method of getting what men want is sure to be the scientific, it is also true that when every area that belongs to science has been freely given up to her religion is only liberated, not obliterated. Whether or not a man will think he needs God to supply his wants will depend altogether on what his wants are. He may get his Rolls-Royce and his yacht, have his fields irrigated, his houses built, his cuisine supplied, his pestilences stopped, without religion, although one may wonder how much of the stability and vigor of the civilization which produces such results has depended on faith in a morally reliable creation. He may even get health without God, although the experience of most of us is that the body is not well unless the mind is and that the mind is never well without faith and hope. But whatever else he may obtain without God he will still live in a world that, like a raft on the high seas, is aimlessly adrift, uncharted, unguided, and unknown. Any one who has ever supposed this world to be so futile and inconsequential an experiment of chance and now has entered into the faiths and hopes of a vital and sustaining religion will regard with utter incredulity the idea that God has become less essential.

If a man cannot honestly believe in God, let him honestly say so, but let him not try to fool himself and us by the supposition that he is giving up a superfluity. Never in man's history has faith in God been more necessary to sane, wholesome, vigorous, and hopeful living than to-day amid the dissipating strain and paralyzing skepticism of modern life.

IX. ETHICS

THE SHIFTING CENTRE OF MORALITY

By STUART PRATT SHERMAN

Stuart Pratt Sherman (1881–1926), after serving for a year in the English Department at Northwestern University, went to the University of Illinois, where he later became chairman of the English Department. He received public notice with the publication of his "On Contemporary Literature" (1917); "The Genius of America" (1923) increased his fame. In 1924 he became editor of "Books," the literary weekly of the "New York Herald-Tribune." His death, at the age of forty-five, deprived America of one of its most widely known critics.

IF Puritanism is, as I have been contending that it is, an essentially non-conforming spirit, then its most formidable adversary should be an essentially conforming spirit. And contrary to the general impression of the facts, the spirit in our present younger generation which is most deeply at variance with traditional Puritanism is not its sporadic rebelliousness but its prevailing readiness to conform. Current criticism, confining itself chiefly to manners and "minor morals" scents a revolt and a flying-off where a deeper consideration discovers rather a slavish conformity.

The social censors have been reporting lately, in high excitement, that our young people exhibit signs of moral deterioration, that they are already crowned with vine leaves and dancing like bacchantes down the primrose way. When one corners a censor and demands point-blank what is wrong, one is not quite adequately answered. What one ordinarily receives is an impressionistic highly colored account of the débutantes of the present year by a débutante of twenty-five years ago, who ejaculates her indignant "Why-my-dears!" over the vogue of rouge and jazz, the cigarettes and the cocktails, the partial emancipation of the lower (instead of only the upper) limbs, the unchaperoned drives by moonlight, and, in short, the extraordinary accessibility, the general "felicity" of the buds. From among these ejaculations there emerges the central assurance of the censor, namely, that she was far, far more difficult to kiss than her neighbor's daughter is. An interesting contention, to which an inquirer of Hamlet's disposition will murmur: "Very like — Very like."

To indict an entire generation on specific charges of this sort is never very convincing. The débutantes who appear at their coming-out parties in bacchantic garb and manners are but an inconsiderable element even in that expensively fashionable set which the Sunday supplement recognizes as Society. And Society itself is but an inconsiderable element in the significant young life of any generation. A small group, flushed and festive, which loves to skirt the perilous verge of decorum, and hang a bit over the edge — such a group is always with us, as any one may easily persuade himself by turning the pages of his Juvenal or his Petrarch or even by running through the files of an illustrated New York weekly from 1860 to 1890. On the basis of rouge and "rag-time" and startling ups and downs of feminine apparel, the ultimate decline of civilization has probably been predicted every thirty years since the time of Queen Semiramis.

The historically-minded critic will be slow to assert that the manners and morals of our younger generation are, on the whole, any worse than those of the older generation, or any better. Yet he may still insist that they are significantly different. For the tendency of young people is to react against both the virtues and the defects of their elders. The father is a hard drinker but the son in disgust resolves not to touch a drop — that sometimes happens. Or the mother reads *The Ladies' Home Journal* and the daughter, *The Liberator:* that also happens. This sort of alternation is not invariable; yet, as we say, an excess in one direction tends to produce an excess in the opposite direction. And between one generation and the next morality does sometimes shift its centre.

Morality has two principal centres.

At one period, we have a morality of which the centre is within the individual. It works from within outward. It holds, like Christianity, that its prime concern is to touch the heart and quicken the conscience and give a right direction to the will. If the heart be right, say the exponents of this morality, right conduct will follow. One does not look to the world for approval; one endeavours to satisfy the inner monitor. One's own standards of right and wrong are more severe than anything that can be imposed from the outside. Therefore one takes for a motto: "Trust thyself. To thine own self be true; thou canst not then be false to any man." If you get morality effectively planted at the centre of a man, he does right though no one is looking. He does right though the heavens fall.

The high tendency of this personal morality is to produce a man like Emerson, notable for his independence, depth, poise, and serenity. Its low tendency is to produce a sentimentalist like Rousseau, whose "beautiful soul" is dissociated from his mundane and muddy behaviour.

At another period, we have a morality of which the centre is outside the individual. It is felt as a social pressure, working from without inward. It is primarily concerned, like ancient Judaism and like all systems of etiquette, with the regulation of external conduct and manners. When this type of morality predominates, if the actions of a man are right and his manners correct, no one worries much about the condition of his feelings. Act right and right feelings will follow; or if they don't, it doesn't much matter. The watch-words are: "Do as the rest do. Conform to established ways. Follow the rules and regulations."

The high tendency of a purely social morality is to cultivate the graces and amenities, and so to produce an urbane and highly polished gentleman like Lord Chesterfield. Its low tendency is to finish the surfaces of character without touching the inward parts, so that the effect upon a sensitive observer, in the case of Talleyrand, was like that of "a silk stocking filled with mud." And an unfriendly critic remarked even of Chesterfield that he taught the "morals of a courtesan and the manners of a dancing master."

Yet let us not forget that this social morality has its merits. It has, above all, a definite method, a perfected technique, for laying hold of the raw, uncultivated man and smoothing his surfaces and adjusting his external conduct to an external standard. Every one has perhaps heard of that lady who always walked into church with such a heavenly smile about her lips that observers thought she must be meditating on some beatific vision, till a friend, more curious than the rest, asked her how she did it. She explained away the mystery by declaring that all she did was to shape her lips, when she entered the church door, as if she were about to utter the word "spruce." The sequel tells how the friend thought to beautify her own expression by the same technique; but she was stopped in the middle of the aisle and was asked in horror, by an acquaintance, what ailed her.

She, much chagrined, explained that she was merely trying the formula which had made the beatific lady look so entrancing. "For Heaven's sake," cried the neighbor, "what is it?" "Why," she replied, "as I come in the door, I simply shape my lips as if about to utter the word 'hemlock.'"

Both of these ladies illustrate very well what I mean by the externality of the method.

At the present time, our ordinary young people are cultivating the external, the socially-centred type of morality. The individual would rather go wrong with the crowd than right by himself. He has a horror of being in any sense alone. He is almost painfully anxious to do as the rest do. Even his "eccentricities" are stereotyped and fashionable. He "revolts" by regiments. Three distinct forces tend to fortify this social morality in a position of predominance over the younger generation: popular philosophy, military discipline, and women.

In the first place, all the popular psychologists are physiologists, looking upon man as merely a nervous organism; and all the popular philosophers are pragmatists, behaviourists, etc., and occupy themselves with the actions and reactions, the responses and inhibitions of this nervous automaton. For them there is no spiritual centre. For them there is really no inside to personality. Everything is valued in terms of visible behaviour. Everything gets its meaning and significance in a network of external relations. Intelligently or otherwise, our young people seize upon current philosophy to help them construct an entire universe for themselves which shall have no "insides." In the violence of their reaction against the idealism and inwardness of their fathers, they rejoice in their intention of living on the surface of things. They will get rid of what their fathers called sin by getting rid of what their fathers called the soul.

The heroine of current fiction has no soul — she has not even a heart; she has only a nervous system. She has no spiritual crises — she has not even emotional crises; she has only nervous reactions. Our popular novelists — our Floyd Dells and Rose Macaulays, and W. L. Georges and Sinclair Lewises and McFees — never present their heroines in the grip of any such grand passions as shattered the heroines of the Brontë sisters. And yet these modern young women go through far more experiences than Charlotte Brontë ever dreamed it was possible for any girl to have. Experiences which would have made the whole of life for Jane Eyre, experiences which would have raised her to rapture or cast her into the nethermost hell — our modern heroines go through these at a week-end, and brush them aside "without batting an eyelid" — as she would say.

The philosophic movement towards an "external" moral centre had doubtless been greatly accelerated by a second force the full consequences of which we are just beginning to feel. It is hardly questionable that army discipline and, perhaps even more, the immense "drives" to which we were subjected in our recent embattled period did much towards establishing in the younger generation its profound deference for this external morality. We hear much about the few dissenters who did not subscribe nor conform, and we hear much about the many honest patriots who did subscribe and conform. But we have had very little study of the effect of military discipline and "drives" upon the vast intermediate mass of unformed plastic young people, practically destitute of individual convictions, who were equipped overnight, by a power not themselves, with uniform convictions and uniform conduct with respect to all manner of subjects which they had never considered.

That abrupt and convulsive shifting of responsibility for belief and conduct from the individual to an organized power outside the individual had its great merits. It frequently clothed the stark naked. But like the asylum that receives the pauper, like the infallible and omniscient church that embraces a thinking soul, it had compensations which were dangerous. If you were not in a position of leadership, you had to initiate and decide nothing. You did what the rest did; and you were "all right." Your scruples were cancelled with a rubber stamp. If doubts pursued you, you took refuge in the crowd, which covered you and shaped you. And you quite forgot that old individualistic maxim: "We sink as easily as we rise through our sympathies."

How the newly augmented powers of women and their quickened class consciousness will affect the situation in the future remains to be seen; but all experience indicates that these new powers and this quickened class consciousness will tend to fortify the alliance of popular philosophy and military discipline against a personal and internally centred morality.   Women in masses are, or always have been, servile under the tyranny of social opinion, and subject to a very gross superstition.   Whenever two or three of them are gathered together, the great goddess They is in the midst of them with Her arrogant foot on their necks.   There is no woman's club or tea or sewing circle or even domestic fireside where Her voice is not heard and where Her words are not solemnly quoted as oracles, ending with absolute finality all masculine dissent.

It is perhaps within the domestic circle that the tryanny of this deity is most ruthlessly imposed and substituted for the free and natural dictates of the private heart.   I will illustrate the procedure. The average man might conceivably dispute, let us assume, with his own wife on fairly equal terms.   He has devoted the better part of a lifetime to studying her special tactics and stratagems, and knows how to meet them.   But the average man is never permitted by a really intelligent wife to carry on any dispute with her.   The moment that he begins an argument, she softly steps aside — or more accurately, side-steps — and "quotes Scripture," quotes this Hydra-headed monster, Whom it is sacrilege to mention by any other designation than the capitalized third person plural.

At the domestic fireside, argument, as distinguished from conviction, usually begins in a man's soul.   In the intimate simplicity of his heart, moved only by considerations of comfort, personal taste, or the family budget, a man will begin thus:

"I believe, Dorothy, we'd better have another electric light put in the dining-room, so that we can see a little better what we are taking in."

She will reply: "Oh, no, my dear; we'll do nothing of the sort. They are using candles now."

Or he will begin: "Well, Dotty old dear, I guess the old car will serve us another season, won't it?"

And she: "Why, John, how can you think so?   It's quite impossible. They are using closed cars now."

Or the poor man will open a fireside rumination thus: "Do you know, Dorothy, when Kitty's in high school —— "

And she will cut in: "But Kitty is not going to the high school. You are absurd.   You know perfectly well that They are sending Their girls away to school now."

Such are the interventions of the great goddess They, trampling rough-shod over the inclinations and powers of the private life. And such is the worship of her, instituted daily on a more and more imposing scale as a large class of timid idolaters becomes a potent organized force in the determination of standards.

Under the combined pressure of philosophy, military discipline, and feminine superstition, the younger generation has been driven to conceive of virtue as merely a facile adjustment to the existing environment. It believes to an excessive degree in certain "standardized" ways of making the adjustment. The resulting phenomena have their comic aspects and their grave aspects, which I shall now explore a little according to a method suggested by this profound aphorism of Stevenson's: "Man lives not by bread alone; but mostly by catchwords." All that is most efficacious in the morality of our time is condensed in its catchwords. I shall hunt for the missing soul of the younger generation by following the bits of slang it has dropped in its flight.

"Abandon hope of social success," I read in an organ of youth a few months ago, "unless you have a car and a 'line.'" For days I enquired in vain of my coevals the meaning of the word 'line.' But the moment I asked a young man of the new times whether he understood it, he laughed, and explained that a 'line' is a complete set of conversational openings and ready-to-wear speeches, practically committed to memory and rehearsed for use on all typical social occasions. If you have a 'line,' you are not at a loss when the door opens, or in the ten minutes' talk with the family or the chaperon or any of the difficult transitional moments in your Napoleonic progress from the first dance to the last good night.

"It is all right," said my informant, "if you don't go to the same place too often."

I mused on a number of things of which I had read or heard, including the training of a successful book-agent, before I thought of the obvious solution. Then I said: "It sounds like F. Scott Fitzgerald."

"It is like him," he replied. "They all study his stuff — get it by heart. He has the best 'line' going."

I ended my lesson with the understanding that 'line' is short for lifeline, a device by which one avoids the danger of misstepping into the deep water which R. L. Stevenson commended to a former generation of students as "truth of intercourse."

This self-distrust of the new generation, this clinging to the social lifeline, this reliance upon external means of grace, is not confined to undergraduates. It pervades the younger society. It is openly recognized and played upon, for instance, in those popular and entertaining magazines which undertake to teach the newly-rich to spend their money as if they had been rich a long time. "Buy a car," advises a canny caterer to democracy, "which will give you that comfortable sense of superiority." O superlative car! "Here are garments," cries another, "which will put you perfectly at ease in any society." O magical garments! Finally consider a full-page advertisement (in a radical journal which scoffs at decorum) of a book on etiquette, running about like this: "If you spilled a plate of soup in the lap of your hostess, should you apologize profusely, or should you pass over the incident in silence? — Buy this book and find out."

If that old censor of social morals, Thoreau, could visit us and inspect these pages, one can imagine him muttering in his Diogenes' beard: "Could not a man who really possessed 'a comfortable sense of superiority' — could he not walk? or if necessary, consider buying a car within his means and adequate to his needs? wear his clothes till they were easy? and, when he spilled the soup, speak what words of consolation God put into his heart?" But Thoreau was of a former generation which sought its comfortable sense of superiority within, rather than in that "ceaseless striving after smartness in clothing," observed by William McFee's London sailor lad as a distinction of the New York man-in-the-street.

Ten thousand finger-posts point the younger generation the way to enter the race for external "distinction," the way to Vanity Fair — ten thousand finger-posts to one honest old-fashioned pilgrim who assured them that it is the privilege of the truly superior man to do what he pleases and what suits his own sense of fitness, simply and nonchalantly. How do heroes converse? "Won't you have a cup of tea?" says King Haakon. "By George, your Majesty," says Mr. Roosevelt, "the very thing I'd like!" You won't find that reply in any book of etiquette; yet it suited the occasion well enough. In general those who always stand on their dignity have nothing else to stand on. It is not the prime minister but the secretarial underlings who step starchily out in frock coats and top hats. Their chief bolts from his office in sack coat and nondescript felt. He has risen above his tailor.

Carlyle had a contemptuous word for all that "superiority" which one can buy at the store: he called it "gigmanity." It is a word that should be taught to our young people as a charm against infatuation with the external show of things. Carlyle found his word in the records of a criminal case. Said a witness: "I have always considered the defendant a respectable man." "What do you mean, sir," queries the judge, "by a respectable man?" "Why, your honor," replied the witness, "*he keeps a gig*." We have substituted for the gig a more elaborate vehicle in which one may ride to respectability — a very smooth-riding vehicle which, to be perfectly respectable, should be equipped, according to current standards, with a laprobe of Chinese civet cat lined with velvet, and an electrically lighted accessories case of gold and pearl.

But consider now a little more closely the young person who expects to be put at ease by a car, a suit of clothes, and a book of etiquette — all of which he recognizes as superior to himself. Follow him to college, whither he is sure to be impelled by his self-distrust and his naïve confidence in a prescribed routine. No organ within him craves intellectual food; but something without him, a continuous social whisper, has suggested that there is salvation in a bachelor's degree. College life is a kind of select soirée, at which it will give him 'a comfortable sense of superiority' merely to be seen. By him we explain why academic culture does not "take." With him in our eye, we expound a curious phrase in wide use among undergraduates.

Every year I talk with a considerable number of young persons, about to enter the junior and senior classes, concerning their program of studies; and I regularly begin by asking what they are doing in certain prescribed subjects, such as foreign languages. Quite regularly seven out of ten of them answer, with a happy smile and a reminiscent sigh: "Thank goodness, I worked *off* my French and German last year."

To which I regularly and hopelessly retort: "But have you worked *up* your German? Have you worked *in* your French? We don't require you to take them for the look of the thing. Can you use them?"

And they quite regularly respond: "Oh, no! We don't expect to use them. We merely took them to *work off* group-requirements."

My feigned surprise that they should think us here "for the look of the thing" is an echo, by the way, of Mr. Kipling, who, as much as any living writer, gave the tone to undergraduate life twenty years ago. Under the spur of his Indian tales and verse, we talked a good deal in those times about doing the "day's work" without excuses. It was the mode then to admire "men who do things." And so our blood was stirred by Mr. Kipling's hard-mouthed bridge-builder haranguing his shiftless Hindus: "Sons of unthinkable begetting, children of unspeakable shame! Are we here for the look of the thing?"

It is at least twenty years since I read that passage; and yet it vibrates still in the memory with an authority which nothing of Mr. F. Scott Fitzgerald's quite possesses. I will present, on the other hand, a bit of recent dialogue from life, which sounds in my ears like a current tune, expressing the spirit of a new generation which candidly admits that it *is* here "for the look of the thing."

At registration time in the fall a very sweet girl from Georgia with a soft Southern voice and soft Southern eyes, fringed like jessamine or honeysuckle, came to me as registration officer, and asked me to waive a college rule in her favor.

"I am very sorry," I said, with customary mild severity, "I can't let you do it. I have no authority in the matter."

"Well," she replied, "who has? Who can?" And she looked into my eyes with searching and almost painful sweetness.

"You might," I said, faltering, "you might go to the Dean. A Dean is the only one that breaks rules. You might ask him, but I doubt if it will do any good. Our Dean is a very firm man. He's a New-Englander, you know, a Puritan, with a stiff conscience."

"Tell me something," she said softly, "will you?"

"Yes," I replied, "if I can." I was ready to do anything for her short of breaking the rule.

"Is this Dean of yours a bachelor or a married man?"

"A bachelor," I answered, "a bachelor of forty."

"Oh, that's all right," she cried gaily, as she gathered up her papers, "I'll *fix* him."

If, now, you take the spirit of this fair Georgian and mold it a little under the pressures of the hour, you produce an outstanding type of the recent feminine "arrivals" in business. She will get on. If she had a shade less of adaptability and a shade more of "soul," she would have her difficulties.

I had recently an instructive conversation with a charming and thoroughly refined young woman, who, moved by the impulse of her time, was seeking "economic independence," and had taken her initial steps in the business world. I asked her what she had learned from her professional life. "The most important thing that I have tried to learn," she replied instantly, but without much gusto, "is how to sell myself."

I wish that I could say that the vile phrase struck me as shocking. But how can one be shocked any longer, whose ears have rung these half-dozen years with phrases struck at the same mint, "slogans" of the "nation-wide" "campaigners," "selling charity," "selling art," "selling the war," "selling patriotism," "selling the flag," "selling the church — yours in business for the Lord," "selling" things visible and things invisible, whatever is now for sale in the heavens above or the waters under the earth — and everything is for sale. Such is the idiom of their souls.

At the present moment, "production" is looked upon as an undertaking for old men. Salesmanship is the one career that kindles the imaginations and genius of the young. It is a perfectly respectable career for one who has something valuable to sell.

We touch now on what is most dangerously wrong in the moral incentives and tendencies of the younger generation. Its one categorical imperative, "Learn to sell yourself," means, being interpreted, "Get your value recognized by society." Publicity managers, business psychologists, sales-engineers, and their kind and kindred, who are legion, have made the atmosphere of our times tense with pressures upon every young person to get his value recognized. If a new popular religion were founded to-day, the first book of its gospel would undoubtedly treat of the psychology of salesmanship. The spirit of this gospel has already invaded the void left by the new universe constructed with no "insides." The young person responds with an intoxication, seldom sobered by any consideration whatever of the really quite primary questions whether he has any value, and, if not, whether by dint of some old-fashioned exertion, he may acquire some.   The emphasis of the selling-slogan is, at least for a young generation, off: it just misses the head of the nail and strikes with a resounding whack close beside it.   Only the attentive notice that it is all noise with no honest drive.

The young person who is inspired to "sell" himself is encouraged by every pressure of his times to concern himself with only one thing, namely, "How to put it across."   He hears on all sides that what he is to put across is of small consequence.   He need not give himself much anxiety, if he is a teacher or preacher about what he is to teach or preach; nor, if he is a journalist or author or artist, about what he is to write or paint.

Efficiency in a universe of salesmen demands no special training or learning in any field whatever, save one —the technique of "touch." If you haven't the touch, you are "Out."   If you have the "touch," you are "It."   This technique is heaven's free gift to the happy mortal who is born "a good mixer," facile and suave in surface contacts.   But it is also masterable by those unintrospective wits, who, wasting no time in meditating either their subject or their object, consider only their "objective," and therefore dedicate their days and their nights to the study of their public, their audience, their clientele.

Learned men in the universities are rapidly establishing the "technique of touch" on universal principles, applicable to all relations between the salesman and the public, from the marketing of short stories to transactions in gold brick.   When this new science is perfected, it bids fair to displace ethics, logic, and the other elements of our bankrupt philosophy.   For those who have acquired the new learning, those who have the "touch," prosper.   They "get away with it."   They "put it across."

Under the new system, success in life is felicitously described as "getting by."   This modest expression indicates that our hero, though slightly elated by his efficiency, is no enthusiast.   He is, on the contrary, just beneath his fine surface, a cynic.   Knowing the hollowness of his interior, he does not respect himself.   Suspecting that those with whom he traffics are equally hollow, he does no respect his public. His criterion of success implies acknowledgment that he is a fraud and his public a fool, who will pass him without challenge provided only that he "puts up a good front." It is understood that I am portraying one whom the "band-wagon" carries to the end of the road.

When I seek for an incarnate symbol of what the virtues of our young generation become when they are pushed to excess, I recall one of its representatives who burst upon us one summer evening in a crowded train coming out of Washington. We were standing, some twenty of us, tired and hungry, jammed in the hot throat of the dining-car, waiting earnestly yet orderly for our turn at a seat. Just as one was vacated, in from the next coach dashed a youth of twenty-one, immaculate in white flannels, chin aloft and eyes hard ahead, like a picture drawn in the old days by Mr. C. D. Gibson for the late R. H. Davis. With a perfectly lordly gesture of the hand, as of one clearing the way for Rupert of Hentzau, and with a quiet but imperative "I beg your pardon," that handsome, that plausible, youth actually tried to break through the wedge of those twenty weary mortals and take that seat for himself. Shameful to relate, the wedge melted before him; he got by — almost to the head of the line, before an iron arm barred the passage, and a firm humorous voice exclaimed: "No, you don't, my boy! You'll have to work your way up, like the rest of us." Whereat that immaculate young importance, instantly collapsing, slunk and wriggled to the rear, while the twenty murmured to one another, "Where did he get that stuff?"

My illustrative personage, real and at the same time symbolical, obviously got his "stuff" from a society excessively dependent for its superiority upon car-makers, tailors, and books of etiquette. The morality of his period has worked upon my hero from without inward, but has not penetrated far. At the centre, where the master should sit, there is a space without form and void. He has nothing, morally speaking, of his own. The time-spirit has clothed him in specious appearances. He travels upon credit which was accumulated in other days, when the Gibson chin was the outward sign of an inward determination. He is, therefore, in the figurative, and probably also in the literal, sense, "Living beyond his means."

I will hazard a guess that at college he studied a "line," "worked off" his French, and attained in his studies a passing mark, which is now generally known as a "gentleman's grade." At the same time he lived softly in a palatial fraternity house contributed by over-indulgent alumni, who themselves paid for their barracks accommo-dations in the old dormitory by tending furnaces, and the like. He had had his father's car at his disposal since his early teens. Natur-ally when he went to college, he required it still for transit from fraternity house to class room and for dances and week-end parties. Of course, if one has a good car, one must live up to one's car.

And so the Old Man, half in pity for his own austere youth, saw his son through in a style that he did not allow himself after a life-time of industry and thrift. "When my boy gets out in the world," the Old Man had said, "he'll have to shift for himself; but we'll give him a start with the best of them. Yes, sir, with the best of them!"

I will guess that our young man is now in the employ of a corpora-tion with very handsome offices, which gives him an apprentice's wage, sufficient to pay installments on his tailor's bill, while it author-izes an expense account allowing and encouraging him to enjoy the clubs, hotels, and costly little pleasures of big business men. All his life he has had unearned advantages thrust upon him; he takes them quite as a matter of course. He has always spent other people's money freely. Now it is a matter of duty to put on all the "side" that he can. He must eat and dress and drive in a fashion to "get in touch" with men whose income tax many times exceeds his income. Under the circumstances, it is altogether too soon to think of laying anything by. If he attempted that, he would have to "drop out of the running." He has, however, "invested" in an automobile, up-holstered with the elegance of a parlor, and is asking his landlord to trust him for the last month's rent.

If he "puts it across" to a girl, formed on the same system — as I think he soon will — she, in her turn, will clutch at the "line" she has been taught. She will demand the right to be married without a ring, to retain her own name, to be secure from the expectation of children, to be allowed to pursue her own career, and to be guar-anteed a "good time." To all of which demands he will yield ready assent. They will have a highly expensive engagement and a still more expensive wedding and honeymoon; and they will then attempt to "jolly things along" together.

They will find that they are unable to keep house comfortably in

his upholstered car.   He will discover that a modern establishment
for two is, in spite of all that our grandmothers used to say, more
difficult to swing than bachelor's quarters.   It will appear that she
is quite his equal as a spender.   At first he may hope for some relief
from the proceeds of that independent career which he has agreed to
allow her to pursue.   But he will learn very shortly that the kind of a
girl who stipulates for a marriage exempt from all the responsibilities of the traditional union becomes the kind of wife who puts all
that she can lay hands on upon her own back, and yet leaves it more
than half uncovered.   She has been trained to dress and display
herself for the kind of man that he is.   But he is not quite equal to
the task of maintaining the kind of woman that she is.   In two years
or less, he will be single again and bankrupt — or an advertising
manager on twenty thousand a year.

I add the alternative; because he may "get by."   But a generation
with a marked tendency towards the production and heroization of
such figures and figurantes should beware of pressing its tendencies
too far.   "The gods creep up on feet of wool."   A spending generation which trades on the moral and material accumulations of its
predecessors, presently finds its stock exhausted.   And though for a
time, by its mastery of "touch" it may still sell water and market
wind, in the long run it will not get by with that stuff.

WAR [1]

By DURANT DRAKE

Durant Drake (1878–) is at present on the faculty of Vassar College as a professor of philosophy. He has taught at the University of Illinois and, in 1923 and 1924, lectured in German, Swiss, and Italian universities. Among his works on philosophy and ethics are "The Problem of Things in Themselves" (1911), "Problems of Conduct" (1914), "America Faces the Future" (1922), and "The New Morality" (1928).

WHAT ARE THE RESULTS OF MODERN WAR?

THE gravest of all the moral problems now before the world is the problem whether it will ever be right again to go to war. Here, because of the intensity of the passions aroused, and the age-long habit of glorifying war, it is singularly difficult to apply the rational criterion of the greatest human happiness. But here, because of the momentous issues at stake, we must be particularly careful to remain cool-headed and free from emotional bias. We must consider dispassionately the results likely to be achieved by possible future wars and ask whether we can legitimately expect that going to war will ever again further the best interests of mankind.

We can probably agree that most past wars have been futile and disastrous, but that there have been occasions when it was best that a nation should defend itself in battle. In most cases it is extremely difficult to know what would have happened if one or both of the peoples concerned had refused to fight. If our forefathers had not fought England for their political independence, or if the North and South had refused to fight over the Secession issue, would our people be better or worse off to-day? No one can surely say. But when the Athenians held back the Persian hordes at Marathon, or when Charles Martel defeated the Saracens at Tours, the world was undoubtedly benefited thereby.

What we may fail to realize, however, is that war has become a totally different thing from what it used to be. Until recently civ-

---

ilization was developed in relatively small oases surrounded by hordes of barbarians who looked with hungry eyes at the rich lands and possessions of their more prosperous neighbours. But now the most powerful nations are among the most advanced; there is no longer any need of defending civilization against savagery. The need now is rather to protect backward peoples from the greed and insolence of the civilized. Guerilla warfare in the old style may recur, for some time to come, between natives and imperialistic rulers. But real war, in the modern sense, takes place between civilized peoples; and it is such warfare that we must discuss.

Now the plain fact is that the destructiveness of war has been multiplied a thousandfold in the twentieth century, and is increasing in geometrical progression. What we call the Great War killed, in something over four years, not far from twenty million soldiers, and indirectly caused, first and last, the death of about twenty million other people. But the technique of war has been improving rapidly since 1918. A fleet of airplanes could now practically wipe out the population of a great city in a night.

The financial loss caused by the Great War has been estimated at about three hundred billion dollars; the cost of living was doubled even in the United States, which had fought for only a year and a half; in Europe it was trebled, quadrupled, and more. Thirty billion dollars' worth of property was destroyed; over three thousand good ships, of more than fifteen million tons, were sunk; thousands of towns and villages were destroyed; economic processes were disorganized for a generation; the very limited world-stocks of copper, platinum, oil, and other valuable resources, were consumed to a very alarming extent.

The total sum of human agony caused by that war was so vast that the imagination can no more grasp it than it can grasp the figures of modern astronomy. But if there are wars in the future they will be carried on increasingly behind the battle-lines, and whole populations will suffer, in all sorts of terrible ways. "If mankind does not end war, war will end mankind."

Out of a great number of corroborative statements from the pens of military experts, the following must suffice; it is written by the Right Honorable Winston Churchill, former First Lord of the British Admiralty:

All that happened in the four years of the Great War was only a prelude to what was preparing for the fifth year. The campaign of the year 1919 would have witnessed an immense accession to the power of destruction. Had the Germans retained the morale to make good their retreat to the Rhine, they would have been assaulted in the summer of 1919 with forces and by methods incomparably more prodigious than any yet employed. Thousands of aeroplanes would have shattered their cities. . . . Poison gases of incredible malignity . . . would have stifled all resistance and paralyzed all life on the hostile front. . . . The campaign of 1919 was never fought; but its ideas go marching along. In every army they are being explored, elaborated, refined under the surface of peace; and should war come again to the world it is not with the weapons and agencies prepared for 1919 that it will be fought, but with developments and extensions of these which will be incomparably more formidable and fatal. . . .

As for poison gas and chemical warfare in all its forms, only the first chapter has been written of a terrible book. Certainly every one of these new avenues to destruction is being studied on both sides of the Rhine [and, we may add, in countries far from the Rhine], with all the science and patience of which man is capable. . . . A study of diseases — or pestilences methodically prepared and deliberately launched upon man and beast — is certainly being pursued in the laboratories of more than one great country. Blight to destroy crops, anthrax to slay horses and cattle, plague to poison not armies only but whole districts — such are the lines along which military science is remorselessly advancing. . . .

Mankind has never been in this position before. Without having improved appreciably in virtue or enjoying wiser guidance, it has got into its hands for the first time the tools by which it can unfailingly accomplish its own extermination. Death stands at attention, obedient, expectant, ready to serve, ready to sheer away the peoples en masse; ready, if called on, to pulverize without hope of repair, what is left of civilization.[1]

This brief glance must suffice as a summary of the direct effects of modern warfare upon human happiness. But when people read and talk of past wars they seldom think much about the murderousness, the wanton destructiveness, the nastiness, the horrible suffering, the setback to civilization. Wars are seldom thought of in terms of the killed and mangled combatants, or in terms of the beaten side, with its misery, demoralization, and despair. Nor is the tyranny of the conquerors usually stressed, the looting, the rapine, the crushing of liberty that is apt to follow the intoxication of victory. Instead, we think of the splendid heroisms, the devoted comradeships, the dogged perseverance and self-denial, and the eventual glorious success of the victors.

[1] Published in a *Bulletin* of the Federal Council of Churches of Christ in America.

The heroisms of war are very real, very pathetic, and very glorious. But at what a price are these virtues fostered! The most important qualities in the soldier are absolute obedience, and ferocity — the will to attack and kill.

The demonstrations of Colonel R. B. Campbell, Director of Bayonet Fighting for the British Army, were very instructive. He would take a platoon of sheepish-looking, poorly developed youths, and, by the exercise of his extraordinary persuasion, rapidly strip away the coverings of civilization from them, and turn them into fighting animals, eyes glaring, teeth bared, trembling, hating. He did not yell, or rant. He talked rapidly, evenly, in a low, confidential, compelling tone. "That's where the liver is, if he runs away. Two inches of steel, no more. . . . And mind you get the right place. . . . In the throat . . . right there . . . two inches. A-a-a-h-h. . . ." At the word the boys charged down on the row of stuffed sacks, stabbing madly but not blindly. As they lunged together the yell went up. . . . "A-a-a-h-h." . . . — a snarling, bestial sound that struck at the jelly of the spine.[1]

As an ex-soldier wrote in 1920, "You have got over your squeamishness. Yes, but it is just that 'squeamishness,' that recognition that the other fellow is also a man, which is religion, brotherhood, morality, and civilization."

When a war is over, the heroisms of battle come to an abrupt end. The callousness persists. Usually a crime-wave follows. The ex-soldiers are restless, insensitive to suffering, longing for pleasure at any price. People generally do not want to think, they want to forget; there is usually a moral slump, a tired acquiescence in graft and privilege and profiteering, and distaste for hard work. Intellectual dishonesty has been fostered by the war-propaganda, hatreds and resentments colour thought, open-mindedness and a scientific attitude toward international problems is harder than ever to secure. The interest in progressive social movements, diverted by the war, is very slow in reviving.

In March or April of 1914, a group of us held a dinner one night at the St. Denis Hotel for some social cause or another — I forget what. But one thing I remember, and that is that Walter Rauschenbusch was our speaker, and that he said words that only a prophet could have uttered.

We are told, he said, that we must be patient, content to move slowly, must bide our time: Rome wasn't built in a day! Don't believe it, he cried. We have not a moment to lose. If we are to do anything, we must do it

---

[1] From an article in *The American Mercury*.

quickly. Now is the hour — perhaps the last hour for us of this generation. For any moment — to-morrow, the day after — a war may break out, and then our chance will be gone. The world will revert on the instant to re-action, autocracy, perhaps to barbarism and savagery. We shall then have to fight, if we can fight at all, not for progress, but for the elemental things which we think achieved forever. But nothing is achieved when war comes. Everything goes! The ground quakes, then caves in beneath our feet. So it's now or never! Once America gets into war with Mexico, Japan — he did not mention Germany, as I recall — our enemies will be in the saddle, to ride roughshod for years.

It was as though a Jeremiah spoke that night! The war came within less than half a year, and with it, just as he prophesied, the ancient abominations. Rauschenbusch saw quickly this doom come down upon us, and died from the sorrow of it. Perhaps his fate was happier than that of those who survived to see their hopes destroyed and their life work at an end.[1]

It is primarily, of course, the young men who are killed in war — though it is quite possible that in another great war whole populations will be indiscriminately slaughtered. In the war of 1914–18 the principal belligerents lost from a quarter to a third of their young men of fighting age. This means an incalculable loss in forward-looking, progressive thought. "What leaders the new age has lost on the battlefields of Europe, what genius, what power of social organization, what spiritual idealism, we shall never know. But that loss is telling upon us to-day in the political arena to which we have now returned, and will tell increasingly, making our national and international decisions more unrepresentative alike of the men who died and of the ideals which, at least in the earlier stages of the war, they thought they were fighting for."

No one can estimate the loss to science, invention and art from the death of gifted young men, like Rupert Brooke, like Alan Seegar, like the young Englishman Mosely, of whom Millikan writes that he

had accomplished as notable a piece of research in physics as has appeared during the past fifty years. Such a mind was one of the early victims of the world-war. He was shot and killed instantly in the trenches of Gallipoli in the summer of 1915.[2]

War under modern conditions kills primarily the physically and mentally fit, the finest specimens of manhood, while the weaklings, the morons, and the defectives remain at home to breed at will. And

[1] J. H. Holmes, in *The Survey Graphic*, vol. 10, p. 550.
[2] R. A. Millikan, *The Electron*, p. 196.

great war has, therefore, a marked dysgenic influence, lowering the quality of the human race on both sides, whichever technically wins. This loss is irreparable.

WOULD ANYTHING JUSTIFY WAR UNDER PRESENT CONDITIONS?

The indictment is terrific. Could anything justify us in joining in such an orgy of murderous destructiveness as war has now become?

Every intelligent person agrees that aggressive war on the modern scale would be unspeakably wicked. The difference of opinion arises with respect to defensive war. Suppose that some great Power were to make unjustifiable demands upon us, threatening, if we refused to comply, to compel us to do so. Should we be justified in going to war with that Power in "self-defence"?

To answer this question intelligently, we must consider the probable results of non-resistance, and compare them with the probable results of war.

Certainly it is no longer true, as it was in the old days, that we may need to go to war to protect our men from slaughter or slavery, and our women from rape or abduction. Incidental atrocities might be committed by an unresisted foreign army of occupation, but they would be insignificant as compared with the atrocities of even a few days of modern warfare. It is inconceivable that any nation now powerful enough to invade and hold the territory of another civilized nation would order its army of occupation to murder, plunder, or destroy property, if the occupation was not resisted. The great mass of every nation are rather kindly folk, who would not stand for cold-blooded brutality, unless their fears and passions were aroused by *war*. It would be impossible to hush the matter up, as is possible sometimes with brutal treatment of remote and uncivilized peoples. If the people whose army was pursuing a policy of wanton destructiveness were kept in ignorance of the facts, the horror evoked in the rest of the world would quickly bring pressure to bear upon them. . . . In short, it is *war* that makes atrocities. If we wish to save our people from physical suffering and death, and our cities and countryside from destruction, we must refuse to go to war, however provoked or ill-treated we may be.

Under modern conditions social order would not be destroyed by a foreign army of occupation, if there were no war. The French occupation of the Rhineland and the Ruhr has produced some incidental cruelties and injustices — natural enough, in view of the deep resentments following a bitter war fought on French soil; but these are negligible as compared with the evils which resistance by the Germans would have brought. In general, life has gone on as usual in the occupied provinces. Life would go on as usual in our country if it were occupied by the armies of a foreign Power; our cities might well be better governed by it than by our own politicians. What the invading nation would desire would be money, or natural resources — coal, iron, oil, or whatever it was in need of. To pay such a tribute would hurt our pride; it would rankle as an injustice (for, whatever the facts in the case, the great majority of us would never believe that we were in the wrong); it would humiliate us in our own eyes. But so far as hurting our pocketbooks is concerned, the amount we should be called upon to pay would be far less than the cost of even a very short war. For war has become incredibly expensive.

It is conceivable that the invading nation might wish to hold our territory under its flag, and thus destroy our political independence. This is extremely unlikely, in the case of continental United States, which is too big a mouthful for any Power to digest. But Porto Rico or Hawaii might be taken, or the Panama Canal, or the Philippines, if we were still ruling them. And in the case of a country not so powerful or so protected by the seas as our own, some neighbouring nation might harbour a lust for expansion at its expense. To be sure, the nations of the earth, with the exception of Russia and the United States, have solemnly covenanted together never henceforth to take by war the territory or infringe the sovereignty of any other nation. But suppose the nation threatening invasion disavows that promise, or is thoroughly distrusted, and suppose the League of Nations seems impotent to enforce the solemn covenant, so that a nation believes that it faces the loss of part of its territory, or the loss of its political independence. Is it justified in going to war in the hope of thereby averting such loss?

What a "war of self-defence" means, under modern conditions, is a war to avert the payment of tribute, or the loss of political independence, or of a portion of territory. The alternative would be, paying the tribute or accepting the partial or complete loss of independence or territory for the time being, and trusting to the force of public opinion throughout the world to remedy the wrong in time. To choose this latter alternative would make against deep-rooted traditional attitudes — the love of political liberty, the sense of "national honour," pride in the flag, the instinct of combativeness. But education could develop contrary traditions, if a serious attempt were made. It is conceivable that a revival of fundamental Christianity might make masses of men as unwilling to fight, on religious grounds, as the Friends were in the late War. It is conceivable that a generation brought up on such books as Wells's *Outline of History* should care more for the peaceful development of civilization than for the perpetuation of their own national name or existing boundaries. It is conceivable that a generation of people enlightened as to the horrors of war should repudiate that barbarous and suicidal method of settling disputes and, appealing to the moral verdict of mankind, should be actually "too proud to fight."

If the majority in every great nation were thus to become truly Christian, or in any other way internationally minded, or merely pacific out of a realization of the horrors of war, the problem would, of course, be solved. But such a happy consummation cannot be counted on in the near future. And the question is, if any one powerful nation may possibly become so jingoistic or greedy as to threaten another nation, should all the nations practise "preparedness" and plan to join battle if invaded? Or should the more pacific nations take the lead and set an example to the others by disarming and pledging themselves under no circumstances to go to war? For unless such antecedent pledges are made and disarmament is effected, it is futile to suppose that a pacific policy could be made to prevail under the excitement of threatened invasion.

It is difficult to forecast the future. But the present writer has come, after much study of the matter, to the conclusion that disarmament and abstinence from military resistance has now become the right course for every nation, irrespective of what other nations do. It seems to him unlikely that any nation henceforth will be able to invade and do any great damage to another civilized nation in cold blood, if that nation refuses to go to war. There are too

many decent people in every nation to support such a policy, if it is
not overlaid by the passions and the propaganda that war would
bring into being.   If such a policy *were* initiated, it would presently
collapse under the double weight of opposition at home and the
combined moral reprobation of the rest of the world.   Furthermore,
it is very doubtful if the occupation of another nation's territory by
armed forces would pay.   Strikes and sabotage, the flooding of
mines and the wrecking of trains, and the thousand possible inter-
ferences with successful exploitation of a conquered land could easily
make the invasion an economic failure for the invaders, without
armed resistance.

"New occasions teach new duties."   The writer agrees heartily
that up to the present decade in the world's history there *have* been
situations so intolerable that war, as it was then waged, was preferable.   And he joins in giving all honour to the brave men who
risked and gave their lives in what they deemed the cause of liberty
and human rights.   But the scales have now been tipped in the
other direction.   The danger to mankind is now far greater from
military "preparedness," with the fears and suspicions thereby
evoked, and the temptation to use the diabolical engines of destruction and the carefully wrought plans which each of the great nations
now holds poised like a sword of Damocles over its neighbours, than
would inhere in a frank and honest policy of pacifism.   The hereditary autocracies, which sometimes provoked wars for the sake of
strengthening their grip on their own people, have now disappeared;
and no nation now really wants war.   Even so, it is too much to
expect the European Powers to disarm at present; ancient fears and
suspicions in that unhappy continent, so long war-ridden, will be a
long time a-dying.   But it is very unlikely that any people in the
world will attack the United States, if we are clearly pacific ourselves.   *We* may be tempted to make war against some nation that
irritates us or infringes what we consider our rights; if we are well
prepared for war, with a fine professional army and navy itching to
show their efficiency, we may well be swept by a wave of misguided
emotionalism into declaring war.   We might or might not win it;
no one knows what secret inventions, what gruesome methods of
murderousness, would determine the outcome.   But in any case we
should be committing the unforgivable sin.

It is a matter of getting rid of outgrown attitudes and adjusting our minds to new situations.   Preparedness for war *was*, till recently, necessary.   Now it has become the supreme danger.   The great Powers are like a band of children playing with dynamite.   It is an expensive game; the great Powers are spending two or three billion dollars a year in playing it, right along.   But this is nothing to what it will cost in a few weeks, or days, if the dynamite should go off. The only sane thing to do is to put the dynamite away and make friends instead of creating fear.   *We* are in the most favourable position for doing that first.   Pride and ignorance stand in the way. For how long?

HOW CAN WAR BE ABOLISHED?

Nothing more imperiously demands our thought and our effort than the campaign to put a final end to war on earth.   The supreme race of history is on; can peace be permanently stabilized before another great explosion occurs?

Education, of course, is the fundamental need.   No nation stands to gain henceforth by a great war; victors and vanquished, they will all lose.   That outstanding truth should be taught everywhere, together with detailed and vivid knowledge of the horrors of the new warfare.

In addition, we should offer such materials of education to our children as will increase their sympathy and sense of kinship with other peoples.   Every one knows that we shall never go to war henceforth with England, or with Canada; we *feel* ourselves too much akin.   It will be harder, but not impossible, to establish similar feeling of essential kinship with the other great peoples of the earth.   More and more we must send our children abroad for study and acquaintance, and welcome foreign youth here.   More and more we must organize international associations of every sort, and attend international conferences.   More and more we must learn to love the art, the music, the great monuments and the natural scenery of other countries, we must come to admire their scientific and practical achievements. We must learn to think of all this as our common human heritage, and feel ourselves to be primarily members of the one great human race, battling its way against the forces of nature towards a glorious future — and only secondarily as Americans, Germans, Frenchmen, or whatever. We are now, on the average, far behind some other peoples in such international-mindedness. We ought to be in the lead.

But this is only a beginning. We must diffuse an understanding of the causes of wars, and work with might and main to counteract them. We must further every possible device that bids fair to lessen the danger of war.

Probably the most dangerous thing in the world now is not lust for conquest, or desire for glory, or combativeness, but fear. We should work, by spreading pacifist sentiment among all peoples, by treaties and pacts like that of Locarno, by disarmament agreements, by strengthening the prestige and power of the League of Nations, to diminish this nightmare of fear, and thereby to lessen the danger that some nation, feeling the necessity of getting the jump on an evil-intentioned enemy, will strike the first blow.

Resentment at old wrongs, at some of the new frontiers in Europe which assign peoples against their will to a sovereignty they do not wish, and at the imperialism of the great Powers, persists, and may at any moment flare up into dangerous excitement. Such wrongs it should be the concern of the League of Nations to consider, and to remedy; all men of good will should help to educate world-opinion to that end.

The steadily increasing population in some countries which are already overpopulated is a serious menace, since such peoples naturally look for a bigger place in the sun. Emigration may serve as a temporary outlet; there are still countries, particularly in South America, that welcome immigration. But at best this is a temporary easing of the strain. The only real solution lies in restricting population, by educating the peoples concerned, raising their standard of living, and teaching them birth control.

There will still remain interested groups that may push for war — professional army and navy men, munition-makers, landowners and capitalists who welcome war as a backfire against democracy, merchants and financiers who may want colonial markets, raw materials free from tariff, concessions for exploiting natural resources, and the like.

This latter group is so dangerous to the world's peace that several changes in national policy should be made by international agreement; and we should work to that end. All colonies should be governed on the "open door" policy, with equality of trading opportunities for the merchants of every nation. All investment fields should be open freely to investors of every nation. All colonial preferential tariffs — such as we have put up at the door of the Philippines — should be abolished, together with all differential export duties. And above all, the nations should agree not to go to war to protect the investments made by their citizens in foreign countries, or to collect debts owed them. All this will be strenuously opposed by the financial interests which gain by the present system of "dollar diplomacy." But from the mere economic point of view all the rest of us would be better off. And we should be free from one of the gravest causes of modern war.

As to the munition-makers and potential war-profiteers, they can be completely undercut by a declaration that if another war comes, wealth will be conscripted. This means, or should mean, that in the event of another war, a pay-as-we-go policy will be inaugurated; instead of selling interest-bearing bonds to the rich, their money will be taken just the same, and they will be given nothing but receipts. If we conscript human life, we have a still greater moral right to conscript money. And it is right that a generation which makes war should pay for it instead of passing a debt on to future generations. Nothing is more hateful than war-profiteers. And if it is definitely known beforehand, because of detailed plans drawn up and legally accepted, that no war-fortunes can be made, and that all existing wealth must be put at the service of the country's need, it is extremely doubtful if war will ever be made.

All of these changes will have to come, probably, by international agreement, as will disarmament. But there is no reason why we should not lead the way. We should be better off thereby, whatever other nations may do.

It is extremely important, too, that freedom of the press be guaranteed, even in time of war — except, of course, for the publication of military news that could help the enemy. All the nations were terribly misled by war-propaganda during the years beginning with 1914. If another war broke out, or were even threatened, we should again be flooded with distorted news. If we want to keep our heads and act intelligently, it is essential that every one should have access to all available facts.

Of course the likelihood is that, if the men at the head of our Government ever decide again to go to war, they will exercise complete control over the press, as in 1917, to "sell the war to the people." But at least now, while we are not hovering on the brink of war, the press, and other educational agencies, might be used by those who are in a position to effect their policies, to sell peace to the people. The conception of a steadfast and resolute peaceableness must be made popular.

An excellent idea, carefully developed by Kirby Page and others, calls for the establishment of a Department of Peace at Washington, parallel with the Department of War. Such a department would carry on an educational campaign for peace, would seek out and make public the facts concerning the practices of our own citizens which seem objectionable to other nations and are therefore a menace to peace, and would in many ways foster international understanding and friendship. The preservation of peace demands the active interest and co-operation of every intelligent person; and that interest needs to be kept alive by incessant effort. This could be done for a fraction of the five hundred million dollars which we are spending annually on our army and navy — not to speak of the two and a half billion dollars a year which is what we spend altogether, for war past and prospective.

But our final word must be this: It is not enough to make people hate war, they must be made to love and enjoy peace. In other words, their daily lives must be made so interesting and colorful that they will not secretly prefer the risks and excitements of war. It is no secret that thousands of men and women had "the time of their lives" in the late war. And millions of others blindly and half-consciously welcomed its coming, because their lives were so hard, or monotonous or unsatisfying.

On August 3, 1914, we waited to hear of war. If the members of that crowd waiting for war could have been honest with an inquirer, they would have had to admit that they wanted war simply because they wanted something new to happen. Their silence was a breathless hope rather than a breathless apprehension, a hope that the monotony of life was going to be broken.[1]

---

[1] John Langdon-Davies, in the *Atlantic Monthly*, vol. 138, p. 115.

War, as an arresting magazine article has recently warned us, is "the explosion point for the discontents of peace."

It is of no use reminding men of the sufferings of war, or that the next war will probably mark the end of civilization. They don't care. If they admitted the truth, they would say that they don't like civilization. War is a symptom of man's profound discontent with himself and his environment; and there will be no end to war until he himself has found peace.[1]

Science, education, religion, art, music, pageantry, sports — everything that brings comfort and joy into human life in its measure tends to counteract the lure of war. Existing natural resources and technical knowledge are adequate for raising immeasurably the standards of living of the masses. To do so must be made a generally accepted moral ideal. "Materialistic," church-people will say; "Bolshevistic," conservatives will say. And meantime we drift toward God knows what future unrest, bitterness, and war. The old moralities have not banished war. Perhaps a morality which definitely prizes human happiness as the *summum bonum* will succeed where they have failed.

[1] I. A. R. Wylie, in *Harper's Magazine*, vol. 154, p. 147.

DRINK

By ARNOLD BENNETT

One of the most prolific of modern writers, Arnold Bennett (1867–1931) has had a varied career as lawyer, editor, and man of letters. Since 1900 he has devoted his time to the production of novels, short stories, plays, essays, and other literary forms. A complete list of his writings would seem almost incredible merely because of its length; however, mention may be made of "The Old Wive's Tale" (1908), "Hilda Lessways" (1911), "These Twain" (1916), "Riceyman Steps" (1923), "Lord Raingo" (1926), "Books and Persons" (1917), "Things that Have Interested Me" (1921, 1923, 1925), and "The Savour of Life" (1928).

ONCE in a village bar-parlour I heard a paunchy, jolly, middle-aged man say: "When I've had a drop too much overnight, do you know what I does? I goes down stairs, and I pours myself out a wine glass full of neat gin, and I drinks it, and that puts me right." Seven travelers once went into the old First Avenue Hotel in Holborn just before closing time, and one of them said: "Let's see. Seven of us. Seven rounds. Seven sevens. Waiter, bring forty-nine whiskey-and-sodas." The waiter did.

Of late I have been motoring a bit on a box seat next to a chauffeur whose chief characteristic seems to be taciturnity. One day it occurred to me to say to him: "What's the beer like around this way?" He was a changed man instantly. I sat a long time one evening with a writer who said to me: "Well, I always drink and always have. I begin with a cocktail before lunch, and I keep on drinking until I get into bed — cocktails, whiskey, burgundy, beer, brandy, liqueurs." This man, admired and esteemed by an immense public, is consistently industrious, has the ascetic appearance of a Trappist monk, talks very modestly in a very quiet voice, and is over sixty years of age. On another evening I spent hours with a well-known American financier. He was of middle age, pale, very quiet in manner, and very modest. He said: "My grandfather drank; my father drank; I drink a good deal; no amount can make me drunk; my health is fine; I work nine hours a day in my office."

Out of my own experience I could multiply such examples of the varied wonders of alcohol. On the other hand, I look about among my acquaintances in various spheres — business, literature, the stage, the bar, politics — and I see everywhere men, and prominent men, whose lives are obviously clouded, and their careers impaired, if not most gravely imperilled, by continual immoderate indulgence in alcohol. And I would say farther that the decent majority of people who drink anything at all would be more interesting companions, more lovable helpmeets, and less silly at the polling booths (especially the municipal polling booths) if they cut down their consumption by half. And I would say still farther that the majority of them would greatly like to cut down their consumption — but can't of their own accord. They simply can't.

Personally I am nearly a teetotaller. I don't drink a pint in a month. I should not fall down dead from shock if I was authoritatively told that I should never get another drop. But I know why those people can't cut down their consumption of alcohol by half. The reason is precisely the same reason as prevents me, despite moral struggles and the invoking of all the powers of uplift, from cutting down my consumption of cigars and cigarettes by half. Am I a slave to tobacco? I am. Are the majority of drinkers slaves to alcohol, in the sense that it controls them more than they control it? They are. (Here, against all that is noblest in my character, I light another cigarette.)

A man drinks, as a man smokes, for two reasons: First, from habit. I have never been able to decide whether habit or self-conceit is the greatest motive force in the world. Second, because it soothes him, producing harmony within him — if only a temporary harmony. Science has exploded the notion that alcohol is a stimulant. Alcohol, like tobacco, is a narcotic.

Would I, if an autocrat, prohibit the use of alcohol? To ask is to answer. A million times no! Alcohol is one of the greatest institutions in the civilized world. It is an object of almost universal affection. It has been the accompaniment of nearly all the finest social events in history. For thousands of years it has celebrated every triumph and softened every defeat. A liquid with this unique record deserves a better fate than to be prohibited. To prohibit alcohol would be to show an odious lack of the historic sense. And think of the innumerable varied forms of it, the varied colors of its shining in the uplifted glass, the varied exquisite physical reactions of it as it slides down the human throat, the varied ecstasies (all too brief!) it produces in the human head!

Moreover, you might prohibit alcohol till you were black in the face with the intensity of your desire for the improvement of others, you could not abolish it. You might as well try to abolish love. There is a fundamental wisdom in human nature which laughs very composedly at the misguided prohibitionary activities of all one-eyed earnest persons. Alcohol may be physically "bad for you," though the men of science, after exhaustive inquiries, seem to have come at last to the conclusion that a little of it is physically good for you — or for most of you. But in other and more subtle and (I should say) more important ways, it is extremely good for you; and whatever the physical price paid, it is worth that price because it is indispensable to a complete life.

Alcohol will always win. Nearly twenty years have passed since I tasted beer (it cost me too much — not in money) but beer remains firmly fixed in my estimation as the most delectable of all drinks, with champagne a bad second, and tea worst third. And I know that one day a glass of beer (good beer, I mean — a rare liquid!) will overset me and persuade me to bear the calamitous cost of it. One might say of alcohol what Matthew Arnold said of Shakespere: "Others abide our question. Thou are free." And also one might say of alcohol that although it has been the cause of immense and widespread misery, it is probably no worse in this respect than passionate love, or ambition, or the thirst for political power.

I have referred to the physical price (by which I mean the price in physical deterioration, sometimes inducing intellectual deterioration) paid for the incalculable benefits of alcohol. That price is tremendous, and I would be the first to admit it. Now the problem before every community of man is: how to lower the price. Let us consider the point. I rule out at once prohibition, because it is no solution at all. You do not lower the price of a benefit by utterly destroying the benefit. Further, it cannot possibly be rendered effective, and its sole effect would be to increase the price (as has been richly proved elsewhere). And further again, even if it would work, it is a humiliating solution.

You can justifiably prohibit certain drugs, because you are thereby safe-guarding the ignorance of mankind against those drugs, and

there is no general desire for them. But men are not ignorant of the
consequences of alcohol. If they drink, they drink with their eyes
open. They know about it. Any remedy which humiliates, by
taking away the right of choice and the need of exercising self-control,
is, and must for ever be, worse than the disease it seeks to cure.
Here, in this connection, I venture to say that more often than anything else I have seen visiting citizens of the United States give vent
to a deep and most resentful feeling of mere humiliation.

No! The harmful effects of the ancient and ineradicable and
grand practice of drinking alcohol must be lessened by quite other
methods. We in this island, with our characteristic talents for compromise and for "getting there" somehow, have already, perhaps
inadvertently, achieved something by raising the monetary price of
alcohol and reducing the opportunities for obtaining it. The State
does not say: "You shan't have it." The State says: "Drink it by
all means, but you will have to put yourself to a little more trouble
in order to get the stuff, and you won't be able to enjoy the precious
privilege without contributing, in exchange for it, quite a large sum
toward the upkeep of the realm!" We may be bled, but we are not
humiliated. The choice is still ours. This device, consistently carried out, has beyond question ameliorated, and is still ameliorating,
the harmful effects of the ancient and ineradicable and grand
practice.

But a more potent instrument towards arriving at the millennium
in the matter of alcohol is, or will be, education. Alcohol, regarded
as a subject of study, is full of interest and full of an immediate practical importance. In these respects it should easily rank as high as
botany or biology or piano-playing. People well know that the
unwise or excessive use of alcohol works evil, but few of them know
how or why — and particularly they do not know how or why alcohol comes to be the most insidious and perilous of all kinds of indulgence. If people did know they would act differently.

More urgent is, and far more effective would be, the education of
character: an affair generally somewhat neglected in our curricu-
lums. Self-discipline is the sole genuine remedy for excess, whether
in the use of alcohol or in anything else. The youth who has been
trained to be master of himself will be the master of alcohol, for he
will know how at once to obtain from it all that it has of good and
reject all that it has of evil.

THE HARM THAT GOOD MEN DO

By BERTRAND RUSSELL

Bertrand Russell (1872–   ) *is, primarily, a mathematician, but it is as a philosopher and critic of modern social institutions that he is most widely known.   He is an Englishman and was educated at Trinity College, Cambridge, where he was afterwards a lecturer.   A few of his books on widely varying subjects are "Principia Mathematica" (with Dr. Whitehead) (1910), "Why Men Fight" (1916), "Mysticism and Logic" (1918), "The Prospects of Industrial Civilization (with Dora Russell) (1923), and "What I Believe" (1925).*

A HUNDRED years ago there lived a philosopher named Jeremy Bentham, who was universally recognized to be a very wicked man.   I remember to this day the first time that I came across his name when I was a boy.   It was in a statement by the Rev. Sydney Smith to the effect that Bentham thought people ought to make soup of their dead grandmothers.   This practice appeared to me as undesirable from a culinary as from a moral point of view, and I, therefore, conceived a bad opinion of Bentham.   Long afterwards, I discovered that the statement was one of those reckless lies in which respectable people are wont to indulge in the interests of virtue.   I also discovered what was the really serious charge against him.   It was no less than this: that he defined a "good" man as a man who does good.   This definition, as the reader will perceive at once if he is rightminded, is subversive of all true morality.   How much more exalted is the attitude of Kant, who lays it down that a kind action is not virtuous if it springs from affection for the beneficiary, but only if it is inspired by the moral law, which is, of course, just as likely to inspire unkind actions.   We know that the exercise of virtue should be its own reward, and it seems to follow that the enduring of it on the part of the patient should be its own punishment.   Kant, therefore, is a more sublime moralist than Bentham, and has the suffrages of all those who tell us that they love virtue for its own sake.

It is true that Bentham fulfilled his own definition of a good man: he did much good.   The forty middle years of the nineteenth century in England were years of incredibly rapid progress, materially, intellectually, and morally. At the beginning of the period comes the Reform Act, which made Parliament representative of the middle-class, not, as theretofore, of the aristocracy. This Act was the most difficult of the steps toward democracy in England, and was quickly followed by other important reforms, such as the abolition of slavery in Jamaica. At the beginning of the period the penalty for petty theft was death by hanging; very soon the death penalty was confined to those who were guilty of murder or high treason. The Corn Laws, which made food so dear as to cause atrocious poverty, were abolished in 1846. Compulsory education was introduced in 1870. It is the fashion to decry the Victorians, but I wish our age had half as good a record as theirs. This, however, is beside the point. My point is that a very large proportion of the progress during those years must be attributed to the influence of Bentham. There can be no doubt that nine-tenths of the people living in England in the latter part of last century were happier than they would have been if he had never lived. So shallow was his philosophy that he would have regarded this as a vindication of his activities. We, in our more enlightened age, can see that such a view is preposterous; but it may fortify us to review the grounds for rejecting a grovelling utilitarianism such as that of Bentham.

We all know what we mean by a "good" man. The ideally good man does not drink or smoke, avoids bad language, converses in the presence of men only exactly as he would if there were ladies present, attends church regularly, and holds the correct opinions on all subjects. He has a wholesome horror of wrong-doing, and realizes that it is our painful duty to castigate Sin. He has a still greater horror of wrong thinking, and considers it the business of the authorities to safeguard the young against those who question the wisdom of the views generally accepted by middle-aged successful citizens. Apart from his professional duties, at which he is assiduous, he spends much time in good works: he may encourage patriotism and military training; he may promote industry, sobriety, and virtue among wage-earners and their children by seeing to it that failures in these respects receive due punishment; he may be a trustee of a university and prevent an ill-judged respect for learning from allowing the employment of professors with subversive ideas. Above all, of course, his "morals," in the narrow sense, must be irreproachable.

It may be doubted whether a "good" man, in the above sense, does, on the average, any more good than a "bad" man. I mean by a "bad" man the contrary of what we have been describing. A "bad" man is one who is known to smoke and to drink occasionally, and even to say a bad word when some one treads on his toe. His conversation is not always such as could be printed, and he sometimes spends fine Sundays out-of-doors instead of at church. Some of his opinions are subversive; for instance, he may think that if you desire peace you should prepare for peace, not for war. Towards wrong-doing he takes a scientific attitude, such as he would take towards his motor car if it misbehaved: he argues that sermons and prison will no more cure vice than mend a broken tire. In the matter of wrong thinking he is even more perverse. He maintains that what is called "wrong thinking" is simply thinking, and what is called "right thinking" is repeating words like a parrot; this gives him a sympathy with all sorts of undesirable cranks. His activities outside his working hours may consist merely in enjoyment, or, worse still, in stirring up discontent with preventable evils which do not interfere with the comfort of the men in power. And it is even possible that in the matter of "morals" he may not conceal his lapses as carefully as a truly virtuous man would do, defending himself by the perverse contention that it is better to be honest than to pretend to set a good example. A man who fails in any or several of these respects will be thought ill of by the average respectable citizen, and will not be allowed to hold any position conferring authority, such as that of a judge, a magistrate, or a schoolmaster. Such positions are open only to "good" men.

This whole state of affairs is more or less modern. It existed in England during the brief reign of the Puritans in the time of Cromwell, and by them it was transplanted to America. It did not reappear in force in England till after the French Revolution, when it was thought to be a good method of combating Jacobinism (i.e., what we should now call Bolshevism). The life of Wordsworth illustrates the change. In his youth he sympathized with the French Revolution, went to France, wrote good poetry, and had a natural daughter. At this period he was a "bad" man. Then he became "good," abandoned his daughter, adopted correct principles, and wrote bad poetry. Coleridge went through a similar change: when he was wicked he wrote "Kubla Khan," and when he was good he wrote theology.

It is difficult to think of any instance of a poet who was "good" at the times when he was writing good poetry. Dante was deported for subversive propaganda; Shakespeare, to judge by the sonnets, would not have been allowed by American immigration officers to land in New York. It is of the essence of a "good" man that he supports the Government; therefore, Milton was good during the reign of Cromwell, and bad before and after; but it was before and after that he wrote his poetry — in fact most of it was written after he had narrowly escaped hanging as a Bolshevik. Donne was virtuous after he became Dean of Saint Paul's, but all his poems were written before that time, and on account of them his appointment caused a scandal. Swinburne was wicked in his youth, when he wrote *Songs Before Sunrise* in praise of those who fought for freedom; he was virtuous in his old age, when he wrote savage attacks on the Boers for defending their liberty against wanton aggression. It is needless to multiply the examples; enough has been said to suggest that the standards of virtue now prevalent are incompatible with the production of good poetry.

In other directions the same thing is true. We all know that Galileo and Darwin were bad men; Spinoza was thought dreadfully wicked until a hundred years after his death; Descartes went abroad for fear of persecution. Almost all the renaissance artists were bad men. To come to humbler matters, those who object to preventable mortality are necessarily wicked. I live in a part of London which is partly very rich, partly very poor; the infant death-rate is abnormally high, and the rich, by corruption and intimidation, control the local government. They use their power to cut down the expenditure on infant welfare and public health and to engage a medical officer at less than the standard rate on condition that he gives only half his time to the work. No one can win the respect of the important local people unless he considers that good dinners for the rich are more important than life for the children of the poor. The corresponding thing is true in every part of the world with which I am acquainted. This suggests that we may simplify our account of what constitutes a good man: a good man is one whose opinions and activities are pleasing to the holders of power.

It has been painful to have to dwell upon the bad men who, in the past, have unfortunately achieved eminence. Let us turn to the more agreeable contemplation of the virtuous.

A typically virtuous man was George III. When Pitt wanted him to emancipate the Catholics (who at that time were not allowed to vote), he would not agree, on the ground that to do so would be contrary to his coronation oath. He righteously refused to be misled by the argument that it would do good to emancipate them; the question, for him, was not whether it would do good, but whether it was "right" in the abstract. His interference in politics was largely responsible for the régime which caused America to claim independence; but his interference was always dictated by the most lofty motives. The same may be said of the ex-Kaiser, a deeply religious man, sincerely convinced, until his fall, that God was on his side, and (so far as I know) wholly free from personal vices. Yet it would be hard to name any man of our time who has done more to cause human misery.

Among politicians "good" men are by no means uncommon. It is not my place to comment on public men in America, but in England we have a very notable example. The present Prime Minister has repeatedly assured us that he is a good man, and I see no reason to doubt his word. He smokes a pipe whenever he is in public — which, in a democratic country, is almost more virtuous than not smoking at all. "You know my record," he says, when appealing to opponents to trust to his honor. Up to the present this record consists in a number of platitudinous discourses on brotherly love, and a book whose central theme is that England is great because the soil of Worcestershire is red and the hay smells good when they cart it home on summer evenings. (In England, owing to the aristocratic traditions, successful manufacturers generally wish to be taken for country gentlemen.) The "virtue" to which Mr. Baldwin aspires is of the type celebrated in Goldsmith's "Deserted Village," smelling of country parsonages and the boots of yokels. It drapes his policy as the roses at cottage windows distract the romantic eye from the unsanitary interior. It impresses not only supporters, but also Labor leaders, whose equally "virtuous" temperament, nurtured in Scotch manse and fishing village, chimes in harmony with our simple and guileless Prime Minister. True-hearted Englishwomen write to the Liberal Press to invest Mr. Baldwin's head with a halo of "great white light," and to urge their countrymen to rise and stand in silence at the name of the national hero — a suggestion to which, I am sorry to say, at least one Member of Parliament has demurred on the trivial ground that it would obstruct parliamentary business. Perhaps our Labor leaders, without ceasing to be genteel, might adopt this method of delaying the anti-Trade Union legislation by which our noble-hearted Prime Minister is proposing to chain down the common people more firmly than ever to long hours in dark mines and dangerous workshops, at starvation wages and with a curtailed legal right of protest.

Mr. Baldwin's well-advertised virtue has been very useful to him in helping the coal owners in the dispute which is still raging in the coal industry. There was a sharp warning of the approaching crisis last year; the respite purchased by the coal subsidy was spent by the Prime Minister in soft words and hard preparations. The Trade Union leaders, while they admired, did not flatter by imitation: their words were hard, their preparations soft or non-existent. When their bluff was called, nothing remained — except the courage and calm common sense of the rank and file, who would have won a great victory but for their leaders' "virtue" and belief in the "virtue" of Mr. Baldwin. The rank and file, of course, are not virtuous: they try to *practice* universal brotherhood and mutual good will. To the relief of all right-minded people, this subversive attempt was defeated by the leaders, who trusted Mr. Baldwin because he is a good man: the General Strike ended with nothing settled, and our modern Cincinnatus returned to the plow — viz.: good dinners and a comfortable country house. At every meal he could thank Heaven that hunger and the misery of starving children were bringing the miners nearer to the point of surrender, and that the coal owners' dividends would be secure whatever else might suffer. But perhaps, after all, this is a miscalculation. No cabinet policy for a hundred years has done so much to promote Bolshevism in England.

Another way in which good men can be useful is by getting themselves murdered. Germany acquired the province of Shantung in China by having the good fortune to have two missionaries murdered there. The Archduke who was murdered at Serajevo was, I believe, a good man; and how grateful we ought to be to him! If he had not died as he did, we might not have had the war, and then the world would not have been made safe for democracy, nor would militarism have been overthrown, nor would we be now enjoying military despotisms in Spain, Italy, Hungary, Bulgaria, and Russia, with the imminent prospect of France to follow suit.

To speak seriously: the standards of "goodness" which are generally recognized by public opinion are not those which are calculated to make the world a happier place. This is due to a variety of causes, of which the chief is tradition, and the next most powerful is the unjust power of dominant classes. Primitive morality seems to have developed out of the notion of taboo; that is to say, it was originally purely superstitious, and forbade certain perfectly harmless acts (such as eating out of the Chief's dish) on the supposed ground that they produced disaster by magical means. In this way there came to be prohibitions, which continued to have authority over people's feelings when the supposed reasons for them were forgotten. A considerable part of current morals is still of this sort: certain kinds of conduct produce emotions of horror, quite regardless of the question whether they have bad effects or not. In many cases the conduct which inspires horror is in fact harmful; if this were not the case, the need for a revision of our moral standards would be more generally recognized. Murder, for example, can obviously not be tolerated in a civilized society; yet the origin of the prohibition of murder is purely superstitious. It was thought that the murdered man's blood (or, later, his ghost) demanded vengeance, and might punish not only the guilty man, but any one who showed him kindness. The superstitious character of the prohibition of murder is shown by the fact that it was possible to be purified from blood-guiltiness by certain ritual ceremonies, which were apparently designed, originally, to disguise the murderer so that the ghost would not recognize him. This, at least, is the theory of Sir J. G. Frazer. When we speak of repentance as "washing out" guilt we are using a metaphor derived from the fact that long ago actual washing was used to remove blood-stains. Such notions as "guilt" and "sin" have an emotional background connected with this source in remote antiquity. Even in the case of murder a rational ethic will view the matter differently; it will be concerned with prevention and cure as in the case of illness, rather than with guilt, punishment, and expiation.

Our current ethic is a curious mixture of superstition and rationalism. Murder is an ancient crime, and we view it through a mist of age-long horror. Forgery is a modern crime, and we view it rationally. We punish forgers, but we do not feel them strange beings set apart, as we do murderers. And we still think in social practice, whatever we may hold in theory, that virtue consists in not doing rather than in doing. The man who abstains from certain acts labelled "sin" is a good man, even though he never does anything to further the welfare of others. This, of course, is not the attitude inculcated in the Gospels: "Love thy neighbor as thyself" is a positive precept. But in all Christian communities the man who obeys this precept is persecuted, suffering at least poverty, usually imprisonment, and sometimes death. The world is full of injustice, and those who profit by injustice are in a position to administer rewards and punishments. The rewards go to those who invent ingenious justifications for inequality, the punishments to those who try to remedy it. I do not know of any country where a man who has a genuine love for his neighbor can long avoid obloquy. In Paris, just before the outbreak of the war, Jean Jaurès, the best citizen of France, was murdered; the murderer was acquitted, on the ground that he had performed a public service. This case was peculiarly dramatic, but the same sort of thing happens everywhere.

Those who defend traditional morality will sometimes admit that it is not perfect, but contend that any criticism will make all morality crumble. This will not be the case if the criticism is based upon something positive and constructive, but only if it is conducted with a view to nothing more than momentary pleasure. To return to Bentham: he advocated, as the basis of morals, "the greatest happiness of the greatest number." A man who acts upon this principle will have a much more arduous life than a man who merely obeys conventional precepts. He will necessarily make himself the champion of the oppressed, and so incur the enmity of the great. He will proclaim facts which the powers that be wish to conceal; he will deny falsehoods designed to alienate sympathy from those who need it. Such a mode of life does not lead to a collapse of genuine morality. Official morality has always been oppressive and nega-

tive: it has said "thou shalt not," and has not troubled to investigate
the effect of activities not forbidden by the code.   Against this kind
of morality all the great mystics and religious teachers have protested in vain: their followers ignored their most explicit pronouncements.   It seems unlikely, therefore, that any large-scale improvement will come through their methods.

More is to be hoped, I think, from the progress of reason and
science.   Gradually men will come to realize that a world whose
institutions are based upon hatred and injustice is not the one most
likely to produce happiness.   The late war taught this lesson to a
few, and would have taught it to many more if it had ended in a
draw.   We need a morality based upon love of life, upon pleasure
in growth and positive achievement, not upon repression and
prohibition.   A man should be regarded as "good" if he is happy,
expansive, generous, and glad when others are happy; if so, a few
peccadillos should be regarded as of little importance.   But a man
who acquires a fortune by cruelty and exploitation should be regarded as at present we regard what is called an "immoral" man;
and he should be so regarded even if he goes to church regularly and
gives a portion of his ill-gotten gains to public objects.   To bring this
about, it is only necessary to instil a rational attitude towards ethical
questions, instead of the mixture of superstition and oppression which
still passes muster as "virtue" among important personages.   The
power of reason is thought small in these days, but I remain an un-
repentant rationalist.   Reason may be a small force, but it is constant, and works always in one direction, while the forces of unreason destroy one another in futile strife.   Therefore, every orgy of
unreason in the end strengthens the friends of reason, and shows
afresh that they are the only true friends of humanity.

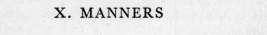

X. MANNERS

THE MUCKER POSE

BY JAMES TRUSLOW ADAMS

James Truslow Adams (1878–   ) *was, until* 1912, *a member of the New York Stock Exchange. During the early part of the World War he was in Europe as a member of the Colonel House Commission, a body which secured data for a projected early Peace Conference. When the United States entered the war, he became a captain in the Military Intelligence Division, and was detailed to special duty at the Peace Conference in Paris,* 1919. *His "Founding of New England"* (1921) *won the Pulitzer prize for being the best book of the year on history. Other works of his are "Revolutionary New England, 1691–1776"* (1923) *and "Provincial Society,* 1690–1763" (1927).

THIS borrowed title expresses better than any I have been able to devise for myself a problem which has recently been put to me by several of my American friends, men who on account of both their profession and positions are familiar with the more cultured portion of the American scene. The question which they put is one that I have been hesitatingly asking myself as I contrast that scene on successive returns from abroad with the one very obviously to be observed in this respect in France or England. "Why," they ask, "is it that a gentleman in America nowadays seems afraid to appear as such; that even university men try to appear uncultured; and that the pose of a gentleman and a scholar is that of the man in the street?" A few nights ago another friend of mine, a literary editor of some importance in New York, complained in the course of the evening's talk that the verbal criticism of many of the writers whom he knew had descended to the moronic classifications of "hot stuff," "bully," "rot," and so on. These writers, often meticulous in the artistry of their own work and thoroughly competent to criticize acutely and intelligently that of others, appeared afraid to do so lest they be considered as literary poseurs. The real pose in their cases was in talking like news-agents on a railroad train; but that appeared to them to be safe, whereas vague danger lurked in conversing as would any intelligent French or English critic.

The mucker-poseurs do not content themselves with talking like ineducated half-wits. They also emulate the language and manners of the bargee and the longshoreman, although where the profanity of the latter is apt to have at least the virtue of picturesqueness, the swearing of the mucker-poseur is apt to be merely coarse. A member of a most distinguished family and a young graduate of one of our best known Eastern universities was overheard the other day in his university club in New York describing his new position in the banking world. The nearest to analysis or description of his work that this young scion of American aristocracy with every social and educational advantage could reach was to tell his friends that it was "the God damnedest most interesting job in the world." Both among men and women of the supposedly cultivated classes such profanity is much on the increase. I know of a man who has recently declined to take foreign visitors to his club for luncheon or dinner any longer on account of the unfortunate impression which would be made upon them by the hard swearing of the American gentlemen, mucker-poseurs, at the surrounding tables. One of the finest scholars in the country, a man who once had distinguished manners, has not only become extremely profane but exceedingly addicted to smutty stories, both, apparently, in the effort to make himself considered a good mixer and as a bid for popularity. If one wishes to acquire an extensive and varied vocabulary of the most modern sort, one has merely to watch the young ladies of the mucker-poseur type playing tennis at Southampton or Newport.

Again, the mucker-poseur aims to act like the lowest of muckers when he — and frequently she — gets drunk. Drinking in this country has ceased to add any charm or grace to social life. On a recent sailing from New York on the *Aquitania* at midnight I counted twelve women first-cabin passengers brought on board, all so drunk that they could not get up the gangway without help. Many years ago, when I was a small boy of twelve, I attended "Field Day" at one of the most exclusive private boarding schools in the East. In the course of the day an address was made by an old graduate on the subject of alcohol. To the surprise and horror of the clerical head of the school, the good-natured but somewhat inebriated speaker said nothing to condemn drinking but he threw out the comment, which is all I can now recall of his speech, that "when you boys do drink, remember always to get drunk like gentlemen." That is something which our present generation of drinkers have completely forgotten.

They act in country clubs in a way which would have been considered a disgrace to the patrons and patronized in a disorderly house of a generation ago. It is not a question of a mere decline in manners but of consciously striven-for pose.

In the case of the young this is more understandable, just as it is more international. I am not here concerned, however, with (or at) the vagaries of the younger and, in so many respects, admirable generation. I am concerned with their elders, men who have lived long enough to have developed personalities of their own, men who appreciate the value of cultivating both mind and manners. Why should they be afraid to appear as cultured gentlemen and assume as a protective coloration the manners and level of thought of those who are beneath them?

The question would be a futile one unless we believed that manners and culture possess genuine significance, a significance for society as a whole as well as for the individual. It is all too evident that a large proportion of the dwellers in our United States do not believe so, but there is a large minority which does. Not to do so argues a failure to think things through and ignorance of history and human nature. This article deals with the contemporary attitude of many believers, and we can but glance briefly, before passing to them, at the non-believers.

One of the most suggestive methods of modern study has been the comparative. By the use of none other, however, are the unwary and the untrained so likely to come to logical grief over a *non sequitur*. The comparative study of habits and customs has revealed that both moral and social conventions have varied from age to age, from place to place, and from race to race. Immediately the unwary and untrained jump to the conclusion that because there appear to be no eternal or universal standards of morals and manners there is, therefore, no value in a local, temporary, and but slowly changing one — a conclusion by no logical possibility to be drawn from the premises. The result of this particular and, at the moment, very popular *non sequitur* has been to cause in many persons a headlong jettisoning of their whole cargo of morals, manners, and conventions, and the bringing about of a muckerly chaos which arouses mirth or terror according to the temperament of the social observer.

It would seem as though no sane person with a knowledge of the past of his own species and any adequate insight into human nature could fail to believe in the absolute need of *some* standards, *some* established values to save us from a derelict wallowing about in the welter of sensations, impulses, attractions, and repulsions which form so much of this strange dream we call life. The standards, the values, will undoubtedly alter from time to time and from place to place; but that does not invalidate the need of having some of them at any one given time and place. Even the now much scorned minor conventions have their effective influence upon conduct, remote or proximate. A story is told of an English gentleman who was sent out as governor of an island where the entire population save for his sole self was black and savage. He dressed for his solitary dinner every night as carefully as though he were about to take a taxi to the smartest residence in Park Lane. He did so not from habit but from a knowledge of human nature. "If," he said, "I should drop this convention of civilized society, I should find myself some day having dropped one and another of the more important conventions, social and moral, and lower myself to the level of the blacks whom I govern. Evening clothes are far more important here than they ever were in London."

As for the second point, lack of culture, it is most evident in the extreme slovenliness in America in the use of the English language. There is, of course, some slang which is not slovenly but which has been born in some flash of genuine insight; and the language is always being enriched by absorbing many such words from below, much as the English aristocracy is by marrying or admitting commoners. But this is not true of the vast mass of slang words and cheap and easy expressions which are intellectually slovenly and nothing else; and anyone habitually using them impairs the keenness of his mind as much as he would the strength of his body by lolling in a hammock all his life. There is no question but that the use of slang, hackneyed phrases, and clichés worn smooth make for intellectual laziness, and if constantly used blur the sense of discrimination. The very first step toward a cultivated mind is the development of the ability rationally to discriminate, to distinguish between varying values and qualities. It is not easy, and most of us Americans rarely achieve it in the cultural field. I have often been struck by the different replies one receives from an American and a Frenchman if you ask them what sort of person so-and-so is. The American will usually find himself helpless and toss off a mere "good scout," "a great guy," "a good egg," whereas the Frenchman, with a moment's reflection, will give you in half a dozen sentences a sharply etched sketch of the man's distinctive characteristics, or what he believes to be such, and classify him accurately as to type. To describe anything accurately — book, picture, man or woman — so as to bring out their unique individual qualities, calls for mental exercise of no mean order. One has to train one's self to do it and keep in training; yet the ability to distinguish, if one of the first steps toward culture, is also, in its higher forms, one of its most perfect fruits. If one dodges every call for discrimination, if one gets no farther in describing a book than "hot stuff," one loses the power after a while even if one ever possessed it. Slovenly language corrodes the mind.

These few observations as to manners and culture are well enough understood by any cultivated person who has had social and intellectual training and who has thought things through. He knows that there are both values and dangers in life, that some things are more valuable than others, and that if he has achieved any such social and intellectual training he cannot lower himself to the general level again without risk. If manners and culture have no value, there is no question involved, but if they have — and we shall now assume that they have — the man who possesses them is above, in those respects at least, the vast mass of men who do not possess them. Why then should he pretend not to, and assume the manners and mental lazzaronism of the crowd? It may be that there is no answer to the question, but as I find those better qualified than myself asking it, it is worth pondering over, and I have come to think that there may be three fundamental influences at work in America which will help us to solve it. One is democracy as we have it, another is business, and the third is the extreme mobility of American life.

In civilization no man can live wholly to or for himself, and whoever would achieve power, influence, or success must cater to the tastes and whims of those who have the granting of these things in their hands. In a democracy, speaking broadly, those who have the power to grant are the whole people; and the minds and manners of the people as a whole are of necessity below those of the chosen few who have risen above the average level by gifts of nature or

happy opportunity. Every social class everywhere has always had
its own standards of morals, manners, and culture. When such
classes are separated by wide social or economic chasms, the only
influences they exert upon one another are apt to be negative. Each
lives in a world of its own, supported by the only public opinion for
which it cares, that of its own class. Each also tends to react against
the manners or morals of the other. The aristocrats of an earlier day
looked down upon the common people and were more than ever
satisfied with their own codes. The common people, in turn, feeling
themselves despised, bolstered up their egos by despising the manners and morals of the class which looked down upon them. Much
of the Puritan movement in England and elsewhere has here its roots.
By no possibility could an ordinary laborer attain to the manners,
social ease, or knowledge of the world of a duke. Ergo, the laborer
by unconscious mental processes well understood by modern psychology, asserted his own worth by denying worth to the qualities
of the classes above him. He could not have the manners of a duke,
therefore, those manners were undesirable anyway. He could not
travel and he could not gain the most valuable sort of education, that
of association with great or cultivated men, therefore, such things
were of no importance. So long as the classes remain separated, as I
said above, their influence upon one another is largely negative, but
when class distinctions disappear in a democracy the mutual influences of members of those former classes or their vestiges in later
generations become a complex in their action as the currents where
tide and river meet.

The effects of democracy in America have been emphasized by
three factors not present in any of the great democracies of Europe.
In the first place, the Americans started almost wholly fresh. Here
were no thousand-year-old institutions and forms of government and
society to be reckoned with as impediments. America was a clean
slate. The settlers did indeed bring with them habits, information,
and memories gained in the old world, but they brought them to a
wilderness.

In the second place, America has been built up exclusively by the
middle and lower classes, from which practically all of us have
descended. Scarcely a man has ever come and settled here who did
not belong to one or the other; and the most distinguished American

families form no exceptions. Every class in history has had its good and bad attributes which have varied with class, country, and period. The English middle class, upper and lower, from which the character of America, with some modifications, has essentially been built up, had admirable qualities but it lacked some of those enjoyed by the aristocracy. For our purpose here we need mention only one. The genuine aristocrat insists upon being himself and is disdainful of public opinion. The middle class, on the other hand, has always been notoriously timid socially. It rests in terror not only of public but even of village opinion. If the religious refugees of New England be held an exception, it may be noted that the genuine ones were far fewer than used to be supposed, and that as a whole the New England immigration may be considered as part of the great economic exodus from England which took thirty thousand Englishmen to Barbados and little St. Kitts while only twelve thousand were settling Massachusetts. Religious refugees have formed an infinitesimal part of American immigration as compared with the economic ones.

The third great influence upon American democracy has been the frontier, whose line was lapped by the waves of the Atlantic in 1640 and after retreating three thousand miles to the Pacific was declared officially closed only in 1890. In the hard rough life of the frontier manners and culture find no home. As Pastorius, the most learned man who came to America before 1700, said, "never have metaphysics or Aristotelian logic earned a loaf of bread." When one is busy killing Indians, clearing the forest, and trekking farther westward every decade, a strong arm, an axe, and a rifle are worth more than all the culture of all the ages. Not only has the frontiersman no leisure or opportunity to acquire manners and culture but, because of their apparent uselessness, and in true class spirit, he comes to despise them. They are effete, effeminate, whereas he and his fellows are the "real men." The well-dressed, cultivated gentleman becomes the "dude," object of derision, who, so far from exerting any ameliorating social or intellectual influence, is heartily looked down upon; and culture itself is relegated to idle women as something with which no real man would concern himself.

There are some of the special attributes of American democracy, and of any democracy in a new land, which it shows in addition to those it would show in any case merely as democracy. In America it was slow in gathering into its hands the reins of power.   For many generations the English aristocratic tradition in part survived, and it may be recalled that we were a part of the British Empire for a longer period than we have been independent.   In general, the "appeal to the people" throughout the colonial period and the years of the early republic was an appeal to "the best people" only.   The first two presidents, Washington and Adams, were as little democratic in doctrine as they were by nature.   Jefferson's doctrinal democracy was largely offset in practice by his being an aristocrat to his finger tips by nature, and it was not until Andrew Jackson that "the people" in the democratic sense came into their own.   At his inaugural reception in the White House his followers climbed upon the silken chairs in their muddy boots to get a look at him, rushed the waiters to grab champagne, broke the glasses, and in the joy of victory gave a number of ladies bloody noses, and even the President himself had to be rescued from his admirers and hurried out through a back door. This historic episode may be taken to mark the turning-point in American manners.   These people had made a president.   Thereafter their tastes would form one of the national influences.

It is this new democracy, a hundred times richer and a shade less raw, which is in the saddle to-day.   What has it done in the way of influencing manners and thought?   Leaving all else aside, even at the risk of drawing a false picture, we shall consider only those points which may help to answer our first question.   For one thing, then, it has knocked the dignity of its elected officials into a cocked hat. Leaving out of the scene many of its chosen, such as the mayor of Chicago or its favorite, Bryan, it forces men to play the mountebank and, whatever the character of the man himself, to appear as one of "the people."   Washington was a very human man but he never forgot that he was a gentleman.   He was adored by his soldiers, but he won their deep affection without ever for a moment losing the dignity of his character and manner.   One has only to imagine what would have happened had a group of his men shouted "Atta Boy, Georgie!" to realize the gulf between his day and ours.   When John Quincy Adams was president, he declined to attend a county fair in Maryland, remarking privately that he did not intend that the president of the United States should be made a side-show at a cattle fair. To-day, the people insist that the president be a side-show; and

Roosevelt, with amused understanding, in his cowboy suit and his rough-rider uniform, used his "properties" as does an actor. Even the supremely conventional Coolidge had to dress up in a ten-gallon hat and chaps, although utterly out of character, and looking so. Just as I write these lines, my attention is called to an announcement in large type in this morning's *New York Times* that it will publish next Sunday "photographs of Herbert Hoover in workaday clothes and a panorama of his ranch." So he, too, is cast for the comedy. Democracy cracks the whip, and even the most conservative of candidates and officials must dance. In the campaign of 1916 it is said that Hughes was politely asked to shave his beard to suit the people. He balked and consented only so far as to trim it. But then, he lost the election.

The people want officials in their own image. Such men as Elihu Root, Joseph Choate, or John Hay are rarely elected, only appointed. To get anywhere in elective politics one must be a "good mixer," and to be a good mixer one must shed a good part of one's culture and a good part of one's manners. Dignity to a considerable degree must be discarded. One must conceal one's knowledge of English and learn the vernacular, except for "orations." Henry Adams, when he became a newspaper correspondent in Washington, said that he had to "learn to talk to Western congressmen, and to hide his own antecedents." It is what every gentleman who desires to take part in elective public life on a large or small stage in the country to-day has to do to some extent except for happy accidents.

Our democracy has fostered education, at least to the extent of almost fabulously increasing the numbers of the reading public. What has been, for the purpose of the present argument, the effect of that? There has been one effect, at least, germane to this discussion. It has greatly lowered the tone of our public press. Such newspaper men as I know agree with me that there has been a most marked decline even in the last twenty years, and they agree with me as to the cause. In the old days a newspaper was largely a personal organ, and what appeared in it reflected for good or ill upon the editor who was known by name to all its readers. In New York the *Sun* was Charles A. Dana. The *Tribune* was Horace Greeley. To-day we know no editors, only owners. The newspaper of to-day aims only at circulation, and with every increase in circulation the quality has to be lowered. The case is well known of the purchaser a few years ago of what had been one of the country's most distinguished journals, who told his staff that thereafter they would have to "cut the highbrow" and write down to the level of the increased public he intended to go after. First the "yellow press," then the tabloids, taught the older newspapers what fortunes awaited those who would stoop to pick them up by catering to the masses. One of the worst tabloids has a circulation of a million copies a day. A newspaper depends on its advertising for its profits. Advertising quantity and rates depend on circulation. Increased circulation spells decreased quality. There is the vicious circle which has been drawn for us by the huge mob which has become literate but not educated.

The discovery of the possibilities of mass circulation has caused the advertisers to raise their demands. Some will not advertise at all in journals with a circulation of less than half a million. Advertising is withdrawn from those journals which heroically venture to maintain their quality at the expense of not increasing their circulation. Financial ruin usually results. The people are evidently getting the kind of papers they want but in doing so they are depriving the cultured class of the sort *they* want, and used to get before America became so "educated." We get foreign cables about the Prince of Wales dancing with Judy O'Grady, or the doings of sex perverts in Berlin, and the treatment of our domestic news is beneath contempt. The other night I examined what used to be one of the leading papers not only in New York but in the whole country and I found no headline on three consecutive pages which did not refer to scandal or to crime. It has been said that the new reading public has not interfered with the old, that there are simply vast numbers of new readers of a different type who are being supplied with what they want. That is not wholly true, and the competition of the new market has had a heavily detrimental influence on the older journals. To-day if a man wishes to succeed in a journalistic career on the daily press he has to scrap even more of his qualities as a gentleman and a scholar than he has to in a career of politics.

The democratic spread of education has also had detrimental effects in other ways. The necessity of finding instruction for the enormous numbers who now go to school, high school, and college has caused a demand for teachers which has far outrun the supply of those qualified to teach. Great numbers of these teachers have even less social and cultural background than have their students. Under them the students may learn the facts of some given subject, but they gain nothing in breadth of culture or even in manners. It is an old story that Charles Eliot Norton once began a lecture at Harvard by saying, "I suppose that none of you young men has ever seen a gentleman." The remark was hyperbolic, as was intended, but it is only too likely to-day that many young men can go through some of our newer "institutions of learning" without seeing at least what used to be called a gentleman. In the professions, more particularly medicine and law, complaint is rampant that they are being swamped by young men who know only the facts of the profession (when they know those) and have no cultural, ethical, or professional standards. A few such could be ignored. When they come, as they are coming now, in shoals, they lower the tone of the whole profession and, without standards themselves, force an unfair competition upon those who try to maintain them.

Perhaps the greatest pressure on the individual to force him to be wary of how he appears to others is in business, for the overwhelming mass of Americans are in the varied ranks of business of some sort or another. One who has reached the top and "made his pile" may, perhaps, do more or less as he pleases, subject only to milder forms of social pressure; but for those on the way the road is beset with pitfalls. Nearly every man wants to make himself popular with his employers, his fellow-workers, his office superiors, or his customers. These are made up of all sorts of men, but the sprinkling of gentlemen and scholars among them is so slight as to be almost negligible for the purpose of helping one's advancement. In America, to an extent known nowhere else, organization is used for every purpose. It is hardly too much to say that there can hardly be an American who is not a member of from one to a dozen organizations, ranging from Rotary, Lions, Kiwanis, Red Men, Masons, Mechanics, the Grange, and dozens more, to Bar Associations, Bankers' Clubs, and social and country clubs innumerable. Some of the larger corporations, notably the banks and trust companies in New York, now have clubs made up entirely of members of their own staffs, with obvious intent.

In many lines of business the effect produced by one's personality at the annual "convention" is of prime importance. For business reasons it is essential that men should be at least moderately popular at all such organizations or meetings. On an unprecedented scale, tacitly understood but not openly acknowledged, there is competition for personal popularity. In many lines, such as stock brokerage where the service is almost wholly personal, it is needful to "play with your customers," the necessity varying not with their social congeniality but with the size of their account. In salesmanship of all sorts the results of the "personal approach" are, of course, of the first importance.

In order to gain popularity with a very large proportion of business men, many of whom have to-day risen from nothing to riches since the War, one thing is fundamentally necessary. You must never appear to be superior even if you are. Too perfect an accent in English may be almost as dangerous as a false one in Latin used to be in the House of Lords. To display a knowledge or taste in art or literature not possessed by your "prospect" may be fatal. On the whole, it is safest to plump yourself down to his level at once whatever that may be, to talk his talk, and only about what he talks. This pressure of the majority on one's personal tastes was amusingly exemplified to me the other day when I was looking for a house to rent in a pleasant Jersey suburb. In the house shown me — as in the case in all the suburbs I know — there was nothing to mark where my lawn might end and my neighbor's begin. All was as open to the public gaze as the street itself. I thought of delightful English or French gardens, surrounded by hedge or wall, screened from the public, where one could putter absurdly over one's plants, read one's book, or have one's supper as much to one's self as in the house. In fact they are out-door rooms, infinitely more attractive than the American "sun parlor." I knew well that no such attempt could be made here, but, nevertheless, I remarked to the "realtor" that it would be pleasant to have a hedge and privacy but I supposed it could not be done on account of the neighbors. "I say No," he answered with pained surprise, "if you are going to be 'high hat' you won't last long here." Just so, and so many things in this country are "high hat" which in other lands simply make for sane and cultivated living that it is no wonder that the business man whose car and cellarette, if not bread and butter, depend so often on his popularity, has to walk warily.

Just why having a garden-wall, speaking one's native tongue correctly, or being able to discriminate in matters of art or literature should be the Gallic equivalent of "high hat" would puzzle a Frenchman, but so it often is in the land of the free. And no one knows his way about the land of the free better than the business man. The pressure may vary with his position and the kind of business he is in, but in general he will soon discover that in any business where personal contact is a factor, the people with whom he deals and upon whose good will he has to lean will insist upon his not being too different from themselves. In Greenwich Village a man may wear a flowing tie and a Spanish hat but it would be suicidal for a bond broker. One has to conform or one is lost. Our two most successful business men are perhaps John D. Rockefeller and Henry Ford. Rockefeller says it is a "religious duty" to make as much money as you can, and Ford has informed us that "history is bunk." The one standard of success in business — and perhaps its stark and easily grasped simplicity is what attracts many Americans — is the amount of money you make from it. There are no foolish nuances. Most Americans are business men. Whatever ideals they may have had in college, and to a considerable extent whatever manners they may have inherited or acquired, they begin to shed, unless their niche is an unusually sheltered one, when the real nature of the excoriating modern business competition dawns upon them. Little by little as they "learn the game" they conform to their customers or associates.

Another characteristic of American life is its extreme mobility. People move up and down in the social scale and round about the country like bubbles in a boiling kettle. Social life everywhere here is in constant flux. I left Wall Street, where I was in business, and a certain suburb where I then lived, fifteen years ago. To-day the personnel of "the Street" as I remember it is almost as completely changed as are the symbols on the ticker. In the suburb where I once knew everyone, at least by name, I know scarcely half a dozen households. People are forever making or losing money, arriving in new social sets, living in Pittsburgh or a mining camp one year and in Los Angeles or St. Paul the next. This has a marked effect on social independence. When a family has lived for many generations in the same place, or, as have many country families in England for centuries, they acquire a social position almost wholly independent of their individual members at a given time.   Indeed, a member is almost an accident and may be as erratic and independent as he pleases.   He still remains a so-and-so of so-and-so, known to all the countryside.   An old hereditary title accomplishes the same result. Here and there in New England villages or in the South there are families who approximate this happy condition, but in the constant movement of the life of most Americans it is necessary for them to depend wholly upon the effect of their personalities and bank accounts.   A man whose family has lived in the "big house" in a small Massachusetts town for a century or two is sufficiently "somebody" there almost to be independent; but should business require him to move to Kalamazoo he is nobody until he "shows them."   The social reputation, immunity, and freedom which long residence in one place gives without effort or thought has to be built again from the ground up, and warily, when one moves to another town where they know not Joseph.   One joins the organizations in the new town, and, again, one conforms.   To begin in a new place by being "different" is dangerous; to begin by being too superior, even if actually, unconsciously, and with no wish to appear so, may be fatal.   Like myself, had I gone to that Jersey suburb and made a little privacy round my garden, the newcomer might be voted "high hat" and not "last long."

In assuming the "mucker pose" the gentleman and scholar does not, of course, descend as low as the "mucker" but he does, in self-defense, for the sake of peace and quiet, for business success, and for the sake of not offending the motley crowd of all sorts whom his neighbors are apt to be in the seething, changing society everywhere to-day, shed enough of his own personality not to offend the average. He avoids whatever others may think "high hat" in manners or culture as he would the plague.   Like Henry Adams he will find himself hiding his antecedents if they happen to be better than the neighbors'.

This possible answer to my friends' question does not necessarily indict democracy and American life.   Both have brought new values into the world of other sorts.   I am merely pointing to one of the possible losses.   For it *is* a loss when a man deliberately uses worse manners than he knows how to use, when he tries to cover up his intellectual abilities, or when he tries to be average when he is above it. A business-democracy has accomplished a great task in levelling up the material condition of its people. It may be asked, however, whether there is no danger of a levelling down of manners and culture. Perhaps the new values gained offset the old ones in some danger of being lost, but it may, even in America, be left to one to question, to ponder, and to doubt. Is the mucker pose really forced on one? People adopt it, evidently, because they think it is the thing to do and essential to make them quickly popular. It does not always work, even in business. A dignified man of science was recently explaining to an applicant for a position some new research work he had been doing. The young Ph.D. was intensely interested. When the scientist concluded he asked the flower of our highest university training what he thought of it. "Hot Dog!" was the immediate and enthusiastic answer, which, in this case, promptly blasted the young man's career in *that* laboratory. It would not have done so generally, however, and we come back to business as conducted to-day, and the character and background of our business leaders, as perhaps, the main contributing cause of forcing the mucker pose.

We can prate as we like about the idealism of America, but it is only money success which really counts. What are ideals or culture or charming manners as compared with business? What do two leaders of opinion at this moment tell us, one from the Pacific and the other from the Atlantic coast? Mr. Hoover, in his address replying to the welcome given him by the people of San Francisco, told them that the most precious possession of their great city was — what? — *their foreign trade!* In New York, the *Sun* in its editorial explaining its intention to support the Republican party, admitted that the prohibition question is "a live campaign topic," and that present conditions may be "intolerable" and "a morass of lawbreaking," but asks whether it is well to risk loss of prosperity for the possible reform of those conditions. In America to-day business life is not the basis for a rational social life but social life is manipulated as the basis for an irrational business one. One makes acquaintances and tries for popularity in order to get ahead downtown. To an unprecedented extent the people who have money in all lines of business are newcomers from far down in the social scale, men with no culture and no background, and often no manners. We may note our new class of multi-millionaire landlords who have built fortunes out of shoe-strings since the War. Two of our now greatest industries have been wholly evolved in the last two decades, and one certainly does not look for culture among the kings in the motor and moving-picture trades. The "people" who came into political power under Jackson made a huge grab at economic power under Grant, but it has been reserved for the present to "make the world safe for democracy." The old class which had inherited manners and culture as essential to an ordered life has abdicated mainly for mere lack of funds. In business for the last decade it has been for the most part the conservatives, who had much to lose, who have lost, and the reckless who have won.

Business may explain the mucker pose, but it may be asked whether those who adopt it are not traitors to all that is best in the world and which has been so hardly built up. An impoverished aristocrat may sell his title in marriage for one generation to rehabilitate his house, but Americans who sell their culture and their breeding to truckle to the unbred in business, who shed these things of the spirit for motor cars and all the rest of the things of the body, are taking refuge in a yet more ignominious surrender. They may thus pick up some of the golden drippings from the muckers' tables, but they do not gain the respect of the muckers whom they imitate and may yet awake to the fact that they have properly forfeited even their own.

MY SON GETS SPANKED

By FREDERIC F. VAN DE WATER

Frederic F. Van de Water (1890–   ) has been a journalist since 1914. He began his career as a reporter on the "New York Tribune," later becoming that paper's night editor. Since 1922 he has been on the staff of "The Ladies' Home Journal." But in addition to his journalistic work, he has become an expert on the New York State Police force, being the only civilian member of that body, and holding the rank of honorary sergeant.

MY nine-year-old son has been tried, condemned, and punished for punching a classmate's nose.

It was not, I gather from the eye-witness testimony of my outraged and retribution-demanding wife, an entirely discreditable performance. I have concluded, after divesting her report of heated imagery, that the blow was a straight right, or, at worst, an uppercut with the weight of the body behind it. This is encouraging. In the past my son has shown a perverse fondness for windmill swings.

Nor was it an unprovoked punch. The classmate had taken our offspring's dearest treasure, a pair of miniature field-glasses through which by myopic squintings one may view a speckled picture of Trafalgar Square, London, had refused to return them and, when importuned, had slapped my son's face. In addition, his classmate was larger than he in every dimension.

Yet my son is in disgrace and, until recently, in tears as well, for I, being also larger than he, have smitten him, not on the nose, thereby upholding poetic justice, pacifying a vindictive mother, and satisfying the demands of fair — well, pretty fair, anyway — chivalry.

For the punched classmate was a little girl.

I have seen her, a fat and sponge-shaped maiden with the sponge's powers of absorption. She plays by choice with the boys of the Fourth Grade, and obtains much plunder thereby; for most of her playmates, already initiated into the mysteries of Politeness to Ladies, relinquish their property rather than hit, or even tell on, a little girl.

So, I have no doubt, will my own child in the future. The thought should be more gratifying. There is something about Sally's smug pudginess that affronts me, though she never has had opportunity to annex belongings of mine.

And yet I have just spanked my child for sharing too sincerely my own antipathy. He will be obliged to apologize to the larcenous Sally when he returns to school to-morrow. That, as well as the spanking, is my wife's idea.

To-day I have not tried to reveal the moral of his punishment. Usually, when the tumult and the shouting dies we consider together the rights and wrongs of the case. This time we have omitted such discussion. I did not dare open it. I felt my position was precarious, that I might topple therefrom at my son's first "Why?" I might be forced to confess that punching a lady's nose was a crude performance, yet more salutary and sensible than many of the over-emphasized standards of chivalric forbearance. And my wife, I know, is on the alert for further evidence of masculine heresy.

Women are, which is why the institution of chivalry has outlived so sturdily its normal background of tournaments and troubadours, crusades and cuirasses, parfit, gentil knights and queens of love and beauty. These properties of medievalism are dead as Ivanhoe. Chivalry endures, and my son, for offense thereunder, gets spanked. Thanks to my paddling his manners toward the other sex will be meeker and milder henceforth, and those of the girls he knows will keep right on being bad. I have bound him to that wheel of courteous behavior on which we men of to-day pay for the sins of our forefathers.

The descendant of Dominant Man who swatted his vassal, woman, more often than was necessary expiates his ancestor's iniquity by squirming helplessly in handcuffs fashioned by woman-fostered ethics.

By spanking my son to-day I have done more than correct a misdemeanor. I have, to some extent, crystallized his future. Vague though that still may be, I can read its outline. From now on, acquisitive little girls will take things away from him with impunity. Horrid little girls will make hideous faces at him, mock the clumsiness and shyness that he inherits from me. Jeering little girls will make his life exquisitely miserable.

When he attains the Terrible 'Teens girls, a little drunk with discovery of their power over males, will do hideous things to the first flowerings of romance in his adolescent breast. In maturity women will bump into him in crowds, jostle him on car platforms, break engagements light-heartedly, forget appointments, delay him, irritate him, disregard him, all without word of apology or recognition of offense, thanks to the spanking I have just administered.

I am sorry for my little boy. He is not yet old enough to be sorry for himself. He has not attained that stage of faintly wilted maturity at which a man wonders why a woman who thrusts herself into a line of purchasers ahead of him should not be thrust out again, why sex equality does not extend to manners, why women enjoy an immunity extending from murders to memoirs.

Chivalry had much to recommend it in 1028, or even in 1908. It has less to-day, in the face of woman's growing independence. It will have little, if anything, to justify it when my son comes of age. Women have proved that they can support themselves most satisfactorily. Why, then, I wonder, must a lad with his first job pay for dances, theaters, meals in order to enjoy the company of girls who are earning possibly more than he? It is custom, I know, but that seems an inadequate answer. And yet my son when he earns his first wages will do it too. Chivalry demands it, and he is going to be chivalrous, even if I have to spank him again.

It is years since I have punched any one in the nose. Being large and blessed with ponderous clumsiness frequently mistaken for power, it is years since any man has given me provocation. A male who treads on your privileges will rectify his error, grouchily or willingly, if you insist. A woman who offends in like manner generally ignores whatever feebly muttered objections you venture. A man knows that behind your objection lies a possible punch in the nose. A woman is sacrosanct under the code of chivalry, and she knows it.

When his châtelaine got on the nerves of bluff Baron Udo de Fitzurse, chivalry curbed and redirected his instinct for felonious assault. His wife remained intact while the good baron girded on his armor and worked off his matrimonial grievance on the nearest dragon or ogre, proclaiming meanwhile that his was the fairest, most gracious ladye in all Christendom. Chivalry was a salutary theory for its time and place. But women are not chattels to-day, and all the dragons have been slain. So, I am a little sorry for my son.

He will hear women preach sex equality. He will see them practice sex superiority.   He will see men hanged for killing men and women triumphantly acquitted of the same offense.   He will cling, by grace of my spankings, to the hallowed code of masculine reticence.   He will read, if feminine memoirs continue their present trend, glibly meticulous accounts by women of their amorous hours.   He and his father and ninety-eight per cent of the American male population would lynch right joyously the man who, following the death of his beloved, revealed in print all the clumsy, pathetic details of the woman's illicit love for him.   Meanwhile, waiting the advent of this super-swine, we read precisely similar disclosures by women, and sympathize.

My son will see women do many other things that would start a fight were men to attempt them.   He will learn that men, the sufferers from feminine presumption, are amazingly willing to punish any of their brethren who resent it — as I have just spanked my own son.

Women as a class are loyal to women, quick to resent affront to one of their number.   The man who makes a woman uncomfortable or unhappy, no matter how much she deserves it, is a brute to other women — and to other men.

I worked in a newspaper office with the most completely incompetent, irresponsible girl who ever had the delusion she was a reporter.   In the month of her employment — a man as helpless and careless would not have lasted a week — she committed all possible newspaper offenses.   That was her sole consistency.   She came in late for assignments.   She forgot to come back from those she received.   Her copy was a latent hornets' nest of misstatement and libel.

When at last she was fired she wept quite publicly, and the men of the night shift who had suffered her negligences and ignorances for thirty days were vastly indignant.   They called the belatedly just city editor who had discharged her a brute with no decent feelings, only they said it less printably.

For such masculine lop-sidedness women are responsible.   In the first place, mothers pump into their male offspring the ideals of chivalry.   They teach their sons that members of the opposite sex are gentle, tender, more delicately and finely fibered, with a higher moral instinct and a cleaner intelligence than men.   In the second place, the overwhelming majority of women justify this statement. Unfortunately, majority is not unanimity, as my son is beginning to discover.   He will find in time that one aching tooth makes the sufferer forget the thirty-one that are sound.   He will spend much of his life marvelling at the consistence of woman's inconsistency.

If he had punched a little boy, his mother might have concealed her pride under a disapproving exterior but secretly she would have been amused and pleased.   She would have told me about it, not in a horror-stifled whisper but with a ring of exultation in her voice. She would have rejoiced that our youngster was learning to defend himself, to stick up for his rights — against other males.

I have never heard of a mother who instructed her son in defense tactics against the depredations of little girls.   It isn't done.   It would be faintly treasonable.   Mothers are firm believers in disarmament — by men.

My son will find out that woman, however, retains her traditional and essential weapons.   Hers is a quicker, keener, more impatient mind, as any husband will testify who has tried to tell a story his wife already knows within earshot of her.   Hers also is an intuition and a stability against passion the average man lacks.   Thus equipped, she outranges and outguns man, whose superior hitting power was once his chief defense.

Thanks to this system, man suffers in childhood.   He goes through exquisite agony in adolescence unless he be more fortunate than one boy I knew.

The list of women he loved vainly from four years old on is long and sad.   The list of women who deserved to be punched is longer and sadder, and many names on the first roster appear also on the second.

He recalls a verse.   It wasn't a very good verse, even for twelve years old, but it was the best he could accomplish, and the most perfect of Keats' was never fashioned in a whiter flame.   Its first stanza ran:

> Oh, Marion, oh, Marion, I love you with all my heart
> And I'll be with you, Marion, till death it do us part.

He stuffed it into his inspiration's pencil box during recess.   He waited, perspiring, ears glowing violently, on the school steps, fatuously certain that an obviously unprepossessing physical exterior would be disregarded henceforth for the sake of the lyric it had fathered.

And while he lingered, his beloved appeared with a tittering group of satellites and, pausing for their edification before him, recited his poem in the nastiest, most jeering voice his ears have ever admitted. The other little girls screeched horrid glee, and within him he felt his vitals wither and drop to dust.

Eventually he fled, stricken. There was nothing else to do. Had a member of his own sex betrayed trust so foully, his course would have been plain, satisfying, pugilistic.

And again, at fifteen, he sat long in the moonlight with Elizabeth. Probably he was funny. Others have found him so in his devout moments, and Elizabeth and the moon together would have lent the Sphinx eloquence. Elizabeth seemed sympathetic and yet, the next morning, the village soda clerk quoted for his benefit and the merriment of bystanding contemporaries the most perfervid of his protestations, word for word. He forswore ice cream sodas for the rest of that summer. He dared not approach that fountain again. His immediate impulse was to seek out Elizabeth and upon her recently adorable snub nose . . . Oh well, women have their prerogatives and Elizabeth passed out of his life, unscathed.

A man who tells is a dog; a girl who reveals is just a flirt, protected by modern chivalry which is far more long-suffering and spacious than its prototype. Guinevere made a fool out of Arthur but she did not boast of it. My favorite among medieval heroes is not Arthur, Lancelot, or Bayard. It is he who is embalmed in a trumpery poem I was forced to learn in grammar school. I have forgotten the name of my hero and the title and the author of the verses that celebrated him, but I do recall that the knight's inamorata asked if he would dare enter an adjacent cage of lions were she to drop her glove therein. He said he certainly would and she tossed the glove in. He recovered it, unhurt, and then, I recall

> He threw the glove
> But not with love
> Straight in the lady's face.

All the spectators applauded. I still do. The sole improvement

I can suggest is that he should have put his hand into the glove first. Medieval chivalry had its moments.

My son, in time, may come to wonder whether consciousness of immunity is a particularly good thing for any one. He will find it an improving exercise for male self-control never to resent feminine boorishness but he will grow to doubt whether this restraint is really beneficial to women themselves.

Eventually he may become the least bit resentful and jealous. A man cannot see women triumphantly performing things which, were he to attempt them, would result in a swift ride to the nearest hospital, without a lurking wrath which, thanks to chivalry's strictures, contents itself with lurking.

Women can argue successfully with traffic cops. I know a girl who ran over one once and, when her justifiably indignant victim pursued and overtook her, wept so prettily that she escaped with nothing more severe than a lecture on traffic laws.

Women can publicly berate men as no male may. I cherish the average human's antipathy to headwaiters, yet I was almost sorry for one who because he stepped by accident on a woman patron's foot was forced to endure, gasping and cringing, a tirade audible to the entire restaurant. When at last she had finished the headwaiter gave me a miserably false smile and shrugged. That is the most a man can do.

Five of us on the late watch in a newspaper office played poker after the last edition had gone to bed. Andy had opened the pot when suddenly the rest of us were aware that a woman, rigid of body and face, had materialized behind his chair. There she stood, voiceless, while we four stared, mute, abashed, as men must be when confronted by the specter of outraged femininity. The fifth, poor hapless Andy, spread his cards in his cupped hands and reiterated, "Opened for a dime." He looked up, saw our faces, and turned.

He seemed as dumb-smitten as we and, besides, she gave him small margin for speech.

"So," her voice rang through the empty office, "this is the way you work late, is it?"

"But, my dear," the culprit protested. "I ——"

"You get your hat," his wife interrupted.

Andy strove to regain at least the semblance of independence.

"Just as soon as I play this hand," he told her with the mirthless, fixed smile of the seasick.

"You'll march right straight home now," she ordered with a ponderous emphasis on every word, and Andy picked up his hat and marched. After he had been led away the survivors told one another what we should do if our wives acted like that. The recitals were impassioned, sanguinary, but it was only the vainglorious babble of men not under fire, and each of us knew all the others were lying.

Furthermore, had Andy embarked upon reprisal, we should have pitied his poor wife wedded to a brute.

The above, I recognize, is comic-strip material yet it is sober fact, reported as accurately as one with newspaper training may write. And I who have just recreated that hideous incident have recently spanked my son for not being more like Andy.

And speaking of comic strips, the irate wife who beats her husband with a rolling pin, or whatever weapon is handy, has an apparently deathless flavor of humor. I have never seen a comic picture in which a woman was smitten by a man, no matter how well she deserved it. Chivalry reigns inviolable, even in cartoon land.

My son may disagree, but there are few more pacific than I. Whatever irritation prompted this has been spent long since. Some of my best friends are women. I shall live on excellent terms with their sex until:

I see a woman deliberately hold up a line before a railway ticket window while she discusses trains at length, trembles for minutes on the brink of decision, at last orders a ticket, waits until it is made out and pushed toward her before she begins to fumble in her purse, deals out money, and continues to block the window while she counts her change, bit by bit, serenely ignoring the impatience of the line dammed up and damning her. I shall think the thoughts suitable to a person brought up by a chivalry reverencing mother until then or until:

I stand in a queue before a box office and see a woman, unthwarted, barge in and purchase seats belonging rightfully to men who have waited long minutes in line, or until:

The next woman shopper calmly appropriates the clerk who had been about to wait on a mere man, picks up something a male has selected, announces that this is just what she wants, and scowls indignantly if the man protests. I shall perpetuate, after my fashion, the Arthurian tradition, blind to anachronism, until the next woman crowds into a station exit against the outpouring crowd, or stands blocking a car doorway while passengers squeeze past her, or takes the seat I offer as if it were something I had borrowed without permission and was returning belatedly.

And even when I survey these offenses again, as I shall certainly within the next week, I shall only squirm inwardly or at most mutter to my nearest male neighbor that women are the limit. He will agree. And that is all that will happen.

Were a man to attempt the violations of fairness, consideration, courtesy cited at random above, he would be dissuaded by the threats and curses of other men or, were he then to persist, some guardian of masculine freedom, what there is of it, would punch him. Men know what will happen if they offend. Women know what will happen if they do. And there we are. And there we stay.

I suspect that if I had praised instead of spanked my son the absorbent and suety Sally would grow into a better and more considerate woman and my offspring himself might become eventually a prophet, an iconoclast, overthrowing Tenth-Century images of chivalric conduct. Yet it is better that I spanked him. The world is unkind to Messiahs, and even the father of a herald of true sex equality would fall heir to an insupportable amount of misery.

THE MATING SEASON OF CO-EDUCATION

By FRANK R. ARNOLD

Frank R. Arnold (1871–   ), *after graduating from Bowdoin in* 1893, *studied at the Universities of Paris, Bordeaux, and Goettingen. Since* 1904, *he has been a professor of French in the Utah Agricultural College and has contributed numerous articles to scholarly journals and literary magazines.*

IF you happen to be a graduate of a monastic New England college and then spend twenty years teaching in a Western co-educational college your point of view on educating the sexes together does much shunting about. You first endure, then pity, but as a rule do not embrace the ambient ardor for putting young men and women through the same cultural mill. Every spring your attitude even becomes that of despair. You sympathize more than ever with Sisyphus as you fight against the triple foe of the college instructor: spring fever, co-educational calf love, and the classic indifference of the eighty-five per cent who, as Doctor Clarence Little told the Michigan alumni in Boston, attend college for reasons other than those of love of knowledge. You get a co-educational complex far different from that of ordinary citizens.

Their view-point on co-education is mainly traditional, depending largely on whether the ordinary citizen is a man or a woman, on whether he first saw the light on the Atlantic seaboard or in the middle West, and possibly also on whether he is a taxpayer. He does not recognize it as a question that will not down and never can be satisfactorily settled. He usually dismisses co-education as a universal Western college blessing and an occasional Eastern college bane, but it is not so simple as all that. It is a problem as hard to settle, with as much to be said on both sides, as that of the epigeneticists and the preformationists. The taxpayer says that only Ohio can expect taxpayers to support three State universities, that no State can afford to give higher education to men and women separately, that taxpayers want to see results, that the easiest result for a taxpayer to grasp is size, and that mammoth proportions in a State university are impossible without an attendance made up of both sexes. Simple and incontrovertible argument for the Babbitts and the other Main-Streeters. Their point of view is worthy of all respect, but the real persons concerned are the students and teachers, and their opinions on the subject are rarely spread abroad. All the same, they are God's own appointed spies on co-education. Most young women students hold the taxpayer's opinion, but from different reasons. According to whether sex blows hot or cold, a girl student becomes an enemy or an advocate of the system. Sex in the case of normal girls is a bigger business, with more insistent demands, a far more alluring game, than careers or intellectual joys, and so there never has been a girl student who, once having tasted the joys of co-education, desires to forego them. Occasionally a girl of the bisexual college system will admit that co-education was all right for her because she knew how to handle herself, but it would never do for her sister, whose life is one constant sequence of innocent love affairs. However, most girl products of the co-educational system probably hold the same opinion as a graduate of the University of Wisconsin who remarked once that a girl couldn't have a good time in college unless she were engaged. She herself had been engaged four times, once each college year, and was an ardent advocate of co-education. She was a good student and on graduating had become a teacher of Latin in an Iowa high school. She kept up the same engaging procedure all through adolescence until she finally married a widower with two children. On a European trip a chance acquaintance asked her to wear his diamond, and she wore it all the time on shipboard but gave it back on landing at Liverpool. She didn't care anything about the man, said he was a bore, that when once you had "gone with" a college man you couldn't stand any other kind, and he was the other kind, and yet she would spend hours in his company, "playing the game." She was a girl of the type known to mothers as "thoroughly nice," and nothing in her conduct was open to criticism except possibly the fixed idea that any man's society was more interesting than a woman's. Sex with her was eternally in evidence, though never rampant, eternally calling for mild satisfaction like that of the Western student who went to Harvard to do graduate work and wrote to a chum that he should go crazy if he didn't find pretty soon some nice girl he could kiss.

The male student, however, is less concerned with sex than business. All the time in constant association with young women students, he often feels that co-education is as distracting as spring fever, as an evil conscience or as a haunting melody, and it is thus because it is so productive of what is known in modern college slang as "female trouble." When you say of a boy student that he has female trouble you mean that he is all upset and unable to work because his girl hasn't written him, or because she is walking past the house, or because she has gone to a dance or a movie with a better man than he the night before, or because she simply will not allow him, in the Shakespearian phrase, to press his suit. How prevalent this distracting female trouble is may be seen by answers to a questionnaire conducted by a Western college paper. Students were asked to send in answers to the query as to whether co-education is a blessing or a curse. It was a subject that they were all so familiar with they had never before even thought of discussing it. The girls wisely sent in no answers. Some of the men's answers were flippant but favorable. Co-education made a man shave every day. It kept him from being a brute. It broke up the adamantine monotony of classes. It made it possible to take a girl to the movies without squeamishness, because you could "stand anything" after having sat through a course in sociology with a lot of girls. Most of the answers, however, brought up the distracting side of the question. Co-education turned the college into a matrimonial bureau. No sense in wasting your time with "Janes," but you couldn't help it when you met them at every turn of the road. Ladies were always lying in wait for a student who wanted to study. What was the use of being "Anned" before you were out of college. One married student even said that co-education was a constant reminder that he had married too early. Women take too much of your time both before and after marriage, was the gist of the whole matter.

It was all the paleolithic cry that the woman tempted me and I did eat. Instead of accepting girl students as an integral part of college life, a necessary concomitant for the development of character, like strong drink and sports, to be used without abusing, the students thought they were being subjected to unnecessary and irresistible devourers of time. And though all had been developed fairly successfully under the co-education régime, the general opinion was that the Amherst or Williams man, with Smith and Mount

Holyoke girls within easy reach, but fortunately not within the gates, was far more favorably situated than the middle Western student whose daily fare was flavored with the feminine at every moment of the day.

Thus the student. The professor, on the other hand, can tell you just how distracting in other ways "female trouble" can be. He uses the simple Hamlet device of looking first on this picture and then on that. Two boys, both with high school love affairs on their hands, went to a Western co-educational college. The first two years they worked well and remained faithful to their high school girls. The next year the high school girls graduated and one boy advised his beloved to go to the State university, as he was at the State agricultural college and both realized that if they were to do any college work they would have to live apart. Freed from sex obsessions, with his girl one hundred miles away and accessible only now and then, the boy made a record in his junior year that showed him to be a good human being even if he were only an average student as far as books go. He bought a Tuxedo, an act of promotion to social virility for a student. He was elected president of his Greek letter fraternity and also of his journalistic club. He wrote and sold five articles for farm papers. He was associate editor of the college paper. Most marvellous of all for a modern college student, so preoccupied with sex, movies, and sports, he had time for reading and used it to read such unrequired books as *The Plastic Age*, *Martha*, *The Sun Field*, *Yvette*, *Arrowsmith*, and *The Recreations of a Psychologist*, a list far from classical but a marvellous feat for a college student of to-day, who usually reads only because he has required subjects and rarely for his own pleasure. The other boy could not keep his girl from following him to his college and with her passed a purely sexual year. He dropped his fraternity life, studied only enough to get passing marks, let the French and dramatic clubs, of which he had been elected president, die of inanition, and read nothing except absolute essentials, never a book, not even a newspaper or a magazine. He had no thought in his head beyond flight to his best girl's arms, and by the end of the year he had no plans in life except to find a teaching position that would enable him to get married. The girl, who was simply marking time and was meant by nature only for a breeder, whose conversation was restricted entirely to exclamations such as "How nice!" and "That's lovely!" had no conception of her *métier de femme* that went so far as putting ambition into her future husband or even sharing any that he might have. The two children were helpless in the grip of sex, and co-education was responsible for a year that was wasted by both except as a valuable human experience from which neither had intelligence and will power enough to draw any profit. The young man's case is perhaps exceptional and is due to the opportunities of co-education, to the lack of will power on his side and of brains on the girl's side, but the case will recur constantly as long as colleges find no way of impressing on their students the elementary fact that co-educational colleges exist not as pleasure clubs with sex in the foreground, but as schools for the training of citizens and human beings. Over the doorways of every educational institution should be carved the verse: "There is a spiritual body" or else "You are human beings as well as animals," and from the first day of orientation courses to the commencement address the college should lay emphasis on the derivation and scope of the word "human."

The observing teacher will also note many false standards that spring up in co-educational institutions as upsetting in their way as the distractions of sex. An agricultural college in a far Western State sent one of its graduates to Oxford. After three years he returned to his college town, settled down as a lawyer, and while waiting for clients did much talking about Oxford before clubs of women or students. One of his most damaging statements to the cause of co-education was the fact that at Oxford he had discovered how delightful is the conversation of men.

"We used to study mornings," he said, "and devote our afternoons to outdoor sports until four, when we would gather in various rooms for afternoon tea and talk. It was then I learned for the first time in my life how extremely agreeable is men's conversation. Until then my idea of pleasure had been to take a girl to a dance, to a movie, or to ride in an automobile. All my pleasure had centred about the other sex, and as none of the girls I knew could 'talk,' as I couldn't 'talk' myself, I really discovered that sharpening one's wits against another's and juggling with ideas is more fun than associating with girls. The French, I understand, consider conversation as a

XI. ÆSTHETICS

THANKS TO THE ARTISTS

By HENRY SEIDEL CANBY

Henry Seidel Canby (1878–   ) received his education at Yale, and was later a professor of English there. For a time he was an editor of the "Yale Review," and then of the "Literary Review." He is now editor of the "Saturday Review of Literature," a magazine which is influential among the intellectual classes. Besides a textbook on rhetoric, his "Definitions" (1922), a collection of critical essays, is well known.

IT would be a wise American town that gave up paying "boosters" and began to support its artists. A country is just so much country until it has been talked about, painted, or put in literature. A town is just so many brick and wood squares, inhabited by human animals, until some one's creative and interpretative mind has given it "atmosphere," by which we mean significance.

America was not mere wild land to the early colonists: it was a country that had already been seen through the eyes of enthusiastic explorers and daring adventurers, whose airs were sweeter than Europe's, whose fruits were richer, where forest and game, and even the savage inhabitant, guaranteed a more exciting life, full of chance for the future.

New England was not just so much stony acre and fishing village for the men of the 'twenties and 'forties. It was a land haloed by the hopes and sufferings of forefathers, where every town had its record of struggle known to all by word of mouth or book.

And when the New-Englanders pushed westward, it was to a wilderness which already had its literature, along trails of which they had read, and into regions familiar to them in imagination.

Say what you please, and it is easy to say too much, of the imitativeness of American literature as Irving, Cooper, Hawthorne, Longfellow, Thoreau, Twain, and Howells wrote it, nevertheless, it was more than justified by the human significance it gave to mere land in America; and it is richer and more valuable than much later writing just because of this attempt. Without Hawthorne and Thoreau, New England would have lost its past; without Cooper and Parkman the word "frontier" would mean no more than "boundary" to most of us.

It is foolish to lay a burden on art, and to say, for example, that American novelists must accept the same obligation to cities and country to-day. But we may justly praise and thank them when they do enrich this somewhat monotonous America that has been planed over by the movies, the *Saturday Evening Post*, quick transportation, and the newspaper with its syndicated features, until it is as repetitive as a tom-tom.

After the Civil War every one began to move in America, and the immigrants, moving in, moved also, so that roots were pulled up everywhere and the town one lived in became as impersonal as a hotel, the farm no more human than a seed-bed. Literature of the time shows this in two ways: the rarity of books that give a local habitation and a name to the familiar, contemporary scene; and a romantic interest, as of the half-starved, in local color stories of remote districts where history and tradition still meant something in the lives of the inhabitants.

It is encouraging to see how rapidly all this is changing. In poetry the Middle West and New England have been made again to figure in the imagination. Rural New Hampshire and Illinois are alive to-day for those who have read Masters, Lindsay, and Frost. In prose Chicago, New York, New Haven, Richmond, Detroit, San Francisco, and the ubiquitous Main Street of a hundred Gopher Prairies have become wayfares for the memory of the reader, as well as congeries of amusement and trade. In particular our universities, which in the 'eighties and 'nineties were darkly lit by a few flaring torches of mawkish romance, have been illumined for the imagination by a series of stories that already begin to make the undergraduate comprehend his place in one of the richest streams of history, and graduates to understand their youth. Poole's "The Harbor" (which served both college and city), Owen Johnson's "Stover at Yale," Norris's "Salt," Fitzgerald's "This Side of Paradise," Stephen Benét's "The Beginning of Wisdom" — these books and many others have, like the opening chapters of Compton Mackenzie's English "Sinister Street," given depth, color, and significance to the college, which may not increase its immediate and measurable efficiency but certainly strengthen its grip upon the imagination, and therefore upon life.

Planners, builders, laborers, schemers, executives make a city, a country, a university habitable, give them their bones and their blood. Poets and novelists make us appreciate the life we live in them, give them their souls. The best "boosters" are artists, because their boosting lasts.

NEW HEIGHTS IN AMERICAN ARCHITECTURE

By HARVEY WILEY CORBETT

Harvey Wiley Corbett (1873–) is an architect who has studied his profession at the University of California, at Liverpool University, England, and at the École des Beaux Arts, France. Besides being on the faculty of Columbia University, he has designed a number of well-known public buildings, and is at present on the board of the Memorial Architectural Commission for the Chicago World's Fair Centennial Celebration in 1933.

EACH year brings a crop of taller buildings, and, since no one enjoys seeing walls tumble down, every one wants to know how tall a building can be. The sky is literally the limit. No skyscraper has fallen. It is safe enough for buildings to go higher than they are to-day. Only they must never lose their usefulness. That, indeed, is the eternal restriction under which an architect works. He may have the most beautiful dreams imaginable, but if his buildings do not serve the purposes for which they were intended, they are architecturally bad no matter how splendid they may seem. Modern man, spending most of his time indoors, must have buildings that are large, specialized, and varied, for the home, whether or not we admit it, is no longer the centre of interest.

Men first used homes as places where they could safely sleep, and sometimes eat. The populations of our modern cities have completed the cycle; they sleep at home and, sometimes, eat there. In the home one hundred years ago, food was provided, clothes were made, business was carried on, amusement was afforded, the sick were nursed, and children were taught. It was, in short, quite self-sufficient. Modern city life has taken from it substantially all these functions. Restaurants provide meals, clothes are made in factories in large quantities, business is carried on in industrial buildings, theatres offer diversion, hospitals care for the sick, and thousands of universities, colleges, schools, and other institutions dispense instruction to both young and old. Suburbs, to be sure, are largely made up of individual dwellings, although even there the demand for apartment houses is making itself felt; but the new suburban developments are planned to benefit each householder by centralizing, for co-operative use, the essential facilities.

In creating the functions of the home on a large scale for community use, the modern architect has to consider how to build for the new needs competently, beautifully, and in a modern idiom. Two factors, which appear with industrialism, enable him to meet the new requirements: steel and the machine. The proper use of both we are but beginning to understand. Until recently, they were used only to meet through speed the urgent demands that the generally increased prosperity and the new social and economic requirements have made of the designer. Steel and the machine have given America, a new country, unhampered by tradition, free to move in almost any direction dictated by commerce or social innovations, a new form of construction.

Architects now approach their work from a totally different angle from that of the past. For six thousand years Egypt, in building, had only one structural principle — the post and lintel; Greece, following, used the same structural principle, though with a refinement and system of detail and proportion that has never since been equalled; Rome introduced the masonry arch in combination with the post and lintel; and until fifty years ago, in spite of all the changing styles, these were the only structural principles employed. Then came steel, and with it skeleton construction, now used throughout the Western world. It has made possible the piling up of storeys to great heights; by enabling work to go forward on many floors at once, it has permitted very rapid building. And the machine, concentrating as it does the energy of thousands of its slaves, now allows the erection in one year of structures surpassing in extent of space those that resulted from centuries of labor by thousands of workmen.

The taking over by society of duties once divided among a multitude of individual homes, requires large and specialized buildings, a condition intensified by the swollen populations of our cities. Hospitals, such as the new Presbyterian Hospital in New York, are needed to care for the sick. To keep residence and business near together requires great apartments, and the scarcity of domestic help makes such co-operative living thoroughly desirable. With increased wages and the eight-hour day, theatres are called upon to accommodate crowds. In education, for which the demand is enormous, the influence of the tall buildings can be seen at the University of Pittsburgh, which has planned a skyscraper to house its halls of learning.

The corporation, the trust, and the super-trust, maintaining headquarters in all the principal cities, have to erect large buildings to house their vast numbers of workers. In municipalities, the nearer their buildings are to one another the easier it is to transact business by means of personal contact, which, in spite of radio, telephone, and telegraph, has remained an important element in commerce. From coast to coast, cities of all sizes appreciate the utility of specialized building, and are not satisfied until they have their own skyscrapers. We are accustomed to think of New York as the city of skyscrapers, but actually America as a whole is a country of tall buildings. Ultimately, small communities always assimilate the styles set by larger ones, modern communicative means makes this process quick; tall buildings are now demanded everywhere. The tall building cannot even be attributed to the topography of Manhattan Island as it sometimes is; like every other honest architectural form, it is the result of fundamental human needs.

Given a need for large buildings, it is fortunate that size can be achieved more practically by piling masses up than by spreading them out. The vertical is always more attractive than the horizontal; it produces an effect of slenderness that is more pleasing. We have vertical stripes on our clothes because we think they add to our appearance. And, conversely, how are ugly clothes — clothes that we do not want copied, the uniforms of convicts — how are such clothes designed? They have broad horizontal stripes. No one would willingly wear anything so hideous. In his buildings, too, man has liked lines that accentuate height and carry the eye upward. Previously, although handicapped by solid masonry construction, he has been fascinated by the majesty and pleasing lift of high buildings. In the Gothic, designed to raise all eyes toward Heaven, he realized his ideal with marvelous feats of engineering. Yet structural difficulties with it were so great that this vertical style did not have much influence on the non-religious architecture of its period. Steel, however, has made every building potentially as high as its designer pleases.

When they were first designing the modern tall buildings, architects, pressed by a seemingly insatiable demand, without time to study appropriate embellishment for the underlying structure, turned, naturally enough, to Gothic, which they adapted as best they could and with some remarkable results. But when Gothic is merely copied slavishly, it is cold and uninspiring; it is impossible to reproduce the conditions and the aspirations of the men who originally built in Gothic. Moreover, Gothic, being primarily an ecclesiastical style, is neither suitable nor expressive of industrial structures.

After this first wave of building activity had passed, architects began to study their problem, to try to evolve new design in character with the new building structure (steel skeleton), with the new proportions (vertical masses), and with the new purposes (commercial enterprises). The steel skeleton is a thing of straight lines and right angles, and American architects now attempted to keep the facings and masses of their buildings true to the structure underneath. Verticality was emphasized; masses were made symmetrical; the whole was treated simply.

The New York building laws gave impulse to original and vigorous design. They pointed the way to a type of city such as the world had never known, a city of symmetrical towers, a city organized to the highest degree of modern efficiency. Under these laws, buildings go straight from the street level to a height that is a factor of the width of the street, depending on the zone in which it lies. Then they must remain within a line drawn from the centre of the street through the cornice. They can slope back, or they can "step" back in storeys. Towers are permitted over an area equal to twenty-five per cent of the lot. Under such regulations, the proportions of all buildings tend to become harmonious.

Horizontal lines carrying the eye of the beholder down long, walled streets, and the ponderous packing-box style of building, were both obviously unsuited to a city so planned, where the high building was recognized as a necessary and permanent accession. The more thoughtful designers eradicated all signs of the horizontal in their buildings, just as the cathedral designers, centuries before, did the same thing in striving for another kind of verticality. Mass and line were made to serve the vertical. The best examples of the new architecture carry the eye upward as inevitably as the walls of a cathedral; yet they are lacking in much embellishment and are strictly considerate of the practical requirements of the buildings as regards natural lighting and conservation of space. The horizontal is used only to fulfil the right angle characteristic of the steel structure. Shadow-brick is sometimes employed to stimulate vertical reveals running the entire height of a building, without the sacrifice of space that would result from actually constructing them. The building rises in a series of simply sculptured masses crowned by an aspiring pinnacle that, owing to the significance of lower lines, still seems to rise despite its mass. The clean lines and simplicity of such structures are imposing; their monumental proportions reflect contemporary society, whose extent surpasses that of any other.

The machine is probably the outstanding trait of the period. Nevertheless, it is still to be so directed that its possibilities of artistic service may be properly developed. The machine is not merely a means of reproducing what has been done before, nor yet of manufacturing materials that appear to be what they are not — like rubber simulating marble. Few have seen fit to use machines artistically; but machines can give materials fresh and native beauty as easily as they can produce gaudy counterfeits. Here again, the designer has been harried by the call from more production, always more. The market in this case is beginning to be surfeited; to sell their wares manufacturers are having to produce more attractive goods than their competitors. The value of simplicity is being recognized. Designers more and more are considering forms that they compose in terms of their structural function, the material out of which they are to be made, and the machines that will shape the material.

The Telephone Building, of which McKenzie, Voorhees, and Gmelin were the architects, is the most interesting modern building in New York because the designers approached their problem from the point of view of designing something with respect for this present Machine Age. They thought in terms of what could be done with the labor of to-day, with the construction of to-day, and with the machinery of to-day, to give each material the form, decoration, and color distinctly its own. That spirit was carried throughout the construction. In matters of detail, the old-fashioned cornice practically disappeared, for, when raised to a height of twenty or more storeys, it served no purpose and was meaningless. But the vertical accent in this building is never lost, even when it reaches its climax, and this is also true of the interior. The marble work, instead of being cut in pilasters with flutes carefully chiselled out, was so designed that machines could shape it. In the Middle Ages, the men who had designed the things that we admire worked with respect for the means available for carrying out their conceptions. The modern architect has to do the same; he must learn to use the machine as a basis of design if his work is to be indigenous to this period.

An ever-recurring criticism of the new architecture is its lack of color, an important element in great buildings of the past. Some attempts, not very successful, at using color have been made. Colored roofs are gaining favor, colored tiles have been employed, and, of course, façades have been embellished variously. But architects have largely confined themselves to dark or light building materials, varied occasionally by shadow-brick. The truth is that the soot and dust and grime of our commercial cities tend to reduce everything to a common gray regardless of its original hue. Such a condition does not provoke experiment. Municipal cleanliness, however, is now being accorded regard almost as high as that given the personal quality, which not many years ago was negligible. Architects are becoming interested in use of color not in blotches but as an inherent part of a building's design. New materials, a sympathetic use of machines, and cleaner cities may make it possible for future buildings to rival in majesty and brilliant splendor anything the Old World ever knew.

Now chiefly occupied in cities, the architect has to consider and help solve problems for which his work is more or less responsible. They have been chiefly two: traffic and the separation of residence from business.

Traffic has always been a matter of concern; a century ago a footbridge was erected across lower Broadway to alleviate congestion. Other things being equal, traffic is proportional to the size of the buildings and the width of streets. Both have been increased, though the size of buildings has grown more rapidly than the breadth of streets, and into this situation has entered the general use of automobiles, a new factor, that has crowded to capacity our business districts. Again, the architect has to face his problem with practical consideration of all the elements involved. The need and demand for large buildings have been demonstrated. The automobile's utility and popularity are known; pleasure cars can be debarred from certain districts, but other types are requisite to large commercial organizations. The answer is, increase the size of streets.

Now, there are two ways of doing this. We can tear down all existing buildings, turn our cities into rubbish piles, cart away the débris, take a fresh start, build ideal cities, and then find them populations. Or we can improve our present cities by intelligently dividing traffic. Streets with arcaded sidewalks one storey up, and within the building line, have been designed. They raise pedestrians above the level of the motor traffic. They give the space now occupied by sidewalks to vehicles. They increase six times the capacity of a street sixty feet wide. Such sidewalks are at once an inherent part of a building's design, and they make a block its basic unit, the end toward which even now it reaches. These sidewalks, decoratively vaulted, would shield pedestrians from sun and rain and snow, while below them would be visible the shiny tops of streams of motor cars like giant beetles. Traffic would be divided naturally. Movement would be free.

In New York alone, thousands are now transported daily to and from their homes. The majority stand crowded together almost without room to be straphangers. They reach their offices in the morning, and their homes at night, after a jostling and crushing that would considerably reduce the market value of cattle. They breathe foul air and turn it into names for persons crushed against them. Sometimes they become accustomed to commuting; more often not.

A building occupying a block could contain a community within itself. It could have a constant cornice line at the first set-back, and this cornice could become an upper sidewalk. Below this point could be business; above it, with promenades and terraces in fresh air and sunshine, could be residences. With small shops in the upper section, people could move about conveniently on their errands. When a man left his office, he could take an elevator to his home. The centres of the buildings could contain elevators and such forms of indoor recreations as theatres, gymnasiums, and swimming pools, for which artificial light suffices. The most congested traffic would be reduced, and people could get the full benefit of the light and air available at the top of our cities.

Such unified functioning is still a thing of dreams, but it is not against the tendencies of modern city life. Business is not satisfied with establishing individual headquarters in large buildings, and it may be that larger buildings will ultimately house related industries. In New York similar types of various commercial enterprises are now grouped together. Finance centres at the lower end of the island, law and the courts about City Hall, the clothing trades above Fourteenth Street, building in the Forties, automobiles about Columbus Circle, and amusements along the general course of upper Broadway. This grouping makes for convenient communication within the various trades, and shopping of all kinds becomes easier. It encourages customers to visit this and that and the other place of business, for those related are in the same vicinity, and sooner or later the most casual window-shopper is drawn like a fly to honey and, perhaps, stuck.

Probably the financing of the gigantic structures suggested could be arranged. Enclosed spaces are now marketable commodities. Formerly men built for their own needs and only in a limited way for those of others. To-day, although real estate generally requires a longer period to bring returns than other investments, they speculate in buildings. Organizations that build primarily for themselves reserve a number of floors for their own use and rent the rest. Others make the erection of buildings both for commerce and residence, and the sale or renting of space in them, their business. The demand for modern quarters and for more room to care for the steady expansion of our cities is so great that such undertakings are lucrative. Real estate is an established business. Our annual crop of taller structures is witness to the willingness of wealth to provide capital for building.

Seeing the widespread destruction of old buildings to make room for new, anyone may well ask how long the new themselves will last. It has been said that if fortunes are not some day spent in repairs, the present steel-frame buildings will collapse. Contrary to such opinions, our tall buildings are structurally quite sound. The life of steel structure is not known, but it has proved durable. As a matter of fact, the large masonry buildings in Europe, such as Saint Paul's

Cathedral, London, are constantly undergoing repairs that are tremendously expensive. A steel frame, on the other hand, can, when necessary, be easily repaired at relatively small cost by jacking up the structure and introducing a new section.

If the first automobiles had been produced with the idea of their lasting for a hundred years or more, imagine what we would be riding in to-day! There would be contraptions with carriage wheels, engines behind, steering rods, and a confirmed habit of stalling. And imagine what Times Square would be at theatre time! But the original manufacturers of motor cars believed that styles would change and their first cars would be improved.

The same idea is now applied to buildings. Rapid construction has changed the architect's respect for old styles and form inapplicable to present needs. Yearly his separation from old methods becomes greater. The old buildings, which were designed to last for centuries, occupied definite places in their communities and inspired builders of ensuing periods; now, with our society in transition, we change quickly, and pressing human needs inspire designers. In America a building is designed for a specific purpose and for a specific time, and American builders recognize that the lives of their buildings may be some thirty years, after which may rise fresh needs better served by newer buildings.

America's failure to produce much of artistic merit prior to 1900 and the celerity with which she has taken up the arts since 1920 are not surprising, for man has time to pursue art, and has wealth with which to encourage its development, only when he prospers. After the war, the American people found themselves with more wealth more generally distributed and more leisure per capita than any people ever had before. A nation was suddenly of age. But it was still growing, and its inheritance, which had been accumulating for three centuries, was to a large extent, and is still being, converted into buildings.

This architecture, rising in response to needs, is recording our customs, our aspirations, our tastes. In it men are striving to beautify buildings without which life, as they know it, cannot continue. It is both spiritual and material. It is a kind of artistic business. Its artistic influence is far-reaching, for the development of architecture inevitably affects that of other arts. Sculpture, painting, and the various crafts are most closely associated with it. Before any art is practised, man has to have buildings in which to sleep and, in modern life, to eat, and trade, and learn to paint, to carve, to write, to compose music, to present suitably the things he creates when they are finished. So other works assume something of the character of their contemporary buildings; and this is happening to-day.

America was ripe for architectural innovations. Her wealth, her lack of old buildings and her need for new ones, her abundance of steel — the new material allowing rapid building for specific purposes — her youth, unbound by traditions, and the ease with which she adapts herself to new methods and conditions — all these play a part in the new architecture that she is producing. Her prosperity enables architects to see their projects realized. The competition that exists among her various activities is a spur which urges architects to employ the most recent methods and devices. Called on to satisfy new human needs, and given new means of building, American architects are evolving an architecture that, original in design and structure, is characteristically American in that it is useful first, then beautiful.

ART IN THE THEATRE

By ROBERT EDMOND JONES

Robert Edmond Jones (1887–   ), after graduating from Harvard in 1910, began designing for the theatre in New York. His work in connection with "The Man Who Married a Dumb Wife," "The Jest," "Richard III," "The Birthday of the Infanta," "Macbeth," "Redemption," and other plays has securely established his reputation as a first-rate theatrical craftsman.

THE first thing I should like to speak about is pride. The pride of the craftsman. What is this theatre we are working in to-day? Who knows? Some people say it is a temple, some say it is a brothel, some say it is a laboratory, or a workshop, or it may be an art, or a plaything, or a corporation. Whatever it is, one thing is true about it. There is not enough fine workmanship in it. There is too much incompetence in it. The theatre demands of its craftsmen that they know their jobs. The theatre is a school. We shall never have done with studying and learning. In the theatre, as in life, we try first of all to free ourselves, as far as we can, from our own limitations. Then we can begin to practice "this noble and magicall art." Then we may begin to dream.

When the curtain rises, it is the scenery that sets the key of the play. A stage setting is not a background; it is an environment. Players act in a setting, not against it. We say, in the audience, when we look at what the designer has made, before any one on the stage has time to move or speak, "Aha! I see! It's going to be like *that!* Aha!" This is true no matter whether we are looking at a realistic representation of Eliza crossing the ice or at the setting for one of Yeats's "Plays for Dancers," carried to the limit of abstract symbolism. When I go to the theatre I want to get an eyeful. Why not? I do not want to have to look at one of the so-called "suggestive" settings, in which a single Gothic column is made to do duty for a cathedral; it makes me feel as if I had been invited to some important ceremony and had been given a poor seat behind a post. I do not want to see any more "skeleton stages" in which a few architectural elements are combined and recombined for the scenes of a play, for after the first half-hour I invariably discover that I have lost the thread of the drama. In spite of myself I have become fascinated, wondering whether the castle door I have seen in the first act is going to turn into a refectory table in the second act or a hope-chest in the last act. No. I don't like these clever, falsely economical contraptions. And I do not want to look at a setting that is merely smart or novel or *chic*, a setting that tells me that it is the latest fashion, as though its designer had taken a flying trip to Europe like a spring buyer and brought back a trunk full of the latest styles in scenery.

I want my imagination to be stimulated by what I see on the stage. But the moment I get a sense of ingenuity, a sense of effort, my imagination is not stimulated; it is starved. That play is finished as far as I am concerned. For I have come to the theatre to see a play, not to see the work done on a play.

A good scene should be, not a picture, but an image. Scene-designing is not what most people imagine it is — a branch of interior decorating. There is no more reason for a room on the stage to be a reproduction of an actual room than for an actor who plays the part of Napoleon to be Napoleon or for an actor who plays Death in the old morality play to be dead. Everything that is actual must undergo a strange metamorphosis, a kind of sea-change, before it can become truth in the theatre. There is a curious mystery in this. You will remember the quotation from "Hamlet":

> "My father! — methinks I see my father."
> "O where, my lord?"
> "In my mind's eye, Horatio."

Stage-designing should be addressed to this eye of the mind. There is an outer eye that observes, and there is an inner eye that sees. A setting should not be a thing to look at in itself. It can, of course, be made so powerful, so expressive, so dramatic, that the actors have nothing to do after the curtain rises but to embroider variations on the theme the scene has already given away. The designer must always be on his guard against being too explicit. A good scene, I repeat, is not a picture. It is something seen, but it is something conveyed as well; a feeling, an evocation. Plato says somewhere, it is beauty I seek, not beautiful things. This is what I mean. A setting is not just a beautiful thing, a collection of beautiful things. It is a presence, a mood, a symphonic accompaniment to the drama, a great warm wind fanning the drama to flame. It echoes, it enhances, it animates. It is an expectancy, a foreboding, a tension. It says nothing, but it gives everything.

Do not think for a moment that I am advising the designer to do away with actual objects on the stage. There is no such thing as a symbolic chair. A chair is a chair. It is in the arrangement of the chairs that the magic lies. Molière knew how to place the chairs on his stage so they almost seemed to speak. In the balcony scene from "Romeo and Juliet" there must be a balcony, and there must be moonlight. But it is not so important that the moon be the kind of moon that shines on Verona as that Juliet may say of it,

> "O, swear not by the moon, the inconstant moon . . .
> Lest that thy love prove likewise variable."

The point is this: it is not the knowledge of the atmospheric conditions prevailing in Northern Italy which counts, but the response to the lyric, soaring quality of Shakespeare's verse.

The designer creates an environment in which all noble emotions are possible. Then he retires. The actor enters. If the designer's work has been good, it disappears from our consciousness at that moment. We do not notice it any more. It has apparently ceased to exist. The actor has taken the stage; and the designer's only reward lies in the praise bestowed on the actor!

Well, now the curtain is up and the play has begun.

When I go to the theatre to see a play performed, I have got to be interested in the people who are performing it. They must, as the saying goes, "hold" me. It is my right as a member of the audience to find men and women on the stage who are alive. I want to respect these players, to look up to them, to care for them, to love them. I want them to speak well, to move well, to give out energy and vitality and eagerness. I do not wish to look at the physically unfit, the mentally defective, or the spiritually violated. They bring to my mind Barnum's cruel remark that normal people are not worth exhibiting. I wish to see actors in whom I can believe — thoroughbreds, people who are "all there." Every day is a living dream: your dream, my dream — and that dream must not be blurred or darkened. The actors must be transparent to it. They may not exhibit. Their task is to reveal.

To reveal. To move in the pattern of a great drama, to let its reality shine through. There is no greater art than this. How few actors live up to its possibilities! Some actors have even made me feel at times that they were at heart a little bit ashamed of being actors. I call this attitude offensive. The right attitude is that of the distinguished old English character actor who, when engaged to play a part, was accustomed to say, "Sir, my fee is so and so much," as if he were a specialist from Harley Street. It is easy, of course, to understand why there are not more good actors on the stage to-day. The *métier* is too hard. This art of acting demands a peculiar humility, a concentration and dedication of all one's energies. But when an actor moves before us at last with the strange freedom and calm of one possessed by the real, we are stirred as only the theatre can stir us.

I am thinking of the company of Irish Players from the Abbey Theatre in Dublin who first gave us the dramas of Synge and Yeats in 1910. As one watched these players, one saw what they knew. I kept saying to myself on that first evening: Who are these rare ones? Where did they come from? How have they spent their lives? Who are their friends? What music they must have heard, what books they must have read, what emotions they must have felt! They literally enchanted me. They put me under a spell. And when the curtain came down at the end of the play, they had become necessary to me. I have often asked myself since that time how it was that these actors could make me feel such strange emotions of trouble and wonder; and I find the answer now, curiously enough, in an address spoken by a modern Irish poet to the youth of Ireland — *Keep in your souls some images of magnificence.* These Irish players had kept in their souls some images of magnificence.

Exceptional people, distinguished people, superior people; people who can say, as the old negro said, "I got a-plenty music in me." These are the actors the theatre needs.

I think it needs also actors who have in them a kind of wildness, an exuberance, a take-it-or-leave-it quality, a dangerous quality. We must get clean away from the winning, ingratiating, I hope-you're-all-going-to-like-me-because-I-need-the-money quality of a great deal of the acting we find to-day. I remember Calvé's entrance in the first act of "Carmen." Her audiences were actually afraid of her. Who has seen Chaliapin in the mad scene of "Boris"? I consider Chaliapin the greatest living actor, by the way. Some of the best actors in the world are to be found on the operatic stage. What a Hedda Gabler Mary Garden would make! It seems as if these actor-singers were set free by the very limitations of the opera — the fixed melodies, the measured steps and pauses. They cannot be casual for one instant. They must be aware. They must know how to do what they have to do. They must have style. And they must have voices.

But I have been speaking of actors, not of acting.

Great rôles require great natures to interpret them. Half our pleasure in seeing a play lies in our knowledge that we are in the presence of artists. But this pleasure of watching the artists themselves is soon forgotten, if the play is well performed, in the contagious excitement of watching a miracle: the miracle of incarnation. Just that. And it is a miracle. I have no words to express what I feel about this subtle, ancient, sacred art — the marvel of it, the wonder, the meaning. The designer creates with inanimate materials; canvas, wood, cloth, light. The actor creates in his living self. And just as the good designer retires in favor of the actor, so does the good actor withdraw his personal self in favor of the character he is playing. He steps aside. The character lives in him. You are to play Hamlet, let us say; not narrate Hamlet, but *play* Hamlet. Then you become his host. You invite him into yourself. You lend him your body, your voice, your nerves; but it is Hamlet's voice that speaks, Hamlet's impulses that move you. We may be grateful to Pirandello for showing us, in his "Six Characters in Search of an Author," the strange reality of the creations of the playwright's mind. Hamlet is as real as you or I. To watch a character develop from the first flashes of contact in the actor's mind to the final moment when the character steps on the stage in full possession of the actor, whose personal self looks on from somewhere in the background, is to be present at a great mystery. No wonder the ancient dramas were initiation-ceremonies: all acting is an initiation, if one can see it so, an initiation into what Emerson calls " the Empire of the real."

But the curtain is up, and the play has begun. We look into a scene that is filled with excitement. See. That man is playing the part of a beggar. We know he is not a real beggar. Why not? How do we know? We cannot say. But we know he is not a beggar. When we look at him we recall, not any particular beggar we may happen to have seen that day, but all beggars we may happen to have ever seen or read about. And all our ideas of misery and helplessness and loneliness rush up in our imaginations to touch us and hurt us. The man is acting.

How is he dressed? (And now I am speaking as a costume-designer.) The man is in rags. Just rags. But why do we look at him with such interest? If he wore ordinary rags we wouldn't look at him twice. He is dressed, not like a real beggar, but like a painting of a beggar. No; that's not quite it. But as he stands there or moves about we are continually reminded of great paintings — paintings like those of Manet, for instance. There is a curious importance about this figure. We are looking at something *theatrical*. These rags have been arranged — "composed," the painters call it — by the hand of an artist. We feel, rather than see, an indescribable difference. These rags have somehow ceased to be rags. They have been transformed into moving sculpture.

I am indebted to the great Madame Freisinger for teaching me the value of simplicity in the theatre. I learned from her not to torture materials into meaningless folds, but to preserve the long flowing line, the noble sweep. "Let us keep this production noble," she would say to me. The costume-designer should steer clear of fashionableness. That was the only fault of the admirable production of *Hamlet* in modern dress. It was so *chic* that it simpered. I remember that in the closet scene, as the Queen cried out,

"O Hamlet, thou hast cleft my heart in twain";

and her son answered,

"O, throw away the worser part of it,
And live the purer with the other half,"

a voice near me whispered, "I wonder if she got that negligé at Bendel's?" And the programme told us that Queen Gertrude of Denmark did, indeed, get that negligé at Bendel's. And, furthermore, that Queen Gertrude's shoes came from the firm of I. Miller, Inc., and that her hats were furnished by Blank and her jewels by Dash, and so on. Think of it! Two worlds are meeting in this play, in this scene — in the night, in Elsinore. And we are reminded of shoes and frocks!

Many of the costumes I design are intentionally somewhat indefinite and abstract. A color, a shimmer, a richness, a sweep — and the actor's presence! I often think of a phrase I once found in an old drama that describes the first entrance of the heroine. It does not say, "She wore a taffeta petticoat or a point lace ruff or a farthingale"; it says, "She came in like starlight, hid in jewels." There she is in that phrase; not just a beautiful girl dressed up in a beautiful dress, but a presence — arresting, ready to act, enfolded in light. It isn't just light, it is a kind of stillness; an awareness, a kind of breathlessness. We ought to look at the actors and say, why! I never saw people like *that* before! I didn't know people looked like *that!*

The subtlety of stage lighting, the far-flung magic of it! When a single light-bulb wrongly placed may reveal, as Yeats said, the proud fragility of dreams!

Shakespeare knew more than all of us. How he uses sunlight, moonlight, candlelight, torchlight, starlight! Imagine Hamlet as he stands with Rosencranz and Guildenstern on the forestage of the Globe Theatre, under the open sky, looking up at the stars, saying,

> . . . this brave o'erhanging firmament,
> this majestical roof fretted with golden fire . . .

I have often wondered whether the Globe Theatre and the Swan Theatre were not oriented toward the east as temples are, in order to take advantage of the lighting-effects of nature. Think of the play of *Macbeth*. It begins on a foggy afternoon before sundown. The day goes. The sun sets. Torches are brought in. We enter deeper and deeper with the play into an extravagant and lurid night of the soul. Or take the trial scene from *The Merchant of Venice*. The scene is played by torchlight. The auditorium is dark. We see the sky overhead. The trial draws to an end. Shylock is defeated. There is a gay little interlude, the byplay with the rings. The stage grows lighter. The torches are carried off. Now the scene is finished. Portia, Nerissa, and Gratiano go away. . . . The full moon rises over the wall of the theatre and touches the stage with silver. Lorenzo and Jessica enter, hand in hand. " . . . On such a night . . ."

The sole aim of the arts of scene-designing, costuming, lighting, is, as I have already said, to enhance the natural powers of the actor. It is for the director to call forth these powers and urge them into the pattern of the play.

The director must never make the mistake of imposing his own ideas upon the actors. Acting is not an imitation of what a director thinks about a character; it is a gradual, half-conscious unfolding and flowering of the self into a new personality. This process of growth should be sacred to the director. He must be humble before it. He must nourish it, stimulate it, foster it in a thousand ways. Once the actors have been engaged, he should address himself to their highest powers. There is nothing they cannot accomplish. In this mood, ignoring every limitation, he fuses them into a white energy. The director energizes; he animates. That is what Max Reinhardt understands so well how to do. He is an animator. A curious thing, the animating quality. Arthur Hopkins has it; Stanislavsky has it; Belasco has it. One feels it instantly when one meets these men. One sees in them what Melville calls "the strong, sustained, and mystic aspect." The best stage director I ever heard of, incidentally, is Captain Ahab in Melville's *Moby Dick*. Modern directors would do well to read this book.

Now I come to the playwrights. I am not one of the calamity-howlers who believe the theatre is in a dying condition. The theatre is no more in a dying condition at this moment than life itself is in a dying condition at this moment. On the contrary: the American theatre, like the advertisements of the *revue Americana*, is "a star-spangled wow." But to my way of thinking, many of the playwrights of to-day are being swamped by their own ability; snowed under by their very cleverness. They know how to say, with astonishing brilliancy, what they have to say. But what have they to say?

There are fashions in plays just as there are fashions in scenery, hats, or socks. This year it has apparently been the fashion to "de-bunk." What is called "a cross-section of American life," whatever that is, is, as they say, "de-bunked." Well, I think debunking should begin at home.   Before one starts to de-bunk America one should take care to de-bunk oneself.   It is a much harder job, of course, to de-bunk oneself.   Truth is a shy thing, a hidden flame.   But it is an immutable natural law of the theatre that what one is shows through what one does.   A week of strenuous dress-rehearsals and people are exposed as they are.

A few weeks ago, in Vienna, I looked at the Sunday theatrical section of a New York newspaper for the first time in several months. Now, the theatre is my work and my life; and I expected either to be infuriated by these pages or to be made so homesick that I would start back to New York the next morning.   Nothing of the kind happened.   The general impression I got was something neat and adequate and snappy.   One would say, "Yes, they do things very well."   There was a kind of thin, meagre competence about the lay-out that was worse than sterility.   Everybody understood how to do. That was clear.   But nobody was doing.

One word struck me: it was repeated in the critics' reviews and quoted again and again in the advertisements: the word *human*.   A gripping *human* drama.   A play of deep *human* emotions.   And so on. Good God!   Have we all become so dehumanized that we will pay to see a drama merely because it is human?

And now I have come to my real point.   I know that there are young people in this country who will really create for the theatre of their time, who will bring something into existence there that has never existed before.   A few.   Not many.   The theatre will be fortunate if it can claim a half-dozen of them.   But it is this half-dozen to whom we look to lift our common experience into a higher region, a clearer light.   We do not want shrewdness or craftiness or adroitness from them.   We have had enough mechanism in the theatre, and more than enough.   Let them go beyond this: let them give us the sense of the dramatic moment, the immortal moment.

Think of this moment.   All that has ever been is in this moment; all that will be is in this moment.   Both are meeting in one living flame, in this unique instant of time.   This is drama; this is theatre — *to be aware of the Now*.

Of all people in the world, Sir Philip Sidney said, poets are the least liars.   Poets are reporters.   They set down what they see.   I will give you an example from *Hamlet*:

"O good Horatio, . . .
    If thou didst ever hold me in thy heart
    Absent thee from felicity awhile."

Absent thee from felicity awhile.   Here are some of the most beautiful words ever written in the English language.   But this is not all. These words are a plain record of fact.   Hamlet, drawing his last breath as he spoke them, was not interested in phrasemaking, nor was Shakespeare.   Hamlet did not think up an exquisite phrase at that moment.   He spoke out the real vision of felicity, immortal.   He saw the clear light, the happy forms.   He saw the felicity.   He called it *felicity*.   He did not invent; he did not orate; he saw, and reported.

I could give you hundreds of examples.   Poets know that what they see is true.   If it were not so they would have told you.

Nothing can stop progress in the American theatre except the workers themselves.   To them I say: There are no limitations there except your own limitations.   Lift it.   Get the personal *you* out of your work.   Who cares about *you?*   Get the wonder into it.   Get your dreams into it.   Where are your dreams?

One word more.   Great drama does not deal with cautious people. Its heroes are tyrants, outcasts, wanderers.   From Prometheus, the first of them all, the thief who stole the divine fire from heaven, these protagonists are all passionate, excessive, violent, terrible.   "Doom eager," the Icelandic saga calls them.   If you are meant to create them in the theatre — not merely to write a well-constructed play or supply nice scenery, but to create — you will imagine yourself into these heroic moods.   They will carry you far.   For the soul is a pilgrim.   If you follow it, it will lead you away from your home and into another world, a dangerous world.   You will join a band of poets and dreamers, the visionaries of the theatre; the mummers, the mountebanks, the jongleurs, the minstrels, the troubadours.

THE GREAT AMERICAN ART

By THOMAS CRAVEN

An art critic of some repute, Thomas Craven has contributed to "The Nation," "The Dial," and "The New Republic" numerous articles on æsthetics. He is also the author of a novel, "Paint" (1923).

ABROAD it is called the cinema; in picturesque American it is the movie.

Go to London, Paris, Rome, Berlin, and Vienna, and you will find that these sensitive peoples of the Old World, the very ones who are supposed to love and foster the traditional arts, have succumbed to the movie, and not, let it be noted, to films of their own manufacture, but to the exclusively American product — to the acrobatics of Fairbanks, the amours of Valentino, and the unique waggery of Chaplin. The conquest of England has been swift and overwhelming: witness the triumphal entry of Tom Mix into the city of London, and the protestations of British producers. Even the valetudinarian Hardy has broken silence to deplore the American incursion; and from the Island of Free Trade come rumblings of a prohibitive tariff, or a Parliamentary act to restrain the exhibition of all pictures save those controlled by British capital.

At last America can boast of an original art, an art as indigenous as ice-water and the red Indian, an art without antecedents or refining tradition, a spectacular and extravagant affair measured, not as the other arts are measured in terms of intelligence and enlightening influence, but in miles and millions — and most important of all, an art consistent with the ideals and energies of the nation from which it sprang, rising from ignominious poverty to win in a few years the patronage and exploitation of the elect. You will remember, perhaps, that the founder of the Astor fortunes, John Jacob himself, was a dealer in furs, and that out of hides came an aristocracy; similarly was Mr. Adolph Zukor, the great movie magnate, a furrier, and to-day he stands out as the progenitor of a new and more powerful social order — an aristocracy of art.

It was in 1893 that Mr. Edison devised a machine by means of which light was projected through a succession of photographic films upon a screen, thereby endowing the American people with a new medium of expression. Strange to say, the Americans did not adopt the medium with the alacrity which might have been expected. The kinetoscope was a clumsy instrument apparently of slight commercial value, and the initial development of its resources was slow and unpromising. In 1910 improvements both in the camera and the films assured the merchants of substantial returns, and production increased ominously; in 1913 the eccentric comedy and the western melodrama came into vogue, and the new industry became an important factor in our national culture. But as yet the moving picture had no pretensions to art — it was simply a novelty and an ingenious and profitable plaything. In 1915 Mr. D. W. Griffith produced the first feature-film, *The Birth of a Nation*, and the movie passed into the realm of art. During the last decade the industry has multiplied to such bewildering proportions as to require a John Maynard Keynes to explain its financial magnitude. Fortunately it is primarily the art of the movie with which I am concerned, and when I say that the vested interests are estimated at more than one billion, five hundred million dollars — the fourth largest business in America — that every week one hundred thirty million people pay six hundred million dollars to enjoy this new art, and that ninety per cent of the films shown abroad are American, I shall have said enough.

The simplest concept of art is the theory expounded by Tolstoy, according to whom art is a means for communicating certain states of the soul, but mind you, elementary states — the homiletic infection of parables, the sentimentality of Dickens, the pathos of lowly illustration, and the touching piety of folk-songs. Tolstoy believed that most of the alleged great art of the world is nothing more than organized artifice, and that its appeal to the senses is based on pernicious hypnotism, or the power to evoke the sensual instincts. To him art was a moral agent, and he refused to countenance anything beyond the comprehension of peasants. One would think, inasmuch as the movies are largely conceived and performed by peasants, or their American equivalents, that the new art of pictures would fit into Tolstoy's scheme, but such is not the case. I find no evidence in the films that any one has ever seen, felt, or experienced anything worth communicating.

From a less primitive point of view, art should contain a measure of intelligence and should demand of its audience a certain amount of understanding and cultivation; through the honest conviction which brings it into life, it should be a protest against cheapness and vulgarity; it should, by reason of its beautiful forms, rouse in man the spirit of emulation, make him intolerant of baseness and shams, and sharpen his susceptibilities — in short, it should act as a civilizing influence. The movie does none of these things. It is the only art in history which exacts nothing from the beholder, and renders impossible the participation of the higher faculties.

There is yet another form of art, a sham art wherein accepted decency and conventional morality are employed as motifs for scurrility and wantonness. Under the mantle of righteousness, and with the sanction of its official censors, the movie engages as "a sense of duty" to expose evil and the dark alluring ways of sin, pursuing its course to the very limit of barbaric extravagance. Artificiality lies at the root of all its productions, and nothing real or convincing ever comes out of its gilded studios. Partly through the nature of the medium and partly through the stupidity and connivance of the exploiters, it ruins every genuinely dramatic situation; it cannot tell the simplest story, point the shallowest moral, or portray the most commonplace sentiment without transforming it into complicated and glittering horrors.

We must, however, apply a higher and more philosophical test to the movie to appreciate how fully it has arrived at the true significance of art. As a reflex of life it has no parallel, nor has the creative labour of any past period — the sculpture of the Greeks, the painting of the Renaissance, the drama of Elizabethan England — approached it in ability to reach the hearts of the people. It is an art which actually works; it travels to the four corners of the earth bearing a message within the scope of housemaids and children. I do not insist that it represents contemporary manners with absolute fidelity, or that its western heroes or drawing-room characters have their counterparts in real life; it is not so literal as that, but transcending nature, as art should, it symbolizes the hopes and aspirations of the unfortunates. Hence the vast popularity of the "society film." These orgiastic conceptions of high life whet the social appetite of scheming, restless femininity the world over. The modern industrial slave, given money and leisure, would model his life after the frivolous debauchery and lavish amativeness depicted by the movies; and the producers, having been slaves themselves — not so long ago — are thoroughly alive to the fact and play upon it. It is an advertised fact that one of the most celebrated actresses of to-day, and a producer in her own right, after the completion of a film, tries it on her retinue of servants before releasing it: if the lackeys approve, the success of the film is taken for granted.

The above paragraph will help to explain the remark of a leading manufacturer to the effect that the business caters mainly to women and depends upon them for its immense profits. Throughout the entire organization the spirit of effeminacy prevails. Except in directing, which, it would seem, demands not brains but the physical stamina necessary to goad and control the mummers, women are predominant. They have no false impressions about their work or about other women; they understand precisely the dreams and desires of their sisters in the audience, and set about fulfilling them; they write the *scenarios*, continuities, and titles; and the cutting of the films — an exceedingly important process — is entrusted to young girls. In addition, women are the best critics of the movies. Their writing, for the most part, is trivial, but it is none the less pertinent. They know what the game is about, which cannot be said of male scribes. Latterly, a number of our young Hazlitts have veered into movie criticism with the expectations of princely rewards, but how ludicrously they have floundered about seeking a point of view! I need not dwell on the effeminacy of the actors. I know that it is difficult to make an actor look like a man, but in the movies the idea is to make him look like a woman. In German and Scandinavian pictures I have seen actors who managed to retain their masculinity — they were not disfigured with hideous make-up, and they were only moderately "temperamental."

For the success or failure of a film the director is held responsible, and rightly, since he is invested with autocratic powers. He is usually a "ham-actor" who entered the movies when competition was less strenuous, and who had the aggressiveness to advance himself to a commanding position. The director is a peculiar fellow. He can be, and often is, illiterate; he need have no knowledge of plastic, graphic, literary, or dramatic art; but he must have unbounded confidence, great forensic strength, and the ability to lord it over the actors with Napoleonic fearlessness. His work begins when the preliminary constructive details are finished — the best-seller bought and retold, the *scenario* prepared by the women experts, the cast selected, the costumes gathered, and the elaborate settings designed. He has no plan of action and proceeds entirely by impulse. Considering his qualifications, is it not wonderful what he accomplishes? The answer is that he has unlimited funds at his disposal, and that he is surrounded by assistants more capable than himself. If, perchance, he must "picturize" a masterpiece, say a novel by Balzac, he instructs one of his servants to find out who Balzac was, hires a woman to read the book and relate the story to him, hires another woman to improve upon it and to "adapt it to the screen," and then packs his troupe off to France for local colour. If he capriciously desires to throw a million dollars away, there is no one to stop him; if he calls for the United States Naval Academy, the Coliseum, or the city of Versailles, his employers are convinced that he is a prodigy of imagination, and arrangements are forthwith concluded. But why a man like Mr. Zukor, a master furrier who would not have permitted his cutters to fashion a single garment without guarding every stroke and seam, should not investigate the progress of his pictures and curb the extravagances of his directors, is a mystery I cannot fathom. Of course, if the director turns out a series of failures, he is himself turned out, but the mischief has been done. From the charges of the Federal Trade Commission it would appear that the big producers have a different and more summary method of preventing failures: they would, by virtue of a complete monopoly of all branches of the industry, force the small exhibitor to accept their films, or close his doors.

On the whole the distinctions between the autocrats of the studio are of no great consequence. The subtlest is Ernst Lubitsch whose pictures are admirably put together, coherent from start to finish, and devoid of wasted space. Rex Ingram has the best taste in sets and backgrounds, and Erich von Stroheim is the least frivolous. Von Stroheim, with a Germanic passion for detailed accuracy, has more than once demonstrated the impossibility of rendering the emotional effects of literature by pictorial methods. In *Greed* he exerted a truly heroic effort to capture the epic quality of Mac-

Teague, spending years on the job, duplicating the scenes and following the geography of the novel with the utmost patience and exactitude. The result? An ineffably dreary performance containing not a single flash of the genius of Frank Norris. D. W. Griffith, the "master of the movies," has done nothing in recent years to justify the title. We must thank him for the "superfilm," the "close-up," the "long-shot," and the "fade-out," and for the excruciating *Way Down East*. His latest pictures are the usual trash. I quote from his address to the American Motion Picture Advertisers: "What a tremendous instrument for truth! . . . This is no business to joke about, to speak covertly about, to be ashamed of. It is as beautiful and sweet and decent and clean as any business or any profession has ever been in the history of the world." The one lonely exception, not only among directors but among actors, is Charlie Chaplin of whom I shall have more to say presently.

The movie, as I have pointed out, is the only art which cannot, or will not, use intelligence. In the business are a number of subordinate functionaries who have grown up in the studios, and who must undoubtedly have practicable ideas for improving the films, but as yet they have been unable to subdue the commercial instincts of their employers. The present tendency of the producers is to make a show of outside talent and to trade on the publicity of best-selling novels; and greedy authors have heeded the call expecting to conquer the new medium without effort and to repeat their popular successes instantly. But the literary folk have fared badly. Clayton Hamilton, as a critical adviser, was a total loss; Rex Beach failed to grasp the mechanics of the art; Mary Roberts Rinehart was shipwrecked; Fannie Hurst, after deprecating the butchery of her masterpieces — which she had sold to the movies for tidy sums — now condescends to write prize-winning trash; and the versatile Hergesheimer, composing directly for the screen, has done nothing to be proud of; the great Maeterlinck's only script was thrown into the scrap-heap; and Michael Arlen, who had no sooner disembarked than Mr. Jesse Lasky begged him to accept fifty thousand dollars for the promise of a *scenario* or two, is on probation. The idol of Mayfair is a canny purveyor and should have no difficulty in supplying Hollywood with amoristic morsels. I cannot do justice to the solitary eminence of Director Rupert Hughes, the only man of letters who has found himself in the movies — you will have to see his picture.

It is not surprising, when we remember that about seven hundred feature-films were put in circulation last year, that the producers should be desperate for material. They will buy anything at any price. If a popular novel or play has no pictorial value, it is consigned to the *scenario* staff for treatment; if, as sometimes happens, it is a work of honest purpose, it will probably have to be rewritten anyhow in order to pass the vice-fiends of the various States. (In Massachusetts, for instance, a movie baby may be born out of wedlock on week-days but not on the Sabbath!) The absurdly inflated prices paid for raw material have had a debasing effect on literature, and latterly, men and women of more than ordinary ability have sold themselves to the sensational movie stuff. On the other hand we have the proud, irrelevant whining of certain authors against the filmed versions of their books. What do they expect? The better the book the worse the movie. Isolated cases like *Greed* or *Anna Christie*, in which the director has conscientiously striven to preserve the spirit of the original, have no relation to literature, and little or no validity as pictures.

In the æsthetics of the movie we are confronted with several interesting problems. Those who have followed the films — and who has not? — must long ago have lost patience with the ambition of the directors to re-create works of fiction. Characterization in the novel is an intricate and laborious process, fundamentally a psychological development. Slowly, through devices varying with the temperament of the author, a figure is set in motion, begins to move and breathe, and to attain a life of its own. Exactly how a character acquires stature and reality is a debatable issue — the author himself is unable to analyse his talent and is as likely to fail as not — but one thing is certain: the novelist must have power over his medium, which is verbal, must have a feeling for words and the ability to convert them into living instruments of expression. But I doubt if the most acute and sympathetic reader ever visualizes a character: he responds to that part of a created figure which is also himself, but he does not actually see his hero. (Ask a dozen readers to describe the physical appearance of Hardy's Tess, and note the results.) For this reason all illustrations are disappointing. I am pretty familiar with Don Quixote, but I cannot somehow project him into the external world; I have seen many drawings of the old knight, but none of them agrees with my own conception which, having been shaped by words, is not graphically clear. The painter, if he is more than a mechanical copyist, in creating a character, infuses himself into the work, thus constructing a Don Quixote utterly at variance with all the Don Quixotes in the world.

And yet the moving-picture companies persist in trying to reproduce literature, and will spend millions of dollars on a single venture. The most that can possibly be extracted from a piece of fiction is the bald outline of action, and the plots of distinguished novels, as the movies have conclusively shown, are melodramatic. Nor will the directors get it into their heads that the backgrounds of novels are also literary creations, and that the camera cannot, by transcribing "on location" the hills and vales of Dorset, convey the scenic atmosphere of Thomas Hardy. When the stars are assembled and smeared with grease paint, the director lashes them into action, and the one-eyed camera obediently registers their grotesque contortions, catching only the externals of form, and giving us, instead of reality, a negative world of silhouettes. The movie bears as much relation to literary characterization as photography does to mural painting. Its trials in this direction may be attributed, first, to the energetic ignorance of directors who esteem themselves artists, and second, to the avarice of producers who, as I have already pointed out, have learned the value of pandering to the appetites of women.

It has remained for a man of genius to discover the obvious province of the movies, and to employ the "silent drama" as an original vehicle. Charlie Chaplin has never had any delusions about the "high art of the screen"; with him it has always been a low and earthy art, and he has proceeded to perfect it on that basis. A born actor trained in the Keystone Comedy school where *scenarios* were unnecessary and plots superfluous, he had the wit to see that the essence of the movie (does not the word itself suggest it?) is pantomime, and that it must create its own effects, and supply its own material, independent of the other arts. Chaplin has sensibly avoided the emotional values of literature; his films are practically empty of narrative; and his plots, if they can be so called, are only wandering chains of comic situations in which his genius for clowning is allowed full play. He is content to be himself, not once, to my knowledge, having attempted to disguise his personality in the character of another, or to interpret a rôle which, without words, simply does not exist. Like all great comedians he is not above coarseness; the humour of his pictures cannot be translated into words, and his curious antics, when described, are childish and nonsensical. But to see him at his best — in parts of *The Pilgrim* — is to enjoy the most intelligent entertainment the movies have yet provided. The recent apotheosis of Chaplin was to be expected. Dilettantes and critics joined in the hymn of sanctification, and the ablest of our clowns became a conquering god. In *The Gold Rush* there are signs that Chaplin is beginning to feel the burden of his greatness and to listen to the praise which designates him as "a man of sorrows whose pathetic feet express the eternal suffering of mankind." Let us hope that he will stick to his coarseness and not be persuaded by the quack æsthetes to produce Euripides.

The fact that the movie has achieved its most interesting results in comedy does not imply that it is limited to this field. *The Last Laugh*, a German film shown in New York last spring, though egregiously sentimental, was an excellent piece of pantomime, and could not have been conceived in any other form. On a larger scale we have the spectacular picture, the movement of crowds, pageantry, and historical episodes, all of which might be very pleasing to the eye but for the directors. The average director's imagination runs to the three-ring circus. Incapable of inventing a sequence of events, or exposing consistently and without deviation the ideas of others, he drags in everything that is queer and costly. What an edifying spectacle could be evolved from certain phases of American history, if the director could be made to understand their significance, and to tell the truth in orderly pantomime! But he would probably resort to trick effects and to the miracles of photography. The technical sleights of the movies are legitimate and amusing, but as imagination they are on the same plane as the magic of Houdini.

In its present state of criminal extravagance the moving-picture industry will not get anywhere. Of the annual harvest of feature-films, how many will ever be seen again? If the experiment of the International Film Arts Guild, in reviving old pictures, has been of any service, it has proved that the movies, in the last ten years, have made little or no progress. True, the photography has gained in clarity and mechanical finish, but it has lost some of its original honesty, just as the slippery modern print has departed from the dignity of the old daguerreotype. Let us compare *The Birth of a Nation* with *The Big Parade*, two pictures of the same *genre*. Technically the latter is the better picture, but it employs the same conventional sentiment and the same pictorial devices as its prototype, accomplishing in a more expert fashion the discoveries of Mr. Griffith. It is undeniable that the war material in *The Big Parade* is, if not more moving, inestimably more accurate than the carnage of *The Birth of a Nation*. This is because Mr. Laurence Stallings, the author of the *scenario*, wrote from experience, and experience bitterly remembered, and used his whole intelligence to impart the hideous realism of the modern shambles. The scenes, I take it, are identical with those in France, and the attacks manœuvred in conformity with military science, but the horrors of war do not come out. Photography is far too thin a medium to carry such horrors, and one leaves the theatre remembering, not the agonies of the combatants, but beautiful flashes of pantomime and odd scraps of comedy.

Nor is there a vast æsthetic difference between *The Cabinet of Dr. Caligari* and *The Beggar on Horseback*, to name two pictures of the most eccentric type. Both seek to arouse bizarre emotional effects by means of complex technical machinery, and both are freak pictures. The Caligari film is more striking in its sets which are arranged in broken planes in the manner of the Cubists, and which give an inkling of what a real artist might do if allowed to coöperate with a director.

The truth is that the movie of to-day is intrinsically the same old ten, twenty, and thirty cent show, and will increase in sumptuous prosperity as long as the public is willing to finance the mad expenditures of the producers. Not until actors, directors, and all concerned are paid in proportion to their worth, and intelligence is displayed in the selection and manipulation of materials, shall we behold any progress.

THE ANATOMY OF JAZZ

By DON KNOWLTON

*Don Knowlton, who graduated from Western Reserve, is the son of
Fanny Snow Knowlton, the composer. Although he received a thorough
training in classical music, upon the publication of "Alexander's Ragtime Band" he turned his attention to jazz, learning to play various
musical instruments, and for two years was a member of a jazz
orchestra. He is now a publicity expert in Cleveland.*

I

FIVE years ago it was proper to loathe jazz. To-day it is the
smart thing to hail it as the only truly American contribution to
music, and to acclaim it as Art. Either attitude is ridiculous.

Jazz bears much the same relationship to music as does the limerick
to poetry. It is a form of musical expression, and an extremely circumscribed form. In fact, I know of no other variety of musical
composition in which so little latitude of construction is allowed.
In this country to-day the form has been developed to the ultimate,
within its limitations — but that fact does not make jazz as an
institution worthy of a special corridor in the musical hall of fame.
Of the thousands of jazz compositions most are abominable — as
are most limericks. There have been some excellent "rags" written,
just as there are a few good limericks, and these are deserving of
recognition as being especially fine pieces of workmanship, considering the vehicle of expression used. But Hamlet could not well die
to a limerick, and neither may the æsthete soar on the wings of jazz.
The devotee of Wagner and Stravinsky who condemns jazz uncon-
ditionally displays merely an utter ignorance of its purposes and
structure; and the "jazz-hound" who cries that American "blues"
should follow Beethoven in the musical encyclopedias betrays a total
loss of musical perspective.

II

For all the publicity so efficiently instigated by Irving Berlin, it
seems probable that the basic principle of jazz — namely, its essential rhythmic exaggeration — is a contribution of the negro.

Syncopation in popular music first came into evidence in the old "coon" songs of minstrel-show days.   Remember *But I Want Them Presents Back?*   Next came such childishly simple attempts as *Under the Bamboo Tree* and *Rainbow*, songs that could not attain popularity to-day, which succeeded because they were the first to stress syncopation in a form which could be reached by the masses.   Then along came Irving Berlin — and we were off.   The ragtime piano player and then the jazz orchestra developed, until to-day we have "symphonic" jazz.

Old-timers such as *Alexander's Ragtime Band, When the Midnight Choo-Choo Leaves for Alabam, Omar Khayyam,* and *Maple Leaf Rag* began to establish a conventional form for jazz.   Since that time there has been no essential change in its structure, the development having been confined almost entirely to internal elaboration.

The idea of exaggerated syncopation was first presented to America in a more or less respectable way.   "Coon songs" and real negro melodies were not considered damaging to one's social or business reputation.   Syncopation itself had a well-developed and honorable lineage at the time.   If the socially elect had adopted syncopation, it might have been *comme il faut* from the outset, and we might have heard the Boston Symphony Orchestra rendering a legitimate jazz symphony years ago.   But musicians of the radical type were developing scientific dissonance.   Strauss discovered new uses for the cymbals, and Bloch conducted a series of fashionable experiments in the resistivity of the human ear.   So syncopation was picked up by the dance hall, cabaret, and vaudeville group, who of course turned it toward their particular purposes.

Jazz has won and held universal popularity, I believe, not merely because of its exploitation by the lower musical order, but because of its own intrinsic qualities.   These are: first, fundamental rhythm; second, simple harmonies; third, standardized form.

Note that I have not included "melody" in my mention of the intrinsic qualities of jazz.   This is not in the least because melody is not essential, but because it belongs to jazz no more and no less than it belongs to any other form of music.   To write a story, one must have something to say: this is the tune.   Shall it be said in ballad, symphony, anthem, or blues?   Jazz is one form of expression; the tune is the thing expressed.   The effect depends vastly more upon the method adopted than it does upon the tune itself.   Take that good old Methodist hymn *Shall We Gather at the River*. Play it on the organ, with its old-fashioned draggy sonorousness; snap it into a Boy Scout March; try it for a one-step; slow it up, syncopate it, throw in a few minors where majors used to be, and you will almost think you have a "Mammy" song. Everything in music has a tune, otherwise it could not move from beginning to end. Jazz tunes may be distinctive, but I doubt it. As Sigmund Spaeth has pointed out in *The Common-Sense of Music*, many of the best jazz melodies have been appropriated from the old masters. Composers have always had for one of their mottoes, "Never throw away an old melody." But the tune does not make jazz. On the contrary, jazz breathes life into many a tune which alone could not carry itself for four measures without dying of stagnation.

It requires no mental effort to enjoy jazz. A moronic musical intelligence can absorb without effort all that it has to offer. The text of the "lyrics" appears to be incidental. The musical form of the thing is what has captivated the masses, because they can understand it. Its simplicity is amazing. The marvel is that so many variations have been accomplished within the prescribed limitations.

For the purposes of this discussion, we will omit the waltz, which is not jazz, and the so-called "ballad." Just how is the typical "rag" built?

III

A popular song stands or falls upon its chorus. Its verse is merely introductory. The standard chorus consists of thirty-two measures, broken into eight phrases of four measures each. At the end of the first sixteen measures is a cæsura. The eight measures following the cæsura usually repeat substantially the theme of measures one to eight (as in *Alexander's Ragtime Band, Jealous, The Girl I Love Belongs to Somebody Else*, and a thousand others), although sometimes this repetition occurs in the last eight measures (as in *Yes, We Have No Bananas*, and *I Want to Be Happy*). In any event, the repetition of the opening refrain is certain. Measures thirteen, fourteen, fifteen, and sixteen end with a rising inflection; measures twenty-nine, thirty, thirty-one, and thirty-two conclude with a positive statement. The musical thought-content of a typical piece may be paralleled crudely in words by the following:

> I like eggs for breakfast —
> Do you like eggs?
> I like eggs for breakfast,
> And eat them every morning.

It requires just about as much literary erudition to digest the above as it does musical intelligence to understand jazz. Hence its popularity.

IV

Jazz harmonies are amazingly standardized. Popular songs (in the chorus, which is all that counts) never change key. They all use thirteen chords or less (with variations in some of them, such as lowering a major third to a minor, or adding that note one tone below the basic note of the chord, which gives direction to the progression). Some songs are built upon three chords (such as *I Want to Be Happy*). Many are based upon four. I know of very few indeed which use all thirteen. Most employ six or seven. No matter how elaborated the modulations in modern "symphonic" orchestration, they are based upon these thirteen chords or less, with the exception of transitions from one piece to another, borrowing from the classical, and similar passages in which the arranger has gone outside the strict field of popular music.

This simplicity of structure of course accounts for the fact that anybody who has any "ear" at all can "fake" jazz. In playing the banjo, mind you, a change of key involves no change of fingering. The player simply slides his hand up or down the neck of the instrument until he strikes the proper basic pitch. There he plays his thirteen chords (with their few variations) exactly as he does in any other key.

The case is much the same with the ukulele, and hence the mail-order advertisements that guarantee "Ukulele Mastered at Home in Six Lessons." The instruction book gives the fingering for the more frequent basic chords, and numbers each. Then it indicates accompaniments, not by note, but by chord number! The "uke" accompaniment to the first eight measures of *By the Light of the Stars* might be written thus:

1 1 1 1 2 2 1 1

each numeral covering one measure.   Naturally, advertisers are careful to pick simple pieces, and do not go into such complications as minors or the chord which the "faker" calls the "barber-shop." But it is actually true that after some five or six hours of application, the business-college beginner can follow on her "uke" by this method such tunes as *Barney Google* or *Follow the Swallow* while father retires to the coal cellar and mother has visions of a Musical Career.

V

Rhythm is the backbone of jazz.   While I hesitate to go so far as some and ascribe a Freudian motivation and a phallic symbolism to jazz, nevertheless, the fact remains that the beat of the tomtom which drives savages into orgiastic ecstasies and the beat of the drum which sets the pace for the dance orchestra are identical.   Jazz serves primitive rhythm on a civilized platter.

Some popular music uses the old *one*-two, *one*-two rhythm (*Oh, Katerina, Parade of the Wooden Soldiers*), but this is not the typical jazz rhythm.   It is simply the old marching time, popular now as always. The real jazz tune goes *um*-pa-*tee*-dle, *um*-pa-*tee*-dle to each measure — four dotted eighths on the accented syllables and four sixteenths on the alternate syllables, to a basic one, two, three, four.

"DOWN HOME RAG"

Upon this foundation are superimposed certain alterations of rhythm which are the true components of jazz.

First comes what I term "anticipation," which consists of a sort of hurrying of the melody, whereby the latter beats the bass to the stroke of the rhythm by a fraction of a second.

Second, is true syncopation.   This, as I have said before, is a well-established musical device and is merely exaggerated in ragtime.

Of itself it does not make ragtime, popular and musical opinion to the contrary notwithstanding. If syncopation created "rag," Brahms's *Lullaby and Good-Night* would be a dance-hall favorite. Syncopation in jazz serves a two-fold purpose: it makes it possible to accent certain words in the "lyrics," as in "I *want* to be happy, I *want* to be happy"; and it attracts the listener's interest by its divergence from the normal, which is maintained in the bass or by the drum — the underlying one, two, three, four, which carries the entire structure. Syncopation is of value not intrinsically, but merely in its variance. Alone, it is meaningless. The irresistible sweep of the fundamental rhythm makes syncopation stand out violently against the background. This is the reason why a jazz tune is so flat and unconvincing in the absence of piano or orchestral accompaniment. The contrast upon which syncopation depends for its startling effect is lacking when only one of the two necessary rhythmic elements is expressed.

"KITTEN ON THE KEYS"

Thirdly, there is the imposition of a *one*, two, three element in rhythm upon the one, two, three, four fundamental. This, I believe, is the only characteristic of jazz which is truly of American — or rather, of Afro-American — origin.

A negro guitar-player once asked me, "You know the difference between primary rag and secondary rag?"

His primary rag was syncopation; his secondary rag was this superimposition of *one*, two, three upon the basic one, two, three, four. Graphically, it may be expressed thus:

1 2 3 1 2 3 1 2	*3 1 2 3 1 2 3 1*
1 2 3 4	1 2 3 4

Although originally presented in the melody as in the *Down Home Rag* and sometimes accentuated there even to-day, as in *Kitten On the Keys*, the idea rapidly shifted from melody into accompaniment and, as it is a rhythmic rather than a melodic principle, it has found its exponents principally in the banjo and the drum. Its true function seems to be one of superimposition upon the melody and primal rhythm alike. The negro guitar-player was right — it is a "secondary rag." And it is this subsidiary *one*, two, three on top of the underlying tempo that makes shoulder-muscles twitch, that bedevils hips, that provokes wiggles and twists on the dance floor, and causes blue-noses to cry out that jazz is a great immoral influence. The soprano saxophone has been blamed for the sins of the secondary rag. In fact, that silvery screecher merely releases impulses which the constant tickling of *one*, two, three upon one, two, three, four has brought clamoring to the surface.

The relegation of this rhythm to the accompaniment is illustrated by the score opposite, showing the opening measures of *Hot Lips*.

The skillful drummer even varies this rhythmic variety. He may omit from the *one*, two, three a stroke in sequence, making it *one*, (blank), three, *one*, (blank), three — or, *one*, two, (blank), *one*, two, (blank) — and so forth. The rhythm may be expressed merely by a *one*, two, three stroke upon a single object (such as the tomtom) or may be accentuated by striking three objects in rotation, such as *cymbal*, tomtom, wood-block, *cymbal*, tomtom, wood-block. Literally beneath this rhythmic superstructure — to be exact, with the drummer's right foot — the fundamental one, two, three, four continues without interruption, setting the pace and creating the tempo-foundation for the entire orchestral effect.

In this connection the references to Krehbiel in Gilbert Seldes' *The Seven Lively Arts* are interesting:

Krehbiel, to be sure — does refer to the "degenerate form" of syncopation which is the basis of our ragtime, and that is hopeful because it indicates that ragtime is a development — intensification, sophistication — of something normal in musical expression. The free use of syncopation has led our good composers of ragtime and jazz to discoveries in rhythm and to a mastery of complications which one finds elsewhere only in the great composers of serious music. In describing the Dahoman war dances at the Chicago World's Fair, Krehbiel says: "Berlioz in his supremest effort with his army of drummers produced nothing to compare *in artistic interest* with the harmonious drumming of these savages. The fundamental effect was a combination of double and triple time, the former kept by the singers, the latter by the drummers, but it is impossible to convey the idea of the wealth of detail achieved by the drummers by means of exchange of rhythms, syncopation of both simultaneously, and dynamic devices."

" HOT LIPS "

Krehbiel caught the thing — a simple superimposition of one rhythm upon another. Yet it is doubtful whether Seldes realized the significance of the very paragraph he quoted. Seldes' chapter, "Toujours Jazz," is delightful in comment, criticism, reference, and deference to the jazzicists of the higher order, but he does not analyze generic jazz structure; nor does he recognize that it is the rhythmic principle (of savage origin) referred to by Krehbiel which has built jazz, much more than the ingenuity, dexterity, or even genius of the individual composer.

This principle I am inclined to regard as rather new to civilized musical thought. Brahms and others have superimposed 1, 2, 3, 4, 5, 6 upon 1, 2, 3, 4 it is true, and pianists with classical educations, who have slipped back into the more profitable lap of jazz, use to-day that device with considerable effect. But never, outside of American ragtime, have I heard the particular *1, 2, 3, 1, 2, 3, 1, 2* upon 1, 2, 3, 4 in dotted eighths and sixteenths, which is so characteristic of jazz.

However, I have never heard native tomtoms calling a jungle tribe to worship or to war.

VI

Jazz has many other standard characteristics, trimmings hung upon the main frame. Among them may be listed what the orchestra player knows as the "break," usually occurring during the cæsura in the middle of the chorus. Here the melody often is sustained upon a single note, usually the fifth, and the balance of the orchestra is enabled to break forth into a sudden spasm of superimposed rhythm.

Borrowing a device from the most approved musical circles, jazz now and then uses dissonance with great effect. It is amusing to see the followers of Strauss and Stravinsky berating the jazzists for employing the very devices which the former apparently most earnest-mindedly admire. Jazz dissonances are simple and few. They are popularly known as "blues." D E-flat G-sharp A is typical.

All this, mind you, takes place within the limitations of thirty-two measures, phrased in eight groups of four measures each — and expressed in thirteen chords or less!

VII

This limitation of form, by the way, has a quite practical excuse entirely aside from the advantage of mass appeal to the musically unintelligent listeners. To make money upon a popular song, the publisher must sell many thousands of copies. His market consists of the million Maggie Smiths who took piano lessons for a year and then "just played."

Maggie will not practice, and her ear is none too good. Her technic is atrocious. She can barely follow a bass, chord, bass, chord, in the left hand, and the melody, together with a few harmony-determining notes, in the right. Consequently the "popular" song is printed for her in kindergarten form, embodying only the fundamental rhythm plus syncopation. The element of "anticipation" is not there; neither is the *one*, two, three superimposed upon the bass, unless it happens to occur in the melody itself. As a result, the popular song as written is a poor thing indeed. Nobody would buy it for its own sake. It must first be popularized by being presented to the public in full form — that is, with the two missing rhythmic qualities included. The trade calls this "song plugging." The public buys a song because it has heard it and liked it — but the printed song which it buys is quite different from the song which it heard. It buys a primer edition only.

The piano player at the sheet-music counter never plays a song as written. She adds (as do all good jazz pianists) "anticipation" and "secondary rag" — she inserts "breaks" and dissonances — she plays three times as many notes as appear upon the printed copy from which she purports to read.

Professional "song pluggers" hired by publishers appear at movies, theaters, dance halls, sheet-music counters, and radio stations, and everlastingly ding the song into the public memory; and of course their accompaniments, piano or orchestral, contain all of the elements of good jazz.

But it is in the dance orchestras that the most complete transformation of a popular song is effected. Have you ever heard a rousing good "rag" at a dance, bought the number at a music counter the next day, taken it home and played it — and wondered why your interest has been caught by such an empty and meaningless succession of noises? The fact is, that the thing you bought at the counter and the thing you heard at the dance were alike in name and skeleton only. The sheet-music edition of the piece bore the same relationship to the orchestration as the framework of a house bears to the completed dwelling.

The man who arranges popular music for dance orchestras is rapidly becoming, in jazz fields, even more important than the composer. It is the arranger who provides life and color and contrasts and lively dissonances and blasts of indigo harmony and contrapuntal runs. He is given a bare stage, and upon it he builds a paradise.

The arranger, while adhering to the formal limitations of jazz, employs in its decoration all of the devices which he can steal from classical music. He opposes progressions with the dexterity of Bach; he snatches a frenzy from Liszt; he borrows a bit of the lyrical purity of Mozart, and inserts Wagnerian crashes in the brass. I recall one orchestration of *Spain*, in which the saxophones carry a pure lead, the piano pounds through the old Spanish rhythm of "L'Amour" in Bizet's *Carmen*, the drum maintains the fundamental one, two, three, four of all ragtime, and the banjo superimposes the "secondary rag." The ingenuity of the arranger is amazing. For the orchestra the simplest piece is built up with the utmost care, and jazz orchestrations are as correctly done, as well balanced and as effective in rendition as are those produced for our symphony orchestras.

The days of playing by ear are rapidly passing. Each man must play his part as written, for it has been carefully calculated with respect to every other part. And not only that — these arrangers, betraying their origins, have inserted, in introductions and "breaks," passages lifted bodily from the classics, which cannot be "faked." Many a time, in the last two years, I have been startled on the dance floor by a measure or two from one of the standard works of Mac-Dowell, Gounod, or Rachmaninoff.

In fact, they are going even farther. Not long ago, at one of Cleveland's noonday dancing places, a thirteen-piece orchestra played the "Storm" from *William Tell* exquisitely. Their rendition retained all of the essential qualities of the original orchestration, altered only to such an extent as to fit the requirements of a small band, and to conform to the essential one, two, three, four rhythm of the dance. At the conclusion of the number, a sweet young office-blossom rushed up to the conductor and gurgled:

"Gee, that's a peach of a number! Can I get it at Woolworth's?"

No, she cannot get it anywhere in a form in which she can play it, for *William Tell* is not built upon a kindergarten structure, and so cannot be reduced to a form of sufficient simplicity to be within reach of Maggie Smith. On the other hand, *Ukulele Lady*, essentially simple, and conforming to standard jazz limitations, can be built up by orchestration to produce an effect surprisingly equivalent in musical values to that of *William Tell*. When Maggie buys and plays *Ukulele Lady*, she is satisfied because the sounds which she makes on her piano are sufficiently similar to her dance-hall recollections to reproduce in her mind, in part at least, the effect of the piece when she first heard it, with all elements included.

VIII

With all this truly able orchestration, why are the "lyrics" of popular songs so inane?

I do not believe that it is because they must be supremely twaddle-some in order to appeal to the masses.   Rather, I think it is because the men who are capable of writing real verse have not been willing to descend to jazz "lyrics," and the latter have been done, not by writers of English, but by musicians, vaudeville actors, and cranks. The popular song writer is notoriously "low-brow."   Years ago, some one started the spoon-hug-kiss-slush theme in ragtime words, and it has stuck, apparently, not so much because the public insisted upon it, as because it was the only theme which was given to the public.   The "lyricists" of jazz knew nothing else.   It was conventional.   That the public would welcome a bit of humor in place of sentimental garbage is evidenced by the success of *Yes, We Have No Bananas*, which not even the most methodical of Methodists can construe as immorally suggestive.   It is the music and not the words which has carried jazz.

A TYPICAL JAZZ " BREAK "
It employs both superimposed rhythm and dissonance

On the other hand — perhaps because the word-writers of popular songs were not sonneteers — the lyrics of jazz possess a quality which makes them infinitely more singable than the words of any other type of song.   They are sung exactly as they would be spoken.   Musical emphasis is identical with conversational accent.   Certainly this is natural and healthy.   In jazz, the jaw-straining soprano cannot yammer through a vocal skinning-the-cat upon what would normally be an unaccented syllable in everyday speech.   The popular song gives each word and each syllable its proper stress — no more, no less.

Obviously, in order to do this, words and music must be written together. The words are not set to music; neither is the music set to words. In this, jazz has followed honorable precedent. To the coincidence of musical and conversational accent the comedies of Gilbert and Sullivan owe much of their enduring popularity. May I recommend that in this respect our modernists of the studio-and-recital aristocracy might well take a leaf from the book of jazz?

IX

The discouraging thing about jazz is the fact that it has been viewed in such false perspective — either condemned completely or inordinately exalted.

The encouraging thing about jazz is that in its orchestrations it is initiating countless thousands into sound principles of harmony and counterpoint, and thus definitely raising the average level of musical intelligence. Snort if you will, but the fact remains that the shop girl who has heard Paul Whiteman has taken a step toward appreciation of Beethoven's Seventh Symphony.

XII. LITERATURE

"WELL READ"

By HENRY SEIDEL CANBY

Henry Seidel Canby (1878–   ) received his education at Yale, and was later a professor of English there. For a time he was an editor of the "Yale Review," and then of the "Literary Review." He is now editor of the "Saturday Review of Literature," a magazine which is influential among the intellectual classes. Besides a textbook on rhetoric, his "Definitions" (1922), a collection of critical essays, is well known.

WHAT is a well-read man? Is he like the "well-dressed" man of the advertisements, who wears exactly what the majority of expensive dressers are putting on at the moment? Bacon had no such meaning in his famous essay. Good reading cannot be merely imitative, though it may be inspired. Second-hand tastes are not tastes at all, but appetites. No one will quarrel with these platitudes.

But another platitude does arouse controversy. Beware of the man of one book, says the old aphorism. Whenever a new book is published, read an old one, is a variant of the same statement. Stick to the pure gold of literature and let the tinsel go, is just a third wording of the same idea, which stated in plain English says that the well-read man is he who reads nothing but what time has proved to be the best. Beware of him, for he carries a heavy charge drawn from greatness.

These slogans are popular with scholars, teachers, and librarians, and naturally, for they are really the armament of defense complexes. Readers are like sheep, running in herds toward the last grass to turn green, no matter how rank or how thin it is. To read the new is always easy for them, to appreciate the old always difficult. The *Iliad* was never popularized until John Erskine's *Private Life of Helen of Troy* made Homer a novelty, good for the movies. Old books have to be taught; new books teach themselves. Hence, when the scholar speaks his contempt for new books, the rubbish of our times, he is on the defensive. He exaggerates the demerits of his own day in order to emphasize by contrast the classic excellence which most readers so willingly neglect.

What then is a well-read man? Certainly not a reader who reads only modern books. He has no background and no standards of comparison. He gets the milk of good books, but not the cream, and he is the ready dupe of every shallow imitator. No one disputes this.

But the opposite is equally true. The man who reads no new books is not and cannot be well read. He may spend his nights with Addison and his days with the *Divine Comedy*. He may read the *Faerie Queene* three times or work upon the Greek tragedians until the barriers of language fall. He may be soundly based in all the great classics, but if he reads no modern books he is not well read. If the greatest clerks are not the wisest men, this is one of the reasons — their knowledge sometimes stops short of their own times. And if criticism written by scholars has so often been wrong, this again is one reason why.

The question can be argued either backward or forward. The only age which a man knows of his own knowledge and with some certainties at least, is his own. He cannot see it as a whole, but he knows some parts, and knows them with indisputable accuracy and with an emotional rightness that is more than reason. Our best history is documented guessing, our best interpretations of earlier literature miss much that Shakespeare or Milton or Goethe meant to their own ages. A reader must read in the light of his own first-hand knowledge of life, and the less he knows of life, the less he will get from the vital heart of the classics. This does not mean that the reader of Sophocles should attend incest cases in the local police court. It does mean that the perception of contemporary life, which to a devoted reader will most often be focussed by modern books, must be vivid, if he is to see the gold of earlier writers as more than dead metal.

Or put it another way, and assert that literature is a continuous process without breaks, and therefore without a point at which classics cease and "modern rubbish" begins. Academic critics in every generation have spoken of such a point as if it really existed. Usually it is indicated in the youth of the speaker: sometimes in the century just past. There is no such point; there is only a change in focus. Books get too near us; we see too many of them; no one has provided glasses for us; it is easier to talk of modern rubbish which began to accumulate after the last great writer died.   This of course is nonsense, very solemn nonsense.

We will challenge, therefore, the title of well read in any one, no matter how erudite, how steeped in the best of earlier literatures, who has no discrimination in, because no vital contacts with, modern literature.   Among English readers we will distrust the critic of Shakespeare who has not read Shaw, as much as the critic of Shaw who has not read Shakespeare.   We will listen to no lectures on the psychology of Racine by critics who have not read in Freud and Jung (imagine Racine not reading there!).   Nor are we more interested in the philosophy of behaviorists who know only behaviorism.

But are there intellectual hermits in our civilization?   Does not the man of one book read modern novels on the sly?   Is not the scholar who despises modern stuff and nonsense deterred by the cost, the number, and difficulty of judging new books without the guidance from tradition to which he is accustomed?   Is the contempt for one's own time in literature only a pose?   It may be, or it may be just the scholar's way of saying that most new books, in the light of eternity, are rubbish, which is too obvious to argue about.   But if a pose, it is a pose dangerous to good judgment.   Those who despise their own literature will never understand it, and if they do not comprehend their own times, what certainty, or probability even, that they will be masters of antiquity!

1) Truth
2) Beauty

THE NOVEL AND THE SPIRIT

By ZONA GALE

Zona Gale (1874–   ) is mainly known as a novelist, having been a writer since 1906. She occasionally writes short stories and essays. As a dramatist, too, she has gained some renown, her play, "Miss Lulu Bett," a dramatization of her novel of that name, receiving the Pulitzer Prize for 1920. A few of her better-known works are "Friendship Village" (1906), "The Loves of Pelleas and Etarre" (1908), "Birth" (1918), and "Faint Perfume" (1923).

A FEW years ago it was the habit of the New York newspapers to instruct their reporters that, whatever the nature of the story which they brought to the city room, one rule must be regarded: the story must be reduced to the briefest possible statement and this statement would constitute the first paragraph of the newspaper account.

Thus: Clarence Thorne, eight-year-old son of Mr. and Mrs. C. E. Thorne, living at 500 West 500th Street, was run over by a sprinkling cart yesterday afternoon at four o'clock as he was playing before his parents' door, and was instantly killed.

Recently I read in the *New York Times* an account of a similar accident and the account ran like this:

The children living in West 500th Street wish that yesterday had not been a holiday because, if it had not been so, little Clarence Thorne, eight-year-old son of Mr. and Mrs. Clarence Thorne living at No. 500, would have been busy at school with his books instead of playing at hopscotch in the street before his parents' door where yesterday afternoon at four o'clock he met his death.

This opening paragraph tells the story, to be sure, briefly and yet in so different a tone from its first statement that the paragraph may be said to regard a new ruling.   Very few years have crept between the two fashions but the whole feeling of the treatment has changed.

Certain habits of the novel vary quite as nimbly.   As in *Père Goriot*, when the misfortunes of the Pension Vauquer have gathered and multiplied, one guest after another has dropped away, even that admirable Vautrin of whom they made a convict, and to Madame Vauquer, receiving blow after blow, the final one is administered by

Sophie, the maid, who enters and cries out that the cat is missing: "Madame, I have not seen Mistigris all day." "Ah, this! . . ." cries Madame. The poor creature lifted her hands to her head. . . .

Imagine Mr. Sinclair Lewis seeking to heighten a situation by a device like that. In such an hour Mr. Lewis would be far more likely to introduce Sophie saying that the green grocer had come for his order and would Madame have beans.

But however the mode of expression of a news story may vary, the character of the news itself remains unaltered. News is news. All the news is the news. News may be colored or suppressed but to the city room and the public it is none the less news and has remained essentially the same since news-writing has attained a professional status. It is only recently that the novel has attained to this honest estate. For though the novel has been slowly extending its technical frontiers, changing its style even as the newspaper, yet it is only of late that the novel has, so to say, begun to try to include all the news.

It is a great moment in any art when the artist transfers his attention from the extension of his method to the extension of his material. From a preoccupation with technical areas and rebellion at their limitations, the novelist seems now to have come to the unique delight of the artist, namely, such strong excitement in the presence of life that he must suppress that excitement. And if it is said that he has always been doing this, yes, he has done this for crises, for moments of extreme action, for acute situations, for the comedy, the tragedy, the zeniths, and the nadirs; but never before has he done this for life's sheer deadly death-dealing routine. As a gatherer of materials he now rivals the newspapers and is saying: "*All* the news for the novel, whether the public knows it as news or not." He is on his way from the old artificial selectiveness to a new selectiveness of still unknown standards.

Consider these three family groups and their comparative value to the fiction writers of to-day and yesterday:

The setting for the first is a little house where lives alone a man in the eighties, alert, humorous, tolerant, well, who refuses to give up his home of a lifetime to go to live with children and grandchildren in the same town. "Here I stay," he says decisively, "I will go forth and back but here I stay." And among all the many members of that family there is a relationship so tender that it would not be welcome material for any modern novelist. — Over the hill are three or four houses tenanted by members of a second family and these are continually at war. They do not admire one another's in-laws and a pending property distribution darkens the sky. Winds of bitterness and clamor rock those houses and the town hears the impact. Rich material this, for any novelist of any period. — But now in the "residence part," as the townsfolk say, there is a third group of whom the town has a stock observation: "Aren't the Blanks a lovely family?" In this family are the father, a business and church pillar of hackneyed composition; the mother who does her best as a matter of course and never questions either; the three adult daughters, potentially charming women, without the initiative or the independence to accept life; and the one adult son Gracchus — a model. "Gracchus Blank is such a nice man," says the town. In that home the thoughts of 1895 are household words. A patriarchal family, with money. And the town says: "Aren't the Blanks a lovely family?"

Now of these three families the first, the tender family, and the second, the bitter family, have often furnished legitimate news for the novelist. So has the third, the patriarchal family, *as viewed by the townspeople*. But the novelist of to-day has discovered the breakfast table and the luncheon table and the evening lamp of that third family, not in crises, but day by day. And he has discovered what goes on within the pillar and the painstaking mother and the three daughters and Gracchus, the model, judged, not by the standards of the town, but to some extent by the standards of the new knowledge concerning renunciation and repression and hypocrisy and business and the church. And the transvaluation of that patriarchal family thus requires a new geometry and all but requires another space. Not, observe, that family in crises so much as that family at breakfast, living its routine life much as you and I live ours.

Of course the novelist has always handled such a family if he could satirize it, blur it, trick it, caricature it. But to record it has not interested him. Indeed under the old theology, the old sociology, the old psychology, he could not record it because he did not see it. So he was content to cover circumstance with something of the bright veil which we throw about the late doings of the dead.

Especially has he been content to use those bright veils in the ceremonies incident to his two most ancient incantations. Two valid incantations the novel has always known, the novel of every land which knows the novel: namely, romantic love in an exhaustless number of colorful arrangements; and moral aspiration. On these virtually all novels have depended for their breath. Love and honor.

And among us these two enchantments have been pronounced in but one tongue and according to one tradition, the Anglo-Saxon. Not only has the American novel clung steadfastly to these two interests but for years it never departed from the Anglo-Saxon interpretation of these two interests. Now of late the American novelist has made two discoveries.

The first discovery is that the American novel may treat of romantic love and moral aspiration not according to the Anglo-Saxon tradition but according to the Anglo-Saxon habit of life — quite another matter.

The second discovery is that love and idealism are after all only two of the factors of existence; and that a large part of even the Anglo-Saxon life is occupied with neither the one nor the other.

Here are thus opened to the novelist masses of fresh material in whose treatment, so far as the Anglo-Saxon habit of life is concerned, it is impossible for him to be imitative. It is the opening up of a new country. His country, his own people as they are and not as they *Realism* think they are. His native sources of supply.

These native sources of supply are not identical with 1776 and 1849 and 1865 and 1917. Nor, in spite of the sins of many, do they depend upon the use of bad English. Gradually in New England, in Virginia, in Indiana, in Kansas, in California, in New York, mine after mine of these native supplies has begun to yield its peculiar ore, an ore not so much dependent upon the dynamite of plot as upon a mere surface shovel to reveal its shining. For it is merely the immemorial richness of human relationship as touched specifically by two influences. One, and that one of lesser importance, is regional color. The second and inestimably the more vital is the national genius. Regional color has often been far too thickly overlaid, has become the "local discoloration" into which Wilde saw local color degenerating. To the national genius the novel of any nation will always be delivered.

The distinctive fashion in which the desire for growth and change expresses itself is the manifestation of the genius of a nation. In the

American national genius we have a spirit now considerably crippled but still recognizably at one with the spirit of the colonies and therefore now definitely at variance with many traditions, both native and world traditions, crystallized in unforeseen forms. For it seems that the right of the individual to life, liberty, and the pursuit of happiness is not limited, as we had earlier supposed, by his politics and his religion. And with this emphasis the national novel is now concerned, in common with the novels of the rest of the world. The novelist who is creative is bound to extend the principles of the national genius and is found applying it to all else which affects the growth of the individual: Marriage, the great American home, relatives, institutions, conventions, traditions, and the accepted virtues in the routine of his civilization. But if crude aspects of this routine are presented by him, or crude characters questioning this routine at any point, somebody is going to say: "I don't like that book. It isn't about pleasant people. I shouldn't care to know them. Why write about them?" Conceivably it may not be about pleasant people. What are we going to do about it? Change the novel or change the people?

Recently in an evening of discussion on the English novel I heard a distinguished professor of science declare that all he wanted of a novel was help in forgetting himself. That seems a crass confession akin to one that might be made by a devotee of the motion picture. Developed drama or a symphony does not help one to forget oneself — they deepen one's sensibilities. It is this which one may ask of any art. It is this which one may ask of the novel. In that case the man of science was right, though not in the way that he meant. For to deepen one's sensibilities is of course to take one out of one's lesser self into one's wider incarnations.

It is precisely this process which, by a method known to the most elementary logic, the modern English novelists including the American novelists have more or less unconsciously begun to attempt. See, they say, not your greater incarnation but its opposite, for so long not considered news for the novel at all. Read of the complacent deaths which you live; if you like, count them — if you can. And thus drop deeper into your pit where you may better see the star of our potential life. Of course as a matter of fact they say nothing of the sort. They merely let us enter the dark and they leave us there to dream of the light if we have it in us.

The following is quoted from a recent American novel.

"The butcher had a hooked nose and when he smiled his nose seemed to press down his thick brown moustache that framed his even teeth so beautifully. He settled his apron over his stomach and gazed at her hungrily above the glass top of the counter as though he were trying to hypnotize her into buying some of the coral pink sausages which reposed beside a block of ice in the transparent case. . . . The meat shop was white as death. It smelled of blood and saw-dust. . . . 'I want a — can you give me a nice rib roast to-day? What do you ask for those hens?' Mrs. Farley always hesitated when she spoke. Her vague squinting eyes traveled undecidedly over the big pieces of meat, the shoulders, the forelegs, the haunches, . . . the fowls dangling in a row a little before the meat. 'I will take two of the hens,' said Mrs. Farley. 'Be sure you give me fat ones,' she added frowning. She fumbled . . . for the money. She made her way through the bitter-smelling gloom." And so on.

Intolerable, certainly. But the novel did not manufacture the butcher-shop. It merely confessed it. Or this:

"Dr. Beach had gone but the nurse was still in the room. She had her back turned towards the door and was folding up some clothes. The gas flame had been extinguished. The window curtains were open. Objects in the room were plainly visible throwing no anchorage of shadow. Lawrence went towards the bed. He set his feet down carefully as if he were afraid of being heard. When he reached her he saw that she had not moved. She would never move. A sob of agony and relief shook him. He kneeled by the bed. She had not moved. Stillness revolved about him in eternal motion."

Obviously *The Narrow House* did not manufacture that terrible sob of agony and relief. Or the terrible commonplace of the story which led up to it. Our novels have been accustomed for long to the good taste of hypocrisy. We have never been willing to admit life in art any more than in life.

However, there is now no hypocrisy, there are no veils, there is not even good taste in the novels intent on leading us into the dark and leaving us there to listen to its terrible breathing. All the news about living goes into these novels. And it is with this wholesale process that the use of the commonplace is concerned. In a majority of the realistic American novels of to-day we have a voice not of evil but of the commonplace.   It is as if all the banalities of our lives — brushes, combs, coat-hangers, the defiling and scouring of dishes, the idiotic recreations, the stodgy generalizations, the sad commercialism, the tragic nothings which collect about us were suddenly to cry out in a single voice in these books.   And you hear the naïve antiphonal chorus: "I don't like those books. . . . I wouldn't care to know the people."   It is wholly unimportant whether or not we like the people. In some of our moments all of us are those people.   Such novels are merely saying: "Look at us."   And why should not the realistic novel say that which is being said by a laboring music, a fourth dimensional art, and an ambiguous social order: "Look at us.   Us gods, fallen into more kinds of pits than seem possible."   These are no trumpet voices, no pulses of propaganda.   They are mere recording voices, conversational, table-talking voices saying: "My dear gods, not only in your crises but at your very breakfasts you are in a pit of your digging."

We have, then, in the American novel of to-day the facing of the Anglo-Saxon habit of life, the admission that it concerns itself with other things than love and aspiration, a tardy turning to our native sources of supply, the recognition of the value of the commonplace, and at last an honest expression of the national genius.   But is there anything which the American novel signally lacks?   What other material, in what way conditioned, might the novel require in its business of imaginatively recording us?   Are there any sources of materials which we here in America are neglecting?   Is there any omission by which we are flawing our fiction as hypocrisy once flawed it?   Has the American novel a malady?

The malady of our novels is an immemorial malady, namely, their lack of power to express beauty.   Beauty as a force.   Inhering beauty. Almost, one adds, incommunicable beauty.

"Beauty old yet ever new, eternal voice and inward word."   The momentary lift and urge which comes from the reading of that line carved on the New York library façade, what novel can ever capture and sustain that?   Perhaps it cannot yet be sustained in a novel, cannot even be borne by us, as it could not be borne to see a god.   And yet it is a part of life, operative in beings.   And there is that other line carved on the same façade: "But above all things truth beareth

away the victory." Without beauty a record of truth is like the
Borglum gargoyle at Princeton — the ill-equipped thing, having
one arm and one wing. The novel which has not beauty has but
one aspect of truth. And where in the American novel have we
beauty?

We have it occurring here and there in volumes which will present
themselves at once — well-remembered bits from Mrs. Wharton,
from Howells, from James; from a half dozen of the moderns. Something of beauty lurks in the work of many whom we moment by moment recall. But not enough beauty. Beauty has never yet been
captured even approximately by any of them. Not captured, one
may say, so nearly in the novel as Henry Adams captured it in "the
Hall of the Dynamos" — and there at the last it eluded him too.
In the novel as America has developed it, there is offered as yet no
veiled wonder.

As between that which we called beauty in the novel fifty years
ago and phases of that which we call merely realism now, you and I
may prefer the merely realistic, phases of which indeed may have
become our idea of beauty. Beauty changes its form. Consider one
worn instance of beauty, an instance to which we were long accustomed to refer as the loveliest chapter in the Victorian novel —
the meeting of Richard Feverel and Lucy by the weir. We still love
it but do we not love it indulgently, as we love Cruikshank? Lift
beside it a page of Conrad, a mere hurrying wing of a sail in the dark
and brooding figures black against a red moon, intent in talk which
is half eloquent elision — and we know that beauty, such as we have,
has changed its form. Or in *The Rescue*, the meeting of the two
women, the catching up of the reality behind the racial difference,
the reaching up to an evolutionary meaning, the dramatization of
the cleft cut by centuries of breeding, the delicate shadowing forth of
all that is to come, the fascination of the fragile yet firm effects won
by every flawless sentence; and from restraint that always rhythmic
clip back to the gorgeous tapestry of the tropics, all this sustained with
other and yet other strands interwoven — the unconscious genius of
love in Linyard, the genius of his friend of the one great passion; the
whole forever pointing, pointing to the inevitable imperious — but
how melodramatic! — conclusion: "Steer north!" This is beauty
as we know it now in the novel; and incidentally it is of the essence

of Conrad. By it we mean infinitely more than the beauty of a mosaic. We mean the beauty of an organism.

But even organic beauty such as is fundamental to *The Rescue* is to be transcended. There is beauty already actually incarnate in life, but in novels seldom operative and never treated as casually existent, like flowers. For refinements of human conduct have run far ahead of their reflection in the novel — the novel is still intent on crude aspects of behavior already by at least a measurable proportion of the race left behind.

To be sure, the use of the Ten Commandments as direct fictional motives has been outgrown. Characters in fiction who ordered their lives under the conscious stimulus of the Ten Commandments would be ridiculous. The Ten Commandments as immediate dictators of action obviously have no literary value. It is only in that area that lies beyond precept, in the shadowy caves of cross current and counter current that the novel can employ them at all.

But among these derivatives the novel seems usually to seize upon crass examples. Witness that highest moment in *The Rescue* — Linyard's resolute "Steer north!" The moment when the yacht has left the island and has taken away all that Linyard cared for in the world:

... Carter approached him and spoke quietly: "The tide has turned and the night is coming on. Hadn't we better get away from these shoals, sir?" ...
Linyard came out of his absorption with a deep tremor of his powerful frame like the shudder of an uprooted tree.
"How was the yacht heading when you lost sight of her?" he asked.
"South, as near as possible," answered Carter. "Will you give me a course to steer for the night, sir?"
Linyard's lips trembled before he spoke, but his voice was calm. "Steer north," he said.

Here is one of the exalted moral beauties of the novel — renunciation. And yet in *The Rescue* — and how much more patently in the novels of any other — what a grandiose gesture it is. "Steer north" is clear melodrama. Renunciation represents a stage in human conduct, but it may be a crude stage. We have James and Conrad as apostles of renunciation and on their heels comes a psychology isolating and defining repression so that already there dawns for us the gospel of transmutation; not to deny or to renounce but to transcend; not to waste force but to transform it; not to thwart but to exceed; to turn passion into power. Here are fields for the fortitude and the delicacy of the novelist beside which undiscriminating renunciation is as crude as blind obedience. Here fall *nuances* of creative conduct beside which "Steer north" bears an odor of bad taste, insisting too much — as does the Golden Rule, that precept for the child in process of becoming so sensitized that he will do unto others the right for its own sake. But these and their like are favorite nobilities of the novel — the glorified detective story with a man himself as both culprit and keeper; or of late as pleased fugitive from the whole case.

Now there are in the world countless persons of humor and variety for whom certain crude moral struggles no longer exist. There are those in whose conduct money questionably touched could enter no more than murder; by whom the truth is spoken quite as simply and naturally as good English; in whom good faith is not an accomplishment like harp-playing but a function like sight; those in whom the social consciousness is a passion beside which any personal profit can live not even as an impulse; those who do not brawl in their families or shout "me first" in any of its tongues. Those whose reactions are in the main socialized, spiritualized, humanized. And who — the point is here — are conscious of but a quite ordinary functioning. No grandiose gestures from them! Merely records of reaction, rich in humor and misadventure and delight and deep waters; the old, dreaming beyond dreams; youth, with its new æsthetic; the middle generation, understanding neither; folk of pressing preoccupation, inarticulacies, flashes of insight; of heart-breaking misapprehension, memories, inevitabilities; who go re-kindling old fires; what have these tragedies to do with raw "right" and "wrong"? Great areas of living involve for such folk as these no *crude* moral choices at all. But they are rarely admitted to the pages of a modern novel, at least without a fanfare. The moral matter-of-course becomes in the novel heavily featured. Good faith and the social passion, for example, are there employed in isolated self-conscious moments, not called casual but made crucial; or else are challenged, revalued, abandoned.

Eventually we shall have, we must believe, occasional novels taking for granted a certain degree of moral health and going about a brighter business. Indeed this may be the only way in which we shall succeed in getting rid of self-conscious idealism as a root-*motif* of the novel, an idealism to which the Anglo-Saxon novel reader clings as tenderly as the Anglo-Saxon in his daily life likes to believe that he himself clings. We shall be rid of this *motif* not by challenging order or by stopping in the welter on this side, but by writing of these who have transcended chaos.

"Do you not see," offers the devotee of the "red-blooded" novel, "with the use of such materials you'd have no novel? Because you'd have no struggle."

But we hear the unimaginative say that if the economic struggle were removed, life would not be worth living. The novel in which a crude moral struggle, either lost or won, is the highest *motif* is as primitive in art as is the economic struggle in life.

Also the reader of the red-blooded novel holds that such serene folk are too rare to become suitable fiction material. Even if they are rare they should have in the novel a place as secure as the pathologic and drunken who seem always to be welcome. The sophisticated reader ventures that by such novels we should be dangerously approaching, in the usual spiral of experience, an apotheosis of the condition through which the novel earlier took its way: the perfect family relationship, the perfect lover, perfection *ad nauseam*. Even if this were true it would not matter. The novel must deliver itself to material which bears no relation to self-conscious perfection. It is precisely the weakness of Anglo-Saxon morality and novel-making alike that they can imagine no such occasions.

Yet in experience it is not until "temptations" are left behind that really beautiful living can begin. Previous to that time everything is crude and experimental. All the loveliest *nuances* of relationship lie in the region beyond such voices. Human experiences reveal new faces in this clear air. Whole planes of experience are to be treated for which only the reasonably evolved can possibly furnish material. And always there is the free spirit within in fleeting union with an exquisite and inexorable spirit without — the great inner history, useless, or no more than incidental to the novel so long as the shackles of a crude idealism have not fallen away. Nor need these adventures by any means be confined to the sophisticated, the formally choice. Homely hearts and hearths furnish their high proportion of unconscious fineness — the unconscious, which always matters most. Theirs are the choices to some extent already bred into the race.

The chief concern of the American novel of to-morrow will be to uncover the beauty of our essential commonplace living as the novel of to-day has triumphantly uncovered its ugliness. To uncover beauty not by denying ugliness — the novel of to-day has made that forever impossible — but first by accepting all of life, something which we in America have never been willing to do either in art or in life; and then by a new selectiveness. It is only after a broadly affirmative art arises that a really selective art becomes possible. The modern realistic novel performs the inestimable service of extending our admissions, our affirmations. It has chosen to affirm the commonplace, the sordid, the ugly, because that is most obvious; also it is far easier to record; is, in fine, the natural gesture away from sentimentality and hypocrisy and smugness. Of course the gesture has been too violent. As Conrad says in his *Notes on Life and Letters:*

It seems as if the discovery made by many men at various times that there is much evil in the world were a source of unholy joy unto some of the modern writers. It gives an author — goodness only knows why — an elated sense of his own superiority. And there is nothing more dangerous than such an elation to that absolute loyalty towards his feelings and sensations an author should keep hold of in his most exalted moments of creation.

And it is true that the novel here in America, having at last eaten of the tree of good and evil and of the commonplace — doubtless unknown in Eden — has learned to admit not only that life is not all apples, but has occasionally led us to suppose that orchards bear exclusively cores — or even worms.

There is, however, nothing ultimately pessimistic about our present records of the commonplace. Nothing inexorable is expected by these modern novels to crush us. There is in them no sense of fate — that is not the way of the national genius. Even Mr. Hergesheimer in his records of a debased society, though he is ironic, is still rather wistful. All these novels are merely saying: "Look at us, gods in the pit — but a pit of our own digging. And we are worth digging out. If we were not so we wouldn't have mentioned it."

This so far is the sum of their affirmations; a broad enough extension if one considers the inhibitions of the 'nineties when our novels were either formed for vigilance committees or else were "light."

So in the revealing of life to which every generation of novelists succeeds, their entire work has as yet hardly touched at life's inner magic. And the greatest of this magic, it is predictable, will be the magic of love. It may be against love that the sins of our modern novels are greatest. For it may appear that love is only one aspect of that heightening of faculty and perception towards which the race seems to be tending. Or what if it is true that the extensions of faculty of the race are to be developed by those in the heightened perception known as "being in love"? Consider what may lie in store for us when novels shall reflect these courts. Picture that sort of love story and compare it with our love stories of now, with the hackneyed lure of the Third-at-the-threshold, the use of the pathologic, the drunken. To these the novel is still serving its brief bondage.

Poetry, pictorial and plastic art, and music, all so much more highly developed than fiction or than the society which fiction now depicts, have always risen to that medium of expression which now we seek for the novel — expression which does not merely record beauty but rises to the actual planes of beauty itself.

It is upon these lovely areas that fiction must adventure. It must know beauty, it must be beauty. Not the beauty of the flesh but the beauty of the cell and of its unknown urge. Inhering beauty. The utter beauty of our essential living.

POETIC PEOPLE

By MAX EASTMAN

Max Eastman (1883–   ) is a modern poet, as well as a critic, and a former professor of philosophy at Columbia University. As editor of "The Masses," a liberal periodical, he gave expression to his resentment of the existing social inequality. His best-known work is "The Enjoyment of Poetry" (1913).

A SIMPLE experiment will distinguish two types of human nature. Gather a throng of people and pour them into a ferryboat. By the time the boat has swung into the river you will find that a certain proportion have taken the trouble to climb upstairs in order to be out on deck and see what is to be seen as they cross over. The rest have settled indoors to think what they will do upon reaching the other side, or perhaps lose themselves in apathy or tobacco smoke. But leaving out those apathetic, or addicted to a single enjoyment, we may divide all the alert passengers on the boat into two classes: those who are interested in crossing the river, and those who are merely interested in getting across. And we may divide all the people on the earth, or all the moods of people, in the same way. Some of them are chiefly occupied with attaining ends, and some with receiving experiences. The distinction of the two will be more marked when we name the first kind practical, and the second poetic, for common knowledge recognizes that a person poetic or in a poetic mood is impractical, and a practical person is intolerant of poetry.

We can see the force of this intolerance too, and how deeply it is justified, if we make clear to our minds just what it means to be practical, and what a great thing it is. It means to be controlled in your doings by the consideration of ends yet unattained. The practical man is never distracted by things, or aspects of things, which have no bearing on his purpose, but, ever seizing the significant, he moves with a single mind and single emotion toward the goal. And even when the goal is achieved you will hardly see him pause to rejoice in it; he is already on his way to another achievement. For that is the irony of his nature. His joy is not in any conquest or destination, but his joy is in going toward it. To which joy he adds the pleasure of being praised as a practical man, and a man who will arrive.

In a more usual sense, perhaps, a practical man is a man occupied with attaining certain ends that people consider important. He must stick pretty close to the business of feeding and preserving life. Nourishment and shelter, money-making, maintaining respectability, and if possible a family — these are the things that give its common meaning to the word "practical." An acute regard for such features of the scenery, and the universe, as contribute or can be made to contribute to these ends, and a systematic neglect of all other features, are the traits of mind which this word popularly suggests. And it is because of the vital importance of these things to almost all people that the word "practical" is a eulogy and is able to be so scornful of the word "poetic."

"It is an earnest thing to be alive in this world. With competition, with war, with disease and poverty and oppression, misfortune and death on-coming, who but fools will give serious attention to what is not significant to the business?"

"Yes — but what is the *use* of being alive in the world, if life is so oppressive in its moral character that we must always be busy getting somewhere, and never simply realizing where we are? What were the value of your eternal achieving, if we were not here on our holiday to appreciate, among other things, some of the things you have achieved?"

Thus, if we could discover a purely poetic and a purely practical person, might they reason together. But we can discover nothing so satisfactory to our definitions, and therefore let us conclude the discussion of the difference between them. It has led us to our own end — a clearer understanding of the nature of poetic people, and of all people when they are in a poetic mood. They are lovers of the qualities of things. They are not engaged, as the learned say that all life is, in becoming adjusted to an environment, but they are engaged in becoming acquainted with it. They are possessed by the impulse to realize, an impulse as deep, and arbitrary, and unexplained as that "will to live" which lies at the bottom of all the explanations. It seems but the manifestation, indeed, of that will itself in a concrete and positive form. It is a wish to experience life and the world. That is the essence of the poetic temper.

Children are poetic. They love to feel of things. I suppose it is necessary to their preservation that they should be, for by random exercise of their organs of feeling they develop them and make them fit for their practical function. But that is not the chief reason why they are poetic; the chief reason is that they are not practical. They have not yet felt the necessity, or got addicted to the trick, of formulating a purpose and then achieving it. Therefore, this naïve impulse of nature, the impulse toward realization, is free in them. Moreover, it is easy of satisfaction. It is easy for children to taste the qualities of experience, because experience is new, and its qualities are but loosely bound together into what we call "things." Each is concrete, particular, unique, and without an habitual use.

Babies have no thought, we may say, but to feel after and find the world, bringing it so far as possible to their mouths where it becomes poignant. They become absorbed in friendship with the water they bathe in. The crumple noise of papers puts them in ecstasy, and later all smells and sounds, brightness, and color, and form, and motion, delight them. We can see them discover light by putting their hands before their eyes and taking them away quickly, and again, at a later age, discover sound by stopping their ears and opening them again.

Who does not remember in his own childhood testing the flavors of things — of words, perhaps, saying them over and over until he had defeated his own wish, for they became pulpy and ridiculous in his mouth? Anything which invades the sense like cinnamon, or sorrel, or neat flowers, or birds' eggs, or a nut, or a horn, is an object of peculiar affection. It is customary in books about children to say that they care little for the actual qualities of an object, and are able to deal with it as though it were anything that they choose to imagine. But I think only the positive part of this statement is true. Undoubtedly their imaginations are active in more various directions, and they draw the distinction between the real and the ideal in perception less clearly than grown-up people do. But the most pronounced characteristic of children is that they are perfectly free to feel the intrinsic qualities of things as they merely are. What we call objects are for the most part practically determined coördinations of qualities. And what we call the *actual* quality of an object is usually the quality which indicates its vital use. When we say

actual, therefore, we really mean practical.   But so far as actuality
from the standpoint of the things is concerned, the children come
nearer to it, and care more about it, than we do.   To us a derby hat
is for covering the head, and that is about all it is; but to them it is
hard, smooth, hollow, deep, funny, and may be named after the
mixing-bowl and employed accordingly.   And so it is with all things.
The child loves a gem with its pure and serene ray, as the poet loves
it, for its own sake.

Nor is it only such qualities as may be said to give pleasure that he
seeks, unless pleasure be defined as seeking, for he wants all experience.   He wants all that he can stand.   He is exploring the whole
world of sense, and not rarely upsets his stomach and his entire
system in a zest for the reception of sensations that are instinctively
abhorred.   Two children of our neighborhood will wear to their
graves the brand of a red-hot scarf-pin as a testimony to that first
love of experience.   They did not want torture, I suppose, but they
wanted to see what it is to be tortured.   And so it was in varying
degrees with us all.   It seems to me, when I look back, as if we were
forever out behind the barn finding out what something or other was
"like."

It has been a vast problem for those concerned with æsthetic and
other theories, why people love tragedy when they are not in it.
But if their theories would only allow that these organisms of ours,
which have been gnashing and struggling together God know what
billions of years for a chance to live, have really an interest in living,
there could be no problem.   The problem is, seeing this wild zest for
life and life so tragic — the problem is, why people do not love
tragedy when they are in it.   And in truth they do.   From the pure
sweetness of early romantic sorrow to the last bitter comfort of an old
man bereft, who mutters to his soul, "This is a part of the full experience of a man!" — from first to last, up to the cannon's mouth, and
down to the midnight grave, the poetic impulse survives.   We love
to taste life to the full.

In energetic but idle hours it survives joyfully.   And in youth
these were the predominant hours.   At all times we were ready for
exuberant realization.   We were not indifferent to the morning.   We
did not wake at the greeting of a last night's proposition in commerce
or knowledge, but at the smile of the sun.   The stuff of our thoughts

was not sentences and numbers, but grass and apples and brown honey. Such excellent objects parading before our minds in a thousand combinations and colors left us no time to develop these general conclusions with which we are now filled. We could not banish our prairie thoughts from the schoolroom, though they liked it as little as we, and the hour of recess was the hour of life. And in the hours of life how greedy we were! Every sense was open with indiscriminate material flowing in. Our eyes trained for every seeing, our ears catching the first murmur of a new experience, we ran after the world in our eagerness, not to learn about it, but to taste the flavor of its being.

> Oh, the wild joys of living! the leaping from rock up to rock,
> The strong rending of boughs from the fir-tree, the cool silver shock
> Of the plunge in a pool's living water, the hunt of the bear,
> And the sultriness showing the lion is couched in his lair,
> And the meal, the rich dates yellowed over with gold dust divine,
> And the locust-flesh steeped in the pitcher, the full draught of wine,
> And the sleep in the dried river-channel where bulrushes tell
> That the water was wont to go warbling so softly and well.
> How good is man's life, the mere living! how fit to employ
> All the heart and the soul and the senses forever in joy!

This agility and fervor of realization extends early to the exercises of all the senses. And then as we grow a little older it comes inward, and we tremble to catch our own emotions on the wing. Fear, for instance, is a being of intense fascination, and even so impelling a power as the instinct of self-preservation is suspended by the poetic impulse — suspended in order that its own very nature may be experienced in feeling. Can you not remember the keen edge of a venture into the barn-yard, a tumultuous dash across to the corn-crib which offered a refuge impregnable to those mild-mannered cows? Anger is a moderate pleasure to most healthy persons, but in youth it is a thing to thirst after and brag of. It is life itself. Mulishness is an engaging state of being. Cruelty and mercy have often the same original charm.

I remember discovering insolence with exactly the same happy spirit of gratification with which I see babies discover light. I was profoundly interested in Nancy Hanks, who had broken the world's record by trotting a mile in 2.04. I believe that I *was* Nancy Hanks most of the time, and anybody who wanted to converse with me or put me in a good-humor would begin upon that topic. But at last I became aware that I could do something quite different from being gratified by all their talk, and I was carried away by the discovery. My opportunity came during supper, at the gracious hands of a maiden aunt:

"Do you know who Nancy Hanks was named after?"

"No," I shouted, "I don't know and I don't care a *darn* — see?"

My memory of the punishment which followed, and how I became aware that there are limits to profitable exploration in such fields, is dim, but of the excited pleasure of the adventure, and my underlying friendliness toward the old lady throughout I am quite certain.

They are great days when we first discern these powerful creatures in us, unnamed and meaningless monsters to challenge forth. Ghost-terror and dizziness and sickness at the sight of blood are among them. Imagine the mind of a young man who knows that there lies a pile of corpses the other side of a smoldering factory wall, and he both hastens to them and flees away from them, until finally this lust after the intense conquers, and he goes and gazes his fill. Do not call that morbid, but an act of exuberant vitality. For there is high-spiritedness in those that are young, not for sensation only, but for emotion. And this too they carry with them, some more and some less, throughout life. Rancor and magnanimity, lust and romance, rapture and even melancholy — drink them to the dregs, for they are what it is to be.

No, no! go not to Lethe ——

It is not only things of the sense and body that a child loves for their own sake, but at a certain age he learns to watch with wonder the paintings of his mind. When he is condemned into his crib, and has to face the loss of the whole lovely world in sleep, then this is the last resource. As long as God lets him, he will devote his somno-lescent power to sensuous memory or anticipation, or just the circus-antics of grotesque and vivid-colored creatures that dance in before him unbidden, uncreated, unexplained. Even if sometimes he does honestly try to think, he finds that he cannot very long cling to the meaning of his thought, because he is all curious to examine those garments of imagery that it wears.

To most adults, I suppose, it is a bare mechanical or rational process to count from one to a hundred; but to an alert child it hardly ever is. It is a winding and bending over a plain, over a prairie, a slow climb, a drip-drip, or an odd march of marionettes, or perhaps it is just the queer sound of the words at his ear. At any rate, the engrossing thing is to estimate the unique character of the process and of each member in it. Eight is a jolly fat man. Six is sitting down. Some people say that they never had any of these pleasures, that they have no mind's eye at all. They cannot see six sit down. Let them try to comfort themselves with the idea that they are more scientific than the rest, not having vivid images to confuse their meanings in the serious business of reaching a conclusion. They are like the people on the ferry-boat who stay downstairs where there are few distractions and they can be perfectly sure to get across. Luckier than they are the people who can enjoy the scenery of speculation, who bring with them out of childhood a clear and spirited fancy.

> —— Great God! I'd rather be
> A Pagan suckled in a creed outworn;
> So might I, standing on this pleasant lea,
> Have glimpses that would make me less forlorn;
> Have sight of Proteus rising from the sea;
> Or hear old Triton blow his wreathèd horn.

The final appearance of the poetic impulse, its intellectual appearance, is also at its height in youth. It is well known that at a certain period, if they are healthy and have a little self-dependence, young persons fall in love with all kinds of unusual ideas. They come forward with an amazing belief, a wise or foolish theory, which they attach to for its own sake, and not out of regard for its practical or real consequence. They take a taste of atheism, anarchism, asceticism, Hindoo philosophy, pessimism, Christianity, or anything that offers a good flavor of radical faith. This is only the same zest for experience. And it will need but a glance at life and literature to prove that such attachment to ideas, with small regard for their meaning in conduct, is not confined to the young. It is a poetic pleasure that people bring with them perhaps farther than any of the others. For most of these pleasures, and especially the more simple and innocent, they soon leave behind, as though it were somehow unworthy to be childlike and love things for their own sake.

We have a superstition prevailing in our homes that the first thing to do upon the appearance of a child is to bring it up. And we see children brought up in the utmost haste by persons who have purchased their own maturity at a cost of all native and fresh joy in anything available. But could we only realize how far the youthful pleasure in every poignant realization is above the accidents of fortune, we should take as great pains to preserve that as to erect the man in our offspring. We should ourselves long to be born again and maintain for the future a more equable union of the practical and poetic in our character.

That such a union is attainable the lives of the greatest show. It is possible to keep throughout a life not wholly disordered, or idle, or cast loose from the general drift of achievement, a spirit fresh to the world. The thought brings us back to Æschylus, a man of heroic proportions who achieved, in an age of turmoil and war, a life filled wonderfully with realizations that were final, the fruit of evolution, and yet not wanting the excellence of great action directed toward a further end. With the participation of that poetic hero in the campaign of defense against the Persians, and in the battles of Salamis and Marathon, it seems as if Nature had indeed achieved her aim. There experience was at its height, but purpose was unshaken. The little library and piazza poets and esteemers of poetry in these days of art will do well to remember the great Greek who died the most renowned literary genius of his age, but had carved upon his proud tomb only this boast, that "The grove of Marathon could bear witness to his good soldierhood, and the long-haired Mede who felt it."

It would be foolish indeed to question whether or not the poetic are capable of purposeful achievement, and the practical capable of intense experience, for we are all, except those lost in apathy, in some degree both poetic and practical. But the example of the hero proves that it is possible for a man who can think clearly and command the differences that lie within him to be both poetic and practical in a high degree.

If we could but free our minds from a contamination with certain modern people who teach themselves that they are presided over by a pretty demon called an Artistic Temperament, we should not only cease cherishing by suggestion the tickle-brain condition into which they decay, but we should have for ourselves a sounder estimate of the place and dignity of the poetic. It is not an attribute of special, exotic, or disordered types, but a universal quality of our nature. No live man is without an arbitrary passion for some experience. Indeed, the defect of many of those most scornful of poetry is not that they are strong in the practical life, but that the attachment to some single state of being has got the better of them. There are fifty thousand morphine-takers in Paris, and all over the face of the earth how many million chewers, and breathers, and swallowers of what, far from being of practical value, is both costly and deleterious, bearing unconscious witness to the poetry of human nature.

The greatly poetic differ from them only in the healthy variety of their loves, prevailing everywhere and always. They are those who live variously as well as vividly in the present. This alone distinguishes them from the millions. This alone distinguishes them from all those excluded by our experiment at the beginning, who confine their enjoyment to smoke while they are crossing the river. They are not without realization. But it is only the childlike and the poetic who make the innumerable intimate acquaintances that are to be made, who welcome all living qualities and perfect them, and finally, perhaps, in a supreme moment of morning sunshine and mist over the city, realize what we may call the essence of crossing a ferry. Their breast thrills, and their eyes drink with rapture the million moving and dancing details of that pageant of life —

—— the white sails of schooners and sloops — the ships at anchor,
The sailors at work in the rigging, or out astride the spars,
The round masts, the swinging motion of the hulls, the slender serpentine
    pennants,
The large and small steamers in motion, the pilots in their pilot-houses,
The white wake left by the passage, the quick tremulous whirl of the wheels,
The flags of all nations, the falling of them at sunset,
The scallop-edged waves in the twilight, the ladled cups, the frolicsome
    crests and glistening,
The stretch afar growing dimmer and dimmer, the gray walls of the granite
    storehouses by the docks,
On the river the shadowy group, the big steam-tug closely flank'd on each
    side by the barges — the hay-boat, the belated lighter,
On the neighboring shore the fires from the foundry chimneys burning high
    and glaringly into the night,
Casting their flicker of black, contrasted with wild red and yellow light, over
    the tops of houses, and down into the clefts of streets.

THE SICKBED OF CULTURE

By FRANCIS HACKETT

Francis Hackett (1883–   ) was born and educated in Ireland. He came to America in 1900, going to New York, where he practiced law. Later he became an editorial writer on the "Chicago Evening Post" and, from 1914 to 1922, an associate editor of " The New Republic." Among his published works are "Horizons" (1918), a book of criticism; "The Story of the Irish Nation" (1922); "That Nice Young Couple" (1924), a novel; and "Henry the Eighth — a Personal History" (1929).

THE newspaper made breakfast rosy. Oats were steady. The coffee market had rallied. Linen was moving better. Lard and ribs were easier. But in the late afternoon I bought the *Atlantic Monthly* and thereupon came to behold the seamy side of this, our mortal adventure. A reactionary tendency, it appears, has developed in the realm of the spirit. There is a sag in culture. Culture is slowly but hideously being extirpated from our midst. The Extirpation of Culture is the very legend of the composition that details our shame. As if it were a weed, a heresy, an abnormal growth, culture is being rooted out and destroyed. Oyez! Oyez! Oyez! Come, sweaty varlets, scriveners, senators, vestrymen, chirurgeons, chymists, draymen, ironmongers and suchlike! Awake to the crisis. Attend to the disgrace and peril of our state.

It is a woman who appears with bitten visage from the sickbed of culture. Ordinarily she refrains from speaking of these things to the gross multitude. She "habitually says nothing to the professional optimists in the public square." But there is a time when the worst must be faced. And it is in this mood of chilled yet passionate reproach that our lady Agoraphobia fetches us to the shaded chamber of the culture we are doing to death. Culture, poor dear, "contact with the best that has been said and thought in the world," has had a time in the vulgar jostle of modernity. As an image of this refinement (not as an image of this refinement's defender), imagine a fragrant New-Englander, a reticule in one mitten, perhaps the odes of Sappho in the other, conscious that she is the "disciplined and finished creature," conscious that she is "intellectually exclusive," conscious also that "culture is inherently snobbish," being asked to fight her passage into a metropolitan subway. "Step lively!" The imperative jars the lady. She gingerly boards the train. On the platform there is contact, but it is not precisely "contact with the best that has been said and thought in the world." Do you wonder, seeing her chaste bonnet somewhat tipsy, her lips compressed, an alarming color tinging her marmoreal cheeks, that Barrett Wendell emits a tiny squeal of pain, that Edith Wharton rolls an eye to heaven, that the shades of Pater and Matthew Arnold flutter unhappily? New England culture is laid between sheets with nothing but the *Atlantic* for hot-water bottle.

And who is to blame for this prostration of our precious culture? The gross multitude. Once culture had seclusion. The social scheme did not allow intrusive minions. "Still less would the conception of the public intellect have admitted the notion. Every one was not supposed to be congenitally qualified for intimacy with the best that has been said and thought in the world." But now, mainly due to "the increased hold of the democratic fallacy on the public mind," the slums pour forth dreadful aspirants to culture, encouraged by traitorous Brahmins; science contributes its stinking acid-stained barbarians; pragmatic philosophers take away the guardian standards of beauty and truth. The angry daughter of the Brahmins descends to slang, the expletive of the continent, in her rage at the invasion. "Science is on top." "The classics are back numbers." We are "overrun by the hordes of ignorance and materialism." Our children sip English from the founts defiled by the poor, "an active and discontented majority, with hands that pick and steal."

Belonging to the upper classes, as she confesses, this gifted prosecutor is certainly entitled to our sympathy. For conceive, she is experiencing in her degree the loneliness of God. Looking down on the inimical multitude she suffers the pangs of isolation. "I begin to think," she observes sadly, "that our age does not really care about perfection." But since "culture must always be in the hands of an oligarchy," perhaps a voice de profundis might be raised to the heights. It is quite permissible, even if the monitor herself is unfortunate enough to use the German word "kultur" like an ignoramus, to be decidedly severe about the bumptious ignorance of the masses. It is quite permissible to argue that upper-class people are "apt" to arrive through riches at the æsthetic truths. But a passion for exclusiveness, a belief in the restriction of cultural susceptibility to the well-nurtured, is all to no purpose if she permits outsiders to come up like flowers. The worst handicap of the neglected culture over which she wrings her fair hands is not "the materialism of all classes," "the influx of a racially and socially inferior population," "the idolatry of science." It is its supersession by another culture to which orthodox culture has not the clue.

To prevent this rivalry there should be a most vigilant campaign against every new human expression. That is the best way to keep the oligarchy entrenched. If the ignorant foreigners, "immigrants who bring no personal traditions," come from countries of oppression, she must decline to believe that they had a literature and a culture. There is only one culture, our own. Perhaps in steerage you can evoke noises from a Lithuanian that sound like human speech. Yes, but soon that Lithuanian will have "the locutions of the slum." Beware of Lithuania. Do not pat the strange dog. He might bite a piece out of your culture. What if the young Jewess on the immigrant ship glows with assent when, without Russian or Yiddish or German, you query: Dostoievsky? Gogol? Tchekov? Lermontov? Tolstoy? Schnitzler? Sudermann? Artzibashef? Ibsen? Strindberg? It is not conversation. It is mere fraternal intercourse through modernity's names. The suppression of such names is the first great necessity of a pinhead conception of culture. And what of Poles and Spaniards and Italians and Scandinavians? What of Constantine Meunier thrusting Walloons into culture? And H. G. Wells with his counter-jumpers and Bennett with his human inchworms, merely keeping the earth fertile, and Shaw with that dreadful winnowing fan in his head? These things must be stopped. Upstairs in the Brahmin mansion there is a delicate lady, disturbed by modernity. She hates pathology and economics. She hates the science which "challenged the supereminence of religion." She honestly cared for things of the spirit, attempted no royal road to salvation. For her comfort it is required that democracy, science, industrialism, suspend their evolutions. It is a good deal to ask, perhaps, but she asks in the name of beauty and moral imagination. These, she takes it, she has loved above all others. It is not her fault if she insists with tight acidity. She hates crowds. She is confined within. She cannot take the air.

THE SPRING LESSON

A REVIEW OF SINCLAIR LEWIS'S *ELMER GANTRY*

By CARL VAN DOREN

Carl Van Doren (1885–   ), a native of Illinois and a graduate of the University of Illinois, has of recent years lived and worked in New York City. After receiving a Ph.D. from Columbia in 1911, he taught English in that University for several years, later becoming head master of a private school. Since 1919 he has given most of his time to literary work, having been associated with "The Nation" and the "Century Magazine." He is now one of the advisory editors of "The Literary Guild of America." Among his books are "The American Novel" (1921), "Contemporary American Novelists" (1922), "The Roving Critic" (1923), "James Branch Cabell" (1925), and (with Mark Van Doren) "American and British Literature Since 1890" (1925).

LET us suppose a case. Suppose George F. Babbitt, having heard that Sinclair Lewis's *Elmer Gantry* is a "preacher novel" and "hot stuff," has decided to read the book. Babbitt is himself not much of a hand to go to church, though he does not mind if his wife goes, and he sends his children to Sunday-school, where they will get good moral teaching an hour a week and will be kept, for that long and maybe longer, out of mischief. For some reason or other, he has always been a little uncomfortable with preachers. They cramp his style. He knows that there are good fellows among them, but, after all, they are preachers, set vaguely apart from the world, and not quite the same as the man that Babbitt sees every day downtown. Moreover, they hold their services on Sunday, which is Babbitt's day of rest. If he went to the morning sermon, he would have to get up earlier than he likes to do for anything except golf. By evening, of course, his day of rest has tired him out. And yet he has never managed to get over the feeling that maybe he ought to go to church more regularly. Every Sunday his conscience whispers to him, from time to time, that he is playing hooky from religion, which is a good thing for everybody.

Without, of course, being aware of his desire, he wishes he had a better excuse for playing hooky than he has ever found. In *Elmer Gantry* he finds it. So this is the way preachers behave! Babbitt has heard cynics wondering whether half the preachers, if the truth were known about them, do not keep a bottle hidden behind a row of Bibles; wondering if, when preachers call on the women of their congregations, with the men-folks away, they spend the whole time talking about spiritual problems. This book makes it look as if the cynics were right in their suspicions. Elmer Gantry can tip the bottle with any man, and he has a way with the women. Babbitt can not help licking his lips as he reads. Imagine seeing this all written down in black and white! There is no doubt about it, he says, preachers are the same as ordinary people, except that they have advantages which the average man never has. Traveling all over the country, for instance, with a lady evangelist, like Sharon Falconer. Getting in with the big guns in every town. Having a chance — Babbitt does not put it quite so neatly — to have all the publicity of a saint and all the privacy of a sinner. Plenty of pay for very little work. This is really too much. A snide game, that's what it is. Babbitt concludes, for the moment, that the preachers will henceforth get small pickings out of him.

On second thought, indeed, Babbitt will probably, like most of his friends, change his mind. Come to think about it, he knows preachers who are certainly not like Elmer Gantry. Anyway, a few preachers like that make no great difference in the long run. The church is a big institution, which ought to be supported by all who have the best interests of the community at heart. Religion is a good thing for everybody. Why, even the lowest savages have some sort of religion. The United States would be badly off without it. Still, Babbitt will be less troubled the next time he drops his wife at the church and himself goes on to the golf course.

No one can ever be quite sure, when the dust of the present scuffle has blown away, whether Sinclair Lewis had his ear closer to the ground than any one else, or whether he himself created the row. It ought to be plain, however, that he has chosen the most spectacular method of attack. The medieval satirists employed it. In an age of faith, they did not examine the faith itself, to see whether it was sound and realistic enough to satisfy the intelligent. They clamored that priests were drunken and sensual, Elmer Gantrys surpliced and tonsured. The common man, who would have grown impatient under the strain of a theological debate and who would have murdered the heretics who might have said his religion was partly superstition, caught up the clamor. The clamor has lasted from that time until this. But in the United States, thanks to the absence of an established church and the presence of many tolerated sects, there has been, since the seventeenth century, no great pressure put upon the easygoing layman by an ecclesiastical organization. Of late this happy condition appears to be undergoing a change. Certain of the more powerful sects, joining their zealous forces, have set out to say what science shall be taught in the schools and how Sunday shall be observed and whether men shall go to church or not. Skeptics have for some time been disturbed by such a development, but, since skepticism calls for a considerable boldness of thought, there are seldom many skeptics in a country. The work of throwing off ecclesiastical tyranny has in the main to be done by persons who are merely emotional and instinctive in their behavior. These are the persons whom *Elmer Gantry* reaches. It tells them, in a familiar idiom, that clergymen are drunken and sensual. The Babbitts must do the rest.

MR. BABBITT'S SPIRITUAL GUIDE

A REVIEW OF SINCLAIR LEWIS'S *ELMER GANTRY*

By JOSEPH WOOD KRUTCH

Joseph Wood Krutch (1893–   ) *has had a varied experience as editor, author, and teacher. His teaching career has brought him into contact with such schools as the Polytechnic Institute of Brooklyn, Vassar, and Columbia. Since 1924 he has been dramatic critic and an associate editor of "The Nation," and since 1926 he has been a member of the board of editors of "The Literary Guild." He is the author of "Comedy and Conscience After the Restoration"* (1924), *"Edgar Allan Poe — A Study in Genius"* (1926), *and the editor of "The Plays of William Congreve"* (1927).

WITH *Elmer Gantry* Mr. Lewis returns to the practice of his own particular trade. In *Arrowsmith* he turned aside in an effort to achieve certain qualities, characteristic of the conventional novel, which his detractors had declared outside his range, and in *Mantrap* he demonstrated that he had not forgotten the requirements of merely popular fiction. The new book is in every way a companion volume to *Main Street* and *Babbitt*. In it the author, sure of the tested effectiveness of a certain technique, and with a zeal undiminished by success, turns his attention to Mr. Babbitt's spiritual guide and adds the third member to his impressive trilogy devoted to the most grotesque aspects of American life. What *Main Street* was to the small town and *Babbitt* to the business man that, neither more nor less, is *Elmer Gantry* to the vulgarest contemporary type of pulpit-thumping materialist.

The book begins with its hero, a coarse young giant, happily engaged in a street fight and in that most blissful condition to which a powerful young man can attain — "unrighteous violence in a righteous cause"; it carries him through his muddled conversion in a denominational college, through the ups and downs of his checkered career as pastor and evangelist; and it ends with his triumphant vindication at the hands of an enthusiastic congregation from the latest of the many near-scandals which threatened his career. Too unreflective ever to know himself, too incapable of thought ever to be really a hypocrite, Elmer is honored and beloved of most of those with whom he comes in contact because he is made of the same coarse clay as they, because no learning, no integrity, and no spirituality sets him apart from those to whom he is paid to minister. He is the type most fit to occupy the pulpits supported by materialists like himself to whom the church is half the defender of petty privileges against subversive forces and half the instrument through which a nominal respect may be paid to virtues inconvenient to practice; and to Elmer himself the pulpit is quite as useful as he is to it since, by virtue of the license which permits him to mount it, he is enabled not only to taste the intoxication of an orator's power but to enjoy as well an income and a position which the mediocrity of his will, the fundamental meanness of his character, and the shallowness of his brain could not have earned for him by any other means.

Mr. Lewis is careful not to leave his picture unrelieved. He does take pains to indicate that every one of the few civilizing influences which the boy Elmer ever received — the most rudimentary forms of art, music, literacy, learning, and ethical idealism — had been, in his experience, connected with the church, and he allows to appear momentarily upon the scene certain ministers of a higher type. But in the book it is everywhere darkness that prevails. Elmer himself has not a single quality which goes to the making of a decent man. He is heartless, treacherous, and cruel; he has nothing resembling even the puritan virtues except the vices of vindictiveness, phariseeism, and hypocrisy into which they can turn; and his career is an indictment of the church as a whole at least in so far as it shows how the mechanism of the church permits the rise of such a man and demands of its servants no qualities which viciousness cannot convincingly imitate. *Elmer Gantry* is as good as *Main Street* and *Babbitt* and it is good in exactly the same way. Here again, as in the two books which made Mr. Lewis's the best-known name among contemporary American novelists, is a completeness of documentation not less than amazing, a power of mimicry which, so far as I know, no living author can equal, and a gusto which, considering the meanness of the material, is all but inexplicable. No mere study, however painstaking and devoted, could make possible the intimate ease with which Mr. Lewis handles the material or the completeness with which he fills in the details of every picture. He seems to know the life he is describing with a thoroughness which could only come from

his having in a real sense lived in it; the contagious rapture with
which he pours out his scenes is the only thing which can keep one
from entertaining a profound pity for a writer compelled to do anything so dreadful.   Some strange twist in Mr. Lewis's character has
enabled him to take a joy in examining, almost participating in,
mediocrity at its most grotesquely intolerable moments, and has
enabled him, miraculously, to make it interesting to others too.

In one respect at least *Elmer Gantry* is superior even to its companion pieces, for up to the last seventy-five pages (which are distinctly
less interesting than the rest) it has a greater variety of incident and
a more sustained interest than either of the other two.   In both
Babbitt and *Main Street* there was a certain static, descriptive quality.
The picture unfolded without developing new interest, and there
was no continuous, steady march of incident, while in the new book
there is a progressive plot which never, until it has almost reached its
conclusion, shows any signs of flagging.   There is, besides, an exposure of Elmer's character which goes further, perhaps, than anything else to justify Mr. Lewis's method — an exposure which seems
detached, unhurried, relentless; too calm and too sure to seem to
spring from hatred or malice, but inspired by a rage which a confidence in his power to describe has calmed.

Elmer Gantry, with its innumerable incidents and its many ramifi-
cations, is indeed a structure far more impressive than most satires, a
sort of cathedral in which every stone is a gargoyle; and though there
will be many who will not be able to read it without the Devil's
question, "But what is art?" it is not likely that any review will
answer that question definitively.   At least it can be said that Mr.
Lewis has done something that no one else is capable of doing.   In a
manner that seems to be merely the almost too literal truth but which
manages nevertheless to contain its own criticism he has, in three
books, recorded a reign of grotesque vulgarity which but for him
would have left no record of itself because no one else could have
adequately recorded it.

NOTES TOWARD A MENTAL
AUTOBIOGRAPHY

NOTES TOWARD A MENTAL
AUTOBIOGRAPHY

THE selection and arrangement of the essays in this volume have been largely determined by actual classroom requirements. Obviously, the theme-plan which follows has also grown out of experience, and is the result of considerable experimentation with many diversified groups of students. Although the editors have never found a universal remedy for all the ills of the composition course, they have found that most students can write if they are supplied with a definite topic and with a sufficient background of ideas upon that topic.

Having read and discussed part or all of the essays in any given section of the book, the student should then endeavor to express his own feelings upon the subject or upon some phase of the subject. It is recommended, of course, that a student should choose only such topics as he can write upon from experience, from observation, from reading, or from combinations of experience, observation, and reading. Any individual discussion of a topic should be definite and logical in thinking, clearly stated, original, and spirited.

At all times, the student-writer should guard against wordiness, illogical reasoning, and vagueness of thought or expression. Even when a rather broad topic is chosen for discussion, the exposition and application of the topic should be specific and personal. As indicated in the Preface and by the title of this part of the book, the general purpose of the suggested plan is to produce a series of papers which will be the individual student's expression of his opinions on the subjects under consideration.

In some cases, the student may wish to answer directly a point of view expressed in a particular essay. Such refutation may be quite interesting and sufficiently valid — if the writer remembers to present facts and establishes a clear, logical relation between such facts.

The suggested list of theme-topics in each section is, of course, far from complete. Students and instructors will be able to amplify the lists considerably, at the same time taking into consideration local conditions and individual differences.

It may be noted that the plan allows for any requisite amount of adaptation to specific needs.   For example, some teachers may wish to omit certain sections altogether, and to place emphasis on the remaining sections.   Two or three papers might be written by each student on any one of the general subjects without exhausting the various possibilities of discussion.

I. PREJUDICES.
   Is America the Best of All Possible Countries?
   The Dangers of the Open Mind.
   "I am broadminded — until you criticize me or mine."
   Racial Prejudice — Does It Affect Me?
   "I am tolerant of everything but intolerance."
   "Only a fool will die for his convictions."
   My Pet Abomination.

II. THE AMERICAN SCENE.
   Our Assumed Freedom of Thought.
   "Money Maketh the Man."
   After the Jazz Age — What?
   S-p-e-e-d!
   "Thy Way Shall Be My Way."
   Is Mr. Mencken Right?
   "How the Other Half Lives."
   An Exploration into "Unknown America."

III. GOVERNMENT.
   All Laws are Good Laws.
   "The minority may be right; the majority is always wrong."
   Government by the Unfit.
   "My Country — Right or Wrong."
   "Patriotism is the last refuge of a scoundrel."
   "No Entangling Alliances."
   "Liberty — Equality — Fraternity."
   The Hundred Per Cent American.

IV. BUSINESS.
   Mr. Babbitt.
   "Business — the Civilizer."
   Unselfish Business.
   Success.
   Honesty in Business.

"The Full Dinner Pail."
The "Service" Idea.
The Mania for Advertising.
The "High-pressure" Salesman.

V. THE COLLEGE AND EDUCATION.
The Cash Value of a College Education.
Democracy in Education.
How I Wasted Four Years in High School.
College as I Have Found It.
"The Social Value of the College-Bred."
The —— Faculty.
The Co-ed: Attraction or Distraction?
Concerning College Men.
"The instruction of fools is folly."
The Benefit of Student Activities.
"The world of learning was never better worth preparing for."
"The Noisy Jargon of the Schools."
The Finished Product — A Scholar and a Gentleman.

VI. SPORTS.
Why a Stadium Has a University.
Vicarious Athletics.
The College Hero — The Athlete.
Football Fanatics.
The Athletic Plant — For Sport or Spectacle?
The High Cost of Good Football Players.
Why I do (or do not) Take Part in College Athletics.
A Defense of Intercollegiate Athletics.

VII. SCIENCE.
The Man of Science — His Place in the Modern World.
The Relation of Science to Progress.
"Some Things That Science Doesn't Know."
From Harvey to Pasteur.
Does Science Benefit Humanity?
The New Chemistry.
Natural Selection — Fact or Theory?
This Monkey Business.
Science in Industry.
How Science Can End War.

VIII. RELIGION.
The Necessity for Religion.
"The Necessity for Atheism."

Why I do (or do not) Go to Church.
What Religion Means to Me.
"A Free Man's Worship."
Does Science Conflict with Religion?
"For non-conformity the World whips you with its displeasure."
The Need for a New God.
Other Religions and Mine — A Comparison.

IX. ETHICS.

Can Law Regulate Conduct?
"The End Justifies the Means."
The Value of the White Lie.
"Self-Reliance."
The Cardinal Virtues.
The Worst Vices.
My Changing Standard of Moral Values.
The Passing of the Double Standard.
"These Wild Young People."
Conventionality — Its Uses and Abuses.
"The Right to be Happy."
"And there shall be no more war."
The Relation of Ethics and Religion.
"What is Truth?"

X. MANNERS.

"I do desire that we may be better strangers."
American Manners.
"Please take my seat."
"I'll punch your nose!"
The Lost Art of Politeness.
On the Rudeness of College Students.
"Well, you'll have to excuse him; he's an American, you know."
"Vulgarity is the first requirement for social success."

XI. ÆSTHETICS.

Jazz!
The Skyscraper — A Symbol of American Life.
A Review of a Current Play.
The Worst Movie I have Seen Recently.
The Best Movie I have Seen Recently.
Why I Never Go to the Symphony.
My One Visit to the Art Museum.
The So-called Æsthetics of Dancing.
"The Glorification of the American Girl."
The Horrors of Vaudeville.
The Comic Strip — An Art Form.

XII. LITERATURE.
Why Read?
Books I Dislike.
My Favorite Author.
A Review of a Current Book.
"Reading maketh a full man."
"No man but a blockhead ever wrote except for money."
Tendencies in Modern Poetry (or the Novel, the Drama, etc.).
The New versus the Old in Literature.
Why I Do Not Like Realistic Novels.
A Defense of Free Verse.
Should Books Teach?
The Usefulness of Literary Criticism.
Should Books Ever Be Censored?